Managing in a Business Context
an HR approach

Managing in a Business Context

an HR approach

Huw Morris • Brian Willey • Sanjiv Sachdev

FINANCIAL TIMES

Prentice Hall

An imprint of **Pearson Education**

Harlow, England · London · New York · Reading, Massachusetts · San Francisco
Toronto · Don Mills, Ontario · Sydney · Tokyo · Singapore · Hong Kong · Seoul
Taipei · Cape Town · Madrid · Mexico City · Amsterdam · Munich · Paris · Milan

Pearson Education Limited
Edinburgh Gate
Harlow
Essex CM20 2JE

and Associated Companies throughout the world

Visit us on the World Wide Web at:
www.pearsoneduc.com

First published 2002

ISBN 0 273 65174 9

British Library Cataloguing-in-Publication Data
A catalogue record for this book is available from the British Library

Typeset in $9\frac{1}{4}$ \ 12pt Stone Serif by 30.
Printed and bound by Bell & Bain Limited, Glasgow

Contents

Instructor's Manual

An Instructor's Manual to accompar
the following address: www.booksi

It is now commonplace and somewhat clichéd to talk about the constancy of change in the business world. Management gurus and business pundits regularly suggest that the old certainties of stable markets, predictable sales and planned growth no longer exist, if they ever did. Foreign competition, rapid technological change and, above all, changing consumer tastes mean that customers can desert an organisation overnight with consequent effects on business performance and jobs.

In addition to the immediate concerns for the economic well-being of organisations, wider changes in the pattern of social and political life have affected how people see their current position and future prospects. The collapse of communism, the growing role of women at work, increasing wealth and an ageing of the population in developed countries are just four of a myriad of changes which have challenged many people's views about how our social lives should be organised and regulated.

Faced with these rapid and significant changes in the world that surrounds us, it is now arguably more important than ever that current and prospective managers and employees are aware of and prepared for these developments. This book, therefore, aims to provide the intellectual tools they will need in order to analyse and evaluate the external pressures which currently confront their organisations.

The principal target market for this book is students studying the 'Managing in a Business Context' component of the Chartered Institute of Personnel and Development's (CIPD) Professional Development Scheme. Although the main focus is practising human resource managers, or those aspiring to perform this role, the book should also be of interest to lecturers and students involved in other related courses, e.g. Certificates and Diplomas in management and MBA programmes.

To these ends this book sets out to:

- discuss different ways of conceiving of organisations and the external environments that confront them;
- examine important contemporary developments in the political, economic, legal, social and technological environments facing British-based organisations;
- suggest some of the implications for human resource managers of contemporary developments in labour, product and capital markets;
- show how further information can be gained about specific industrial sectors and named organisations;
- illustrate how a number of analytical and evaluative tools can be used to examine recent developments in specific organisations' external environments; and

- show how the results of any analysis can be discussed and communicated to other managers and employees.

Achieving these objectives presents a number of difficulties. Any informed analysis and evaluation of the environment surrounding contemporary organisations necessitates drawing together insights and observations from a range of academic disciplines, including economics, political theory, sociology, social psychology, organisation theory and socio-legal studies. Within each of these disciplines there are a range of competing ideological and theoretical perspectives. Unfortunately, the similarities between these traditions are often obscured by differences in terminology and a wealth of academic jargon. As a consequence of this diversity of language there is a danger that any student of this area of study will become confused about the lessons to be drawn from different analyses and prescriptions.

In order to overcome these problems we have attempted to use a relatively standard set of terms throughout the book and to include a glossary to explain some of the more obscure terms. We have also attempted to draw connections between the different chapters and to develop and expand upon ideas as the book progresses.

The book begins by considering what is meant by the term 'business context'. In Chapter 1 we explore how developments in the world surrounding an organisation may impinge upon the decisions and actions of managers and employees. Here we focus on the variety of ways in which the staff of an organisation can prepare for change and plan responses to external problems and opportunities.

Chapters 2, 3 and 4 move on to consider the immediate task environment within which most, if not all, organisations operate. More specifically we consider how an organisation's demands for money, staff and customers affect the choices available to managers in general, and human resource professionals in particular. In these chapters we aim to demonstrate that organisations differ in terms of their ownership, organisation and orientation as well as the ways in which they recruit and retain employees and deal with the consumers of their goods and services. By examining these differences we hope to shed some light on the range of alternatives that currently confront the people who devise, develop and implement personnel policies in organisations based in the United Kingdom.

Moving away from the day-to-day concerns of customers and internal resources, Chapters 5 to 11 of the book consider the wider political, economic, social, technological and legal environments within which organisations operate. The influence of these issues may seem distant from the pressing concerns of filling staff vacancies and meeting orders, but as we shall see, these wider changes can have profound effects. The issues considered in these chapters include:

☐ recent fluctuations in the economic fortunes of the United Kingdom;
☐ changes in the distribution of income, wealth, education and health;
☐ the effects of industrial activity and new technology on human welfare and the natural environment;
☐ the influence of the political system and party ideologies on the policies pursued by European institutions and recent United Kingdom governments; and
☐ the role of the individual and collective employment law in regulating the relationship between managers, employees and trade unions.

The final chapter of the book returns to the themes explored in the opening chapter. In this concluding section we draw together some of the issues discussed and speculate about possible future changes in the corporate environment of UK-based organisations.

Aids to Learning

This book has been designed to include the following pedagogical features to aid the learning process.

Introduction

Each chapter begins with a section which spells out the content, focus and scope of the chapter, to guide the reader through the material that follows.

Learning objectives

The reader is given a list of objectives that should be attained once the chapter and associated exercises have been completed.

Case study

The practical importance of the concepts and skills described in the book is illustrated by a short case study in most chapters, introducing the reader to a number of issues which will be discussed in that chapter.

Analysis and issues

This book aims to draw clear links between theory and practice, and so the main substantive component of each chapter consists of a discussion of competing ideological approaches and theoretical concepts which can be used either to analyse material contained within the case studies, or alternatively to examine developments within an organisation known to the reader.

Figures and tables

Where possible, diagrams and illustrations have been included to help the reader visualise and quantify key elements of any theory or issue under discussion.

Exhibits

These give practical examples, supplementary information and summaries of recent debates on contentious issues.

Exercises

These invite readers to apply the concepts discussed to the operation of a case study organisation or their own employers. Model answers are included, where appropriate, in an appendix at the end of the book.

Chapter summaries

A review of the main points of each chapter is included in the concluding section of each chapter.

Glossary

Key terms and definitions are explained in the glossary at the end of the book.

References

A comprehensive list of the materials cited in the text is included at the end of the book.

Index

The book includes an index designed to enable the reader to search quickly for relevant information when tackling problems in class, examinations or to use as the basis for assignments.

Huw Morris
Bristol Business School
University of the West of England

Brian Willey and Sanjiv Sachdev
Kingston Business School
Kingston University

Authors' Acknowledgements

This book is the product of work undertaken by the authors at different times over a number of years. Most of the material presented is drawn from teaching materials and lecture notes used on the Core Management component of the Postgraduate Diploma and Masters Degree in Personnel Management at Kingston University. As such we owe a considerable debt to a number of people who in their various ways have provided us with intellectual stimulation, secretarial assistance, editorial guidance and financial support.

Past and present students on the personnel management teaching programmes at Kingston have contributed by being willing guinea pigs for many of the exercises contained within this book. They have helped us gain a better understanding of the subject area by asking difficult questions and making astute observations. Their experiences of the realities of people management in a rapidly changing business world have also provided the basis for many of the examples and case studies in this book.

Whatever its contents, this book would not have seen the light of day without the valuable assistance of Peter Haywood, John Logan, Ian James, Dan Russell and Maureen Beard. With good humour and considerable patience they have corrected our grammar and sharpened the focus of our arguments. In addition, a number of anonymous reviewers and our publisher, Jacqueline Senior, have provided insightful comments and useful editorial guidance on various drafts of the book.

Finally, we have benefited from the constant encouragement and patience of our families. Our thanks to our respective families: Rhianon, Wendy, Bronwen, James and Ami; Ann, Ian, David and Helen; Kathy and David.

Publisher's Acknowledgements

We are grateful to the following for permission to reproduce copyright material:

Tables 2.4 and 4.5 and Figures 5.6, 5.8, 7.1, 7.2, 7.3, 7.4 and 7.5 from the Office for National Statistics, Crown copyright material is reproduced with permission of the Controller of Her Majesty's Stationery Office and the Queen's Printer for Scotland; Table 3.1 from *Exploring Corporate Strategy*, 6th edition, by Gerry Johnson and Kevan Scholes, reprinted by permission of Pearson Education Limited © Pearson Education Limited 2002; Figure 3.6 adapted from the Ansoff Matrix in *The New Corporate Strategy* (1987) by H. Igor Ansoff; Tables 4.2, 4.3, 4.4 and short extracts from *All Change at Work. British Employment Relations 1980–1998* (2000) by Neil Millward and John Forth, together with short extracts from *Britain at Work? The Workplace Employees Relations Survey* (1999) by M. Cully *et al*., all published by Routledge, London; Figure 5.7 from the Organisation for Economic Co-operation and Development (OECD); Figure 6.1 from *Technological Change at Work* (1994) by I. McLoughlin and J. Clark © The Open University; Table 6.1 adapted from *Organizational Behaviour: An Introductory Text* (1991) by A. Huczynski and D. Buchanan, reprinted by permission of Pearson Education Limited © Pearson Education Limited; Figure 10.3 from *The Equal Opportunities Review* No. 93 (September 2000 pp. 11–22) published by the Butterworth Division of Reed Elsevier (UK) Ltd.; extract from 'Future perfect? Genetic knowledge will change the world profoundly', from *The Economist*, 1 July 2000 © The Economist Newspaper Limited, London.

We are grateful to the Financial Times Limited for permission to reprint the following material:

Exhibit 2.3 Hard labour to put code into practice, © *Financial Times*, 12 June, 2001; Table 2.1 Share price information for selected food retailing PLCs in 2001, © *Financial Times*, 12th July, 2001; Figure 4.1 Money at Work: Childcare is out of its infancy, © *Financial Times*, 13 September, 2000; Exhibit 6.1 Fundamental change is now a real proposition, © *Financial Times*, 30 March, 2001.

In some instances we have been unable to trace the owners of copyright material, and we would appreciate any information that would enable us to do so.

The business environment and HRM

☐ Introduction

Every organisation is confronted by external pressures which will have implications for the way it manages its internal operations and employees. Skill shortages, competition, government regulation and new technology are just a few of the many problems which affect managers and employees within organisations based in the United Kingdom. While few managers and employees will welcome these developments, it is obviously essential that they are aware of these changes and are prepared to respond to them. By correctly identifying developments in the organisation's external environment and evaluating their possible effects, managers and employees should be better placed to draw up and amend plans to ensure the long-term viability of the organisation with which they are associated.

☐ Focus and scope

This chapter begins the task of examining changes in the corporate environment of UK-based organisations. It demonstrates that there are a variety of ways in which these changes can be analysed. Underpinning these various approaches are different assumptions which will have implications for the way in which the analysis is performed, the results of this evaluation, and any recommendations for future action. This chapter explores these different approaches by reference to four sets of basic assumptions about the external environment:

☐ objective versus subjective interpretations;
☐ continuity versus turbulent change;
☐ choice versus determinism;
☐ absolute versus relative values.

We believe that an awareness of these different assumptions and approaches will enable readers to improve their ability to undertake their own analyses and evaluations of the external business environment, or comment upon the results of assessments undertaken by others.

Learning objectives

Once you have read this chapter and completed the associated exercises, you should be able to:

☐ describe some of the external pressures and problems confronting organisations based in the UK;

☐ outline the assumptions which underpin different approaches to the analysis of organisations and their external environments;

☐ comment on different means of evaluating what to do in specific circumstances;

☐ undertake environmental scanning activities using a variety of different methods.

CASE STUDY

Hodsons

The following case study describes events within a real organisation. The information contained within this case will be used as the basis for a number of skills exercises, as well as a general discussion of the problems associated with analysing the external environment confronting any organisation. We will return to the case study at various points throughout this chapter.

Hodsons is a builders' merchant with close to 50 outlets in the south of England. The company was founded in the early 1900s by the Hodson family and has subsequently grown through the acquisition of smaller competitor organisations. In the early stages of its operation the company specialised in supplying timber to house builders and other professional traders. As the organisation has grown, its product range has expanded and it now sells builders' tools, a range of building materials and a variety of finished and semi-finished household improvement products. The staff of the company have also increasingly sought to source this growing range of products from overseas. As a consequence, tools made in the UK and Europe have been replaced by similar items made for a fraction of the cost in China and India.

Despite the expansion of the business, the Board of Directors at Hodsons, which is still dominated by members of the Hodson family under the leadership of John Hodson (Managing Director), has consciously decided to limit its customer base to professional builders. This approach, together with the decision to allow acquired companies to trade under their former names and to rely upon word of mouth as a means of attracting new trade, has meant that the company's name is not well known outside the building industry.

Hodsons' operations are typically based on high streets in major towns and cities and are staffed by a small team of full-time male employees who have usually spent much of their working life with the company. These sales assistants pride themselves on their extensive knowledge of building techniques and their ability to advise customers as well as to deal with the more mundane tasks of manual stock ordering, storage and sales. The stores are open between 8 am and 5 pm, Monday to Saturday.

During the 1970s and 1980s the company's sales and profitability grew steadily as the UK economy expanded and the housing market and associated building industry flourished. In the 1990s, however, a number of external pressures have produced difficulties for the organisation and have led directly to a decline in overall sales and profitability. Faced with these problems, several senior managers, who had been recruited for their retailing expertise, have been placing pressure on the Board of Directors to reappraise its business plans. One of the most vociferous of these critics is Michael Sellers, the company's Senior Operations Manager. He believes that Hodsons' traditional market base will continue to decline and that large out-of-town Do-It-Yourself centres will continue to take market share away from the company.

By comparison, John Hodson and many of the company's other directors believe that there is still a place for a high-street-based chain of specialist builders' merchants. Furthermore, they do not have a very high opinion of the growing number of Do-It-Yourself centres, which they believe fail to provide their customers with a high standard of service and advice. They have a pride in their company and do not really want their builders' yards to be transformed into a collection of large anonymous 'sheds'. They are prepared to pay the price of reduced sales and profits in the short term, in order to retain their skilled staff and ensure high levels of service in the long term.

In an attempt to overcome these differences of opinion, Michael Sellers has persuaded the Board of Directors to ask a team of business consultants to produce a report identifying the causes of the company's current predicament and outlining advice on the future development of the business. He believes this report will endorse his view by providing an objective view of the problems confronting the organisation. He also hopes that, once this report has been accepted and agreed, it will provide a basis for a radical restructuring of the company.

The consultancy team began its investigation by attempting to define the pressures facing the business. To complete this task, extensive research was undertaken before the preparation of the initial report. This research was based upon interviews with employees at various levels within the organisation, as well as discussions with senior managers from competitor firms and representatives of various building trade associations. The results of this analysis were duly presented to the Board of Directors and a selection of senior and middle managers. It was hoped that, once agreement had been reached about the nature of the problems, some progress could be made in attempting to map out a plan for responding to these difficulties.

Exercise 1.1 **The external pressures facing Hodsons**

Assuming the role of one of the consultancy team and drawing upon your own general knowledge, list what you consider to be the five principal external pressures facing Hodsons.

☐ Analysing the business environment

The Hodsons case demonstrates how external business pressures and problems can affect a company. It also illustrates some of the problems which confront managers, employees and consultants when they attempt to analyse and evaluate these external pressures. Management writers and practitioners adopt different perspectives when they attempt to analyse organisations. Whether we say that these analyses are informed by theory, or just plain common sense, they all share a number of features. They all implicitly say something about the nature of the concepts under observation as well as the relationship between these different concepts. The assumptions which underpin these different approaches can have a profound effect upon the results of any analysis. More specifically these different approaches will produce:

☐ different diagnoses of current problems;

☐ predictions of possible future developments; and

☐ prescriptions for future action.

In order to make sense of the immense variety of these approaches, the following discussion focuses upon differences in four areas:

☐ objective versus subjective interpretations;
☐ continuity versus turbulent change ;
☐ determinism versus free will; and
☐ definitive versus relative values.

Few writers and practitioners adopt an extreme position in any of these areas, but as the following discussion aims to demonstrate, there are significant differences of emphasis.

☐ Objective versus subjective interpretations

A persistent trait in all human enquiry has been the search for universal facts – statements which can be considered true in all circumstances and at all times. In the physical sciences this has led to the statement of categories which precisely define the characteristics of, and relationships between, things. These definitions are considered by many to be objective truths because they remain true regardless of who is there to witness them. For example, awareness of the principles of chemistry or biology will enable us to categorise chemical elements or plant and animal species regardless of time, place or the identity of the observer. To put this another way, it is believed that physical phenomena in the world that surrounds us have an independent existence and the act of observing does not change the nature of these things. As a consequence, it is assumed that it should be easy for researchers and practitioners to gather information in order to gain a better understanding of the world which surrounds them. This perspective is represented diagrammatically in Fig 1.1, where the person is merely an observer of events in the outside world. The person can gain more information about what is happening, and the act of perception may filter what is sensed, but the process of sensing does not alter this external reality.

The belief that the external world is essentially objective is shared by social scientists from a range of disciplines and schools of thought. For example, many *free-market* economists believe in the primacy of markets and argue that the interplay of demand and supply determines, or should determine, what is produced, how it is made and the way in which it is distributed. They argue that markets are a natural phenomenon and that this reality confronts people in all economies regardless of social, cultural and historical setting.

By adopting this perspective it could be argued that Hodsons is experiencing a decline in business because of a change in the nature of demand away from building wholesalers towards 'Do-It-Yourself' centres. If we follow this logic, the

Figure 1.1
An objective view
of the interaction
between people
and their physical
environment

Board of Directors has little choice but to scale back its current operations and alter what it supplies in order to deal with the new competition.

A belief in a universal objective reality is not confined to free-market economists. Many Marxist, Green and feminist writers from the opposite end of the political spectrum similarly argue that there are common truths confronting people in all situations. However, these writers focus upon what they term *capitalism or patriarchy* rather than the market in order to explain the position of people in different countries.

According to many of these critics, capitalism can be characterised as a system which promotes the exploitation of the economically weak by the wealthy. Through the ownership of land, machinery and buildings, the rich and their agents are able to force the poor to undertake work in exchange for wages. These wages do not reflect the true worth of what is produced and as a result profits can be made for the capitalists from the sale of these goods and services. Through the generation and accumulation of profits, the capitalists are then able to strengthen and improve their position. While there may be benefits for some as a consequence of the operation of this system, these are likely to be confined to small groups and to last for relatively short periods of time. These small groups may be élités within one country or, alternatively, within an increasingly globalised economy the citizens of developed western nations. For the critics of this capitalist system, there is a glimmer of hope in their assumption that these inequities cannot persist and grow larger indefinitely. Dissatisfaction amongst the exploited poor, they suggest, may lead to violent unrest and challenges to the system. Similarly, limited resources will force governments, companies, groups and individuals to accept greater regulation of their activities if everyone is not to suffer as a consequence of environmental disturbances.

If we apply these insights to the Hodsons case then there is little that the current employees or their overseas suppliers can do about their present predicament. The problems that they confront reflect the inequities of the capitalist system. According to this view, a solution to these problems can only be achieved when a more fundamental change in the structure of society and the attitudes of individuals is accomplished both within the UK and across the world more generally.

The preceding snapshots are not intended to provide a detailed examination of free-market, Marxist, Green or feminist accounts of the working of modern societies. These approaches will be considered in more detail in subsequent chapters. However, these examples are intended to illustrate that at the heart of many analyses of organisations and societies is a belief in an objective and universal account of human behaviour. If we subscribe to this view, then – like Michael Sellers in the case study – we should believe that there is one best way of interpreting the case study at the beginning of this chapter. Our only task is to find out what this approach is and to implement it. The results of this analysis can then be used as a guide to future action by managers and employees.

Despite the seeming certainty of the objective approach, many writers have questioned whether the world we live in is really understandable solely in these terms. Even within the physical sciences the view that external phenomena should be seen as independent objective entities has been questioned. For example, in the field of quantum mechanics (sub-atomic physics) scientists studying the behaviour of electrons have suggested that in some circumstances electrons behave like particles and in others like waves. Furthermore, when studying the behaviour of these electrons, the way in which events are observed may alter what is judged to have happened. Similarly, in the study of the behaviour of stars and planets (cosmology) a number of physicists have suggested that the universe is not really understandable on a purely objective basis. At its most extreme, this view is expressed in the 'anthropopic principle' which suggests that the universe is only there because we are here to observe it. In short, all physical phenomena depend upon observers generating and placing order over the world that surrounds them.

In the social sciences there are few if any areas where our theoretical understanding of the way people behave enables us to categorise things with the degree of certainty seemingly characteristic of the physical sciences. Much of what we believe about the world may depend upon shared understandings and attitudes expressed in a structured way by means of language. The words which we use to describe these beliefs may be useful in helping us to think about what is going on, but they may also influence the meaning of what is being described. For example, in the case study at the beginning of this chapter a distinction was drawn between Hodsons, the organisation, and a number of external pressures. This seemingly straightforward separation of the company from its surroundings relies upon common sense and legal definitions of organisations as groups of people, employed to work within specific buildings, to produce certain goods and services in pursuit of common objectives. By this measure the external environment consists of all the other people, objects and information which are not directly employed by the organisation. There are problems with this simple definition, however, as the case study itself demonstrates. When the consultancy team is called into Hodsons to advise the Board of Directors about possible future developments, are these visitors part of the organisation or part of its environment? Similarly, when the consultants visit competitor organisations to interview their managers, should these individuals be seen as adversaries or advisers – 'them' or 'us'?

Indeed, some writers have even questioned whether it is appropriate to talk of organisations as distinct entities. According to David Silverman (1970), to consider an organisation as having an identity which can be separated from the people of which it is composed is to be guilty of 'reification' – giving life to something which is abstract. Others have furthered these criticisms by arguing that individuals have to interpret the organisations within which they work and the surrounding environment; therefore, the act of seeing and thinking about the world involves the imposition of order. Here it is suggested that people subjectively create or enact much of the world in which they live. There is no external objective reality, only a socially constructed reality, which depends upon human beings interpreting, negotiating and reaching temporary agreements about an acceptable shared reading of the world that surrounds them.

By this measure the problems confronting Hodsons may be only one interpretation of the pressures confronting the company. The Do-It-Yourself centres may only be seen as a threat to the company because this is a generally acceptable and useful way of seeing the world. A number of other, as yet unrevealed, explanations of the perceived problems may be available and could emerge through discussion among the people with an interest in the future of Hodsons.

Figure 1.2
A subjective view
of the interaction
between people
and their physical
environment

This alternative way of seeing the interplay between members of an organisation and their environment can be illustrated by reversing the direction of the arrows in our earlier diagram (*see* Fig 1.2).

Figure 1.2 aims to demonstrate that people impose order on the world outside them. The environment which we experience is therefore a product of our perceptions, language, thought processes and dealings with other people.

If we subscribe to this view of the external environment being subjectively constructed by people, it soon becomes apparent that there is considerable scope for disagreement about the form of external pressures and their effects. In recognition of this potential for disagreement a number of writers have laid stress on the role of cultural and political considerations in decision-making processes within organisations.

The powerful influence of national, industrial and organisational cultures in shaping attitudes, values and actions has been recognised by a growing number of writers in recent years (Hofstede, 1980; Hampden-Turner and Fons Trompenaars, 1993; Pettigrew and Whipp, 1991; Schein, 1984; Pfeffer, 1992). According to these writers, certain ways of seeing the world will tend to predominate in particular societies, industrial sectors or organisations. These ways of seeing the world will be communicated informally in all social settings via buzzwords, stories, rituals and ceremonies, among other things. As a consequence of the messages received from these sources people become conditioned in their beliefs about how to find out more about their environment, what is deemed to be an acceptable interpretation of the problem, and what will be viewed as a satisfactory solution.

In some eastern cultures, for example, individual reflection and listening to the insights of older and more experienced workers may be seen as the most appropriate means of finding out more about the problem. By contrast, in Anglo-Saxon countries a premium may be placed on what are deemed to be more 'scientific' analyses of the situation based upon the systematic application of a programme of interviews or questionnaires. The extent to which the results of these analyses are accepted and acted upon may further be determined by the way in which the problems are described and analysed.

If we apply these cultural insights to the Hodsons case, the problems which the company confronts can be seen to have deeper cultural roots. From this perspective Hodsons may be seen as typical of small and medium-sized firms operating in the UK. The company has grown under the direction of its original family owners and their beliefs about what is an acceptable form of business to undertake have conditioned decisions in the past. Their ability to lead in this way is dependent upon a national belief in 'managers' right to manage' and the importance of individual entrepreneurs. This has meant that decisions about the long-term future of the business are considered to be the preserve of the Board of Directors under the leadership of the Managing Director. In many other countries implicit cultural definitions of what constitutes an organisation and who should be allowed to influence its operation may mean that a more participative view of how decisions should be taken would have been adopted. In these contexts employees, bankers and other representatives of groups with a stake in the organisation may influence the definition of problems and the choice of appropriate solutions. At the level of the building industry, the form and function of building suppliers might similarly be seen as culturally determined. Traditionally, builders' yards have not been open to the general public and advertising has been seen to be an unprofessional activity. It could be argued that it has taken a challenge to these values, led by retailers who model their behaviour on retailing patterns in other cultures, to alter these views. But these changes may not be inevitable or necessarily long lasting. Concern about the effects of large out-of-town shopping centres on city centre retailers, poorer members of the community and the impact of pollution on the environment may lead to further change. While it is not possible to predict the nature of this change, it could include the promotion of small stores in town centres and/or firms that use telephone and e-mail-based ordering systems and deliver products direct to the customer whether at work or at home.

The way in which Hodsons will ultimately respond to the pressures it confronts might also be seen to be affected by established attitudes and behaviours within the organisation. Under the direction of John Hodson the firm has adopted a relatively conservative and defensive approach to its operations. Against this background it is unlikely that he will wish to sponsor a radical solution to the current problems.

Aside from the influence of dominant patterns of values, attitudes and behaviours at the national and organisational level, there may also be considerable differences at the level of the group and the individual. Thus the beliefs of managers and employees, individually or in groups, can play an important part in determining how environmental threats and opportunities are interpreted. The members of an organisation will not necessarily see their environment in similar ways and therefore they may wish to adopt different courses of action in response to the perceived threats. There is rarely one commonly agreed view of the causes of an organisation's misfortunes, nor is there usually consensus on the means of solving these problems. Whatever the validity and merits of a particular diagnosis, prediction or prescription, the ultimate decision to adopt or reject a proposal will invariably depend upon the interests and relative power of different groups within an organisation. Where consensus is not forthcoming, these different groups will tend to resort to political tactics in order to achieve their desired ends. Whether this be through attempts to control or manipulate recalcitrant colleagues, to negotiate or collaborate with adversaries or to accommodate the interests of dissenting groups, the final form of any solution is unlikely to appear wholly rational to an observer from outside the organisation.

Once again, by applying these insights to the Hodsons case we can see that there are fundamental differences of opinion between Mike Sellers and John Hodson. At the present time, John Hodson and the Board of Directors appear to have accommodated Mike Sellers' criticisms of the current approach by agreeing to appoint external consultants. Whether this compromise will produce a solution which is acceptable to all parties in the longer term remains to be seen. However, it is worth noting that John Hodson appears to have a stronger position within the organisation. As a member of the founding family with many close friends on the Board of Directors he has a higher status and more resources at his disposal than Mike Sellers. If Mike wishes to change things he will be forced to rely on his expertise and charisma in any future negotiations or power struggle.

☐ Continuity versus turbulent change

Another area of difference between analyses of the physical environment which confronts organisations is the extent to which writers portray things as dynamic and changing rapidly or alternatively relatively static and developing slowly.

If we subscribe to a relatively stable and static view of the external world then there is little need to anticipate, forecast or predict what will happen in the future. Things will continue to behave in the same way as they always have, and therefore managers and employees can afford to concentrate on ensuring that operations within the organisation are undertaken in the most effective and cost-efficient manner.

Approaches which emphasise stability have come under increasing attack in recent years. The rate of change is said to be increasing and there are few areas of organisational activity which are unaffected by this trend. Writers from a number of disciplines have suggested that this increase in the rate of change presents managers and employees with new problems when they attempt to analyse and make sense of the environment within which they operate (*see* Handy, 1991, 1994; Kanter, 1985, 1989; and Peters, 1989). Not only are there a myriad of variables, but all of these interact in ways which are often difficult to measure and to use as the basis for future predictions.

Chaos theory is one of the most recent examples of the recognition of the problems associated with complexity and change in the physical sciences (Gleick, 1987). According to advocates of this approach, the behaviour of systems is often dependent upon small fluctuations in variables which are difficult to measure. These fluctuations may then become amplified with dramatic effects on the overall pattern of observed activity. For example, it has been suggested that the behaviour of weather systems is affected by a very large number of different factors, including surface temperature, wind patterns and ocean currents. Furthermore, the way in which these variables interact means that small variations in humidity, wind speed or temperature in one area of the world can have dramatic effects upon the weather in other continents. To use one well-worn cliché 'the beating of a butterfly's wings can produce a hurricane on the other side of the world'. This approach to understanding changes within particular systems has recently been extended to a number of areas of social scientific enquiry. For example, econometricians attempting to understand the workings of equity and commodity markets have suggested that a small variation in the price of one company's shares or a particular product in one exchange could have dramatic effects on other financial markets around the world. Similarly, a growing number of sociologists and other social commentators use the concept of reflexivity to refer to the increasing interdependence between events in different parts of the world and the consequent rapid and unpredictable nature of change in social and economic arrangements in seemingly separate areas of the world (Giddens, 1984).

A belief in the complex and dynamic view of the world implicit within chaos theory, reflexivity and similar approaches to analysing the external world presents us with two problems which could potentially limit the value of any analysis of current developments and future trends.

The first of these problems is overcoming the difficulties associated with getting accurate measurements of relevant variables and indicators. For example, the measures of the recession which have caused problems for Hodsons rely on calculations of consumer spending and building activity within the construction industry, as well as other measures of consumption and production. These figures are collected nationally by the government's Office for National Statistics and a range of trade and industry bodies. The resultant indices provide a snapshot of the overall level of activity within the sector, but this aggregate figure may mask significant variations. While the overall level of timber sales may have declined, some suppliers will have seen an increase in sales. Furthermore, the difficulties associated with compiling this data will often mean that figures are not available for many months. Even when these measures have been collected and published, errors in their compilation may mean that the original figures are subject to significant revision at a future date.

A number of critics have drawn attention to these physical and mental limitations on our ability to gain accurate measurements of changes in the world that surrounds us (Simon, 1976; Cyert and March, 1963). According to these writers, all human decision making takes place within the context of 'imperfect knowledge', 'bounded rationality' and 'uncertainty'. Even the most complex computerised models of the world are limited by the quality of the raw data which is fed into them. Computing engineers use the acronym 'GIGO' to refer to this phenomenon – 'garbage in, garbage out'. In short, this slogan means that if you put the wrong data into a computer you will get the wrong information out. Because all organisations face limitations in terms of the money and time they can invest in collecting information, the data they collect is often incomplete or inaccurate. As a consequence the managers and employees that have to interpret the results of any analysis, whether computerised or otherwise, will usually find that many of the questions they would like to ask are not answerable with the information provided. Even if these decision makers have a perfect and complete set of data with which to perform their analyses, the interpretation placed upon this information will still be constrained by the physical limitations of individual managers' memories and powers of thought. Most of us can only remember between seven and eight things at any one time. Furthermore, our ability to manipulate this information is very limited. Awareness of these problems has led a number of writers to draw attention to the messiness of most management decision making and action. In the words of one writer, strategy formulation and implementation is best seen as the 'science of muddling through' (Lindbloom, 1959).

The second problem associated with any analysis of complex and changing systems concerns what is done with the raw data and information. Any prediction or forecast of future trends will be based upon assumptions about the relationship between different indicators. For example, in the Hodsons case study it may be assumed that a general rise in the level of consumer confidence and an increase in the number of new house sales will lead to an upturn in the construction industry, with consequent improvements in the company's sales position. This relationship is illustrated in Fig 1.3.

However, this simple model with its in-built assumptions about cause and effect relationships between different variables may oversimplify what is really happening within the building industry. The variables may be difficult to disen-

Figure 1.3 Cause and effect: the implied relationship between consumer confidence and Hodsons' sales

tangle from one another; the nature of cause and effect may be more complex than this simple chain implies; and there may be other variables at work.

For example, the number of new house sales will have an effect upon the level of consumer confidence and the amount of building activity will influence the volume of house sales. Furthermore, the availability of mortgages, older housing stock and rented accommodation, among other things, could all affect one or more of the variables. These complexities and interrelationships between the phenomena we observe will inevitably affect our ability to produce effective analyses of current activity and future trends.

Other accounts have challenged the view that events that surround us can be isolated as specific variables which relate to one another in a manner which can be determined. For some writers it is more appropriate to think of the things which we see around us as elements of a complex web, or threads of a woven fabric. Each component of the web or fabric is thus seen as part of an inter-related whole which can only be understood in terms of its relationship to other parts (Collins, 1994).

One form of this analysis is generally referred to as systems theory. Drawing upon models developed in the biological and engineering sciences, this approach encourages us to see organisations as dynamic structures characterised by the flow of information and materials. In order for these organisations to transform raw materials into goods and services, while satisfying the objectives of the organisation's members, all parts of the system must be in balance with one another, and with the environment that surrounds them (*see* Von Bertalanffy, 1967; Katz and Kahn, 1966; Lovelock, 1979).

More radical forms of this analysis suggest that our attempts to fragment and name parts of the world that surrounds us are at best misguided. By defining the world in terms of basic units and then seeking to determine how these elements relate to one another, we can gain only a partial understanding of the nature of reality. According to this view, it is not appropriate to isolate and pick out one aspect of an organisation's environment. All aspects of the organisation and its environment have to be considered together as a whole because they are all interrelated. Furthermore, the nature of the whole is constantly changing. The future is not a continuation of established patterns or cause and effect, but a gradual unfolding of a complex and indivisible whole (Bohm, 1980).

Exercise 1.2 **Representing the external environment**

Refer back to the list of pressures confronting Hodsons and set out this information as creatively and imaginatively as you can on an overhead projector slide or a plain A4 sheet of paper. You may find it helpful to refer to the suggestions in Exhibit 1.1 when undertaking this analysis.

1.1 Representing the external environment

There are a range of ways in which the pressures confronting the members of an organisation can be represented and communicated. A brief description of the most common forms of analysis follows.

Lists

The easiest and perhaps least demanding form of analysis involves merely listing the pressures, either in the order they occurred to you, or on the basis of their perceived level of importance.

Categories

If your list of external pressures becomes very long, or you are anxious to ensure that equal attention is focused on all forms of possible external change, it may be appropriate to order the information on the basis of a series of categories. One of the most common approaches is a *PEST analysis*.

PEST analyses draw our attention to the Political, Economic, Social and Technological (PEST) changes which confront the organisation. The use of these headings is designed to ensure that equal attention is focused upon all these areas of possible external change. A number of writers have amended the PEST acronym to include legal and ecological pressures (PESTLE).

There are two problems commonly associated with conducting a PEST or PESTLE analysis. First, there is the possibility that a particular pressure may be listed under only one heading when it should occur under several. This reflects the somewhat arbitrary nature of the categories being used in this form of analysis. Second, there is a danger that by merely listing the pressures the relative importance of different trends may be overlooked. This problem can be overcome by ranking the pressures in order of importance and allocating a number from I to 100 to each external pressure.

Maps and rich pictures

This is a more elaborate form of analysis which can be undertaken by carrying out the following five steps:

1 Draw up a long list of external pressures and problems confronting the organisation. It may be helpful to write these down on individual small pieces of card.

2 Edit the list to ensure that there are no exact duplications of information or imprecise statements.

3 Group the list or cards into related categories. By rearranging the list or cards on a large sheet of paper or board it should be possible to isolate a number of groups of issues. If one issue within these groups appears to subsume a number of others, cluster these constituent issues around the main heading. For example, the following issues might be clustered under the heading 'economic recession': a collapse in house prices, a decline in consumer confidence and rising unemployment.

4 If issues are difficult to group but are clearly interrelated, arrows can be drawn to indicate the nature of the relationship between these factors. The strength and nature of the connection between particular issues can then be indicated by the width of the line which is drawn and the direction of the arrows entered on that line.

5 The relative importance of particular developments can be indicated by assigning numbers to particular issues to indicate their relative ranking. It should also be possible to indicate whether a particular factor is stable and predictable or subject to rapid and tur-

bulent change by assigning a colour to that issue. For example, yellow and red could be used to indicate 'hot issues' which are likely to change their form rapidly, while blue and purple indicate issues which are 'cold' and unlikely to alter in the foreseeable future.

Images and metaphors

According to Gareth Morgan, pictures, images and the use of appropriate metaphors can provide a powerful basis for analysis of the interplay between an organisation and its environment (Morgan, 1986, 1993). For example, by drawing an image of the organisation as an iceberg or termite hill and extending this image through annotating the diagram, important aspects of the organisation's current position may be revealed. Morgan suggests that this approach works because it encourages members of the organisation to think creatively and outside of the confines of accepted categories and definitions.

Models

This approach attempts to specify the exact nature of, and the relationship between, things. The most sophisticated forms rely upon the statement of equations which define specific measurable variables and indicate the precise interplay between these elements. Where these models and theories have been appropriately constructed and expressed, it should then be possible to draw up a number of propositions or hypotheses which specify exactly what will happen if one or more variables within the equation are altered. If a model or theory is to be tested in this manner it is essential that hypotheses drawn from it can be expressed in a form which allows them to be verified or refuted by reference to information drawn from laboratory experiments or observations in the field. In short, it must be possible to prove that the model is incorrect – it must be falsifiable. Once these tests have been conducted and the component hypotheses and propositions have been demonstrated to provide a reliable explanation of observed phenomena in a range of settings, it should then be possible to use the model as the basis for forecasts and predictions.

In the social sciences a number of models have been developed to explain the behaviour of the UK economy, social classes, and product and market development by companies. Unfortunately, the difficulties associated with collecting reliable information and manipulating this data have meant that, at present, few of these models provide a reliable basis for accurate forecasts of the future. Nevertheless, companies, institutions and other organisations still frequently use these models as the basis for anticipating and planning responses to possible future developments.

Scenario building

Another approach to analysing external pressures is to develop a series of scenarios outlining what could possibly happen in the future. In a rapidly changing world it may not be possible to produce an accurate prediction of the future, but by producing several different predictions it may be possible to challenge managers' existing assumptions and get closer to what will really happen. For example, managers might wish to consider what they would do in the event of a recession, steady growth or an economic boom. By outlining these various scenarios managers will have an opportunity to rehearse the reasons for particular decisions before they are forced to confront them directly.

☐ Choice and determinism

So far in this chapter we have considered how different views about the nature of the physical environment that surrounds us can affect how we analyse our own current position, or the position of a particular organisation, and predict possible future developments. In this next section we move on to consider how much discretion managers and employees have in responding to these external pressures. To what extent do managers individually, and employees collectively, have a choice about what they do in the future? Can they alter the position of their organisation and respond to, or master, the pressures that confront them? Or, are they forced to remain where they are – buffeted and pulled along by external developments over which they have no control? In short, how much choice do managers and employees have when making and implementing decisions?

As we shall see, writers differ in their views on these questions. For some, senior managers and directors can choose from a wide range of possible courses of action and will have few problems in implementing their preferred solutions. For others, perceptions of choice are often illusory as managers are frequently servants rather than masters of their environment. Thus, in practice, it may appear as if managers and employees consciously choose certain courses of action, but in reality what they do is determined by wider forces over which they have no control.

Choice

Those writers who emphasise choice suggest that managers are always confronted with different possible courses of action; therefore they are able to decide for themselves what they wish to do and how they wish to do it. There may be external pressures and influences, but people are always free to ignore, avoid, or meet these challenges as they see fit. This approach is particularly influential within the field of management theory and practice. Indeed, the belief that managers and employees are masters of their own destiny and the future of their organisations has become so pervasive in the UK and USA in recent years that it is often treated as basic common sense.

An important example of this view is provided by the *deliberative* approach to decision making within organisations. The assumptions implicit in this approach underpin many contemporary accounts of how decisions should be taken at all levels, and within all areas, of an organisation's activities. For example, this approach might be used to determine the content and form of the organisation's investment decisions, marketing campaigns, information systems, and human resource management policies. Although the details as put forward by different authors vary, there are a number of common features. Thus in general it is suggested that almost any organisational problems or external pressures can be addressed by going through the following four steps.

1 Possible future scenarios

This first stage involves reviewing information about a particular problem or pressure and associated developments using material gathered from a wide range of sources in order to make intelligent judgements about what could happen over the next ten to twenty years. Through discussion with colleagues on a one-to-one basis, or in groups, this might produce anything up to twenty different outlines of possible developments (these different outlines are referred to as scenarios in Exhibit 1.1 above). Some of these suggestions will inevitably be optimistic and others more pessimistic in tone and outlook. For example, the list of possible future scenarios for Hodsons might include potential national or global catastrophes. For example, among the current list of major threats to humans and their actvities are a worldwide recession or financial crisis, epidemics of CJD, AIDS or influenza, as well as the threats of global warming and ozone depletion, or perhaps more fancifully an asteroid impact. At the other extreme of possible future scenarios are predicted innovations and inventions which might prolong human life and reduce the limitations on economic growth currently imposed by shortages of raw materials and restrictions on improvements in productivity. For example, gene therapy, more successful treatments or possible cures for heart disease and cancer, as well as non-polluting and renewable sources of energy. In combination, these changes might lead to prolonged and significant increases in the volume of economic activity within the UK and global economy, leading to increased consumer affluence and improved demand for the products and services offered by retailers like Hodsons.

2 Probable future scenarios

Between the extremes of possible futures outlined above are a range of other possible developments which are arguably more probable. Drawing on the original list of possible scenarios, it should be possible to review each in turn in order to produce a shorter list of eight or more probable future scenarios. In undertaking this analysis it might be sensible to allocate a probability rating to each of the different suggestions. Thus the chances of an asteroid impact in the next ten years are probably in the order of 1 in 100 000 and can therefore probably be discounted from the analysis. However, other possible developments are more probable. For example, the introduction of regulations limiting the use of cars, growing public concern about the use of timber in house construction and/or restrictions on the importation of timber from developing countries as a consequence of concerns about pollution or the effects of deforestation. Taken together, these developments might reduce the demand for the company's products and limit the supply of timber, with significant effects on the overall level of sales that the organisation could achieve. At the other end of the spectrum of possible developments are the invention of pollution-free and renewable fuel supplies, improvements in forestry methods and increased consumer interest in timber as a housing material. Any one or more of these changes might lead to significant increases in timber sales, but might also be associated with increased consumer interest in large out-of-town stores.

3 Preferred future scenarios

The third stage in preparing for developments to come is the further refinement of the original list of possible future scenarios in order to concentrate on those developments which the company's managers and employees would prefer to see. At this stage, the number of scenarios could be whittled down to three or four preferred scenarios. Returning to the case of Hodsons, this might include:

☐ expansion into new markets, e.g. house improvement and building work;

☐ relocation to out-of-town locations;

☐ merger or alliance with another timber retailer or do-it-yourself store;

☐ retrenchment or consolidation of activities, e.g. a store closure programme or a reduction in staffing, or limitations on the range of goods and services offered at each location.

Obviously, the options listed above are not necessarily mutually exclusive. In other words, it is possible to pursue more than one of the possible lines of development at any one time or to mix elements of each. As a consequence, the managers and employees of the firm might decide that they would prefer to rearrange the options to reflect different combinations, rather than state the options in terms of the stark alternatives listed above. Whatever is finally decided through discussion of these or similar alternatives, it should be possible to rehearse the implications of each approach for particular departments and functions within the organisation as well as considering the pros and cons of each option in relation to one another.

4 Planning for the preferred solution

The final stage in the deliberative approach is to choose which of the preferred solutions the organisation's employees and managers will actually pursue over the next five or more years. In essence this will involve outlining the key features of the preferred state solution and then working backwards over the period of years in which it is planned that these changes will take place in order to outline the necessary intermediary steps that will need to be taken. Further details of the range of alternative approaches and perspectives available for analysing and undertaking this task, as well as evaluating the success of this approach, are contained in Chapter 3.

Determinism

For writers adopting a determinist perspective, various environmental factors (market conditions, technology, culture, organisation structure and internal organisational politics, etc.) either significantly constrain or determine the strategies available to an organisation. As a consequence, managers and employees within companies have few real choices. For example, the theory of the firm which lies at the heart of mainstream economic analysis adopts a deterministic view of how organisations operate. Other things being equal, it is suggested that the amount of goods supplied by individual firms or the economy in general is determined by the interplay of the level of demand and supply. If firms wish to exploit this demand and make a profit they need to ensure that the most efficient balance is achieved between their sales and costs. If they fail to follow this logic then they can be sure that their competitors will, and in the long run they will be driven out of business.

This deterministic approach is not confined to the field of economics; indeed, similar models have been presented by management theorists and sociologists.

In one famous study of the Scottish electronics industry in the early 1960s it was suggested that organisational structure and operating style are strongly influenced, if not determined, by the market pressures facing the company (Burns and Stalker, 1961). The results of this study indicate that in stable market conditions with relatively low levels of product and process innovation, bureaucratic forms of organisation are most appropriate. A key feature of this form of organisation is a clear hierarchy of managerial control and a strict division of labour. By contrast, in more volatile market conditions where there is rapid technological change, flexible and organic forms of organisation are more appropriate. The main elements of this form of organisation are blurred reporting lines and employer reliance upon worker loyalty and a general willingness to undertake a wide variety of tasks in order to get the job done. According to Burns and Stalker, although it is relatively easy to specify the best match between an organisation and its environment, there are problems associated with changing from one form to another. Changes to the formal organisational structure will not radically change the career aspirations of staff or their internal political loyalties. Indeed, these aspirations and ties may act as a major, if not insurmountable, barrier to internal organisational change initiatives.

Later elaborations of this approach have suggested that organisational success is contingent upon achieving the best match between an organisation and its environment. Referred to as *contingency theory*, this approach has led to a number of different lists of external and internal pressures and recipes for dealing with these constraints (*see* Lawrence and Lorsch, 1967; Miles and Snow, 1978; Morgan, 1986). Thus decision makers within any organisation are not completely free to make choices. If they ignore the lessons to be learnt about the best match between market conditions and the activities of their organisation they will perform poorly or go out of business. Thus the aim in these circumstances should be to gain a congruent match between environmental conditions and internal business operations.

More recently, a number of analysts and commentators have used the concept of stakeholding in order to draw attention to the influence of individuals and groups on decisions and actions within a firm. According to these writers, it is helpful to consider the choices and constraints available to managers and employees within a firm by reference to key groups inside and outside the organisation. Each of these groups, it is suggested, will have its own views or combination of views about the current state of the organisation as well as preferences about what should happen in the future. These groups may then seek to influence the form of future initiatives or to limit proposed changes through argument or active resistance.

Through the application of contingency and stakeholder forms of analysis to the Hodsons case study it would appear that the organisation is poorly adapted to its environment. The environment has become turbulent and unpredictable, but the Board of Directors has retained a defensive attitude to goal setting and continues to rely upon bureaucratic and authoritarian management methods. Meanwhile the staff in the branch operations remain committed to their jobs primarily because of the discretion and expertise that they are encouraged to develop and demonstrate at work. If the members of the organisation wish to remain in business and assure their longer-term future they will have to find a higher degree of congruence between their internal operations and the external environment, as well as between the interests and intentions of the directors as one stakeholder group and the branch employees as another. Both of these groups have choices available to them, but these are severely constrained by the natural logic of acceptable matches between environmental conditions and organisational structure and operations.

Other forms of determinist analysis draw upon the biological sciences in general, and evolutionary theory in particular to analyse organisational behaviour. Using models of product and organisational life cycles, they suggest that, like human beings, products and organisations are born, they grow, mature, decline and then die. Steps may be taken to extend the life of a particular product or organisation, but in the end its demise is inevitable (Leavitt, 1975; Greiner, 1972).

In response to these insights, and a belief that the world is increasingly characterised by rapid change and uncertainty, a number of writers have suggested that managers and employees should abandon attempts to rationally plan a response to external pressures. Instead it is suggested they should become more flexible in their approach to planning. This may be achieved by building some variety into the way in which the organisation operates, perhaps by allowing junior managers and employees more discretion and decision-making authority in an attempt to get them to find their own local solutions to wider problems. Alternatively, senior managers and directors may wish to sponsor several different solutions simultaneously in order to reduce the chances of failure.

The most extreme forms of determinist analysis adopt a fatalist perspective by suggesting that people and the organisations of which they are members are prisoners of their environment and have little choice but to go with the flow of the events that surround them. If they do not move in this direction then their organisations will die. Frequently labelled as 'evolutionists' or 'population ecologists', these writers have focused their analysis on the dynamics of change at the level of industries or whole groups of organisations (Hannan and Freeman, 1988). They argue that the form of change and adaptation implicit in the rational planning model is easier said than done. Instead they suggest that competition and scarce physical resources limit the number of organisations an environment can sustain. In short, there can only be so many building suppliers within the construction industry in the UK. Furthermore, the combined pressures of an organisation's existing investment in land and equipment, together with legal constraints on what can and cannot be done, combine with limitations on available information, internal political constraints, and the existing history and culture of the organisation to make change very difficult to achieve. As a consequence, they maintain that organisations survive or fail as a result of natural evolutionary processes, regardless of the actions taken by their managers and employees.

If we apply this final insight to the Hodsons case, it may be that wider changes in the business environment confronting the organisation are so profound and the internal capacity to respond so limited that senior managers have no choice. Their only option is to plan the sale of all or part of the company assets and concentrate their efforts on finding alternative employment for themselves and the other employees.

Exercise 1.3 **Choosing an appropriate response to declining sales at Hodsons**

By reference to the material contained in the Hodsons case study and your own general knowledge of developments in the do-it-yourself and retail building materials industry, outline your own views of possible, probable and preferred business futures for this organisation.

☐ Absolute and relative values

The last of the four sets of basic assumptions underpinning different approaches to the analysis and evaluation of an organisation's external environment focuses on the ethical position adopted by managers and employees or any observer undertaking an assessment of the current position and potential future development of an organisation. By ethical position we mean the moral values that they use when reaching judgements about what is good and bad about a particular problem or pressure and the responses which might be adopted in reaction to developments inside or outside the organisation. As this section aims to demonstrate, there are a range of different positions that these managers, employees or observers can take, from a belief, at one extreme, that there are universal and enduring ethical truths, to a view at the other extreme that the rights and wrongs of particular thoughts and actions can only ever be determined by reference to all the facts of a case and will vary from one individual to another. These two extremes are referred to in this section as absolute and relative approaches.

Absolute

The view that there are absolute moral or ethical principles which should guide the judgement and action of people has a long history in the west. Whether embodied in religious doctrines, legal rules or local customs and conventions, there is a commonly held assumption in most if not all societies that individuals have an obligation to behave in particular ways. However, when it comes to defining what principles should apply, as well as specifying how these principles should be put into effect, theologians, philosophers, lawyers, anthropologists and sociologists have adopted different approaches and often arrived at different answers. For the theologian, the rules governing what humans ought to do are either God given or alternatively derive from the teachings of human representatives of these divine entities. For the philosopher, moral and ethical principles may be revealed through a reasoned consideration of particular approaches in relation to one another. Meanwhile, for the lawyer, principles may be drawn from or applied to the laws in a particular set of circumstances. The anthropologist or sociologist, by contrast, is apt to be more concerned with the way in which particular rules and codes have been derived, the views of those regulated or affected by these principles, and the effects, if any, on the behaviour of those individuals the rules seek to control.

It is beyond the scope of this chapter to deal with the very wide variety of ways in which theologians, philosophers, lawyers, anthropologists and sociologists have sought to tackle the question of what absolute moral and ethical principles guide or should guide the judgements and actions of individuals and groups. However, the following three distinctive approaches are worthy of some comment.

Virtue

For the ancient Greek philosophers Plato and his pupil Aristotle, every person does what their own character prompts. While both of these writers believed that there were absolute notions of justice which exist apart from the thought and actions of individuals, the extent to which these people are aware of the form of these absolutes depends on their character, education and willingness to engage in rational contemplation. In short, some people are better placed to make these decisions than others and they should be given the authority and responsibility to determine what is right and wrong and, as a consequence, make difficult choices on behalf of others.

Rules and duties

This approach rests on the belief that there are certain beliefs and behaviours which are always wrong and others which are invariably if not always right. The work of anthropologists and comparative ethicists over the last hundred or more years has revealed that all societies have codes, customs or cultural norms which seek to influence and affect individual behaviour in the following ways:

- ☐ Forbid homicide and bodily violence except in certain very prescribed circumstances.
- ☐ Protect the property rights of individuals and groups.
- ☐ Regulate and restrict insults or attacks on honour or reputation.
- ☐ Outline the obligations of parents and children, suppliers and customers, employers and employees.

In determining the relevance and importance of these rules in specific circumstances, a number of philosophers have stressed the importance of motivation and the ends being sought when a particular act is undertaken. For example, depriving someone of one of their belongings may not be treated with the same seriousness if it can be argued that there was no intention to steal, only to borrow this item. Similarly, certain acts might be justified if they cause discomfort for a few but enable many more to achieve their own specific ends.

Specific ends

According to the advocates of this approach, the fundamental principle governing ethical decisions should be the pursuit of a particular objective, e.g. pleasure, improved well-being, economic gain or some other form of advantage.

It is commonly assumed that a logical consequence of the pursuit of these ends will be the avoidance of pain, economic loss or some other form of disadvantage. There are many variants of this approach, from the extremes of hedonism with its emphasis on the pursuit of individual pleasure, to the assumption in much of mainstream economics that employees, customers and firms will respectively seek to maximise their income, achieve the maximum satisfaction of their needs and wants, and increase profits.

Relative

Despite continued debate about the use and relevance of absolute values in guiding moral and ethical judgements, a number of writers and commentators have drawn attention to the continuing variety of decisions made by people about what is right and wrong. Reacting to concerns about the power of religious or rational forms of inquiry to reveal what is good and bad, critics of the absolute approach have emphasised the relative basis of values and ethics. A variety of different perspectives and methods have been put forward in an attempt to make sense of the choices people make and to provide some justification or rationale for their different evaluations. The main features of three of the most significant examples of this approach are outlined below.

Situationism

Advocates of this approach believe that while there may be certain general principles governing human thought and action, the relevance and applicability of these principles will vary from situation to situation and therefore it is only possible to make an appropriate judgement when all the facts relating to that situation can be gathered together and considered together.

Utilitarianism

The essence of this approach is most famously captured in the phrase, 'the greatest good for the greatest number'. Following this maxim, it has been argued that past actions or future intentions should be evaluated by reference to the extent to which they produce the most happiness for the largest number of individuals within any society of constituent grouping. In its earliest versions, utilitarianism was criticised for the power it appeared to give to those who would define the majority within any society, what would be deemed to constitute good, and the limits, if any, that might be placed on acceptable levels of harm to minority groups. In response to these concerns, other variants of this approach have sought to draw attention to the importance of democratic and other forms of inclusive decision-making process in determining the trade-off between the pursuit of different ends and the individuals or groups seeking these ends.

Existentialism

This is arguably the most radical of the relative methods of making value and ethical judgements. The roots of this approach can be traced back to the mid-nineteenth century, but it was not until the post-WWII years that it became popular in Western Europe. At this time it found expression in novels of European intellectuals as much as in the writings of philosophers and other social commentators. For the adherents of this approach, morality and ethical judgement cannot be subjected to reasoned analysis and there are no absolute values which could or should guide an individual's thoughts and actions. In the absence of these certainties, individuals are forced to make their own choices, to commit themselves to what they have picked to pursue and to the maintenance of sufficient liberty in order to ensure that they are free to make these choices.

Applying insights derived from the different approaches to value and ethical judgements outlined above to the Hodsons case demonstrates that there are a variety of ways in which the managers of this firm might seek to choose a course of action in the future and justify these choices. For example, it could be argued that Mike Sellers and John Hodson should be left to make the final choices on behalf of the company as a consequence of their arguably superior upbringing and education. It could also be suggested that within the limits of the law, the only sensible course of action would be to choose those options that will maximise the company's profits and employees' incomes in the foreseeable future. Alternatively, it might be argued that the right course of action can only be determined when all of the individuals and groups with an interest in the future of Hodsons have been identified and decisions have been made on their behalf or through consultation with these groups about which courses of action would produce the greatest benefits for all of these different parties.

Exercise 1.4   Choosing an appropriate response to declining sales at Hodsons

Using the information contained in the Hodsons case study and your own general knowledge, produce a list of possible responses to the decline in sales produced by the recession. When you have completed this list, decide which if any of these options are feasible and then determine which is the most appropriate or suitable. You may find it useful to consider some of the suggestions outlined in the preceding section.

☐ Summary and conclusion

This chapter has considered four sets of differences in the basic assumptions which underpin many contemporary accounts of the way in which organisations and their members deal with external pressures and developments. These distinctions between objective versus subjective interpretations, continuity versus turbulent change, choice versus determinism and absolute versus relative values have been described and illustrated with reference to the Hodsons case study at the beginning of the chapter.

Although few writers and practitioners adopt an extreme position on any one of these dimensions, there are significant differences of emphasis in their accounts. These differences have a profound effect upon suggestions about the most appropriate means to:

☐ investigate and analyse external pressures;

☐ diagnose the problems confronting an organisation;

☐ predict future trends and developments; and

☐ propose recommendations for future action.

Different assumptions lead to different approaches, analyses, predictions and proposals and so it has been suggested that before attempting any reading of environmental pressures, managers and employees should consider the assumptions that they are making and ensure that alternative ways of seeing the situation are considered. We may favour one particular approach, but it is important to consider other perspectives. A full analysis of the problems confronting any organisation can best be achieved when all facets have been considered.

As a general rule, before beginning any analysis or evaluation of a problem confronting an organisation it is important to consider:

☐ a variety of methods of gathering data and information;

☐ different interpretations of the problem;

☐ the extent to which it is possible to define and predict future trends and changes;

☐ whether managers and employees within the organisation will be able to take the necessary remedial action.

Exercise 1.5   Analysis of pressures and problems

Compile an analysis of the pressures and problems confronting either your employing organisation or a company with which you are familiar. There are a range of library and other resources which should enable you to complete this task quickly.

☐ The World Wide Web: There are a number of search engines available on the World Wide Web which can help you to find information about organisations and companies. Among the most popular of these search engines are the following:

http://www.msn.com   http://www.excite.com
http://www.google.com   http://www.lycos.com

There are also more specific sites which can be helpful in your search for general business or company specific information:

http://bized.ac.uk/
http://www.clearinghouse.net/
http://www.ft.com
http://www.researchindex.co.uk
http://www.dis.strath.ac.uk/business/
http://sosig.ac.uk/

☐ CD ROM. A number of national newspapers, business magazines and academic journals are available on CD ROM disks either in full text or abstract form. Most university, college and public libraries provide access to these databases locally or via web-based subscription services. By using a CD ROM machine it should be possible to locate recent relevant articles and then download them onto a computer disk for subsequent editing. Useful CD ROM services include FAME (Financial Analysis Made Easy), ABI/Inform (general business and company information compiled from magazines) and Mintel (market intelligence information).

☐ Indexes. If your library does not have a CD ROM machine it should have a number of indexes which list relevant publications under subject headings. The Research Index provides a list of articles which have appeared on specific topics or companies on a fortnightly basis. A similar service is provided by the Business Periodicals Index and the Financial Journals Index.

☐ Organisational sources. You may wish to contact the organisation directly. Most large companies will have a press or public relations office and many have a separate education department which can provide you with copies of the annual report and other literature about the organisation. Obviously these materials will have been drawn up to show the company in the best possible light and therefore you should always read these materials in a critical manner, and compare this information with analyses in the business, trade or professional press.

When you have collected the material, analyse the current position of the organisation and possible future directions using one or more of the techniques covered in this chapter.

02

Ownership, control, objectives and organisation

☐ Introduction

Organisations operating in the UK are very varied. Small corner shops financed and operated by their owners exist next door to large multinational companies with thousands of employees and finance drawn from stock markets around the world. In addition to these different forms of private enterprise, agencies supported by central or local government, together with charities and voluntary bodies, provide a range of goods and services to people across the country. These different forms of organisation share a number of features and yet remain different in crucial ways. Increasingly important are 'Public–Private Partnerships' which blur some of the distinction between the private and public sectors.

☐ Focus and scope

This chapter aims to outline some of the major differences which exist between organisations in terms of their ownership, organisation and objectives. By undertaking this analysis we hope to demonstrate that these factors have a significant impact upon the nature and form of the pressures affecting organisations in different sectors of the UK economy. In addition, the way in which particular organisations deal with specific external pressures will be, at least in part, conditioned by their owners and other individuals with an interest in their operations. Thus, private sector companies which aim to gain a profit from their activities will behave in a very different manner by comparison with large public sector services which seek to provide a service to members of the community.

The chapter begins with an outline of the main differences between private and public sector organisations. We then move on to consider recent changes to the ownership, organisation and objectives of various public and private sector bodies. Here we aim to demonstrate that in the public sector government-sponsored reforms including privatisation have had a significant effect on the operation of current and former public sector agencies. We will also consider the role of 'Public–Private Partnership.' Similar attention is paid to the private sector where we discuss the effects of recent waves of merger and acquisition activity and the gradual expansion of multinational company operations.

Moving away from a focus on general trends, the chapter concludes with an outline of some of the varied methods of operation in specific organisations.

While we may be able to discern general trends at the level of the international and national economy, a fuller appreciation of the operation of specific organisations requires more refined forms of analysis. At this level, therefore, we aim to demonstrate the importance of analysing the different interests of key groups inside and outside the organisation. By identifying these groups we hope to demonstrate their influence on the stated objectives of specific organisations. In undertaking this analysis we also seek to outline ways in which the stated and unstated goals of an organisation may be examined in order to measure progress and expose gaps between the goals as laid down by its senior managers and the actual day-to-day behaviour of employees within that organisation.

Learning objectives

Once you have read this chapter and completed the associated exercises, you should be able to:

☐ define different forms of organisation and comment upon the implications of these differences for the goals pursued by managers and employees;

☐ describe trends in the ownership and orientation of UK organisations;

☐ discuss the factors influencing a specific organisation's goals;

☐ outline the goals being pursued by an organisation known to you; and

☐ consider the ethical issues shaping organisations.

CASE STUDY

Flexington University

The following case study examines the ownership, organisation and objectives of Flexington – a medium-sized university based in the south-east of England. The material presented in this case is drawn directly from the experiences of employees at a number of institutions of higher education. As such it is not based on people and events within any one university, but represents a stylised account of developments within the sector as a whole over the last 90 years. The information presented in this case study will form the basis of later discussion in this chapter.

The changing status of Flexington University

The history of Flexington University can be traced back to the late nineteenth century when members of the local Mechanical Institute founded Stanmead Technical College. This college was set up in response to concerns about the failures of British industry and commerce in overseas markets. Leading members of the Institute believed that these failings were caused by the poor training and education of British workers. Taking a lead from the experiences of German industrialists and trainers, they were determined to establish an institution which would provide high standards of instruction in technical and vocational subjects.

Financed through voluntary subscriptions from the Institute's membership, the college began its operations by renting space in local schools and charging students a nominal fee for evening classes in subjects as diverse as geometry, technical drawing, building construction and electricity. Because of Stanmead College's reliance on private funding, classes were available only when a sufficient number of students enrolled on these courses. Furthermore, students who attended these courses were not awarded nationally recognised qualifications;

instead they had to rely upon local employers accepting certificates of attendance from the college as proof of their skills and abilities.

As the college expanded its operations, it became more dependent upon local government for its funding and in the early 1900s Flexington County Council assumed responsibility for the day-to-day operation of the college. For the next 45 years, the college remained relatively small, although the range of courses on offer changed in response to changes in the skills demanded by local industry.

In the 1940s, the onset of the Second World War placed new demands on the college as a growing number of male and female armaments workers needed training in modern production techniques. At the end of the war, the government introduced an Education Act which committed the country to providing secondary education for all and introduced a requirement for local authorities to provide further education in technical and design subjects.

In the period immediately following the Second World War, the college also began to hasten the process of linking courses to nationally recognised qualifications. This initiative gained extra momentum when the college was allowed to register its students as external candidates for University of London degree courses.

As the college continued to expand, an increasing proportion of the teaching was at the undergraduate level and in 1962 the college split into two. Stanmead College of Further Education focused its work on vocational further education for school leavers, while Stanmead Institute of Technology concentrated on providing academic study for more mature students. Despite these changes, both colleges remained committed to providing training and education in technical subjects.

In 1970, Stanmead Institute of Technology merged with the Roseberry College of Art and Design and the Peabody Teachers' Training Academy to form Flexington Polytechnic. The new organisation was set up in response to a government initiative designed to increase the number of graduates with vocational skills in a range of subjects. At the same time a new body – the Council for National Academic Awards (CNAA) – was set up to oversee the quality of the wider range of courses provided by Flexington and other polytechnics.

Over the next 18 years the polytechnic, although still formally owned and controlled by the local authority, reorganised its operations and concentrated its work within six faculties – Business, Education and Social Work, Science, Art and Design, Technology and Social Sciences. Accompanying this broadening of the work of the organisation there was a gradual change in the balance of work undertaken by these sections of the polytechnic. These changes took place for four reasons.

1 The Faculties of Science and Technology became less significant in the overall work of the institution as manufacturing industry declined in importance within the local economy.

2 The Business and Social Science Faculties became more important as local residents sought qualifications which would help them advance their careers in the growing number of local service-sector industries.

3 Staff increasingly undertook research and consultancy work in addition to their teaching duties.

4 Various departments within the Polytechnic gained approval from the CNAA to offer higher level degrees in various disciplines.

In combination these changes began to blur the differences between Flexington and the older, established universities.

In the early 1980s the government relaxed the rules governing the establishment of universities. In response to these changes, Britain's first private university was established at Buckingham.

Later in the same decade Flexington, like other polytechnics, was encouraged by further government action to increase rapidly the number of students taught on its courses. The older, more established universities were much slower in their response. In recognition of the increases in student numbers within polytechnics, and in an attempt to encourage the older universities to compete, the government decided in 1991 to allow the polytechnics to adopt the title of university. Thus in 1991 Flexington became an independent university with the ability to award degrees and manage its own financial affairs.

During the mid-1990s the level of government financing for undergraduate students diminished as existing funds from the Higher Education Funding Council were spread among an increasing number of students. In response to these financial pressures the governors and managers of the new university launched three initiatives.

☐ Steps were taken to increase the number of overseas and commercially sponsored students at the university. These students would pay higher fees than those individuals who could claim government grants.

☐ Plans were developed to improve the research profile of the organisation in order to attract additional funds from government research councils and private sector sponsors.

☐ The University set up a private company - Flexington University Enterprises Limited (FUEL) - to register patents and copyrights, as well as sell consultancy services and merchandise.

Although these steps led to a doubling of undergraduate student numbers in the early 1990s, this growth was not welcomed by everybody. The parents of many students and the various trade unions representing staff and student interests criticised the government directly for reducing the level of student grants. Meanwhile several academics used the media to question the effectiveness of cheap mass higher education and a number of employers restricted their graduate recruitment to those universities which had not engaged in rapid expansion.

☐ The development of private sector companies and public sector bodies

To make sense of the immense variety of business operations in the UK it is useful to consider some of the ways in which they differ. This section draws upon the work of economic historians, industrial sociologists and business commentators to consider one of the more significant forms of difference.

A common way of distinguishing between organisations is to consider their ownership – who owns the assets or capital of the business (property, premises and equipment). Are they owned publicly with the organisation's assets held by all the citizens of a state, but controlled by government nominees? Alternatively, are the physical resources of the organisation privately owned by individuals, groups or other organisations, with the responsibility for day-to-day operations vested in the hands of a board of directors, trustees, or governors?

Private companies, as we currently understand them, are a relatively recent phenomenon and their historical roots can be traced back to the end of the sixteenth and seventeenth centuries. At this time the UK was beginning to emerge from a feudal agricultural system in which the Crown, Lords and Guilds of skilled workmen owned most of the land, property and tools with which ordinary people worked.

The expansion of international trade in the Tudor and Stuart periods meant that merchants needed the backing of a large number of financiers in order to fund their trading operations. Individually funded businesses and partnerships were unable to provide sufficient investment and faced legal difficulties. If the owners of the business wished to sue one of their customers or suppliers, all of the partners had to be involved in the legal action. Similarly any legal action by another party against the partnership could be taken only if all the members of the partnership were named in the writ.

The restrictions outlined above did not apply to organisations which had received a Royal Charter from the monarch, giving them a legal status which was independent of their owners. In these circumstances any legal action against the organisation could be limited to naming the company and not its individual owners. The first such company was the Muscovy Company of Merchant Adventurers which received a Royal Charter in 1553 from King Edward VI. Over the next three hundred years many more organisations sought corporate status, either through an application for a Royal Charter or from the mid-eighteenth century onwards through the passage of a Private Act of Parliament.

The beginning of the Industrial Revolution at the end of the eighteenth century unleashed a spate of technological innovations. The emergence of steam power, deep-seam coal mining, iron foundries, cotton spinning machines, canals, turnpikes (private roads) and railways produced fundamental changes. In order to exploit these developments a new breed of industrialists required substantial material and financial resources to make their new inventions work. It was against this background that laws were passed in the first half of the nineteenth century which enabled businessmen to establish companies with limited liability. Under these regulations the risk attached to any investment in a company was limited to the value of the investors' shares in the company. If the organisation went bankrupt shareholders would lose their initial stake in the company, but they were immune from further legal action by other parties.

Accompanying the changes in the country's industrial base were improvements in agricultural techniques (the Agrarian Revolution). The systematic adoption of new planting and harvesting methods, the enclosure of common land and crop rotation produced substantial improvements in the productivity of many farms. As the adoption of these new methods gathered pace and combined with rapid industrialisation, people were attracted to the growing number of towns and cities which provided a home for the new manufacturing companies. Within these new and expanding urban centres, the need to provide effective sanitation, health care, transportation, education and housing provided a basis for the development of social welfare provided by central and local government. Early attempts to cope with these problems led to the passing of a number of laws designed to regulate industrial activity and working conditions. At the same time there was a steady expansion in the role of local and central government.

During the twentieth century the role of the public sector was further extended. At this time a combination of economic crises and a poor record of investment and management by particular companies, as well as a desire to promote a more equal society, provided the impetus for the nationalisation of many previously privately owned organisations. This process of nationalisation was also accompanied by the establishment of new public sector bodies or an extension in the role of existing bodies. For example, the BBC was set up to provide radio entertainment, the National Health Service was established to provide a comprehensive system of medical care, and social work and probation services were added to the list of services provided by many local authorities.

Today the British economy contains a variety of organisations with different forms of ownership. These differences are recognised legally and it is therefore possible to distinguish between a number of distinct types of private and public sector organisations. As we aim to demonstrate in the following section, variations in the ownership of these organisations will affect who controls these organisations and the objectives they choose to pursue.

Private sector organisations

Private sector businesses provide the backbone of British industry and commerce. This form of organisation accounts for approximately three-quarters of economic output and over three-quarters of employment within the national economy (*Socialist Trends*, ONS 2001). In addition to profit-making businesses, there are a smaller number of private sector charities, trusts and associations which provide a variety of valuable services. Taken together it is possible to distinguish the following forms of private sector organisation.

Sole traders

These are individuals who have set up a business with a view to making profit. There are few specific legal formalities associated with this form of organisation, excluding notification to the Inland Revenue and, if their sales exceed a specified level, registration with HM Customs and Excise for VAT payments. These businesses have unlimited liability. This means that if the business incurs debts or becomes bankrupt, any part of the owner's property or assets may be sold to raise funds to repay these bills.

In some sectors of the economy this form of organisation dominates business activity, especially within industries where only relatively low levels of capital investment are required, e.g. retailing, building and catering services. Although definitive figures are hard to come by due to the lack of legal formalities associated with this form of organisation, the Customs and Excise records suggest that sole trader status is the most common form of business operation in the UK.

Partnerships

This form of business organisation generally consists of two to twenty people who come together to form a business with a view to making a profit. In the case of large professional practices, limitations on the number of partners may not apply.

Under the terms of the Partnership Act 1890, the name of the partnership has to be registered, unless it only consists of the names of the partners. Like sole traders, partnerships do not have a separate legal identity from their owners and therefore the financial liability of a partnership is usually unlimited. In other words each partner is eligible to share in the profits of the enterprise, and is also responsible for the debts of other partners. The exact division of these profits and debts is usually specified in a formal written agreement referred to as a Deed of Partnership. This document will usually specify the names of the partners, the trading name and address of the business, the aims of their partnership, the amount of any initial investment, and the principles which will govern the division of profits and liabilities.

In certain circumstances, under the terms of the Limited Partnership Act 1907, the business partners may elect to form a limited partnership with the amount of an individual partner's liability limited to the sum he or she originally invested. However, this form of organisation is relatively rare.

Like sole traders, partnerships are required to register with the Inland Revenue and, where appropriate, HM Customs and Excise.

This form of organisation has a number of advantages in comparison with sole trader status. First and foremost, it enables the business to draw upon finance from a larger number of people. It also enables small businesses to set up operations without having to comply with the financial and other reporting requirements which apply to private and public limited companies. On the downside, partnerships rely upon sustained cooperation between the individuals involved within the business. This may present difficulties when the partners disagree about business priorities.

Despite these difficulties, partnerships remain the second most popular form of business organisation within the UK. This form of organisation is commonly adopted by small family-owned businesses and professional practices, including accountants, architects, doctors and lawyers.

Private limited companies

The majority of large private businesses operating in the UK are registered as private limited companies. This process involves the drawing up of Memoranda and Articles of Association and a formal application to the Registrar of Companies.

Private limited companies, unlike sole traders and partnerships, have a legal identity which is distinct and separate from that of their owners, directors and employees. As a consequence, these organisations have limited liability which, as previously mentioned, means that the shareholders who own the company only risk losing their investment in shares should the company go into liquidation. In return for their investment, shareholders may share in the success of a company through the payment of annual dividends (a proportion of the company's annual profits).

Shareholders are also entitled to have a say in the way the company is run. This right is exercised at the company's annual general meeting where the company's Board of Directors is appointed, the previous year's performance is reported, questions are answered and resolutions proposed. The Board of Directors is also required to submit audited accounts and other information to the Registrar of Companies.

Public limited companies (PLCs)

These organisations share the same basic characteristics as private limited companies but differ in two important respects. First, these organisations are required to publish an annual report and statement of accounts which should

EXHIBIT

2.1 Reading the financial pages

The information contained in Table 2.1 is printed in a number of quality newspapers on a daily or weekly basis. This information is broken down into a number of columns of figures to give investors an indication of the current worth of particular companies' shares. The meaning of the figures entered under each of these column headings is generally defined as follows:

☐ **Price** refers to the cost of a single share and is expressed in pence. However, the figure does not include the cost of brokers' fees which any shareholders will incur when they decide to buy or sell shares.

☐ **+ or -** signs specify the change in the price of the share on the most recent day of stock market trading.

☐ **High and low.** These figures give an indication of the highest and lowest prices quoted for the company's shares in the previous year of trading.

☐ **Mkt Cap £m** refers to market capitalisation in sterling - the value of the company on the stock market. This figure is usually expressed in millions and calculated on the basis of the total number of shares multiplied by their quoted price.

☐ **Yld Gr's** is shorthand for the gross yield of shares. This figure refers to the dividend paid to shareholders as a percentage of the share price. In other words, it provides a measure of the rate of return on an investment in these shares. The figure is quoted as gross because no account has been taken of the effects of tax.

☐ **P/E.** The price/earnings ratio gives an indication of the level of investors' confidence in the company. It is calculated by dividing the current share price by the latest available figure for that company's net earnings per share. A P/E ratio of 5.7 would mean, therefore, that the share price is currently 5.7 times the company's earnings per share. In general, the higher the P/E ratio the greater the confidence investors have in the firm's future profits. However, a high P/E ratio can also reflect special factors such as expectations of a takeover by another company. It is worth noting that P/E ratios can be sensibly compared only between companies engaged in similar businesses.

Table 2.1 Share price information for selected food retailing PLCs in 2001 **FT**

Food retailing	Price	+ or -	High	Low	Mkt Cap. (£m)	Yld Gr's	P/E
Iceland	$160\frac{3}{4}$	$-1\frac{1}{4}$	347	$134\frac{1}{2}$	11	1.6	18.4
Safeway	$372\frac{3}{4}$	$-\frac{1}{4}$	421	255	13,612	2.4	16.4
Sainsbury (J)	$428\frac{1}{4}$	$+1\frac{1}{4}$	$452\frac{3}{4}$	283	13,491	3.3	23.8
Tesco	$253\frac{3}{4}$	$+\frac{3}{4}$	293	200	13	3.9	10.1

Source: Financial Times, 12 July 2001

be available for public inspection. Second, shares in these companies are traded on the Stock Exchange which means that they invariably have a greater number of shareholders and are therefore able to gain access to larger financial resources. As a consequence, public limited companies tend to be larger than their private counterparts.

The *Financial Times* and a number of other business publications provide a detailed breakdown of movements in the share prices of these companies. These printed figures appear daunting at first sight. However, the information contained on these pages is useful for gauging the relative performance of specific companies.

The *Financial Times* Stock Exchange 100 Index – known as the *FTSE Index* (pronounced *footsie*) – is an index which provides a measure of the stock market value of shares in the hundred largest registered companies, as measured by their market capitalisation. The index was established in 1984 at a base value of 1000. Within this index the share price movements of larger companies carry more weight than those of smaller companies.

Exercise 2.1 **Reading the financial pages**

Which of the companies listed in Table 2.1 has:

(a) the most expensive shares?
(b) experienced the widest fluctuations in share price in the preceding year?
(c) has the greatest number of issued shares?
(d) the appearance of high shareholder confidence in its future performance?

Voluntary organisations

The voluntary sector – sometimes termed the third sector – is a very disparate grouping. It includes charities, political parties, religious organisations, professional institutes, trade unions and voluntary bodies (e.g. the Women's Institute, St John's Ambulance, Rotary Club). The charity sector alone consists of 185 000 bodies enjoying certain tax privileges supervised, in England and Wales, by the Charities Commission. The voluntary sector forms some 7 per cent of GDP and employs 530 000 employees. These organisations differ from private sector organisations in a number of respects:

1 Their affairs are often overseen by representatives elected by the members of the organisation on the basis of one member, one vote. By contrast, the election of directors of private companies is carried out on the basis of one vote per share; thus larger shareholders have a greater number of votes. Once elected, voluntary body representatives are responsible for managing these organisations according to policy decisions democratically taken by the wider membership at annual conferences or similar meetings.

2 The primary objective of almost all voluntary bodies is to further the well-being and interests of a specified group within society. In the case of charities, these organisations provide a means for channelling resources

between those who donate funds to those that need this money. As a consequence, they are unlike businesses because they rarely sell a product or a service and it is not their intention to generate a profit.

3   Voluntary bodies often rely on the work of large numbers of unpaid volunteers.

The scale of activity undertaken by these organisations is partly revealed by the following figures:

☐   Thirty-seven charities in the UK had incomes in excess of £20 million in 2001.

☐   Membership of many professional bodies grew in the 1990s. The Institute of Chartered Accountants (England and Wales) has a registered membership of 120 000 and the Chartered Institute of Personnel and Development 83 000.

☐   Trade union membership in the UK stood at approximately 7.3 million in 2001.

Those voluntary bodies which are able to register as charities enjoy considerable tax advantages as they are generally not required to pay VAT on sales, or corporation tax on retained surpluses. Because of these financial advantages there are strict controls governing which types of organisation may register as a charity and the means by which they can organise their activities and raise funds.

Public sector organisations

At its broadest the term public sector is used to refer to government and state-sponsored organisations. Within this general category, three distinct groups can be isolated: central government, local authorities and public corporations.

Central government

Central government bodies include all those ministries and departments which are the direct responsibility of a Minister of State, as well as the Quasi Autonomous Non-Governmental Organisations (Quangos) which are free from direct parliamentary control. At present, there are approximately 20 central government ministries, e.g. Defence, Health, Treasury, Trade and Industry, Education and Skills as well as the Home and Foreign Offices. Each government ministry and department is overseen by a ministerial team; the most important of these teams include a Secretary of State who has a seat in Cabinet. Many central government departments consist of a number of divisions; for example, the Department for Education and Skills oversees the work of the Further and Higher Education Funding Councils, the Employment and Training Agencies.

The funding of the various government departments is determined in the three-yearly Comprehensive Spending Review, when ministers from the various spending ministries submit their claims for the following three years to the Treasury. The functioning and efficiency of each of these ministries is open to written and verbal questioning on the floor of the Houses of Parliament. More detailed scrutiny is undertaken by Parliamentary Select Committees comprised of ordinary Members of Parliament drawn proportionately from each political party.

Local government

Local government in the UK operates according to a patchy system of one-, two- and three-tiered arrangements. In some areas of the country, therefore, there is one level of local government, in others two, and in a few regions three. These levels of operations go under a variety of names including metropolitan, county, district and parish councils. The first three of these bodies are responsible for the local provision of roads, environmental health, controls on development, education and housing, etc.

The management of local authorities mirrors the organisation of central government with a split between the roles of elected councillors and council officers. Councillors are responsible for the formulation of overall policy. Council officers are charged with the execution of this policy and the day-to-day management of the council's services.

Since 1979 there has been a considerable reorganisation of local government within the UK. In 1986 the seven metropolitan county councils of London, the West Midlands, Greater Manchester, Merseyside, Sheffield, Leeds and Tyneside were abolished. Eight years later local government in Wales and Scotland was reorganised following the report of the Local Government Commissions for Wales and Scotland. In 1999 a Greater London Authority was once again created. Debate on further regional government in England has increased since the establishment of the Scottish Parliament and Welsh Assembly in 1998 (see Chapter 8).

Public corporations

There are over 50 public corporations and nationalised industries which engage in a range of activities (e.g. Bank of England, Royal Mint, hospital trusts, the BBC and the Royal Mail). These bodies have been created by statute or Royal Charter and this legal identity enables them to operate like businesses within the private sector with one important exception – their debts and liabilities are effectively underwritten by the State.

Public corporations gain their revenue through sales of their products/services or through central government grants or loans. The managing boards of these bodies are appointed by ministers who have the power to give general directions, but are not supposed to be involved in day-to-day management decisions. These bodies are also subject to public scrutiny through House of Commons Select Committees (e.g. the Treasury and Public Accounts Committees), the National Audit Office and special reports commissioned from management consultants or the Monopolies and Mergers Commission.

Public and private sector ownership and control

In the preceding section we have seen that organisations currently operating in the UK may be divided into two broad categories of private and public sector ownership. The first of these categories includes companies and voluntary bodies which, according to their legal status and size, will be managed and controlled either directly by their owners or indirectly by appointed or elected directors. For example, voluntary bodies will generally be owned by their members and managed by elected officials who are charged with ensuring that the organisations achieve their stated welfare and charitable aims. By contrast, within the commercial world, sole traders with small businesses will generally oversee the day-to-day management of their business according to objectives they have set for themselves. Meanwhile, within larger private sector enterprises which have adopted private or public limited company status there is likely to be a split between ownership and control so that the people who own the business are not necessarily involved in managing its operations. Indeed, the individual shareholders of many large British companies may have little or no direct say over who represents their interests in the boardroom. In these situations the management of the organisation is often left to a group of professionally trained directors who are appointed by the largest shareholders and charged with maximising the company's financial performance.

Within the public sector the position is somewhat different. Here, the assets of the organisation are held in trust by central or local government on behalf of their electors. However, the day-to-day management and control of these bodies is overseen by government ministers and local councillors directly, or indirectly through their appointed managers, civil servants or local government officers. As a consequence, the objectives of these organisations are often fashioned by the political priorities and policies of politicians and their parties.

Exercise 2.2 **Public or private?**

The ownership and control of Flexington University, and its forerunner colleges, underwent a number of changes during its development. By reference to the list of different forms of public and private sector organisation, construct a grid similar to Table 2.2 and fill in the boxes to indicate the ownership, control and objectives of the organisation at different points in its history.

Table 2.2

	Ownership	Control	Objectives
Stanmead Technical College			
Stanmead Institute of Technology			
Flexington Polytechnic			
Flexington University			
Flexington University Enterprises Limited			

☐ Organisational and operational changes in the public, private and voluntary sectors

Having examined current legal definitions of organisations operating in the UK, we now move on to examine recent changes in the organisation and operation of public sector bodies and private sector businesses. As we noted in the introduction to the preceding section, the legal regulation of organisations and their operations has changed gradually over time. This process of change continues today. Our intention in this section is to demonstrate that these changes have altered the way in which private and public sector organisations define and deal with their external environments. Thus privatisation and other reforms have exposed many former public sector bodies to competition with the private sector for funds from investors and business from customers. Similarly, in the private sector, internationalisation has led the directors and managers of many businesses to redefine their operations on a global scale. In this new environment they no longer see the UK as the sole source of sales, capital or staff. As we hope to demonstrate, these and other changes have had profound implications for our understanding of how these organisations currently work, and how they might operate in the future.

Changes in the public sector

Under the Thatcher, Major and Blair administrations changes in government policy fundamentally altered the operation of public sector services and public corporations in the UK. In this section we consider four of the most important changes under the following headings: privatisation; deregulation, liberalisation and marketisation; PPPs/PFI (Public Private Partnerships/Private Finance Initiative); and financial constraints, commercialisation and managerialism.

Privatisation

Privatisation is a widely used term which has come to be associated with steps to increase private forms of capital ownership, raise public revenue and increase efficiency. The measures introduced in this area have included:

- ☐ the sale of public corporations or parts thereof to private sector businesses or investors (e.g. Rover Group to British Aerospace);
- ☐ the transfer of public corporations to the private sector through the sale of shares (e.g. British Telecom and British Gas); and
- ☐ management or employee buyouts (e.g. National Freight Consortium). (*see* Table 2.3.)

Although in excess of £30 billion has been raised through the sale of these companies, significant costs were incurred preparing these organisations for flotation. In the period preceding each new sale of shares in a former public sector body, money was spent on cutbacks and restructuring within these

Table 2.3 Major privatisations since 1979

Company	Date	Company	Date
British Petroleum (1)	1979, 1983 and 1987	BAA	1987
British Aerospace	1981	Rover Group (3)	1988
Cable and Wireless	1981	British Steel	1988
Amersham International	1982	National Bus Company (4)	1988
National Freight (2)	1982	General Practice Finance Corp	1989
Britoil	1982	Regional Water Authorities	1989
Associated British Ports	1983	Girobank (5)	1990
Enterprise Oil	1984	Area Electricity Boards and National Grid	1990
Jaguar	1984	National Power and PowerGen	1991
British Telecom	1984	Scottish Hydroelectric	1991
British Shipbuilders (1)	1984 and various other dates	Scottish Power	1991
British Gas	1986	East Midlands Airport	1993
British Airways	1987	National Coal Board	1994
Royal Ordnance (3)	1987	British Rail	1996
Rolls-Royce	1987	National Air Traffic Services	2001

Notes: (1) Shares in British Petroleum and British Shipbuilders were sold in a number of tranches to different investors at various dates during the 1980s. (2) National Freight shares were sold to a consortium of managers and employees. (3) Royal Ordnance and Rover Group were sold to British Aerospace. (4) The National Bus Company was sold as 72 separate local bus companies. (5) Girobank was sold to the Alliance and Leicester Building Society. (6) The government also divested itself of minority shareholdings in British Sugar, ICL, Ferranti and British Technology Group.

organisations, as well as writing off debt and on occasion financing lengthy industrial disputes with unions (e.g. the miners' strike of 1984–5 and railway disputes in 1994).

Despite the sale of shares to the private sector, governments retained a 'golden share' in many of these companies for the first few years of their operation. This special share gave the government ultimate control over the future direction of a company and could be used to block any takeover attempt which it judged to be against the national interest.

Accompanying transfers of ownership from the public sector to the private sector were other measures involving the transfer or quasi-privatisation of public sector services – for example, direct service organisations in local authorities, agencies within the Civil Service, and incorporation status in the higher and further education sectors. These new organisations were formally listed as privately owned, or treated as if they were, even though the assets of these organisations could not be sold without the permission of the appropriate government agency. Ministers believed that by changing the ownership of these organisations in this way managers would be encouraged to adopt a more entrepreneurial, innovative and cost-effective approach to delivering services.

Among public sector services, the most significant form of privatisation was the sale of council houses. As a result of legislation introduced in the early 1980s, almost 1.5 million council tenants exercised the right to buy their homes. Annual sales peaked at 226 000 in 1982, but fell to less than half of this level in 1985 and 1986. Between 1986 and 1989, sales increased in each year before falling throughout the late 1980s and early and mid-1990s.

Deregulation, liberalisation and marketisation

Accompanying changes in the ownership of organisations were measures designed to:

- [ ] remove direct governmental control of public corporations and services (*deregulation*);
- [ ] promote competition between private and public sector organisations (*liberalisation*);
- [ ] introduce the discipline of the marketplace within public sector monopolies (*marketisation*).

The intention behind all of these moves was that through competition the quality of service provided would be increased while costs decreased. It was assumed that under these conditions public sector managers would improve their expertise and ensure that resources were directed to improve the services and products demanded by customers. Furthermore, that customer choice would be improved by breaking up public sector monopolies and promoting competition.

Under *deregulation*, the direct influence of government ministers on the definition and direction of public sector corporations was either relaxed, replaced by other systems of control, or became less visible. Under the slogan of 'rolling back the frontier of the state', the traditional model of central government control of management decisions within public sector enterprises was relaxed in many areas. For example, the centralised planning of energy provision by ministers and civil servants within the Department of Energy was gradually replaced by business plans determined by managers within the industries concerned. Similar initiatives are apparent within public sector services where agency status removed many bodies from direct governmental control. Despite these changes, regulation has not been completely removed. In many instances direct control of an industry or service has merely been replaced by other indirect methods of regulation. This trend has been referred to by some commentators as a gradual process of deregulation and re-regulation.

During the 1980s and early 1990s, therefore, the privatisation of many public sector utilities was accompanied by the creation of statutory bodies charged with the regulation and policing of these new private sector companies – for example, Ofwat, Oftel and Ofgem to oversee the operations of the 12 regional water companies, British Telecom, British Gas and the electricity industry respectively. Similarly, within the public services, direct governmental control was replaced by a system of financial control. Finally, it is worth noting that, although government ministers in the Thatcher and Major administrations were apt to talk of their success in 'removing the dead hand of government' from the operation of newly privatised companies and public sector services, government influence still affected the decisions of managers and officials within these organisations.

A number of other measures, which we refer to here as *liberalisation*, allowed private sector companies into markets traditionally reserved for public sector bodies. Examples of these initiatives included the promotion of independent production services in the television and radio broadcasting industries, and the removal of competition controls in the bus industry. The momentum behind these initiatives was increased in the early 1990s by the more active application of competition policy by the European Union. This policy was designed to break up monopolies in any sector of industry, whether public or private.

The most radical of *liberalisation* policies was the compulsory competitive tendering (CCT) of functions in many areas of the public sector. As a consequence, the National Health Service, Civil Service and local authorities were required to seek competing tenders (bids from private sector companies as well as estimates from their own workforce) for refuse collection, street and building cleaning, laundry services, vehicle and ground maintenance, the management of leisure facilities and various personnel management functions.

The final set of policy initiatives – *marketisation* – attempted to introduce the discipline of the marketplace in a number of public sector services that for political reasons remained virtual monopolies. Examples of this included the break-up of the water, electricity and rail industries prior to privatisation, as well as the introduction of an internal market within the NHS. District Health Authorities and some general practitioners are now allocated funds and are able to shop around to get the most cost-effective service from local and general hospitals.

The Blair governments replaced CCT by 'Best Value'. Best Value seeks to broaden the performance criteria used to evaluate local government services and end the legal requirement to put them out to tender. Competition (what is sometimes called 'contestability') is still central but will not in itself demonstrate best value. Value for money criteria will be supplemented by benchmarked measures of effectiveness and service quality. The 'Best Value' initiative has influenced some councils in outsourcing many of their services – including HR – to the private sector.

Public–Private Partnerships and the Private Finance Initiative

In 1992 the then Conservative Chancellor of the Exchequer launched the Private Finance Initiative (PFI). By June 2001 almost 400 PFI deals had been signed with a capital value of £17 billion. In the period covered by the comprehensive spending review (1999–2002) PFI will account for 14 per cent of total publicly sponsored capital spending. PFI spending is heavily concentrated in certain areas of the public sector, including transport, health and increasingly local government. While the PFI arguably represents a small proportion of total capital spending, it is the dominant model of procurement for *new* hospitals or prisons; 19 out of 23 major hospital projects that had reached financial closure by summer 2000 were commissioned by using the PFI route. Furthermore, the NHS plan (February 2001) suggested that almost all new hospitals would be built using PFI.

PFI projects fall within the definition of Public–Private Partnerships (PPPs), a wider term which includes various types of joint venture as well as PFI projects. The Commission on Public–Private Partnerships (CPPP) defines PPPs as 'a risk sharing relationship between the public and the private sectors based on a shared aspiration to bring about a desired policy outcome' (2001:40). The principle of PFI is that a public sector body obtains a service rather than an asset. A private sector contractor (often created for the purpose) funds any asset required and is then paid for the service provided. The public sector client pays a fee over the life of the contract to the private provider which is contingent upon services meeting specified standards. The initial private finance is repaid by streams of income from the public purse. PPPs are controversial and have been subject to widespread criticism (*see* Gaffney *et al.*, 1999; Pollack *et al.*, 2001).

The Labour government believes that the quality of public services is improved through involving the private sector. It enthusiastically promotes PPPs; in its 1997 manifesto it declared that 'Labour pioneered the idea of public/private partnerships' and it would 'reinvigorate' the idea (Labour Party, 1997). For its second term, the Labour government argued that 'Where private-sector providers can support public endeavour, we should use them. A "spirit of enterprise" should apply as much to public service as to business' (Labour Party, 2001). There is a general emphasis on demoting the significance of questions of public or private, arguing that it is 'outcomes, not ownership that matters'. The CPPP report is a vivid example of this approach, maintaining that 'the whole significance of public ownership is overblown' and that 'the question of who should own the underlying assets used in public services is increasingly a second order issue' (2001:33). Like CCT before it, but on a larger scale and with a broader scope, PFI represents a fundamental shift in the focus of the public sector, away from being a direct provider to becoming a procurer and regulator of services.

Financial constraints, commercialisation and managerialism

The Thatcher and Major governments believed that public sector services should be encouraged to behave more like their private sector counterparts. In order to achieve this objective, a number of policies were developed and implemented to promote financial prudence, a commercial orientation and so-called professional management practices.

Financial prudence was promoted by the establishment of principles to govern investment decisions and the establishment of financial targets. Examples of particular initiatives in this area included the following.

☐ The imposition of investment appraisal formulae within public sector corporations. For example, prior to privatisation British Rail was encouraged to use strict pay-back criteria when planning future capital expenditure. This meant that any investment funds had to be repaid within a short period of time.

☐ The use of cash limits within the Civil Service and armed forces, together with council tax capping for local authorities.

☐ The reduction of public sector subsidies covering drug prescription charges, museum and art gallery maintenance and school meals services.

Accompanying these measures to promote financial stringency were other steps designed to foster commercial attitudes and practices (*commercialisation*). Thus, a number of public sector services introduced new services which were funded by direct charges to their clients – for example, rapid land searches by local government officers, company information provided by central government agencies, video and books produced by the BBC, and conference facilities within publicly owned buildings. Other public sector bodies went even further and set up separate enterprise companies/trusts which seek to attract external funds either through external sponsorship or joint investment projects involving private and public sector capital.

The final set of initiatives, which we have labelled *managerialism*, aimed to develop the management skills of civil servants and other public sector workers. Examples of these changes included the following.

☐ Business representatives appointed to the boards of almost all public sector bodies, including school governing bodies, and the appointment or secondment of professionally qualified managers to run public sector services like NHS hospitals.

☐ The devolution of management decision making and budgetary controls to cost and profit centres. Under this system each component part of the organisation was required to generate a pre-specified level of profit or operate within centrally determined cost limits. This system replaced a more centralised system of cost and profit controls in which surpluses in one area could be used to subsidise other less economic but socially worthwhile objectives pursued by other departments within the organisation.

☐ A requirement for public sector bodies to produce regular corporate plans specifying objectives and monitoring their achievements against these objectives. In addition, reviews of the performance of these bodies were strengthened by an extension of the role of government-appointed inspectors, including the Audit Commission and the National Audit Office.

☐ A gradual withdrawal from an established series of national systems for determining the pay and conditions of public sector workers through negotiation with trade unions. These national systems were replaced by a more fragmented and less uniform system in which the pay and conditions of public servants were determined through local negotiations with trade unions and unilaterally by local managers.

Exercise 2.3   **Changes in the public sector**

By reference to the case study at the beginning of the chapter, list examples of changes in the public sector that have affected Flexington University and those that have not. From the examples of experiences in other areas of the public sector, what changes might the senior managers at Flexington expect to see in years to come?

Changes in the voluntary sector

The voluntary sector was also affected by many of the initiatives outlined above. During the 1980s and early 1990s an increasing range of services traditionally provided by the State were transferred to the voluntary sector. Furthermore, legislation and other policy measures were used to encourage these organisations to embrace the new spirit of commercialism and managerialism. Examples of these moves included the flotation of the Abbey National and Halifax Building Societies, the introduction of charity credit cards and the changed approach of many trade unions. The Labour government is keen to increase the role of voluntary services in the provision of public services.

Changes in the private sector

The private sector in the UK, like the public sector, witnessed changes in the ownership and orientation of companies over the past two decades. Many of these changes were a continuation of established trends – for example, a decline in the size of the agriculture, extraction and manufacturing sectors and an expansion in the size of the service sector, an increase in the number of small firms, and a continuation of growth in the size and importance of large companies. Within large businesses these changes were accompanied by a gradual concentration of share ownership within the hands of pension funds and insurance companies.

Other changes had more recent origins. The growing interest in quality and customer service, as well as concerns about business ethics, arguably demonstrated a shift in the orientation and focus of business leaders and their employees. In this section we explore these developments in more detail under the following headings: composition and size; multinational enterprises mergers and acquisitions; ownership; customer culture; and business ethics. It is worth noting that the last of these two changes were not confined to the private sector and similar changes were observed in the public sector.

Composition and size

Economists traditionally divide the work performed within an economy into three sectors which they refer to as the primary, secondary and tertiary sectors.

☐ *The primary sector* consists of organisations which extract basic raw materials from the earth and includes agriculture, forestry, mining and fishing.

☐ *The secondary sector* is comprised of firms which process raw materials into finished products. This category includes manufacturing, construction and energy-producing companies.

 The tertiary sector covers the distribution of goods and provision of attendant services. Examples of the types of organisation in this sector include hotel and catering, security, financial and banking services.

Since the beginnings of the Industrial Revolution the importance of the primary sector to the British economy has been in relative decline. Although Britain remains self-sufficient in the production of oil and a range of agricultural products, advances in technology and cheaper imports from overseas have combined so that agriculture is now responsible for less than 2 per cent of the total domestic economic output and 5 per cent of employment.

2.2 Is the decline of the secondary sector a cause for concern?

Economists and politicians have not generally worried about the decline in the importance of the primary sector. Although some have expressed concern about an overreliance on imports in times of international conflict, and others have fears about the future of the countryside if farming is no longer viable, steps to prevent the further decline of the primary sector have not been seen as a political priority.

A more general source of concern and debate has been the continued decline of the secondary or industrial sector. Here economists and politicians differ in their assessment of the present situation and future developments. Those that express concern about the decline in the industrial sector usually raise one or more of the following arguments.

☐ The decline in the industrial sector within the UK has been more rapid than in other advanced western economies.

☐ The industrial sector is the main source of wealth generation within the economy. It is here that productivity increases most rapidly.

☐ It is through the sale of manufactured goods overseas that we are able to raise the money to pay for the import of primary goods and the supply of tertiary services at home.

☐ The industrial sector provides highly skilled and highly paid jobs which are not available in the hotel, catering, security industries and other elements of the tertiary sector.

☐ Most research and development activity is undertaken by industrial firms. If the UK loses its own manufacturing base we cannot rely on foreign firms bringing their know-how and new techniques to this country.

In response, those less concerned about the decline of Britain's manufacturing industry raise the following counter-arguments.

☐ All developed economies have experienced a change in the role and relative importance of their industrial sectors.

☐ The decline in this sector was more rapid within the UK during the 1980s and 1990s because exports in this sector declined as exports from the North Sea Oil increased. As the overall value of all exports should be equal to the value of imports, an increase in the primary sector will be matched by a decline in another area, in this case manufacturing.

☐ The tertiary sector, like the industrial sector, includes a wide range of different business activities. While hotel and catering and security services may not produce highly skilled, well-paid jobs within profitable businesses, finance, banking, music, video and information technology services do require high skill levels, highly paid staff and considerable investment in research and development if they are to generate high levels of sales and revenue for the country.

☐ The UK cannot and should not wish to compete with countries which are developing or maintaining their industrial sector through an overreliance on cheap labour and cheap land.

The secondary sector has also been of declining importance within the UK over the past 30 years. Output and employment in this sector peaked in the late 1960s and declined constantly, although at varying rates, thereafter. Meanwhile, the level of employment and output within the service sector expanded throughout the post-war period with the exception of the recession in the early 1990s.

Multinational enterprises

Another element of the changing size and structure of UK businesses has been the rise of the multinational enterprise. The UK economy is more dependent upon the activities of multinational enterprises (MNEs) than almost any other nation in the world. As a proportion of total activity within the domestic economy, the production and sales of British MNEs exceed that of MNEs based in any other country with the exception of the Netherlands. In recent years, this *internationalisation* or *globalisation* of UK companies has accelerated in response to steps taken to form a single European market and as a reaction to increased international competition from companies in the Far East and America. The first of these pressures has fuelled an increase in cross-border mergers and acquisitions within the European Union as companies have sought to establish a wider operating base with outlets in many of the member states. The second set of influences has prompted a number of companies to relocate their operations to areas with greater sales opportunities or lower operating costs. According to Reich (1991), these pressures may lead to the gradual rundown of UK MNE operations in their home country. In other countries this phenomenon has been referred to as the *doughnut effect* – MNEs with small or nominal head office facilities in their home country while the bulk of their investment, operations and employment are located overseas.

Among the foreign-owned MNEs operating in the UK, the largest number have their origins in the USA. Some 13 per cent of all private sector workplaces are predominately foreign owned.

The arrival of an MNE is often welcomed by the government of the host country as it will generally involve new investment and the creation of employment. Furthermore, MNEs may bring new technology and management expertise. In order to attract MNEs, however, governments – both national and local – often offer substantial investment subsidies and tax exemptions; indeed, the incentives offered to Nissan, Toyota and other Japanese companies have often approached a third of their set-up costs. Once the new facilities have been established future decisions about investment and employment at that site tend to be taken by people outside the country concerned. For this reason MNEs have been criticised for four reasons. First, it is argued that MNEs limit their overseas operations to low-technology and low-skill tasks. Second, it is claimed that MNEs will price their products and move money between countries in order to avoid taxation which may disadvantage the host country. Third, it has been suggested that these organisations are like seagulls. They land in a new area, gain sustenance from local grants and subsidies and then take flight the moment trading conditions worsen or larger grants become available elsewhere. Finally, it has been argued that the large size of these companies and their spread of operations make it impossible for national governments to regulate business behaviour effectively.

Mergers and acquisitions

An important cause of changes in the structure of private sector industry and the size of firms has been merger and acquisition activity. There is a technical difference between a merger (when two companies fuse together to form a new company) and acquisitions (where one firm takes over another); in keeping with the common use of these words, however, the following section makes no distinction between these terms.

The number and value of acquisitions have fluctuated substantially from year to year. Over the past 90 years, the UK has experienced five waves of acquisition activity – the 1920s, 1967–69, 1972–73, 1984–89 and 1993–96. Each of these waves of activity has corresponded with an upturn in the general fortunes of the UK economy, but the magnitude of each successive wave has grown larger. Even accounting for inflation, the value of merger transactions has increased with each surge of acquisition activity, with companies often prepared to take on substantial debts to finance takeovers. A growing proportion of mergers has involved UK companies joining up with foreign-owned firms. An example is the merger of British Steel with the Dutch-based Hoogovens, now known as Corus. Vodafone has grown rapidly in this manner through mergers with Airtouch of the USA and Mannesmann of Germany.

Mergers and acquisitions are usually classified under one of three headings according to the form of the takeover. *Horizontal mergers* involve companies acquiring other firms engaged in similar activities, e.g. a high street grocery chain purchasing another chain of stores. *Vertical mergers* refer to situations in which an organisation buys a controlling interest in its suppliers or customers, e.g. a car manufacturer buys a car dealership or steel producer. The third category is known as a *diversified merger* and involves the purchase of a company engaged in a seemingly unrelated business, e.g. a cigarette company buys shares in an insurance company.

In addition to differences in the form of merger activity there are also differences in the approach adopted by the bidding company. Thus takeovers may be hostile, friendly or contested bids. Similarly, the company formed by the merger of two organisations may result in complete integration, the slotting in of a new division or loose inclusion within a holding company.

Accompanying the merger waves of the late 1980s and mid-1990s there was also an increased interest in forms of collaboration between companies that did not necessarily involve one company purchasing another. The development of franchising, licensing and joint venture arrangements often provided a formal basis for collaborative arrangements between a large number of organisations. Indeed, a number of companies developed the technique to such an extent that they were able to build large business empires on the basis of these arrangements, e.g. McDonald's, the Body Shop.

Under a licensing or franchising arrangement the right to use various patented techniques, trademarks or copyright-protected materials is sold to another organisation for a specified period of time. For example, many Benetton shops are operated under franchise arrangements under which the owner of a particular shop is required to purchase goods from Benetton and to sell these items in a specified manner.

By contrast, joint venture arrangements tend to be reserved for specified short-term projects in which two or more partners agree to share resources and expertise in order to develop or sell a particular product or service. Airbus Industries provides a good example of this phenomenon; in this case four European aerospace companies agreed to share the costs of developing a range of European civilian aircraft.

Ownership

The ownership of British companies has gradually changed over the past one hundred years or more as owner-managed companies have developed to become large PLCs whose shares and financial resources are provided by other institutions. Today, the pattern of corporate ownership in the UK can now be characterised as a complex web of interlinked share holdings and finance arrangements. Companies no longer just buy each other's products and services; they also often provide finance for each other through shareholdings, joint ventures and other cooperative arrangements. This gradual trend towards the institutional ownership of UK industry continued throughout the 1980s and 1990s, despite the much publicised desire of the UK government to promote share ownership among the general population. While the number of individual shareholders increased dramatically from 7 per cent of the population in 1979 to 25 per cent in 1991, the value of these shares as a proportion of all shareholdings decreased (see Table 2.4).

Table 2.4
Percentage distribution of shareholdings in British PLCs by value

	1963	1975	1981	1992	1997
Individuals	54.0	37.5	28.2	20.0	16.5
Non-profit making bodies	2.1	2.3	2.2	2.2	1.9
Public sector	1.5	3.6	3.0	1.2	0.1
Banks	1.3	0.7	0.3	0.2	0.1
Insurance companies	10.0	15.9	20.5	20.7	23.5
Pension funds	6.4	16.8	26.7	31.1	22.1
Unit trusts	1.3	4.1	3.6	5.7	6.7
Other financial institutions	11.3	10.5	6.8	2.8	2.6
Companies	5.1	3.0	5.1	3.3	2.0
Overseas	7.0	5.6	3.6	12.8	24

Source: Share Ownership, (Office for National Statistics 1999)

A survey by the government's Office of National Statistics (ONS, 1999) revealed that 41 per cent of individual shareholders have a small number of shares in a few companies, usually ones that have been recently privatised. These are generally quickly sold to make a quick profit.

Despite the increased value of shareholdings by institutional investors, John Scott has shown on the basis of data from the UK and USA that share owners rarely control a sufficient percentage of the company's shares to influence the decisions of the board of directors (Scott, 1985). In his studies he has demonstrated that, as the role of institutional investors has increased, these organisations have not sought to gain a controlling influence over the management of companies. Thus few companies are directly controlled by their owners. This research supports the findings of an earlier study by Berle and Means (1932) which suggested that as companies have grown in size over the last one hundred years a split has occurred between those that own the organisation and those who manage its day-to-day operations – *the divorce of ownership and control*. On the basis of this research it has been suggested that large companies are apt to act in the interests of their managers rather than their shareholders. Other research has indicated that one consequence is that managers are likely to concentrate on increasing sales, the size of their companies, or more sceptically their own salaries, including money derived from short-term share options, rather than focus on the long-term viability of the company.

Other writers have suggested that, despite the divorce of ownership and control, there are still powerful pressures on company directors to ensure that they manage their firms in the interests of shareholders. These pressures arise from the threat of a hostile takeover by another company or the withdrawal of financial support by institutional investors. In the UK, there is also said to be a culture of *financial short-termism* which exerts considerable pressure on company directors to ensure that their company's shares are performing well even if investment in research, development and training has to be sacrificed as a consequence (Hutton, 1995). This culture is further to supported by the practice of allowing key individuals, usually with the same cultural and educational background, to hold board-level positions in several companies. This means that similar approaches are adopted in seemingly very different companies.

Customer culture

During the 1950s, 1960s and 1970s, a number of writers commented on the emergence of very large, private sector companies which had been able to grow through selling standardised products which were assembled by unskilled and semi-skilled labour. These products were then sold to the emerging mass markets of the developed world through the use of advertising and other mass marketing techniques. This approach to the organisation of business operations was referred to as *Fordism* in recognition of the influence of the Ford Motor Company in the development of this approach. Although this approach to the organisation of companies and industries offered the prospect of cheaper goods and services for customers in the western world, it was not without its critics. Indeed, a number of writers in the 1960s and 1970s suggested that these large companies failed to serve the interests of their customers (Packard, 1957; Galbraith, 1967). In particular, it was alleged that these companies manufactured products which would not last very long in order to ensure that their customers came back to buy replacements at regular intervals. Furthermore, it was suggested that these organisations used mass advertising to promote changes in fashion and to encourage customers to buy products they did not really need. This, it was argued, contributed to the development of an increasingly *consumerist* society. Finally, it was argued that the senior managers of these organisations decided what customers would want and used the dominant position of their companies within specific industries to ensure that customers were forced to buy their products.

In more recent times, other commentators have claimed that this traditional Fordist approach to production is becoming less widespread as western companies have been forced to respond to increased international business competition, changes in technology and more sophisticated customer tastes. They maintain that in place of the traditional Fordist model a new *post-Fordist* model of industrial organisation has emerged (*see* Table 2.5). Here companies, individually or through close links with other organisations, concentrate their efforts on supplying the needs of specific groups of customers by using highly

Table 2.5
A comparison of
Fordism and
post-Fordism

	Fordism	Post-Fordism
Market	Mass markets of largely similar consumers	Niche markets of customers with specific needs
	Manufacturers dictate to retailers and consumers	Consumers and retailers dictate to manufacturers
Product	Limited range of standardised products	Large variety of specialised products
Production method	Large-scale assembly line operations using machines dedicated to specific tasks	Small-scale batch operations using machines which can be adapted for a number of tasks
Research & development	Separated from production and concentrates on developing new products	Linked to production and concentrates on constantly developing and improving products
Inputs	Material intensive	Material saving, information intensive
Work	Strict division of labour between semi-skilled and unskilled employees who complete manual work and managers who undertake mental work	Highly skilled workers with an integration of mental and manual work
		More routine work performed by sub-contractors and suppliers
Management	Extensive managerial hierarchies	Limited managerial hierarchies
Competitive strategy	Compete by working at full capacity	Compete through selling high-quality, innovative products

skilled workers to produce specialised products using adaptable machines. These organisations make extensive use of new technology to identify changing consumer tastes and to contact potential customers through targeted advertising or direct marketing via mailshot or telephone. This highly focused approach means that these organisations are highly reliant on accurate information and marketing analyses to ensure that they do not waste materials producing goods that nobody wants. This information is constantly fed back to employees so that they can adapt products to meet each new change in customer fashion.

Whether this post-Fordist approach is as widespread as some commentators would suggest remains in doubt; however, there is some evidence that elements of this new approach have been adopted by many large and medium-sized companies. In particular it has been noted that many British companies implemented total quality management programmes during the 1980s and 1990s. These initiatives were designed to promote a greater understanding of a customer-orientated culture among the staff of their organisations.

Exercise 2.4 Changes in the private sector

How have the changes outlined above affected the behaviour of a private sector organisation known to you? Try to be specific about the measures and their effects.

☐ Business ethics and HRM

'The last temptation is the greatest treason: To do the right thing for the wrong reason'

T.S. Eliot (1935) *Murder in the Cathedral*

'The social responsibility of business is to increase its profits.'

Milton Friedman, (1970)

Debate on the relationship between business and ethics is far from new. Both the Catholic and Protestant churches prescribed what was legitimate business practice. Whether embodied in religious doctrines, legal rules or local customs and conventions, there is a commonly held assumption in most if not all societies that individuals have an obligation to behave in particular ways. The great Victorian critic, John Ruskin, argued that:

It being the privilege of the fishes, as it is of rats and wolves, to live by the laws of supply and demand; but the distinction of humanity, to live by those of right. (1862) 'Unto This Last'

Politicians such as Liberal prime minister in the nineteenth century, Gladstone, argued for 'the rule of ought'. However, since the end of the cold war 'ethics' has acquired a much higher prominence, particularly in relation to the activities of multinationals. A new socio-economic landscape emerged with the end of the cold war. The post-war Keynesian model of social democracy was faltering, the state was retreating from activities in which it had once played a prominent role – industries such as rail, water and coal were privatised and the private sector has a growing role in delivering public services (Kuttner, 1997; Hutton, 1995). There was new ascendancy of corporate power (Korten, 1995; Monbiot, 2000) and, it is argued, this ascendancy is of a much more intrusive nature (Lloyd, 2000; Klein, 2000). Ethics has a greater importance arising from the new landscape of post-cold-war capitalism.

Some commentators are hostile to ethical considerations having any role in business decisions. They argue that business ethics is a contradiction in terms. For example, the free-market economist Milton Friedman argues that taking account of issues beyond the profit is 'pure and unadulterated socialism' (1970), although he maintains that firms must in this course of action conform to 'ethical custom'. However, this is not a mainstream view, indeed in the United States all of the Fortune 500 companies now have codes of conduct.

There is an ethical aspect to most human resource issues whether they are explicitly recognised or not. Most HR managers have implicit ethical beliefs and values. HRM is an especially fertile field for ethical issues as it entails examining matters where questions of 'fairness' and equity are paramount, notably sex and race discrimination, privacy, fair labour standards and whistleblowing issues. The HRM department for the footwear manufacturer Adidas has made performance in human rights a factor in calculating annual bonuses for some managers.

What is ethics?

Ethics is an area of inquiry that dates back to the ancient Greeks (*see* Box 2.1). Like its kin in medicine and law, business ethics consists of a rather uneasy application of some very general ethical principles to business practice. Without care, ethics could easily become a catch-all word representing all that is seen as 'good' or 'moral'. Petrick and Quinn (1997) usefully argue that 'ethics is the study of individual and collective moral awareness, judgement, character and conduct'. It raises questions as to whether we should or should not perform certain actions and whether those actions are virtuous or vicious, right or wrong.

Box 2.1

Ethics in ancient Greece

For the ancient Greek philosophers Plato and Aristotle, every person does what their own character prompts. While both of these writers believed that there were absolute notions of justice which exist apart from the thoughts and actions of individuals, the extent to which these people are aware of the form of these absolutes depends on their character, education and willingness to engage in rational contemplation. In short, some people are better placed to make these decisions than others and they should be given the authority and responsibility to determine what is right and wrong and, as a consequence, make difficult choices on behalf of others.

By ethical position we mean the moral values that they use when reaching judgements about what is good and bad about a particular problem or pressure and the responses which might be adopted in reaction to developments inside or outside the organisation. As this section aims to show, there are a range of different positions that managers, employees or observers can take from a belief, at one extreme, that there are universal and enduring ethical truths, to a view at the other extreme that the rights and wrongs of particular thoughts and actions can only ever be determined by reference to all the facts of a case and will vary from one individual to another. These two extremes are referred to in this section as absolute and relative approaches.

There are three prominent frameworks for examining ethical issues – the utilitarian, the Kantian and the Rawlsian/stakeholder approach. Each is outlined briefly in Box 2.2.

Why ethics? The rise of corporate social responsibility

Ethics has become a more important issue in an age of 'turbo-capitalism' when a more vibrant, vigorous capitalism coincided with the retreat of the state. Globalised corporations are less constrained or regulated than before; international trade agreements and deregulation within national markets are widespread (Giddens, 1998). A spate of mega-mergers has seen the emergence of even-larger corporations

Box 2.2

The Utilitarian, Kantian and Rawlsian/Stakeholder approach to ethical issues

Utilitarian: Deriving from the work of Jeremy Bentham, the essence of this approach is captured in the phrase, 'the greatest good for the greatest number'. This maintains that the morality of actions is to be judged by their consequences. An action is moral if, when compared with any alternative action, it produces the greatest amount of good for the greatest number of people directly or indirectly affected by that action. This allows people to be treated as a means to an end, if the end is the greatest good for the greatest number. This approach is perhaps the most common; we should perform an action 'because it enhances economic performance'. If the interests of shareholders and employees clash, a resort to utilitarian reasoning is common. This approach struggles to cope with the problem of knowledge of all consequences and has difficulty in defining 'good' and 'unjust' consequences.

Kantian: Based on the work of the eighteenth-century philosopher Immanuel Kant, this argues that what makes an action right or wrong is not the sum of its consequences but the fact that it conforms to moral law. It is not good enough to perform a morally correct action, because this could stem from self-interested motives that have nothing to do with morality. Rather, an action is moral if it conforms to moral law that is based on pure reason. So, in the employment context, a workforce of core and periphery workers can be justified on Kantian grounds if the workers are treated with equal regard and rights, if the terms are equalised pro rata and the contract is freely chosen. It is argued that this approach can be flawed in that it appeals to utilitarian consequences to demonstrate the rightness of rules, particularly when there is a clash of moral rules.

Rawlsian/Stakeholder: According to this view, the good must be distributed with mutual consultation and so that no organisational stakeholders are complete losers while others are clear winners. Management must place priority on the long-term interests of stakeholders and the survival of the organisation. Such approaches to ethics place less emphasis on 'good' and more on the 'right' (or the just distribution of the good). Some argue that this approach has difficulty in reconciling matters when short-term and long-term interests conflict with each other.

(Vodaphone–Mannesmann/BP–Amoco/AOL–Time Warner/Daimler–Chrysler). With the new resurgence of corporate power and as their role within society has grown, so too have issues about their accountability and concerns as to their activities. As their role has grown in shaping societies, so too have the demands for transparency. Their sheer scale and prominence means that Coca-Cola is inevitably involved in issues of water scarcity, Ikea in issues of deforestation and Ford in issues surrounding emission levels and recyclability of its cars. As firms play a greater role in public life (providing education and health care in some parts of Britain), so they have been subject to calls for greater public accountability.

Firms also seek a deeper relationship with their consumers than just selling products to them (Leadbeater, 1999). Thus Coca-Cola seeks 'to associate it with values . . . such as freedom and integrity'. Tommy Hilfiger argues that 'By respecting one another we can reach all cultures and communities' the company says 'We promote . . . the concept of living the American dream.' Starbucks wants, according to its marketing director, to 'align ourselves with one of the greatest moments towards finding a connection with your soul' (cited in Klein, 2000). Even good 'citizenship' claims (made by BP, McDonald's and BAT) entail a higher level of responsibility and duty than that normally undertaken by companies; a wider role. As corporations associate their products with certain fundamental values, so some argue, they are entitled to be judged by higher standards.

The central concept of much of recent business ethics debate is the idea of social responsibility. This arises in part from widespread concern about the ethical conduct of firms. As the role of firms has grown in the global economy, so too has concern about their influence and accountability. The activities of firms such as Nike, the Gap, Monsanto and McDonald's are closely scrutinised, partly because of their growing economic importance and role within societies. The Golden Arches of McDonald's have overtaken the Christian cross as the second most widely recognised symbol in the world. Only the five rings of the Olympic Games – which McDonald's officially sponsors – are better known. In 1986, McDonald's claimed that 96 per cent of children polled could identify Ronald McDonald. Only Santa Claus did better. One in ten Americans are now believed to have got their first job at a McDonald's (Vidal, 1997). In 1994 UNCTAD reported that multinationals employed around one-fifth of the world's workers outside the agricultural sector in the industrialised countries.

Private sector firms are increasingly important in areas such as health, education and pension provision. Railtrack provides a good example. Its priorities, decisions and accountability are a matter of widespread public concern. If business becomes a partner with government over managing a hospital in the Private Finance Initiative or if the ownership and maintenance of the rail and telephone networks are subcontracted to it as, for example, with Railtrack and BT, it is likely that the degree to which it is discharging a public interest will become a matter of wider debate.

Corporate social responsibility is about the values and standards by which firms operate. Some argue that the new centrality of business in contemporary life means that business must acknowledge that it too has citizenship responsibilities. Victory in the ideological battle means that paradoxically it has never had greater obligations to act with integrity and wider social purpose. There is a growing trend for companies to publish social reports, in which they account for their social, environmental activities as well as their financial ones, and to allow these to be verified externally.

Stakeholding and shareholding

Those who see the firm as having responsibilities beyond shareholders are often associated with 'stakeholding'. The orthodox view of the firm maintains that since the purpose of the capitalist firm is to maximise profits, only those stakeholders who bear risk directly, the shareholders, should have the right to determine policy. Other key stakeholders have right of exit alone. Financial ownership justifies control. This view is reflected in statements from the CBI, the Hanson Trust and most graphically from the former chief executive of Sunbeam, Al Dunlap.

> management's overriding objective is to increase earnings per share annually ... Increasing shareholder value will increase the wealth of the company and thus, of society
>
> (Hanson Trust)

> While business has relations with customers and employees, its responsibilities are to its shareholders
>
> (CBI)

> Stakeholders! Whenever I hear the word, I ask 'How much did they pay for their stake?' Stakeholders don't pay a penny for their stake. Shareholders do.
>
> (Al Dunlap)

Stakeholding is a notoriously slippery and elusive term; rooted in economics, it is underpinned by the core idea that the rights of ownership entail obligations. Issues of inclusion and governance are at its heart. The stakeholders of an organisation are those who are affected and have legitimate expectations and rights regarding the actions of the organisation, and these include the employees, the consumers and the suppliers as well as the surrounding community and the society at large. This approach to the firm argues that it must discharge obligations to the wider community as well as to its owners; that the decisions of a firm must reflect the interests of its employees, suppliers and the areas in which it operates as well as its shareholders.

Social responsibility, so considered, is not an additional burden on the corporation, but part and parcel of its essential concerns, to serve the needs and be fair to not only its investors/owners but those who work for, buy from, sell to, live near or are affected by the activities that are demanded and rewarded by the free-market system. Many companies claim to adhere to this new cultural business requirement, but others are said to believe it can be discharged through better public relations or tokenistic nods towards what most directors see as little more than politically correct behaviour with little value.

CASE STUDY

McLibel

McDonald's sued two environmental activists for libel, complaining about the contents of a leaflet. McDonald's was forced to disclose huge amounts of information on its labour practices, its environmental record, its a animal welfare procedures, and was subject to unprecedented scrutiny. McLibel stands as the longest English case of any kind at 313 days.

Among the findings in the court case were:

- According to Edward Oakley, a McDonald's senior vice-president, 'nutritious food' meant 'foods that contain nutrients'. When the man responsible for the 'nutrition guides' in McDonald's stores was asked if there was any food he knew of that wasn't nutritious, he said, 'I do not know if you would call it food or not, but you could put up an argument for black coffee or black tea or water.'

- David Green, senior vice president of Marketing [USA], argued that he thought Coca-Cola was nutritious, because it provided water, and that was part of a balanced diet.

- The defence had no luck in getting McDonald's to hand over company documents showing the bacterial content of the beefburgers. After several months, Rampton [McDonald's QC] told the court that they had been inadvertently held for safe keeping by Group 4 Security and had inadvertently been destroyed by them.

- In the McLibel case, McDonald's executive Ed Oakley explained that the McDonald's garbage stuffed into landfills is 'a benefit, otherwise you will end up with lots of vast empty gravel pits all over the country'.

- McDonald's was revealed [in San Francisco, in 1974] to have used lie detectors to ask about employees' union sympathies.

- A senior McDonalds' employee claimed that the company's 'rap sessions' (meetings for workers to give their views to a manager or supervisor) meant that there was no need for unions, and he denied any crew felt 'exploited' or 'pushed around', or felt they got 'low pay', because 'no one has said to me they do'.

- Edward Oakley, senior vice-President of McDonald's UK, also responsible for the Quality Assurance Department at McDonald's, admitted that the 'animal welfare policy is, in fact, just a policy to comply with the laws of the various countries in which McDonald's operate'.

- Oakley said he thought that chickens kept in small battery cages were 'pretty comfortable' and that 'hens kept in batteries were better cared for' [than free range ones].

Source: Vidal, J (1997) *McLibel, Burger Culture on Trial*, London: Pan

The rise of an ethical agenda

Corporate ascendancy has not been unmitigated. Countervailing trends have, to a degree, limited the power of multinationals. As corporate power has grown, so too has anti-corporate activism. It is arguable that a more ethical agenda is emerging. This has four clear manifestations:

1 Better corporate governance

There are growing demands for better corporate governance within companies, fuelled by the sense that unaccountable and untransparent decision making is unacceptable. A series of government inquiries have been held (the Hampel, Greenbury and Cadbury inquiries). Greater shareholder activism is also a emerging trend, where shareholders are intervening more in issues ranging from remuneration of executives to the impact of the organisation on the environment.

2 Rise of NGOs

There is increasing pressure on business by ever more effective and numerous non-governmental organisations and lobby groups to make policy socially and environmentally responsible. The number and power of non-governmental organisations (NGOs) has grown substantially; in 1975 there were 1400. In 1995 there were 28 900. When Heineken pulled out of Burma in 1996, the CEO said: 'Public opinion and issues surrounding this market have changed to a degree that could have an adverse effect on our brand and corporate reputation.'

3 Consumer power

There is greater willingness by consumers to use their consumer power to support their ethical and moral concerns. Fledgling movements put pressure on institutional investors to invest according to some ethical criteria. There are now £2.6 billion of savings funds explicitly mandated to invest in companies who demonstrate social, environmental and ethical responsibility in their business policies. The Universities Superannuation Scheme, Britain's third largest pension fund controlling assets worth £20 billion, has recently said it will confront companies over their environmental performance and unjustifiably low, 'sweatshop' wages. It is to recruit specialist researchers to monitor companies' behaviour, and while it will sell shares as a last resort insists 'we are more concerned to influence the way companies do things'. In April 1996 Harvard University rejected a proposed $1 million vending deal with Pepsi, citing the company's Burma holdings. According to the Investor Responsibility Research Centre in 1997, 'some 20 US cities and towns . . . adopted "anti-sweatshop" ordinances that require that goods purchased by those city governments – including uniforms for police, fire and public works personnel – be made without sweatshop labour.' All companies trading with regimes incurring human rights abuses risk consumer boycott and opprobrium. Heineken had to withdraw from building a brewery in Burma 'in response to a high response to a high profile campaign against it in the US. Firms like Monsanto and Heineken surrendered to pressure quickly rather than lose brand reputation from defending an indefensible position. According to research by the Co-op Bank, as much as £8bn of consumers money is spent or invested on 'ethical' products and services.

A code was drafted by the Council on Economic Priorities (CEP), a consumer watchdog in New York, along with several large corporations. The CEP plan would inspect factories for adherence to a set of standards covering key issues such as health, safety, overtime, child labour and the like. Under this model, brand-name multinationals like Avon and Toys 'R' Us, rather than trying to enforce their own codes around the world, simply place their orders with factories that have been found in compliance with the code. Then, the factories are monitored by a private auditing company, which certifies factories that meet the code as 'SA8000' (SA stands for social accountability).

4 International standards

While still in an early stage of development, international labour and environmental standards are emerging. In 1992 the Rio Summit endorsed the idea of sustainable development. In 1998 the United Nations issued a global compact, challenging companies to conform to the principles and obligations for business enshrined in various UN treaties – notably on labour, social and environmental standards. A code on child labour drafted by Unicef, the ILO and an association of Pakistani manufacturers was signed by all the major soccer-ball manufacturers; it provides for outside monitoring as well as education and rehabilitation for the child labourers. The World Bank has begun work on standards of corporate governance. In Britain, the Ethical Trading Initiative has been developed (*see* Exhibit 2.3). The case for social and environmental audits to supplement the annual report and accounts is being accepted by a small but growing number of multinationals. The Institute of Social and Ethical Accountability has developed a social auditing process which has been used by the Body Shop, the Co-operative Bank, Camelot and others.

2.3 | EXHIBIT

Hard labour to put code into practice `FT`

Enforcing ethical guidelines for worldwide production is more difficult than anybody thought, says Roger Cowe

If good intentions were enough to rid business of unethical methods of production, child labour and slavery would no longer exist. At the last count, there were more than 200 corporate codes of conduct aiming to ensure that western consumer goods are manufactured under acceptable conditions.

Sadly, intentions do not always get you very far. In many developing countries, where the west's leading brands are manufactured, child labour continues and health and safety conditions are miserable. Even companies such as Nike that set out a code of conduct cannot be sure that the reputation of their brands will not suffer a revelation about dangerous or oppressive working conditions in a factory somewhere along its supply chain.

Drawing up a code can be done by executives sitting in head office. The hard part is to ensure it is implemented. No matter how many instructions, contract stipulations and factory inspections, unscrupulous employers in countries such as Vietnam, China or Indonesia may escape the scrutiny of the western companies that are their customers – if not that of the occasional hidden television camera.

Hence a UK initiative backed by the Department for International Development, which has during the past three years sought to develop a way of making such standards stick. The Ethical Trading Initiative (ETI) is a tripartite body, with members drawn from business, campaigning groups and trade unions. ETI has developed a code (see below) based on International Labour Organisation conventions. But its main effort has been to test approaches that will help companies to ensure that their suppliers abide by those standards.

Most companies that have attempted to monitor compliance with their codes of conduct have used either external audit firms or their own specialists – sometimes giving this duty to technical staff who frequently visit suppliers' factories. For example, C&A set up an in-house specialist audit team. Adidas recently announced that the US-based Fair Labor Association would audit one in 10 of its suppliers as an external check on its own audit procedures.

But Dan Rees, manager of the ETI secretariat, says this kind of audit is bound to miss some breaches of labour codes.

'They may be good at checking what they can see but how do you know that there is no sexual harassment or child labour? Auditors are good at measuring health and safety issues and aspects of the code that are checkable by management information. But they are not so good at interviewing workers and finding cost-effective ways of checking whether what they hear from management is what the workers are experiencing.'

The scale of the problem has been evidenced by the annual assessments of suppliers, which ETI member companies sign up to when they join. Last year the member companies assessed 6,500 workplaces. They identified about 1,000 issues that required investment or significant corrective action as well as a further 500 that are yet to be resolved. In there words, there were breaches of the ETI code in almost a quarter of the factories inspected – and since these are the most progressive companies, their suppliers ought to be ahead of the game.

In spite of the high media profile of child labour, only 10 of these 1,000 incidents involved under-age workers. Health and safety issues such as machinery guards and protection against fire accounted for 60 per cent of the 1,000 breaches, followed by questions of working hours and wages.

It was also sobering to discover that while east Asia still poses significant problems, the country with the second largest number of incidents was the UK. Top of the league of shame was China, with Vietnam and Turkey in third and fourth places.

The ETI base code summarised

- ☐ Employment is freely chosen – no involuntary labour, no financial deposits with employers or lodging of identity papers/passports
- ☐ Freedom of association – a right to trade union activity
- ☐ Safe and healthy working conditions – including training for workers
- ☐ No child labour – normally under 15
- ☐ A living wage – at least enough to meet basic needs a week
- ☐ Reasonable hours – normally no more than 48 hours a week, with at least one day off
- ☐ No discrimination on race, caste, national origin, religion, age disability, gender, marital status, sexual orientation, union membership or political affiliation
- ☐ Regular employment – no use of home workers, contract labour etc to avoid social security and other obligations to employees
- ☐ Humane treatment – no physical or verbal abuse, harassment or other intimidation
- ☐ Implementation – member companies commit to independent verification, annual reporting to ETI, and corrective action including termination of supplier contracts where serious breaches persist

Source: Financial Times, 12 June 2001

Exercise 2.5 (a) Identify the strengths and weaknesses of the ETI.
(b) What are the most important parts of the ETI code? Give reasons for your answers.

☐ Summary and conclusion

In this chapter we have described and analysed some of the principal differences between organisations in terms of their ownership, organisation and objectives. More specifically we have sought to demonstrate that private companies, voluntary bodies and public services adopt different forms of organisation and pursue distinctive objectives. Thus the directors and managers of large multinationals are apt to show more concern for the interests of their shareholders and other financial investors than people in positions of power within charities, trade unions and other voluntary bodies. Similarly, officials within public sector organisations are more likely than the managers of small businesses to place an emphasis on the concerns of political parties and pressure groups.

Meanwhile, few of the shareholders in large UK-based companies own sufficient shares to directly influence the policies pursued by the company's senior managers, in the public sector politicians and their appointees continue to exert considerable influence over state-owned agencies and other services. Even newly privatised companies and deregulated services continue to be subject to some direct government control, albeit in a less direct and effective form.

As this discussion has shown, the nature of the external environment confronting specific organisations in the public, private and voluntary sectors is likely to vary significantly. Thus, the range of options open to the managers and employees planning a response in these organisations to external changes is likely to be constrained in different ways. For example, the managers of private sector multinationals may choose to react to poor trading conditions, increasing labour costs, or interventionist legislation by moving their business operations to another country. By contrast, managers in the public and voluntary sectors do not generally enjoy the same freedoms.

In addition, the decisions of managers within a large private company are frequently influenced by concerns about their organisation's share price and financial performance. While public sector managers also have to retain the confidence and support of their backers if they experience difficulties, they are rarely faced with the same threats of an aggressive takeover or the withdrawal of funds.

For these reasons it is important to have a fuller understanding of the ownership and objectives of an organisation before beginning the task of reviewing the possible problems and pressures in its external environment. To ensure that this understanding is based on an analysis of the unique influences and particular objectives of a specific organisation, this chapter ended by outlining how to identify the stakeholders in an organisation and their influence on the range of objectives it pursues.

☐ Web references

A think tank with close links to the Labour government. The CPPP report is accessible here
   www.ippr.org.uk

A think tank that has been published research hostile to PPPs.
   www.catalyst-trust.co.uk

The official McDonald's website
   www.mcdonalds.com

An anti-McDonalds website
   www.mcspotlight.org

03 Strategy

Chapter

☐ Introduction

The term strategy has become something of an all-purpose buzzword in recent years. A casual browse through any management or business magazine will reveal a variety of ways in which this word can be used, from strategic cost accounting to strategic waste control. So pervasive is this term that, according to some cynical commentators, it is now possible to elevate the importance attached to the most mundane of activities by adding the term strategic. However, as the use of this word has grown, its meaning has become confused and obscured.

☐ Focus and scope

This chapter aims to define some of the variety of ways in which the term strategic is used and to examine some of the more popular approaches to analysing organisational strategy. The chapter is divided into the following four sections:

☐ What is strategy?
☐ The spectacle of strategy: the case of Optico
☐ Problems associated with defining strategy
☐ Ten different approaches to defining and analysing strategy

Learning objectives

When you have read this chapter and completed the associated exercises and further reading you should be prepared to:

☐ comment critically on three definitions of strategy;
☐ outline the main features of the ten approaches to strategy;
☐ use a range of analytical techniques to assess and evaluate the strategic decisions and actions taken within the case-study company Optico.

☐ What is strategy?

The term strategy is derived from the Greek *strategia* and was originally used to refer to the role of a general. When the term strategy passed into the English language in the nineteenth century, it was commonly used to describe the planning and direction of military campaigns. In the later half of the twentieth century, the term strategy was taken up by business writers and commentators to refer to *the art or skill of planning within companies towards an advantage or desired end* (*Oxford Shorter English Dictionary*, 1995).

Over the past 50 years, with the growth of social science research and business education, the term strategy has taken on an ever-wider set of meanings. With this wider usage it is difficult to provide a single, succinct and comprehensive definition of this word. However, despite this ambiguity, the following five key themes tend to recur in discussions about what constitutes strategic decisions and actions.

- ☐ *Scale*. Strategic decisions and actions are likely to have major resource implications.
- ☐ *Scope*. They are apt to involve coordinated and integrated action covering several different elements of the organisation's current activities.
- ☐ *Duration*. They will tend to be long term in nature.
- ☐ *Uncertainty and risk*. Because it is difficult to anticipate the reaction or intentions of customers, suppliers, competitors or regulatory agencies, the allocation of sizeable resources over prolonged periods of time will tend to expose the organisation to high levels of uncertainty and risk.
- ☐ *Change*. The outcome of the strategic decision-making process will tend to involve significant change in equipment, staffing arrangements or other aspects of the organisation's physical and human resources.

CASE STUDY

The spectacle of strategy: the case of Optico

Optico is a company with a long history. The beginnings of the current organisation can be traced back to 1800 when John Eslan, a Dutch émigré, first set up shop in London's East End to manufacture and supply telescopes to seafarers. As his expertise in the design of lenses improved, he also began to sell monocles and spectacles.

The company grew slowly but steadily over the next 150 years and in the early 1950s there were 40 shops across the UK. As the company grew, initial concern with cash flow gave way to a greater concentration on establishing a reputation for providing quality products and services, while earning sufficient profit to support the owners and their employees.

In the early 1950s there were no statutory controls regulating who could test eyesight or supply glasses and, although pharmacists and doctors frequently undertook these tasks, the sale of off-the shelf glasses within high-street shops was relatively commonplace. In this environment the Eslan shops were distinctive because they focused on testing eyesight and supplying prescription spectacles.

During the 1950s the optical industry became subject to increased regulation. The recently formed British Optical Association (BOA), a body established by opticians to monitor and maintain standards within the industry, began to lobby government for the introduction of regulations preventing unqualified people from undertaking eyesight tests or fitting glasses. Playing on public fears about blindness induced by undiagnosed diabetes and glaucoma, this emerging professional body finally persuaded the then Conservative government to introduce the Optician's Act 1957.

Under the terms of this statute, all future eyesight tests would have to be completed by a qualified opthalmic optician. Furthermore, the fitting of glasses would be reserved for opthalmic opticians and a new category of staff which came to be known as dispensing opticians. To ensure that standards within the industry were maintained and that opticians had professional qualifications based on appropriate training, the Government established a new body, the General Optical Council, (GOC), to regulate the industry and profession. Over the next ten years the GOC restricted opthalmic optician status to members of the British Optical Association. This professional body in turn raised its entry standards from five O levels to postgraduate status over a seven-year period. In addition, the BOA introduced ethical guidelines for its members which prevented opticians from supplying glasses to patients who had had their eyes tested by another practitioner. These guidelines also restricted advertising and prohibited retailers from displaying the price of spectacles or lenses in the windows of their stores. Any breach of these regulations could lead to the optician concerned being struck off the BOA's register of members and thereby prevented from working in the industry in future. Modelling practice on other established professions like dentistry and general medical practice, the BOA argued that the commercialism associated with advertising, marketing and price competition diverted attention from an optician's primary objective of protecting and improving patients' eyesight. The introduction, over the same period, of National Health Service funded eyesight tests, and a limited range of subsidised lenses and spectacles, meant that patients did not pay for tests and could obtain cheaper glasses.

In combination, the changes listed above meant the end of what had once been a relatively unregulated industry in which may different types of supplier vied with one another to provide spectacles to customers across the country. This pattern of trading had been replaced by a heavily regulated profession of opticians who shared the same training and abided by the same commercial rules. As these new regulations began to take effect, the profit levels reported by optical practices began to rise steadily, with corresponding increases in the pay of their staff.

Attracted by these profits, Harson Industries, a large cigarette manufacturer, bought Optico in the late 1960s. Harsons had grown rapidly in the post-WWII war period as smoking became more popular, but fears about the health risks associated with smoking had encouraged the Board of Directors to diversify the company's activities to other areas. Thus in the late 1960s and early 1970s they bought controlling interests in Status, a light engineering company specialising in pressure cookers, Fatchen, an insurance company, and Cornershop, a chain of newsagents. The aim was to ensure that the company had a steady stream of income which would not be heavily affected by any further concern about the dangers of smoking. In practice, the choice of companies being acquired was heavily influenced by the background and contacts of the non-executive board members at Harsons. More than one of the deals was agreed in principle after a chance meeting between a director from Harsons and his or her counterpart from one of the soon to be acquired companies.

Operating under the umbrella of the Harsons group name, but with considerable autonomy over the planning of their future direction, the Board at Optico set about implementing a policy of aggressive expansion by acquisition. Money borrowed from the parent company enabled Optico to grow by purchasing many of its family-run competitors. By 1982, Optico's Board controlled a national network of 360 small high street branches which each employed approximately five staff (one opthalmic optician, one dispensing optician and two or three receptionists). The network of branch operations was supported by three factories which could normally supply customer orders within two weeks of the initial eye sight test. In two of these factories lenses were ground and fitted to spectacle frames. The vast majority of these spectacle frames were imported from overseas. Meanwhile, in the third factory staff concentrated on the production of contact lenses.

By taking advantage of its own in-house production facilities, Optico was able to reduce its costs and therefore make higher profits than competitors charging the same prices. In addition, the heavily regulated nature of the industry meant that the company could provide staff with stable and secure employment, while the absence of marketing and advertising pressure left the company's senior management free to concentrate on expanding operations and improving internal procedures. Under these conditions, opthalmic opticians with little or no formal business or management training were able to maintain control of the company and there were few if any formally qualified financiers, marketing specialists or personnel managers to be found anywhere in the company. Any posts with these titles were commonly held by opthalmic opticians who had been promoted from one of the company's high street branches. The company was also able to draw on sizeable profits in order to buy a controlling interest in chains of opticians in Spain and Italy where there were far fewer regulations on the supply and sale of spectacles.

In the early 1980s, Optico went through a period of rapid and profound change. At this time the newly elected Conservative government announced its intention to deregulate the optical industry. The Health and Social Security Act 1984 removed restrictions preventing unqualified staff from fitting spectacles and lifted the ban on marketing and advertising within the industry. Additional legislation four years later limited eligibility for subsidised spectacles and free eye sight tests to children and social security claimants. This second legal reform in the 1980s meant that it was once again lawful for high-street retailers to sell glasses to members of the public, whether or not their staff were qualified and regardless of whether the customer had received an eyesight test.

The gradual removal of the NHS funding for eyesight tests and spectacles reduced Optico's revenue by a third over a three-year period. Meanwhile, the lifting of restrictions on who could sell spectacles opened up the industry to many high-street retailers who had established a presence in other areas. The changes also opened the way to an influx of new companies and competitors from overseas. These new entrants to the optical market brought with them expertise in areas which had previously remained unrecognised and underdeveloped at Optico. Focusing on perceived customer demands for cheaper spectacles and faster service, these new organisations opened larger shops and installed production facilities on site. This investment in equipment was backed up by extensive press and television advertising campaigns. The new business methods meant that most customers could visit an optician's shop and buy and obtain their spectacles on the same day. More complex or elaborate orders still took anything up to two weeks.

Faced with increasing competition, declining revenue and reduced profits, the senior managers at Optico called in a team of management consultants to advise them on the way ahead. After a lengthy study the consultants' report was produced and accepted by the board at Optico. The consultants' report suggested that the company should be reorganised. The overseas operation and one hundred or more unprofitable stores in the UK would be sold off and the remaining outlets would be grouped into four divisions according to their size and location. Larger stores in areas of the country where customers were particularly price-sensitive would be renamed Cheaper Specs and these outlets would be encouraged to concentrate on selling larger quantities of ready-to-wear glasses. A much smaller number of shops in prestigious locations would concentrate on providing high-quality eyesight tests, patient consultations, designer frames and specialist lenses. The upmarket image of these stores would be reinforced by renaming these stores Hamilton and DeGrey. The third category of store would involve the company in the development of a new approach to retailing. A small number of very large stores would be opened in city centre and out-of-town shopping centres. Labelled Eye Stores, these shops would stock a very extensive range of frames and lenses supported by lens and frame-fitting facilities so that customers could order and collect their glasses on the same day. The company's remaining stores would retain their original name, but would benefit from a change in the company's logo, a television advertising campaign, shop refitting and an extensive programme of sales training for staff. It was hoped that these initiatives would help the organisation to present a new, coordinated and consistent corporate image to current and potential customers. Finally, although a majority of the company's existing staff and senior managers retained their jobs, in exchange for funding for these initiatives from the parent company Harsons, the Board at Optico agreed to recruit specialists to head up their finance and marketing departments.

The initiatives outlined above took some years to implement, but by 1990 were all firmly in place. Although it is difficult in these circumstances to attribute success or failures to specific initiatives, these changes were accompanied by a modest revival in the company's fortunes. By 1995, Optico's new holding company had once again assumed a position of market dominance. The company's network of high-street stores, which had been scaled back to just over 200 stores in the late 1980s, was once again expanding and by the mid-1990s there were close to 400 outlets. As the company once again reasserted its former position of market dominance, many of its newer competitors were forced out of business or taken over by Optico.

Optico's parent company began to experience problems in the mid-1990s, and in 1996 Harson's board of directors announced their intention to refocus the company's activities on tobacco manufacture and distribution. As a consequence of this change of approach, Harson's existing subsidiaries were to be sold. Faced with a threat of a hostile or non-friendly takeover, the Board at Optico quickly set about organising their own management buyout. With the aid of a number of venture capital firms in the City, the money needed to finance this buyout was quickly raised and in June 1996 the board formally took control of the new independent company. Between them the board members held 10 per cent of the shares in the new company and institutional investors held the remaining 90 per cent.

Over the next year Optico continued to operate much as before, although the non-executive director representatives of the company's new financial backers took a greater interest in the firm's overall performance than Harson's representatives had in the past. By mid-1998 these new non-executive directors had begun to grow impatient with what they saw as the amateurish behaviour of the company's existing senior management and the poor levels of return on their investment. They felt that opticians, rather than business people or professional managers, occupied too many important positions in the company. In the autumn of 1998 these concerns could no longer be hidden and with the aid of the company's chairman, the non-executive directors replaced the company's managing director, deputy manager and director of store operations. The chairman then took on the responsibilities of these staff until a firm of headhunters could find replacements to fill the vacant posts.

Exercise 3.1   By reference to the five strategic themes listed above (i.e. scale, scope, duration, uncertainty and change), identify and list the major strategic decisions taken by the boards of Harsons and Optico in the preceding case study.

☐ Problems associated with defining strategy

Although the five themes listed at the start of this chapter help us focus our thinking about the form and content of strategic decisions, these definitions also reveal five significant problems with simple definitions of strategy.

First, it would appear that the precise boundaries between strategic and non-strategic decisions will vary from organisation to organisation, and over time. For example, the decision to invest £100 000 in the development of a new service might be an important strategic decision in a local hospital, but a relatively routine matter in an organisation as large as BT.

Second, we can all think of real or hypothetical circumstances where an important strategic decision could be not to do something. For example, the decision not to expand the organisation's operations in response to increased consumer demand, or alternatively not to cut prices in response to new competition. These decisions may be taken consciously, or they may be the implicit consequence of not addressing particular developments within or outside the organisation. In these situations none of the criteria listed above would necessarily apply, except that the alternative, whether considered or ignored, would have been big in terms of scale, scope, duration, uncertainty or change.

Third, situations may arise where significant changes occur within an organisation, but these developments cannot be linked to any preceding strategic decision. It may be that these changes are subsequently said to have been the consequence of deliberative management action, or it may be that no one wants to take responsibility for what happened.

The fourth problem is that the five themes do not tell us anything about how strategic decisions should be taken, or how the results of this decision-making process should be acted upon. In other words, who takes or should take which decisions and how are they or should they be implemented? Furthermore, how much freedom do these decision makers and action takers really enjoy? Are they able to alter the size and scope or their organisation's activities, or are they merely functionaries responding to wider economic, legal, social, political and technological changes?

Finally, what are, or what should be, the objectives of any strategic decision-making process? A cursory examination of the operations of any two organisations would suggest that decisions and actions, whether consciously taken or implemented by default, are directed towards some objective, whether stated or not. In view of this observation it is obviously important to consider the aims and objectives of strategic decision making.

☐ Different approaches to defining and analysing strategy

To deal with the problems associated with finding a precise definition of the term strategy it is useful to think of some of the different ways in which this term has been used in recent research and textbook discussions. As the following account aims to demonstrate, there are at least ten different approaches, each of which highlights a different aspect of the strategy-making process. These different approaches should not be seen as mutually exclusive, but rather as different facets of a very complex phenomenon. While one approach, or combination of some of these methods, may provide the most effective description of the strategy-making process in a particular situation, or the most useful prescription for further activity, this does not imply that this approach has universal validity. Nor should it be taken to mean that the other approaches are without merit or value. Instead, it is more effective to think of the ten different approaches as analytical and evaluative tools, each of which is suited to particular tasks and circumstances.

The ten approaches which form the basis for this section have been adapted and extended from work originally undertaken by Henry Mintzberg (1987). In one of his many famous contributions to research in this area, he identifies five approaches to the analysis of strategy labelled: plans, ploys, patterns, position and perspective. In order to bring this work up to date, the following account adds a further five approaches derived from other research and writing in this area. These other approaches are labelled purpose, potential, possibilities, programmes and politics. Due to the constraints of space these different approaches have been combined under the following six headings:

☐ Strategy as purpose

☐ Strategy as position

☐ Strategy as potential

☐ Strategy as possibilities

☐ Strategy as plans

☐ Strategy as ploys, programmes, politics, patterns and perspective

Strategy as purpose

The vast majority of writers and researchers dealing with strategy-making within organisations suggest that the first step is, or should be, some attempt to provide a written specification of the purpose and long-term aims and objectives of the organisation. The terms used by different writers to describe this statement of the organisation's purpose include the driving force, strategic intent, mission or vision (Tregoe and Zimmerman, 1980; Hamel and Prahalad, 1994; Campbell and Alexander, 1997). Despite the variability of the labels attached to statements of organisational purpose, there is some agreement that this document should, as a minimum, deal with the following two important questions.

☐ Who are we in business for? Who are the key individuals and stakeholder groups influencing decisions and actions within the organisation?

☐ Why are we in business? What goals does or should the organisation pursue?

Stakeholder analysis provides a useful means of tackling the first of these questions. The first step in this form of analysis is to identify the key individuals or stakeholder groups who have, or wish to have, an influence over the future development of the organisation. These individuals or groups may be employed within the organisation or they may work for external agencies.

There are no complete master lists of the stakeholders influencing all organisations, but a number of writers and organisations have attempted to draw up lists of the main groups. Common categories in these lists include: employees, managers, directors, suppliers, owners, customers, regulatory agencies, trade unions, professional bodies, financiers and the local community. In practice, detailed stakeholder analyses tend to include many more categories and invariably attach names or labels to each group in order to improve the precision of this form of assessment. When all of the names have been listed they can then be arranged in a bubblegram or venn diagram (*see* Fig 3.1).

Having established which groups have an influence over the future of the organisation, the next step is to assess their relative power. In practice, stakeholders rarely have a direct impact on the objectives of an organisation, but they can have powerful indirect effects and may heavily constrain the range of choices open to managers. For example, owners denied sufficient return on their investments may withdraw their funds, employees with few opportunities for career progression may leave to join another company, and if the managers of an organisation ignore the wishes of the local community or regulatory agencies they may find themselves subject to greater statutory controls. Even suppliers have a choice about whether to provide goods and services to the organisation.

There are no definitive rules to help those charged with strategic analysis determine the relative power of various stakeholders; however, in most circumstances it should be possible to rank or score the level of influence exerted by each group. For example, owners might be ranked first, managers second, employees third, customers fourth and suppliers fifth. Alternatively, the different degrees of influence exerted by these groups could be scored on a 100-point scale. Using this approach, owners might be given a score of 40, managers 30, employees 20 and suppliers 10. These differences in influence could also be represented by the size of the circles or bubbles in the stakeholder diagram.

The third stage in the analysis of an organisation's purpose brings us to consider the objectives of different individuals and stakeholder groups. In essence this means tackling the second of the two questions listed previously; namely, what goals does or should the organisation pursue? Researchers and consultants

Figure 3.1
A stakeholder
analysis of Optico

analysing how directors and senior managers have tackled this question have offered a number of different analytical tools to help managers categorise the ultimate objectives pursued by key individuals and stakeholder groups associated with their organisation.

When it comes to deciding what the organisation's ultimate objectives are, many directors and senior managers suggest that the primary aim or driving force behind their organisation's operations is the attainment of one of more *financial measures* of progress, e.g. share performance, profit, return on investment or cash flow. By contrast, in other organisations the main focus might be some measure of *market performance*, e.g. sales, market share or market development. A third set of possible objectives relates to the organisation's *products and internal logistics*, e.g. productivity, product quality and research and development. The final set of objectives concentrates on the satisfaction of *social and ethical concerns* inside and outside the organisation, e.g. customer satisfaction, employee welfare, community and supplier relations. These different types of objective are mapped out in the wheel of objectives (*see* Fig 3.2).

The wheel of objectives is a device designed to enable directors, managers and other employees to depict and analyse the objectives of their own organisations. This form of analysis may be undertaken by completing the following six steps.

1   Directors, managers or employees rank-order the objectives listed on the outer perimeter of the wheel by reference to their experience of the organisation over the past five years. The most important objective is given a rank of 1 and the least important a rank of 12.

Figure 3.2
The wheel of objectives

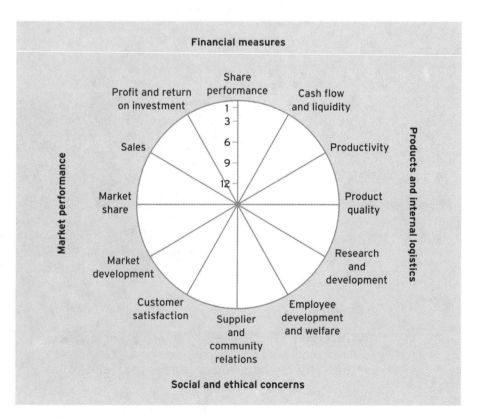

2   If two or more objectives are ranked equally, both items are given the same score but the ranking of the next objective starts one step lower on the appropriate spoke of the wheel. For example, if share performance and new market development are both ranked 1st, then the next objective, research and development, should be ranked 3rd.

3   Having completed the ranking of all twelve items, the directors, managers or employees then draw a cross at the appropriate point on each spoke of the wheel. Thus, if share performance is ranked 1st they should draw a cross on that part of the spoke labelled 1. They then repeat this exercise until all of the spokes are marked with a cross at some point along their length.

4   When each spoke is marked with an 'x' a line can be drawn to connect each of the crosses on adjacent spokes. When this line has been completed it should resemble a distorted circle.

5   The wheel can then be used again to rank-order the objectives contained in the organisation's mission statement. Alternatively or additionally, the procedures can be repeated in order to rank an individual's own preferred objectives for the organisation in future.

6   Finally, the different assessments can be compared. How do the assessments of the organisation's past objectives, mission statement and the individual's preferred goals for the future vary?

For many writers the definition of an organisation's purpose should make some reference to *the principal domains within which it intends to do business* (Digman, 1990). Following this line of reasoning, the mission or vision statement for an organisation like Optico might make reference to being the largest optical retailer in the UK. Other writers suggest that a broad statement of strategic intent linked to the objectives of key stakeholder is more appropriate because it does not limit the organisation to accepted definitions of industry and market boundaries. As the following section aims to demonstrate, establishing the limits of the market or industry within which an organisation operates is a very difficult task.

Exercise 3.2   By reference to the material contained in the case study at the beginning of this chapter, use the wheel of objectives diagram in Fig 3.2 and follow the first four steps outlined above to plot the objectives of Optico in the late 1950s and again in the late 1990s. How, if at all, did the objectives of the organisation change?

Strategy as position

The second major approach to the analysis of strategy focuses on the current and future environmental, market, industry and competitive positions of the organisation. The central questions addressed by analyses following this approach is:

what business are we in and what business do we want to be in? In other words, what products and services are or could be provided by the organisation, to which customers? What customer needs will this approach satisfy? How does this strategy compare with those adopted by the organisation's competitors? By addressing these questions appropriately, it is suggested that the managers and employees will be better placed to position their organisation to:

☐ exploit new and existing markets and products;
☐ outperform other organisations and avoid unnecessary competition.

There is a variety of different analytical tools and devices which can be used to tackle this question but due to the constraints of space it is only possible to deal with three of the most popular methods in this section:

☐ product market position;
☐ industry position;
☐ competitor analysis.

These methods build on the analyses outlined in Chapter 1, but focus much more specifically on the market and industry position of an organisation rather than the effects of broader political, economic, social and technological problems and pressures.

Product market position

Attempts to define the product market position of an organisation are fraught with difficulty. Traditional approaches to this question have tended to focus on the concept of *substitutability*. Put simply, this means that any two products are deemed to compete in the same market if the customer is prepared to swap goods provided by one firm with those produced by another organisation. However, this seemingly simple definition presents its own problems. For example, a cursory examination of Optico reveals that not all its customers would readily exchange the items bought from this company with those produced by a competitor. In other words, it would appear that the market for spectacles is subdivided. Here, customers vary according to the products that they wish to buy. Some people want a cheap pair of reading glasses, while others want contact lenses, fashionable frames or specialist spectacles made for sports wear, sunny climates or difficult working conditions. Furthermore, some customers want a personal eyesight test before buying their glasses while others are content to buy ready-made spectacles off the shelf.

Moving away from retail markets to consider raw material and wholesale markets, where one organisation sells goods or services to another, there may be other factors at work. For example, these markets might differ according to the location, wealth, performance requirements, purchasing procedures and scheduling of the purchasing company.

To deal with these differences between customers and companies, marketing specialists have developed the concept of market segmentation (*see* Table 3.1).

Table 3.1 Some criteria for market segmentation	Type of factor	Customer markets	Industry/organisational markets
	Characteristics of the customer or organisation	Age Sex Race Income Family size Life-cycle stage Location Life cycle	Industry Location Size Technology Profitability Management
	Location of purchase or use	Size of purchase Brand loyalty Purpose of use Purchasing behaviour Importance of purchase Choice criteria	Application Importance of purchase Volume Frequency of purchase Purchasing procedure Choice criteria Distribution channels
	User's needs, requirements and preferences for product characteristics	Product similarity Price perferences Brand preferences Desired features Quality	Performance Assistance from suppliers Quality Service requirements

Source: Johnson and Scholes 1993: 102

According to these analyses, the degree of product substitutability may be affected by a number of factors, including the characteristics of the customer, the location of purchase and the end use of the product provided. As a consequence of these and other differences, any form of market analysis needs to consider these factors when assessing the market position of a product.

Whether markets are defined in general terms or by reference to segments, there is always a danger that inappropriate definitions can cause more problems than they solve. For example, many optical industry analysts have questioned whether there really is a market for spectacles at all. These commentators suggest that the real market is for improvements in the customer's vision. It is then argued that if medical procedures advance sufficiently it should soon be possible to correct most people's eyesight by minor surgery. If this analysis is correct it means that the managers and staff at Optico need to consider what the effects of this change would be for their business in the future.

Turning away from definitions of the market which rely on characteristics of the customer, another commonly used form of market definition concentrates on defining the market by reference to the policies and practices of producers. In other words, markets are not defined by the needs, demands and wishes of consumers, but rather by the marketing and selling behaviour of their suppliers. An example of this approach is provided by the concept of the *marketing mix*. The simplest form of this analysis, developed by a group of academics at Harvard University in the 1930s and 1940s, is commonly referred to as the 4Ps. This acronym is used to refer to four aspects of the offering made by an organisation to potential customers:

□ *product*: variety, branding, design, styling and packaging;

□ *promotion*: public relations, advertising, sponsorship, sales campaigns and mailshots;

□ *price*: recommended retail price, discounting, credit arrangements and other payment methods;

□ *place*: market coverage, distribution methods, transport arrangements, accessibility and organisation of sales force.

Industry position

Although the terms market and industry are often used interchangeably, for authors like Kay (1996) the two are not synonymous. Industries often contain a number of organisations which serve similar markets, but these markets may be quite different from one another. Furthermore, organisations which consider themselves to be members of quite different industries often serve similar markets. For example, the organisations in the optical industry dealt with in the case at the beginning of this chapter attempt to meet the needs of customers who wish to buy glasses with prescription lenses, eyecare products and sunglasses. By providing these goods and services they are in competition with many organisations that sell sunglasses within the high-street clothing industry, as well as chemists who sell eyecare products in the high-street pharmaceutical industry. Although these organisations are subject to similar pressures where their markets overlap, they are organised along different lines, operate in different locations and are subject to different industry pressures. For example, they are apt to belong to different collective organisations when seeking to represent their views to government and other organisations. They will also tend to have different trade journals and magazines. As a consequence of these and other pressures, it is likely that managers and employees will compare the operation of their organisation with standards set in what they believe to be their industry. Pettigrew and Whipp (1991) refer to these differences as industry recipes. By this they mean that the range of acceptable strategies within any organisation is often set by reference to the actions of other organisations in the same industry.

Popular guidelines for the task of undertaking an industry analysis are provided by the work of Porter, a professor at Havard Business School and a prominent business author (Porter, 1980, 1985).

According to Porter, an essential first step in any form of strategic analysis is a thorough assessment of the organisation's position within existing industries. For Porter, the level of competition and attractiveness of a particular industry is determined by the opportunities which exist to generate profit. Building on this insight, Porter argues that the potential profitability of any industry is determined by the interaction of the following five forces (*see* Fig 3.3).

□ *The extent of competitive rivalry*. This is a measure of the degree of competition between existing companies in the industry and involves determining how many firms operate in particular market segments, the relative size of these firms, the rate of market growth and the presence of any barriers to specific firms leaving the industry. Competition is apt to be greatest in situ-

Figure 3.3
The five competitive forces that determine industry profitability (*Source*: Porter, 1985: 5)

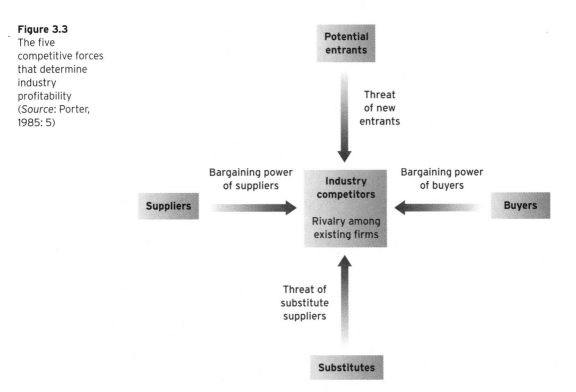

ations where there are a large number of similar-sized firms competing for business in a declining market where there are significant physical or financial barriers to individual firms leaving the industry.

☐ *The threat of new entrants.* This will be highest when existing firms within the industry are unable to exploit one or more of the following five resources: economies of scale, legal regulations preventing competition, preferential access to distribution channels, distinctive products or services, or lengthy experience in the market or industry.

☐ *The threat of substitutes.* As previously mentioned, the threat of substitution is greatest where potential customers can gain the same benefits from buying two seemingly unrelated goods or services. Thus, when there are many potential substitute goods or services available from companies in other industries, the competitive pressures facing the organisation will be greater and the potential for generating profit will be lower.

☐ *The power of buyers and the power of suppliers.* The last two forces affecting the competitive position of a firm and the attractiveness of the industry in which it operates are the power of buyers and the power of suppliers. Although these two groups are normally separated, common factors determine their relative power within the industry. The first factor is the concentration and availability of alternative sources of supply. Put simply, customers and suppliers will tend to have higher levels of bargaining power *vis-à-vis* individual companies in the industry when other firms are available to supply their needs or buy their goods and services. Thus, where one firm monopolises an industry, suppliers and buyers will be forced to do business with a company which might exploit this position by reducing the price it pays for supplies and increasing the price of the product it sells. The second factor affecting the power of suppliers and buyers is the threat of backward or forward integration. *Backward integration* refers to the situations in which a firms buys a controlling interest in its suppliers. By contrast, *forward integration* refers to the situation in which supplying firms buy a controlling interest in their customer's business.

Competitor analysis and benchmarking

Another form of industry analysis concentrates on identifying the main competitors facing an organisation and assessing what if anything can be learnt from their approach. Commonly referred to as competitor analysis or benchmarking, the first step in this process involves selecting organisations which managers and employees believe the organisation currently resembles or would like to emulate in the future. Market researchers typically approach this task by asking small groups of people how they view the organisation and the products and services it supplies. In making this assessment they are encouraged to make comparisons with other organisations. For example, a market researcher working for Optico might ask a focus group of customers or employees to compare this company with well-known high-street retailers. Research along these lines might begin with the following questions.

☐ How do Optico's stores compare with its main rivals in the optical industry?

☐ What are the similarities and differences between Optico and other high-street retailers, e.g. Boots, Marks and Spencers, Bhs or Littlewoods?

☐ What, if anything, could Optico learn from the approach taken by these other organisations?

More elaborate forms of benchmarking involve specifying key criteria, like those identified earlier in the wheel of objectives, and then systematically comparing the results achieved by organisations in the industry by reference to each of these dimensions. This form of analysis is difficult to perform in the private sector because of the problems associated with gaining access to reliable information which has been compiled in a consistent manner. However, the use of this type of benchmarking data has become widespread in the public sector, and information is now available on many of these dimensions for managers and consultants wishing to compare the performance of hospitals, schools, universities and other public bodies.

Exercise 3.3   Using the material contained in the case study at the beginning of this Chapter and your own general knowledge about the optical and retail industries, undertake a market, industry or competitor analysis of Optico's current position.

Strategy as potential

The third approach to strategy focuses on the capabilities and potential of the organisation. Like analyses of an organisation's external environment, market and industry position, the simplest approach to assessing the resources and operations of an organisation involves compiling a list, or drawing a diagram to represent key internal resources and problem areas. However, this approach presents problems. Most importantly, it is difficult to ensure that the list or diagram provides a concise and comprehensive overview of all of the significant resources and capabilities within the organisation. These problems can be overcome, at least in part, by involving a wide range of people in the analysis. It may also be helpful to group the results into categories. For example, the organisation's internal resources might be analysed in terms of *strengths* and *weaknesses*. These resources may then be compared with external *opportunities* and *threats*. The combination of these two forms of analysis is commonly referred to by the acronym *SWOT*. However, even with the use of SWOT analysis, there is no way of ensuring that all of the relevant factors inside and outside the organisation have been listed, nor that those that have been written down are really significant.

To deal with these difficulties, a range of models and conceptual frameworks have been offered by different authors to guide the thoughts and actions of staff undertaking internal resource analyses. Among the most popular methods are:

☐ core competencies;

☐ distinctive capabilities;

☐ value chain analysis.

Core competencies

For Hamel and Prahalad (1994), the concept of core competence provides a useful antidote to the traditional reliance on defining an organisation's resources and operations in terms of their products, financial resources and infrastructure. It also encourages the managers and staff of any organisation to consider directly the source of their competitive advantage. As they point out, the market value of the majority of large companies typically exceeds their asset value by a ratio of between 2.1 and 10.1. They attribute these differences to the core competences of these companies; the skills and knowledge built up by managers and staff which provide them with advantages over their competitors. Hamel and Prahalad suggest that core competences vary significantly between organisations in different industries. The one common characteristic of these competences in all settings is that they refer to the ability of staff or internal systems to produce functions that customers value. By functions they mean the needs satisfied by the good or service produced by the organisation.

Distinctive capabilities

According to Kay (1993), any form of strategic analysis should begin with an analysis of the organisation's *distinctive capabilities*. Taking issue with Porter, he argues that industries are not more or less attractive or profitable, but that organisations are in a stronger or weaker position on the basis of their possession of one or more of the following four distinctive capabilities:

☐ *Innovation* – the development of new products and services. If this capability is to provide the organisation with sustained competitive advantage, the organisation needs to find some method of protecting the innovation from copying by rivals.

☐ *Architecture* – is used to refer to the internal operating procedures and systems used within the organisation. For example, purchasing policies, the organisation of production, customer databases, distribution channels and billing procedures, etc.

☐ *Reputation* – refers to the corporate or brand image of the organisation and its products or services in the eyes of suppliers, customers, regulators and other key stakeholder groups. The benefits of a good reputation may include high levels of customer loyalty, extensive credit facilities from suppliers and above average valuations of the goodwill in the organisation's balance sheet and share price.

☐ *Strategic assets* – may be sources of supply, proprietary technologies or privileged access to key groups of customers. For example, exploration or mining rights, patents, copyrights, trademarks and prime property locations.

The possession and development of these distinctive capabilities can help an organisation to achieve higher levels of value-added than its rivals. Kay prefers value-added to profit as a measure of performance because it is less susceptible to manipulation and includes other benefits of improved performance, e.g. higher spending on research and development, training and wages. However, as he goes on to point out, the distinctive capabilities outlined above will provide competitive advantages only if sustainable and appropriable. This means that it must be possible to defend the advantages from imitation by competitors and the benefits of higher value-added must be realisable by the firm rather than passed on to suppliers in the form of higher prices for raw materials or on to customers in the form of lower prices for finished products.

Value chain analysis

The last of our three chosen methods of assessing an organisation's resources and operations was developed from management accounting principles by Porter (1985). He suggests that a fuller understanding of an organisation's strategic capabilities can be gained by analysing the costs and value-added by its various internal operations. To help managers and other staff undertake this analysis, Porter divides the internal operations of operations into two basic units: primary and support activities (*see* Fig 3.4). These activities are then subdivided respectively into five and four separate subunits.

Detailed value chain analysis involves three further steps. First, critical activities within each sub-unit of activity are identified and the value added by these

Figure 3.4
The value chain
(*Source*: Porter,
1985: 46)

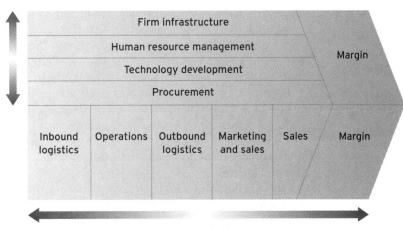

operations is assessed from the perspective of the final customer. As Porter emphasises, the value chain within any individual organisation is part of a larger supply chain in which raw materials are converted by different organisations into finished products and then distributed and sold to the final customer. As a consequence of this division of activities between firms, it is not always easy to assess costs and values from the perspective of the final customer, but it is nevertheless essential if the organisation is to maintain competitive advantage. The second stage in value chain analysis involves isolating the factors which determine the costs and value added by various activities. Finally, the linkages between the various activities are mapped and analysed in order to identify those combinations of internal processes which are both difficult for competitors to imitate and also generate the highest margins between cost and value-added. According to Porter, by focusing on the maintenance and development of these core strategic capabilities, managers and staff within the organisation should be able to retain and enhance its competitive advantage. This form of value chain analysis is similar in content and application to what has elsewhere been referred to as *Business Process Re-engineering*.

Exercise 3.4 By reference to the material contained in the case study at the beginning of this chapter, list the core competences or distinctive capabilities of Optico in the late 1990s.

Strategy as the evaluation of alternative possibilities

The fourth of our approaches to strategy formulation and implementation concentrates on the process of evaluating the benefits and pitfalls associated with different courses of action. Like the techniques reviewed in earlier subsections, these methods differ from one another in terms of the degree of judgement they leave open to those undertaking strategic analyses.

For many writers a defining feature of any consideration of the process of strategy making is an understanding that the actions of managers or employees involve choices (conscious or unconscious). The point is that whatever the problem, pressure or priority facing these individuals, the way that they deal with this issue will invariably involve deciding to do certain things and ignoring or dismissing the other options. If we accept this view, that most if not all strategy formulation involves a choice between alternative courses of action, it should be possible to improve the organisation by paying more attention to how these decisions are made, and more specifically, by developing our abilities to make decisions and implement changes which are generally seen as appropriate and legitimate.

In this section three methods of evaluating the possible options facing an organisation are considered. These three techniques are labelled:

- multiple attribute utility tests (MAUT);
- portfolio analysis
- make or buy analysis.

Multiple attribute utility tests (MAUT)

The simplest form of analysing the options confronting an organisation when faced with a particular problem or pressure is to undertake a MAUT or payoff analysis. This form of analysis can be undertaken by completing the following six steps.

1 Through group or discussion, analysis of competitor behaviour and a review of the literature, identify between two and five options for dealing with a particular problem or pressure. For example, in the case of Optico at the beginning of this chapter the threat of new competition in the mid-1980s could have been dealt with by one or more of the following options:

- doing nothing;
- consolidating the organisation's activities in order to concentrate on those activities that add most value;
- increasing the organisation's marketing and advertising activities;
- reducing the price of the product and services offered;
- targeting key groups of customers or market segments.

2 List a series of criteria against which the various options can be evaluated. These criteria could be derived from an assessment of the organisation's goals using the wheel of objectives or some other similar list. According to Johnson and Scholes (1993), the most appropriate criteria for assessing the options in any set of circumstances are:

- suitability: the extent to which the option deals with the problem;
- feasibility: the ability of the organisation to devote sufficient resources to the implementation of the proposed solution;

❏ acceptability: the degree of support for the option from key individuals and stakeholder groups.

3 Draw up a matrix with the various options listed horizontally and the criteria arranged along the vertical axis (*see* Table 3.2).

Table 3.2
A MAUT analysis of Optico's strategic options in the mid-1980s

Evaluation criteria	Do nothing	Consolidate	Marketing	Reduce prices	Target markets
Suitability (Weighting × 1)	5 (5)	4 (4)	1 (1)	2 (2)	2 (2)
Feasibility (Weighting × 2)	1 (2)	2 (4)	3 (6)	3 (6)	3 (6)
Acceptability (Weighting × 3)	4 (12)	5 (15)	1 (3)	2 (6)	2 (6)
Total score	10 (19)	11 (23)	5 (10)	7 (14)	7 (14)

Note: This MAUT evaluation has been compiled by ranking each option against each criterion, with 1 being the most appropriate option and 5 the least appropriate. The rankings have been weighted so that feasibility and acceptability are two and three times less important than suitability. This has been achieved by multiplying the rankings associated with these by 2 and 3 respectively. The raw rankings are listed first and the weighted rankings are displayed under figures in brackets.

4 Having set out the options and the methods of assessing their appropriateness, the next step is to rank or score these different options. For example, the ranking of 1 for the most appropriate option and 5 for the least relevant. Alternatively, a total score of 100 for each criterion could be allocated proportionately to each of the options, the highest scores going to the most attractive options.

5 Weight the criteria in order to ensure that the importance of various objectives is reflected in the ranking scoring of particular options. For example, the pursuit of increases in market share in the short to medium term might be deemed to be more important than share performance, the level of profit or return on investment. These differences in the value attached to particular objectives can be reflected by weightings, but it is important to note that the way in which this should be done will vary according to whether the initial assessment of options has relied upon rankings or scores. Thus, if the options were ranked, the weightings should be introduced by multiplying the numbers attached to the less relevant criteria by an appropriate factor. For example, return on investment and profit could be multiplied by two while the market share criterion is left unweighted. If the options have been scored, the procedure is reversed, with the numbers allocated to each option under the most important criteria being multiplied by what is deemed to be an appropriate weighting, while the numbers allocated under less important criteria are left unaltered. Following this approach, market share might be multiplied by two, while return on investment and profit are left unaltered.

6 The total weighted rankings or scores for each option can be calculated before a decision is made about which course of action to pursue.

Multiple attribute utility testing or payoff matrices are used widely in job evaluation, recruitment and redundancy selection and to a lesser extent when evaluating tenders and making purchasing decisions. This approach has advantages over less formal methods because it ensures that the same criteria are applied in a systematic, visible and understandable manner to each of the options.

Portfolio analysis

Large conglomerates and multinational firms offer a wide range of products and services to many different markets. In these organisations a key decision-making area facing senior managers and the board of directors is: what businesses should we be in? In other words, which of the organisation's operating divisions or companies should benefit from what levels of investment and which units should be rationalised or sold off? Within each operating unit of multidivisional firms or, alternatively, within single business organisations, similar decisions ought to be made about which products, services or functions should be made in-house and which should be purchased from suppliers or provided by the customer. To help senior managers deal with these decisions, a range of portfolio planning techniques have been developed by business consultants and researchers.

Among the most popular of these decision-making tools are the Boston Consulting Group matrix (BCG) and Ansoff's technology/market matrix. The key features of each of these approaches are as follows:

BCG matrix

The BCG matrix can be used to analyse the position of a division within a large organisation, or alternatively to consider the position and prospects for offerings from one division or a single business organisation. Offering is used here to refer to products, services or functions. The position of the division or offering is mapped by reference to its current market share and the level of overall growth in this market (*see* Fig 3.5). On the basis of this analysis, divisions or offerings can be grouped into four categories: cash cows, which can be milked to provide funds for investment; dogs, which can be rationalised, run down or sold off to another organisation; stars, which require continued investment to maintain their position in the market; and question marks, which either require investment or should be sold off.

Technology/market matrix

The range of options available to an organisation wishing to develop its operations in the future is outlined in Igor Ansoff's Product/Market Matrix (*see* Fig 3.6 on page 82). The three dimensions in this matrix are market need, product/service technology and market geography. The first of these dimensions refers to the customer demand for particular functions from the goods or services offered by the organisation, e.g. improvements in their eyesight or the offer of personal transportation. The second dimension focuses on the technology of the organisation's products or services, e.g. spectacles, contact lens, or in the case of transport, aeroplanes. The third dimension draws attention to the geographical range of the organisation's activities, e.g. regional,

Figure 3.5
The Boston
Consulting Group
matrix
(*Source*: Porter,
1985: 12)

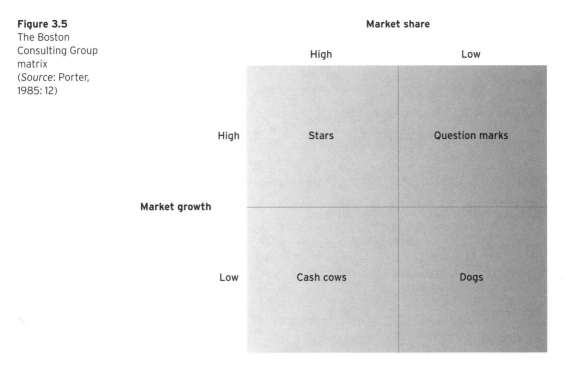

national, European, or international. By combining these three dimensions, eight possible options are identified. These different courses of action are illustrated in more detail in the second diagram in Fig 3.6.

In the short term, there is a limited range of options available to the managers and employees wishing to change the present portfolio offered by their organisation. They may choose to do nothing, to consolidate their operations or to use advertising and other marketing initiatives to gain greater market penetration. However, in the medium to longer term, they may pursue a policy of diversification using new technologies to serve new market needs. Alternatively, they wish to branch out into new businesses by using new technologies to serve new market needs. Furthermore, the organisation's present approach or diversification strategies may be extended from existing home markets to overseas locations by pursuing a policy of internationalisation. Obviously, these options have different resource implications and are associated with lower or higher degrees of risk. The most radical, and perhaps riskiest, strategy is a move to unrelated conglomerate operations. In this situation new technologies are applied to new market needs in the organisation's home market or overseas. This option is represented in the first diagram of Fig 3.6 (overleaf) by the move from the lightly shaded box in the bottom left-hand quadrant to the more darkly shaded box in the top right-hand quadrant.

Make or buy analysis

There is a range of options available when it comes to deciding who should produce component parts of the goods and services provided by an organisation.

Figure 3.6
Ansoff's
technology/market
matrix

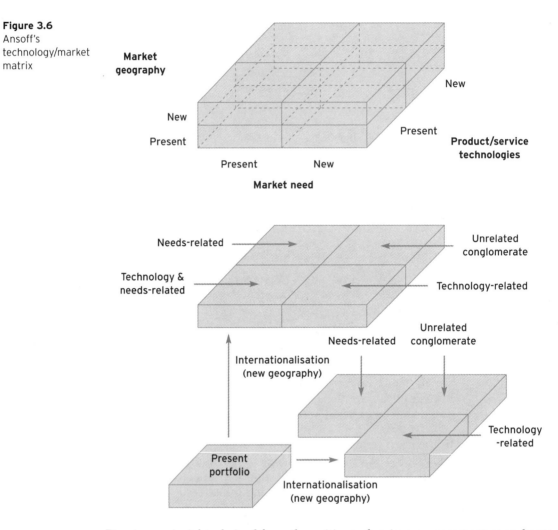

Drawing on insights derived from the writings of various management consultants and academic researchers, it is possible to identify two important components of this decision: first, the location of production, i.e. whether the goods or services are to be made in-house or bought from external suppliers; second, the duration of these activities, i.e. whether these arrangements are intended to be short term or long term. The combination of these two dimensions reveals four basic options (see Figure 3.6). The goods and services can be made in-house by permanent operating units or temporary project groups. Alternatively, these products may be supplied on a short term basis by subcontractors or long-term by partner organisations (whether these are licensees or licensors/franchisees or franchisors).

The factors affecting the choice between these alternatives are many and varied, but will invariably include the level of risk, return, resources, expertise and separability associated with each element of the activity. For example, where there is a risk that the organisation's reputation or strategic assets may be damaged or appropriated by a subcontractor or commercial partner, the operations will tend to be kept in-house, unless the returns associated with this activity are deemed to be sufficient to justify the risk. Similarly, where the

Figure 3.7
Make or buy
analysis

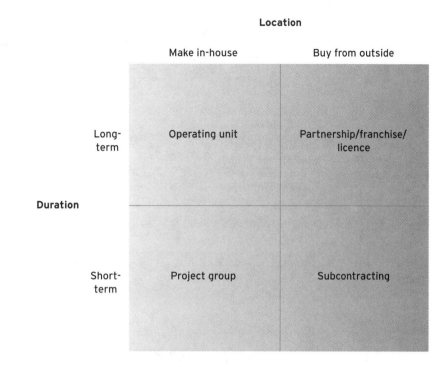

work requires levels of resources or expertise which exceed those currently available within the organisation, it will tend to be put out to contract or conducted through alliances with other organisations. Finally, the decision to make or outsource will be influenced by the extent to which it is possible to separate the personnel required to make various elements of the finished product or service. Where there are significant linkages, the organisation will tend to keep the activity in-house. Alternatively, where the resources and expertise are low and the associated risks are high, it may be better to acquire or merge with another organisation.

Exercise 3.5 By reference to the material contained in the case study at the beginning of this chapter, identify instances in which one or more of the models outlined above may have influenced the strategic decisions of managers at Optico.

Strategy as plans

Advocates of this approach suggest that an organisation's strategy is, or should be, contained within detailed written plans drawn up by senior managers and approved by the board of directors. Guidelines for those wishing to adopt this approach usually suggest that the development of strategy should be divided into a series of discrete steps which combine the approaches outlined in the preceding four sections in a logical sequence (*see* Fig 3.8).

Figure 3.8
Strategy as
planning

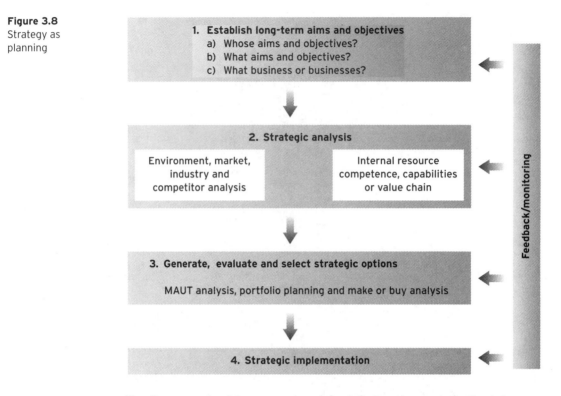

The first stage in this process involves defining the organisation's long-term aims and principal business or businesses. In the case of Optico, these aims and objectives might be included in a mission statement as superior market growth and shareholder value from outstanding performance in the retail optical business.

The second stage combines external environment, market, industry and competitor analyses with internal reviews of the organisation's own competences and capabilities. Once these analyses have been completed, it is assumed that it should be possible, during the third stage, to generate a number of possible options for future action. These various courses of action can then be evaluated by reference to the organisation's own long-term objectives before the final choice is made and plans are set in place to implement this proposed solution.

Writers and researchers who see strategy as primarily concerned with the development and implementation of plans tend to see strategic decision making as the preserve of the managing director and other members of the board of directors aided by senior managers who specialise in strategic planning. For example, Igor Ansoff (1987) suggests that strategic decisions can be distinguished from administrative and operating decisions because they are taken centrally within the organisation and concern choices about the allocation of resources between different product and market opportunities. Furthermore, these decisions tend to be taken in circumstances of uncertainty and risk in which the decision makers are likely to be ignorant about some of the potential decisions taken at lower levels within the organisation under conditions of less uncertainty. This second category of decisions focuses on the managerial structure of the organisation, arrangements for obtaining raw materials, the design of production and the marketing of finished products and services. Finally, operating decisions focus on the day-to-day scheduling of staff, supplies, production and marketing. These decisions are often programmable and self-regenerative. In other words, there is an identifiable timetable for dealing with these decisions and choices tend to be repeated unless altered by strategic and administrative decisions at higher levels within the organisation.

Ansoff's approach has been highly influential and, as a consequence, other authors have adapted his approach to differentiate between different forms or levels of strategy formulation, e.g. corporate, business and operational strategy (Johnson and Scholes, 2002) or first-, second- and third-order strategy (Purcell and Ahlstrand, 1994). These writers suggest that corporate or first-order strategies focus on the long-term direction of its activities, how it will be run structurally and financially and how resources will be allocated to different constituent parts of the enterprise. Business or second-order strategies concentrate on the structural issues associated with which products or services should be developed and offered to which markets, by which parts of the organisation. Finally, operational or third-order strategies deal with different functional areas of the organisation's activities, e.g. purchasing, production, marketing, sales, service, research and development, human resources and finance.

The distinction between different levels of strategy has also been used to help guide directors and managers when faced with the problem of translating broad statements of intent into appropriate, coordinated and effective action. Thus, many management consultants suggest that corporate, business and operational strategies can be brought together and integrated within five-year plans which are annually reviewed. This planning process brings together three parallel processes (*see* Fig 3.9).

First, the specification of business and operational objectives by the managers and employees within different parts of the organisation. These objectives are then reviewed and approved or rejected by reference to the organisation's overall objectives.

The second component of this process is a review of the organisation's business objectives and associated plans. As part of this process, directors and senior managers will be encouraged to consider possible extensions or reductions in the range of activities performed by the organisation. This might involve divestment from some activities and investment in new initiatives or joint ventures, mergers or acquisitions of other organisations.

The third element is a review of the organisation's longer-term corporate objectives and strategy in the light of the business and operational decisions that have been made and assessments of possible future developments.

Finally, it is suggested that the results of these three activities should be written up and distributed to all the managers and employees within the organisation. This written statement of objectives can then be used as a basis for discussion, appraisal, training, and reward. It should also guide day-to-day decision making within the organisation.

Strategy as programmes, ploys, politics, patterns and perspective

Writers associated with this approach draw on the results of case studies and other analyses in order to document the source of changes within organisations.

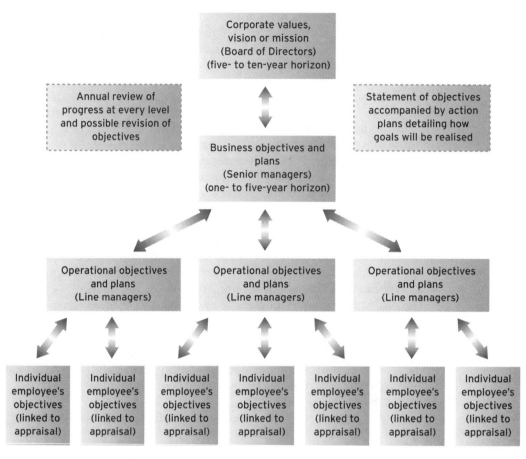

Figure 3.9 Planning and practice

As these accounts seek to demonstrate, action within organisations is rarely the result of a process of analysing the organisation's purpose, position, potential or possibilities. Furthermore, it is extremely uncommon for these changes to come about as a consequence of an organisation's annual planning cycle. For these writers the mismatch between the prescriptions of the five approaches outlined in earlier sections of this chapter and the reality of day-to-day decision making and action in organisations may be explained by one or more of the following four factors.

Cost

Collecting, analysing and evaluating information costs money, and managers and their employees rarely have sufficient resources at their disposal to devote to this task. The definition of an organisation's objectives, analysis of its position and potential, or evaluation of possible ways forward, requires considerable amounts of staff time and financial resources. Furthermore, if these tasks are to be successful the results of these activities have to involve or be communicated to all the staff in the organisation. Faced with these demands, it is not surprising that managers in most organisations would rather concentrate on what they see as the more pressing demands of producing and selling the goods and services which provide the organisation's income.

Availability of accurate information

Even when sufficient resources are made available to engage in strategic analysis and evaluation it may be difficult to get accurate and up-to-date information. The data required to perform some of the simpler tasks outlined in earlier sections may involve staff in hundreds of hours of work. By the time this data-gathering exercise has been completed, there is no guarantee that the problems or pressures the project set out to deal with will remain the same. There is also a danger that the information collected may no longer be accurate.

Bounded rationality

In order to fit the information collected from any strategic analysis into the frameworks and models outlined in the first five sub-sections of this section chapter, it is necessary to simplify the nature of the problem or rationalise the range of solutions considered. This simplification is required because the people conducting the analysis and receiving its results will find it difficult to cope with complex models and methods. Research by psychologists has consistently demonstrated that most people find it difficult to remember and cope with the analysis being performed. On the basis of these results it could be argued that the models and frameworks outlined earlier in this chapter have become popular because they are easy to remember, rather than because they provide an accurate guide for strategic thinking.

Commitment and compliance

If strategic analysis and evaluation are to lead to any significant changes in the direction of an organisation, it is essential that managers and employees are committed to, or comply with, the resulting plans and guidelines. However, the assumption that staff will be prepared to follow this lead is contentious. As we saw earlier, the goals and directions of an organisation are influenced by various individuals and stakeholder groups. In certain circumstances it may be possible to accommodate these different views and reach a compromise which satisfies their different demands, for example by allowing these different groups to participate in the analysis of the organisation's position, potential or possible ways forward. However, quite apart form the cost of this exercise, there may be situations in which it is impossible to gain support from all of these groups. Even when a majority of the stakeholders, or the most influential amongst these groups, agree with the plans proposed, there may be difficulties associated with getting the other groups to comply with the results of this analysis or evaluation.

An acknowledgement of the influence of one or more of the four factors listed above has led many researchers and business commentators to describe much so-called strategy making by reference to one or more of the following five approaches:

☐ programmes;

☐ ploys;

- ☐ politics;
- ☐ patterns;
- ☐ perspective.

Programmes

The term programmes is used to refer to a range of off-the-shelf solutions touted by management consultants, business commentators and academics. The labels attached to these programmes include organisation development, total quality management, human resource management, business process re-engineering, lean production, the learning organisation, performance management, empowerment and strategic management itself. The content of these programmes varies considerably, but all combine guidelines and techniques for managers and employees which it is suggested will cure a range of organisational ills.

In practice, it would appear that fashion plays an important part in determining whether these programmes are taken up and implemented by managers. The hype that accompanies the coining of a new term, or the development of a novel technique, often encourages managers to jump on the bandwagon. These managers would appear to believe that the danger of not understanding and applying the latest management fad is that the competition will exploit any benefits that flow from this programme and gain an advantage over their rivals. However, following fashion and fads also exposes the organisation to two problems.

In order to exploit any potential benefits it is necessary to commit resources to the programme before the real benefits of this approach have been widely established. There is therefore a danger that the programme will be implemented before the pitfalls associated with this approach are fully realised.

Following fashion will not provide the organisation with a unique advantage over its competitors. According to Hamel (1997), there are three types of organisation in any industry or market cluster. He refers to these types of organisation as rule makers, rule takers and rule breakers. Organisations in the first group tend to be few in number and generally owe their existence to the development of new ways of doing business which have had a significant influence on the current shape and operation of particular industries. The second group tends to have many more members and consists of the followers who consciously or unconsciously accept the rules governing how business is done in the industry and tend to copy the programmes introduced by the rule-making organisations. The final group consists of a very small number of organisations who are less willing to accept existing definitions of industry barriers and methods of operation. These rule breakers are more prepared to adopt innovative approaches and, while many fail, the few that succeed tend to be the next generation of rule makers in the industry.

Ploys

In practice, many of the changes implemented by organisations owe their origins to operational decisions taken by junior managers and other employees. If the resulting changes in the organisation's activities grow sufficiently in magnitude, then they tend to become considered strategic. At this stage it is not uncommon for senior managers to amend the organisation's objectives to accommodate these changes. For example, research examining why and how companies launch new products, internationalise their operations, enter into joint ventures or merge with other organisations suggests that these initiatives frequently begin with tactical initiatives by relatively junior employees (Hendry, 1994).

The result of these studies suggest that the distance between the top of the organisation and the day-to-day realities of operations prevents many senior managers and directors from developing an awareness of trends and possibilities within the business. This distance also frequently prevents these staff from having the contacts that are necessary in order to secure deals with other organisations. In these circumstances, middle and junior managers will tend to exploit their contacts and develop firm proposals before putting this to senior managers and the board for approval. Faced with a *fait accompli*, the managers responsible for shaping the future direction of the organisation are faced with only three options: accept, reject or refer the proposal back for further development.

If there are any chances that the proposal will be successful it is quite likely that it will be accepted for the following five reasons. First, the junior employees bringing forward the proposal will often mould their recommendations so that they appear to be in keeping with the spirit if not the letter of the organisation's stated objectives. Hendry (1994) refers to this situation as a solution in search of a problem. Second, it is difficult for senior managers and members of the board to verify independently the claims contained within the proposals. As mentioned earlier, analysis and evaluation costs money and takes time. Third, most proposals of this sort will be well worked out before they are put to senior managers, and may also be time-sensitive. The combination of these factors means that in practice there may only be a small window of opportunity for implementing the proposed changes. A fourth reason for the willingness of boards of directors to accept proposals is that rejecting the proposal may demoralise the staff concerned and undermine their commitment to the senior managers' other objectives. Finally, there is always a danger that the staff bringing forward the proposal will leave and take their ideas to another organisation.

Politics

Office politics are a perennial focus of novels, plays, television sitcoms and other literary forms, but these aspects of everyday work are largely ignored in the accounts of strategy making offered by academics and management consultants. These authors may mention the importance of office politics when explaining the form and content of organisational policies, but few go on to describe and analyse how these processes operate. For example, Purcell and Ahlstrand comment that 'by far the most influential personnel directors we met were those with a close working relationship with the CEO. Their power was more personal than personnel' (1994: 109). By this they mean that where HR issues have an influence on an organisation's business strategy, this tends to be the result of a political alliance or friendship between the managing directors in companies which are said to have adopted a strategic approach to personnel issues.

Various researchers have offered different ways of analysing the power and influence of groups within an organisation (French and Raven, 1959: Marchington; 1978, Pfeffer, 1981). For example, according to French and Raven (1959), the form of many decisions and actions result from key individuals or groups exerting power over others in the organisation. In discussing this process they identify the following sources of individual or group power:

☐ *Reward* – the use of resources as rewards, where the recipient values the chosen method and believes it can be delivered. This may include salary increases, promotion, increased job satisfaction and social recognition.

☐ *Coercive* – the capacity to enforce discipline or material and psychological punishment. This may include loss of pay, demotion or humiliation in front of the individual's peer group.

☐ *Referent* – the personal characteristics of the manager. This may include charisma, personal charm or leadership qualities.

☐ *Legitimate* – the organisational rules and regulations which stipulate the nature of relationships between people at work. For example, organisation charts, job descriptions, role profiles, constitutions, and terms of reference which outline which individuals or groups are formally granted the authority to make certain types of decision.

☐ *Expert* – the existence of power as knowledge, skill or expertise. This may include the possession of degrees, certificates or experiences which others feel qualify the individual to make important decisions. Of the few studies of micropolitical processes in organisations which have been undertaken, the majority have tended to concentrate on major stakeholders and significant disagreements between these groups; there has been relatively little attention to the day-to-day wrangles which normally characterise decision making in organisations. The few exceptions to this rule tend to suggest that many organisational changes come about as a consequence of ongoing processes which combine negotiation, accommodation, compromise, coercion and occasional conflict.

Patterns

The advocates of this approach argue that the haphazard nature of decision making and action in most organisations means that it is only really possible to discern strategy in retrospect. In other words, the techniques and models outlined in earlier sections may be useful aids to managers who wish to analyse decisions which were, or were not, taken in the past, but are of little help when assessing what could happen in the future.

Advocates of this approach often rely on notions of culture and/or management style of an organisation, industry or national level in order to explain the sources of change within organisation (Peters and Waterman, 1982; Miles and Snow, 1978; Pascale and Athos, 1986; Hofstede, 1994; Purcell and Ahlstrand, 1995). However, these writers differ in their assessments of the extent to which it is possible for the senior managers of an organisation to manipulate or significantly alter the dominant culture within the organisation. For Peters and

Waterman (1982), it is possible for these managers to alter the destiny of their organisations by learning from the example of others. For the other writers, culture and management style reflect the complex, interconnected totality of the way in which the organisation operates and it is therefore difficult to alter this culture in a directed and planned manner.

Two of the most influential exponents of this pattern or culture-based approach to strategy are Miles and Snow, who studied a range of different organisations and identified four basic types which they labelled prospectors, analysers, defenders and reactors (*see* Table 3.3).

Table 3.3
Different types of organisational culture and their influences on strategic decision making

	Dominant objectives	Preferred strategies	Planning and control systems
Defenders	Desire for secure and stable niche in market	Specialisation Cost-effcient production Marketing emphasises price and service Tendency to vertical integration	Centralised detailed control. Emphasis on cost-efficiency Extensive use of formal planning techniques
Prospectors	Location and exploitation of new product and market	Growth through product and market development Constant monitoring of environmental change Multiple technologies	Emphasis on flexibility Decentralised control. Use of *ad hoc* measurements
Analysers	Desire to match new venture to shape of business	Steady growth through market penetration Exploitation of applied research Followers in the market	Very complicated coordinating roles between functions Intensive planning
Reactors	React to change	Mixed, inconsistent and often inappropriate	Poorly managed or non-existent

Source: Adapted from Miles and Snow (1978)

Perspective

Advocates of the last of the approaches dealt with in this section criticise the very concept of strategy itself (*see* for example: Hyman, 1987; Walby, 1990; Hassard and Parker, 1994). Although there are significant differences between these writers, they all suggest that the concept of strategy and other associated discourses in management serve to conceal rather than reveal the structures and processes of decision making and action within organisations.

These writers criticise the conventional view that groups of senior managers and directors within individual organisations are the masters of change. Instead, they suggest that many of the decisions and actions taken within organisations are driven by the wider economic and ideological forces of capitalism, patriarchy, racism or other deeper-seated patterns of resource, power and status inequality. These Marxist, feminist and other radical critics argue that most new initiatives within organisations are driven by the logic of the system, whether this emphasises increased management control, the deskilling of employees and the degradation of labour, exploitation of the environment or the oppression of women and minority groups (Schumacher, 1973; Braverman, 1974; Edwards, 1978; Burawoy, 1985; Walby, 1990).

For these writers, whatever the sources of the system, the logic of the structure and processes at play is hidden from the many managers and employees, either because they choose to ignore it, or because the language of strategy obscures it. Indeed, for many postmodernists, the concepts and words that are used wrongly imply that financial and market objectives are of primary importance and assume that managers can be omniscient and omnipotent. As such, it is argued, the categories and definitions used channel the nature of the discussion and limit the insights which can be gained. For example, it is suggested, the frequent use of military and sporting metaphors in the discussion of strategy highlights the competitive nature of this activity and draws attention away from discussion of the cooperation that often exists between enterprises in the same industry.

Even when these critics of conventional approaches to strategy concede that individual managers may have choices, they are apt to suggest that these choices are constrained by the structure of the system and inevitably produce contradictory outcomes (Hyman, 1987: 30). For example, the requirement to analyse and dissect problems into functional and departmental areas, but also to provide integrative and co-ordinated solutions. Similarly, the requirements to build relationships based on trust within organisations, while simultaneously pursuing cost reductions by cutting employment levels and outsourcing activities. Finally, the requirement to produce increases in profit through improvements in productivity while matching market pay rates and improving conditions for employees.

For writers adopting this perspective, it is not just that definitions and analyses of strategy arrive at the wrong conclusions, but also that they start with the wrong assumptions and use flawed methods of analysis and evaluation.

Exercise 3.6   By reference to the case study material at the beginning of this chapter, provide examples of developments with Harsons or Optico which exhibit characteristics of the programmes, ploys, politics and patterns.

☐ Summary and conclusion

This chapter has reviewed ten different approaches to the definition and analysis of strategy under six headings. In the course of this review, the implications of different approaches for the planning and implementation of organisation change have been considered. As was noted at the outset, none of these different approaches should be considered to provide a complete explanation of the process of strategy making and implementation. However, in combination these approaches do reveal different facets of dimensions of the processes of work.

☐ Recommended reading

Johnson, G and Scholes, K (2001) *Exploring Corporate Strategy: Text and Cases*, London: Pearson Education.

Mintzberg, H, Quinn, J and Ghoshal, S (1995) *The Strategy Process*, London: Prentice Hall.

Moore, J (1992) *Writers on Strategy and Strategic Management*, Harmondsworth: Penguin.

Whittington, R (1993) *What is Strategy: Does it Matter?* London: Routledge.

04 | The labour market

Chapter

□ Introduction: a changing labour market

The pace of change in the labour market is, arguably, greater than ever before. *The Economist* makes the grandiloquent claim that 'Nothing in human life has changed more in ten centuries than the world of work. Most trades now practised in rich countries did not exist 250 years ago.' (*The Economist*, Toiling from there to here, 31 December 1999). Since the war the labour market has been transformed. The early 1950s was an era of full employment, of male breadwinners, of mass manufacturing where industries such as coal, steel and shipbuilding employed hundreds of thousands – these were to decline dramatically (*see* Table 4.1). Trade unions were relatively strong, employment was relatively stable; the 9–5, five days a week, job-for-life model was far from uncommon. The contrast with today is striking. Nearly half the workforce is female. 'Atypical' forms of employment – part-time work, temporary work, short-term contracts – are commonplace (*see* Table 4.1). Services have – with a vengeance – displaced manufacturing as the main sector of employment; there are now more childcare workers than car workers in Britain. Subcontracting labour is far more widespread, as is the demand for graduate employment. After decades of downsizing, restructuring and re-engineering we are said to be both more flexible and at the same time more insecure.

Below we examine some of these trends: sectoral change and changes in ownership, the feminisation of the labour market, and the rise of 'flexibility', insecurity and the 'work–life' balance.

Table 4.1	Year	No. of coal-miners	Year	No. employed in the steel industry
The decline in the numbers employed in the coal and steel industries	1954	700 000	1978	186 000
	1974	300 000	1988	51 600
	1994	10 000	2003*	22 000

Sources: Coal - Kelly (1998) Rethinking Industrial Relations; Steel - *Guardian*, 2 February 2001
*Forecast

☐ Focus and scope

We begin by examining trends in the labour market. These include sectoral change and changes in ownership, the decline of trade unions, the feminisation of the labour market, the rise of 'flexibility', the issue of insecurity and finally, the 'work-life' balance.

Learning objectives

Once you have read through this chapter and completed the associated exercises, you should be able to:

☐ comment on recent trends in the UK labour market;

☐ collect labour market information from a range of sources;

☐ outline the causes and consequences of status differences between groups within the labour market;

☐ discuss issues such as 'family friendly' employment practices and the 'work-life balance'.

☐ What is work?

The world of work is continually undergoing a complex array of changes and shifts. Underpinning it is the more fundamental question of what is 'work'. This issue lies behind the key distinction between 'paid work' and 'unpaid work'. Activities such as lawn mowing or childcare can both be said to be 'work' but they can be unpaid (if you do it yourself) or paid (if you hire someone to do it), even though the actual activity undertaken may be identical. It is not 'work' as such but paid work that is the central concern of personnel managers, what is often called the 'wage–effort bargain'.

The Cambridge economist, Alfred Marshall, defined it as: 'any exertion of mind or body undergone partly or wholly with a view to some good other than the pleasure derived directly from that work' (cited in Thomas, 1999). This is arguably flawed, as physical exercise would count as work if it were done for reasons of health rather than for reasons of pleasure. The Oxford historian, Keith Thomas, sees 'Work has an end beyond itself, being designed to produce or achieve something; it involves a degree of obligation or necessity, being a task that that others set us or that we set ourselves; and it is arduous, involving effort and persistence beyond the point at which the task ceases to be wholly pleasurable' (Thomas, 1999).

The traditional view of 'work' was that it was something everyone would naturally avoid. Humankind was seen as being naturally idle. It was taken as axiomatic that human beings preferred leisure to work. People, it was said, worked only out of necessity. In the words of St Paul: 'if any would not work, neither should he eat' (First epistle to the Thessalonians, 3:10). Without stick or carrots, human indolence would reassert itself. An instrumental attitude to work prevailed; it was a means to an end, a temporary surrender of liberty for material reward. Indeed, the French word for work, *travail*, supposedly derives from *trepalium*, an instrument of torture.

More recently this conception was seen as psychologically misconceived. Potentially work was a liberating activity, leading to self-realisation and freedom. Work is the main source of income for households and individuals. But work can also provide networks of friends and acquaintances, a sense of participation in society and opportunities for development.

☐ Sectoral change and changing ownership

Between 1979, the start of the Thatcher era, and the advent of a Labour government in 1997 the labour market landscape had been transformed. The period witnessed a decline of manufacturing and increasing dominance of service industries, the contraction and reorganisation of the public sector, the shift to smaller workplaces, the rise of foreign ownership and the increased use of non-standard employment contracts. The influence of trade unions was sharply reduced.

Massive sectoral change took place in these two decades. Table 4.2 outlines some of the shifts; a sharp decline in manufacturing as a source of employment is evident, as is the rise of private services. Pressures to cut the levels of public spending and public sector employment have been insistent since the late 1970s. Public sector employment peaked in 1979 at 7.5 million and declined as a consequence of privatisation, competitive tendering and efficiency savings to 5.1 million in 1996 – a fall of 31 per cent. These trends are expected to continue; virtually all of the sectors in which job growth is expected are service sectors.

Table 4.2
Employment in various sectors (% of employees)

	1980	1984	1990	1998
Private sector manufacturing and extraction	38	27	27	25
Private sector services	26	29	38	44
Public sector	36	43	35	32

All establishments with 25 or more employees
Source: Millward *et al.* (2000)

The ownership and patterns of control in organisations have important implications for management structure and work organisation. Important differences are likely to arise depending on whether a workplace operates in the private sector, attempting to maximise returns for shareholders, or in the public sector, operating within the confines of predetermined budgets. But even within these sectors there are important differences in the character of ownership and control. Within the private sector there are partnerships, non-government organisations, cooperatives, private companies and publicly listed companies. The public sector has experienced dramatic changes in the character of ownership and control since the late 1970s. As well as privatisation, authority has been devolved to local managers in education and health through a system of grant-maintained schools and the creation of NHS trusts.

Takeovers and mergers in the private sector have been widespread. Between 1990 and 1998 nearly a third (29 per cent) of private sector workplaces were subject to change of ownership. Just under half of these changes (46 per cent) came about through a takeover or merger (much more common in services –

58 per cent – than in manufacturing – 25 per cent). Mergers and acquisitions are particularly important in the UK. Britain is the most acquisitive nation in Europe, responsible for US$386bn worth of takeovers in 1999, by comparison to second-placed Germany's total of $261bn. In 2000 the largest-ever European takeover occurred as Vodaphone Airtouch took over the German mobile company Mannesmann for £113bn. In 1995, in Germany, there had been only four contested takeovers since 1945; in Britain there has been an average of forty a year (Hutton, 1995). (Since then the German rate has increased). A further third of all changes of ownership arose as a result of the establishment being sold by the parent organisation. A fifth (18 per cent) of public sector workplaces in both 1990 and 1998 reported some change in the ownership of the establishment during this period. The proportion of private sector workplaces that were wholly or majority owned or controlled by foreign organisations more than doubled over these two decades, from 6 per cent in 1980 to 13 per cent in 1998 (most of this growth took place during the 1990s) (see Chapter 2).

☐ The restriction of union power and the reassertion of managerial prerogative

The principal aim of the Conservative governments' labour market policy between 1979 and 1997 was to bolster employers' 'right to manage' and promote greater 'flexibility' in the labour market. It was hoped that this would enhance competitiveness and encourage employment growth. To this end, there was a progressive weakening of the framework of statutory employment protection and a gradual tightening of restrictions of activities of trade unions. Union membership fell sharply, from 65 per cent of all employees in 1980 to 36 per cent in 1998 (see Table 4.3). Union presence is now most common in the public sector; just one in four private sector employees belong to a union; few young workers are union members. The proportion of workplaces with a union presence fell from nearly three-quarters in 1980 (73 per cent) to just over a half in 1998 (54 per cent), a fall of almost one-third. Collective bargaining ceased to be dominant, largely because unions have failed to organise in new workplaces (derecognition has had a marginal impact). In turn, direct communication between management and employees has become much more common. Industrial action has also diminished markedly; in 1998 it was rare indeed, with only 12 days per thousand employees being lost in the year, less than 1 per cent of the average level in the late 1970s.

More recently, the unions have witnessed a modest revival; membership is rising once more, and greater efforts are being made to organise neglected sectors. 'Partnerships' with employers seem to have had some success; the WERS survey found that 'workplaces with union recognition and a majority of high commitment practices appeared to have more stable workforces and more productive workforces.' [Cully et al., 1999].

While trade unions are a shrinking presence, nothing seems to have replaced the trade unions as a mechanism of employee 'voice'. There remains a 'representation gap' (Towers, 1997). 'Voice' mechanisms can ensure the effective representation of labour and thus diminish 'exit' and facilitate a better use of labour. Mechanisms for collective consultation are still more likely to be found in unionised workplaces. Just a third of workplaces without any union members had a consultative committee in place at the workplace or at a higher level in the organisation, compared to three-quarters of unionised workplaces. The sometimes predicted advent of employee representatives in workplaces without union members has simply not materialised. In 1990, 11 per cent had them; in 1998 the proportion was little different (12 per cent). A common claim of many organisations is that staff is their 'biggest asset'. This sentiment is not always reflected in practice. According to PIRC (Pensions Investment Research Consultants), just one in four (24 per cent) of the top 100 British companies had a board-level director with responsibility for human resources. A recent wide-ranging study by the Anglo-German Foundation [Vitols et al., 1997] compared human resource practices in Britain and Germany. It found that the supervisory boards and the work councils of the latter helped ensure 'that human resource problems are discussed at the highest levels of management when considering strategic decisions'. In Britain, 'strategic decisions were often made at the board level without adequately considering the human resource implications. A frequent role of human resource managers was thus to implement and "sell" to the workforce decisions in which they had not been directly involved'. German mechanisms of 'voice' were seen as allowing the interests of labour to be factored into decision making.

Table 4.3 Aggregate union membership density (%)	Sector	1980	1984	1990	1998
	Private	56	43	36	26
	Public	84	81	72	57

Source: Millward et al. (2000)

The Conservative governments of the 1980s and 1990s did not completely succeed in their agenda, as there were countervailing influences from Europe. The latter led to an extension in the coverage of sex discrimination legislation, the introduction of the principle of equal pay for equal value, enhanced protection and consultation during business transfers and the extension of regulations governing health and safety consultation and working time.

☐ Feminisation of the labour market

Perhaps the most far-reaching and significant labour market change has been the changing role of women. The proportion of female employees in Britain rose from 42 per cent in 1980 to 47 per cent in 1998(Cully et al. 1999). The decline of manufacturing employment, accompanied by expansion in private services industries, has been accompanied by a decline in full-time traditionally male jobs and an increase in part-time jobs mainly filled by women. Across the US and the EU the changing shape of the family, a changing domestic division of labour, shifting social attitudes and educational policies have facilitated a sharp growth in the participation of women in the labour market and a corresponding decline in the male breadwinner model. The greater role of women in the composition of the workforce has been dubbed 'the feminisation' of work. A high proportion of these women (44 per cent in 1998) work part-time (part-time work is especially common among mothers). In some areas of Britain, such as Yorkshire and Humberside, women workers already constitute more than half the workforce. More recent forecasts estimate that women will form the majority of the British workforce by 2006. Among employee relations managers, some feminisation seems to have occurred; by 1998, 39 per cent of employee relations managers were women, compared to 12 per cent in 1980.

However, the labour market is highly segmented by gender. Men and women work in different sectors of the economy (industrial segregation); so too they work in different occupations (occupational segregation) within sectors. Some jobs are so predominately male or female that there are, in effect, separate labour markets for them which produce differing outcomes on things like pay. Two good examples of industrial segmentation are education and health. In the health-care sector 82 per cent of employees are women and in education it is some 68 per cent; conversely, in construction it is 15 per cent. Women account for three-fifths of employment in the public sector and a little over two-fifths in the private sector. Within sectors there can be occupational segmentation. This is where certain groups of workers predominate in certain posts. A survey by trade union BECTU vividly illustrates this. It found that while its male members worked as producers, directors, sound and lighting engineers, and camera operators, women were concentrated in departments such as wardrobe, makeup, hair, costume, production support, and research/writing. Although women managers increased their share of all management jobs from 12–14 per cent in 1980 to 21–24 per cent in 1990, they occupy a narrow range of these jobs. Women's employment in professional and management jobs has been observed to tend to concentrate in occupational niches which are more likely to be associated with the exercise of expertise rather than power.

Occupational segmentation often manifests itself in men occupying the more senior positions. Thus, in the boardrooms of Britain's top 100 companies (as measured by the Financial Times Stock Exchange), women account for only 5 per cent of all board directors. There are only 10 female executive directors (out of 552). Many boards have no women members at all. Similarly in 1999, while 19 per cent of police constables were women, only 5 per cent were Chief and Assistant Chief Constables. Commentators often speak of a 'glass ceiling' excluding women from the most senior posts.

There are sharp variations in the success of women in the labour market. Whether women participate in the labour market and whether they work full or part-time is clearly correlated with occupational qualifications and childbirth. In 1997, 86 per cent of women with 'A' level or higher qualifications were economically active, compared with 52 per cent of those with no formal qualifications. In 1998, 55 per cent of women in the UK were active in the labour market, compared to 75 per cent of women without children.

A substantial pay-gap remains between male and female workers. For women working full-time, the gap had narrowed from 73 per cent of male earnings in 1976 to 84 per cent in 1999. This was largely due the Sex Discrimination and Equal Pay Acts. But for part-time workers the gap is far wider, although this has been narrowed by the introduction of the minimum wage. Women's employment patterns are characterised by discontinuity, related to taking breaks for child rearing, often returning to work on a part-time basis. This tends to sharply reduce women's lifetime earnings, particularly among women with fewer qualifications.

While women's participation rates in the labour market have grown, there has been a sharp decline in male participation rates in the labour market, particularly in age group 55–65. Half of the males in this age range are 'economically inactive'. (Note that this is not the same as unemployed. Most have taken early retirement or have left work due to illness or disability.)

☐ Flexibility and insecurity

In the past two decades labour 'flexibility' became a goal and guiding principle of government. Job security became a dominant concern of many in employment; 'employability' the panacea for those who lost their jobs. 'Flexibility' is one of the great buzzwords of our time, but it is also a controversial one. The very term has positive overtones; being flexible is a good thing, its converse, 'inflexibility', a negative attribute. Surveys such as WERS and bodies like the Low Pay Commission prefer the more neutral 'non-standard work' (although one could contend that this itself represents a 'male' pattern of employment, namely full-time work). Atkinson's portrayal of a 'flexible firm' is controversial but also highly influential. He identified various kinds of 'flexibility', including numerical flexibility – the employer's ability to adjust the size of the workforce in line with short-term variations in the demand for labour; functional flexibility – shifting employees between tasks; geographical flexibility, concerning the mobility of workers (homeworking and teleworking); and temporal forms (shiftworking, short-term contracts etc.). Firms were using these to accommodate fluctuating levels of demand.

Flexible forms of employment grew in the 1980s and 1990s (*see* Table 4.4). Self-employment rose rapidly; one in four workers are part-time workers; the proportion of all employees working part-time (defined as 30 hours or less per week) rose from 21 per cent in 1981 to 25 per cent in 1998. Most of the growth in part-time work took place in the 1960s and 1970s. However, the presence of part-time work varies enormously across different types of workplace; 16 per cent employ no part-timers (51 per cent of those in electricity, gas and water); in 26 per cent of workplaces part-timers form a majority (up from 16 per cent in 1990). Firms like the coffee retailer Starbucks use wholly part-time workers. Temporary jobs doubled as a proportion of employment from 4 per cent in 1984 to 8 per cent in 1998.

Table 4.4 Changes in non-standard working	1980s		1998
Self-employment	7%	[1980]	12%
Part-time*	21%	[1981]	25%
Temporary workers	4%	[1984]	8%

*Defined as 30 hrs or less per week
Source: Millward *et al*. (2000) All Change at Work

Fixed-term contracts were used in almost half of all workplaces (a third of private sector workplaces and nearly three-quarters of public sector ones). Temporary agency workers are in just over a quarter of workplaces.

Flexibility and insecurity are frequently seen as two sides of the same coin. It is sometimes argued that the greater the degree of flexibility, the higher the level of insecurity; that for many work has become more fragmented, fractured and fraught. It was argued that during the Thatcher and Major governments 'More and more risk has accrued on workforces as successive Employment Acts have reduced employee protection and as companies have come under intense and growing pressure from pension fund and insurance company shareholders to deliver the highest financial returns over the shortest period in the industrialised world' (Hutton, 1995). There is a debate about the extent and nature of insecurity. What is clear is that the perception of insecurity at work has grown. The OECD reports a threefold increase in media references to insecurity in the G7 economies between 1982 and 1996 and an increase in 'perceived employee security' in the 1990s in all OECD countries for which data is available. According to the OECD, between 1985 and 1995 British workers registered the sharpest decline of confidence in employment security in Europe. New forms of employment are altering the 'psychological contract' at work, such that the latter (Cappelli *et al.*, 1997) has come to resemble 'a spot market where employees are encouraged to focus on their immediate self-interest as employers promise to do the same'.

Heery and Salmon (2000) define insecurity on a three-fold basis: in terms of job tenure/contracts; the subjective experiences of employees; and the context in which job loss takes place. They find that insecurity has grown. As to job tenure, there is evidence of a modest decline in total job tenure over the past twenty years, with a more substantial decline for male workers. Among men, job tenure has fallen by 12 per cent in a decade. The risk of unemployment has risen for both men and women; 5.6 per cent of British employees experienced a spell of unemployment between 1973 and 1977, and 15 per cent did so in 1988–92 (more than a fifth of males experienced unemployment in this period) (Gallie *et al.*, 1998). The structure of employment has changed. There has been a modest but clear decline in the number of employees in full-time permanent employment (from 67.4 per cent in 1984 to 61.7 per cent in 1997) and an increase in the various forms of non-standard employment. According to Dex and McCulloch (1997), one-half of women and a quarter of males held non-standard jobs by 1994. Finally, the broader context of employment has changed. Changes in welfare provision have reduced financial support to the unemployed and the employment laws between 1979 and 1997 reduced the employment protection available to employees.

The management consultant Charles Handy has described some firms as being 'shamrock organisations'. Embodied in the first leaf are the organisation's culture, its knowledge and direction. The second leaf consists of non-essential work that may be farmed out to contractors. The third leaf is the flexible workforce – temporary and part-time workers who can be called upon to meet fluctuating demands for labour.

□ The work-life balance: working time and family leave

Distinguishing time for employment from other types of time is a feature of industrialisation (Thompson, 1967). The measurement of time itself has varied; in Madagascar time might be measured by 'a rice-cooking' (about half an hour) or 'the frying of a locust' (a moment). In seventeenth-century Chile time was often measured in 'credos': an earthquake was described in 1647 as lasting for the period of two credos; while the cooking time of an egg could be judged by an Ave Maria said aloud. Working time has long been a source of conflict. Across Europe, Mayday became a national holiday to commemorate campaigns to limit the working day to eight hours on 1 May 1890 (Hobsbawn, 1998).

Britain has a 'long hours working culture', particularly among male workers. In the mid-1980s, reversing a century-long trend in which the working week gradually shortened, it began to grow once more. In 1998 some 13 per cent of employees worked in excess of 48 paid hours a week, a higher proportion than any other country in the EU. A third (32 per cent) of managers and administrators did so. Concern about this trend is widespread. Graphic instances such as the Clapham Junction rail disaster in 1988 found that the senior technician responsible had been working a seven-day week for the previous 13 weeks, highlighting the issue still further. Working fathers are especially more likely than other men of a similar age to work long hours. Table 4.5 outlines the differences between British and continental European length of working week. The Working Time Regulations appear to have had little impact on the length of the working week.

Table 4.5
Working time in
Britain, France
and Germany.

	Male	Female
UK	45.2	40.7
France	40.2	38.6
Germany	40.5	39.3
EU average	41.3	39

Source: Social Trends 31 (Office for National Statistics 2001)

Furthermore, a generation of people currently in middle age will form a particularly vulnerable 'care sandwich' which requires them to look after their own children and pay taxes towards their parents' welfare, while also making provision for their old age. These care issues have become particularly problematic with the rise of dual income households. Between 1979 and 1991 the number of dual earner households rose from 53 per cent to 67 per cent and the number of traditional male breadwinner families fell from 40 per cent to 23 per cent. In 1979, only 24 per cent of women returned to work within 9 to 11 months of the birth of their child. By 1996, 67 per cent of women did so (24 per cent full-time, 42 per cent part-time). Furthermore, childcare provision in Britain is notoriously expensive and scarce. There is only one registered childcare place for every six children under the age of eight in England. Mothers generally rely on informal types of childcare, providing care themselves mostly, but also using their partner, mother or mother-in-law, especially when their children are pre-school age. Revising working time, some have argued, is an opportunity to better attune the world of work to other human needs, such as the demands of parenting.

MONEY AT WORK: Childcare is out of its infancy: COMPANY BENEFITS FOR PARENTS: Employers are extending flexible deals and help with costs, says Debbie Harrison **FT**

By DEBBIE HARRISON

The days when employees see their children only at weekends may be numbered. More employers are introducing 'family-friendly' benefits and flexible working terms in an effort to attract and retain good staff.

Money is not the only issue, although there are important tax and National Insurance breaks if the benefits are structured to meet Inland Revenue guidelines.

Equally important are lifestyle considerations. As any working parent with young children appreciates, there is no such thing as trouble-free childcare, but a considerate employer can help reduce the inevitable stress.

Peter Clews, employee relations manager at investment bank JP Morgan, says the company is busy making improvements to its family-friendly benefits. "The work/life balance is a big issue and there is a lot of competition for good staff in what McKinsey calls 'the war for talent",' says Clews.

The bank has a flexible working scheme for its 4,000 London employees, some of whom are allowed to work from home for part of the week. The average age at the bank is 31 and many staff have young children.

Under a deal introduced this year, female employees receive 18 weeks maternity leave on full pay no matter how long they have been with the company, while male employees can take 10 days' paid paternity leave (up from five) at any time.

Employees can also take up to 13 weeks of unpaid parental leave for any child – not just children born after last December, which is the statutory requirement. A confidential helpline is available for employees with family problems.

Clearly, however careful – and expensive – the childcare arrangements, things do go wrong. The most helpful employers, therefore, reserve a number of emergency places at a nursery close to work. This is one of the benefits offered by JP Morgan, which, together with ING Barings, Chase Manhattan, Lehmans and Deutsche Bank, use The Nursery Works group of nine nurseries in London.

As the companies are involved in the management of the group, the Revenue treats the arrangements in the same way as approved worksite nurseries. Emergency places tend to be free for employees while those who take a full-time place claim tax relief on the fees at their marginal rate of tax and do not pay National Insurance on the fees. This brings the standard monthly fee of about £1,000 down to to £600 for a higher-rate taxpayer.

ING Barings launched a range of family-friendly benefits in 1999 for its 1700 employees. The company is a 10-minute walk from The Nursery Works' Spitalfields Children's Centre, where it reserves two full time and 20 emergency places.

Andrew Stavrou, vice president of pensions and benefits at ING Barings, says: 'We can offer more permanent places if employees want them, but many are reluctant to bring their young children into London on a daily basis. However, they are reassured to know there is an emergency place should a last-minute problem arise.'

Emmanuel Antman, corporate finance manager with the investment bank, has used the emergency service several times when the family's nanny was off sick or on holiday. He says: 'The nursery is open from 8.30am until 6pm. All you have to do is telephone before 8am to check there is an emergency place available.'

At National Magazines the staff profile – 78 per cent are female with an average age of 32 – explains the company's commitment to family-friendly policies. NatMags, which publishes *Cosmopolitan*, *Harper's & Queen* and *Country Living*, pays a monthly childcare allowance of £210 to employees with a child under five.

It also pays a bonus of five weeks salary for employees who return from maternity leave and provides 10 days' paid paternity leave. The company offers 15 weeks' maternity leave at full pay and returning mothers are allowed to work part-time on full pay for the first two weeks.

Pharmaceutical giant Pfizer offers an emergency nanny service, a holiday play scheme and a childcare/parenting helpline run by Bupa. More than half of Pfizer's 4500 UK-based employees have young children with care needs.

'Family friendly' benefits tend to be associated with childcare, but for many employees in their 30s and 40s there is an elderly parent to worry about as well. Pfizer is unusual in that it also offers assistance to employees who are responsible for elderly relatives.

Source: Financial Times
(13 September 2000)

Figure 4.1 Money at work

> **Exercise 4.1** (a) How typical are the examples listed above of workplaces more generally?
>
> (b) Devise three arguments for and against family friendly practices.
>
> (c) Outline the distinction between 'family friendly' practices and those concerning the 'work-life' balance.

☐ Women, work and family responsibilities

The patterns of the working lives of men and women are very different. One of the most striking contrasts between men's and women's paid employment is in their patterns of economic activity by age. Whereas the proportion of men who are working or formally seeking work rises steadily with age until 45, thereafter declining slowly to 54 before dropping swiftly, the participation rates for women are depressed between the ages of 20 and 34. This difference is associated with childbearing and rearing. Many women take time out of the labour market in order to have children, and most of those who return do so, at least in the short term, on a part-time basis. Full-time working peaks (both as a proportion of women working and as a proportion of all women) in the early twenties (and even here it accounts for only about half of all women), and declines rapidly between the mid-to-late twenties and the mid-thirties. Men, by contrast, almost exclusively work full-time between the ages of 25 and 60. The availability of suitable childcare is one of the determining factors in whether a mother works full-time, part-time or not at all.

There have been growing calls for 'family friendly' working arrangements, that is, employment practices which permit employees with family responsibilities to balance these with their commitments (it is not necessarily the same as flexible working, although there may be some overlap). Underlying arguments for 'family friendly' policies is a recognition that 'standard' full-time is not easily compatible with responsible parenting, that the majority of mothers as well as fathers of dependent children are employed in paid work and that the conflicts generated by such patterns may be socially and personally dysfunctional. Taking time out of the labour market or deciding to work part-time dents earning potential. It is argued that only when fathers and mothers bear equal responsibility for parenting can men and women share equal status at work (Reeves, 2000). The impact of childbearing can vary markedly. The more a mother earns before pregnancy, and the higher the household income, the greater the likelihood that she returns to work. The career paths of high-status women who take only a short break (for example, maternity leave) and return to full-time work can cope relatively smoothly with the impact of motherhood, whereas women who return part-time and/or after a substantial gap in paid employment suffer substantial detriment.

Concern about some of these difficulties lies behind recent legislation to reconcile work and family life. Directly deriving from the EU's parental leave directive, the Employment Relations Act 1999 introduced some family leave measures (*see* Table 4.6).

Table 4.6
Family leave

Maternity leave:	Ordinary: 18 weeks (expected increase to 26 weeks)
	Additional: available after one years' service
	Statutory Maternity Pay (expected to be available for 26 weeks at £100 per week from 2003)
Parental leave:	13 weeks for parents of children under 5 years
	18 weeks for parents of child in receipt of Disabled Living Allowance
	Qualifying service of one year (can be with a previous employer)
	Leave unpaid
	Statutory Paternity Pay of 2 weeks (in addition to the 13 weeks) (expected to be at £100 per week)
Adoption leave:	Expected from 2003
	26 weeks
	Statutory Adoption Pay of 26 weeks (expected to be at £100 per week)
Adoption leave:	Expected from 2003
	26 weeks
	Statutory Adoption Pay of 26 weeks (expected to be at £100 per week)
Dependancy leave:	Reasonable time off for emergencies

(The up-to-date entitlements can be checked on the Department of Trade and Industry website: http://www.dti.gov.uk/er)

In adopting the directive the government explicitly sought a 'light touch'. It has been criticised for adopting a minimalist approach, in requiring a year's continuous service for entitlement to parental leave (whereas 13 weeks is minimum allowed under the directive), and that directive allows eight years as an upper limit, while the government went for five years.

The takeup of parental leave has been very low – just 3 per cent of those eligible have used it, mainly because it is unpaid. In contrast, the new paid paternity leave scheme is expected to have a 70 per cent takeup level. Britain was one of six countries in the EU where parental leave is unpaid. It is highly questionable whether an unpaid scheme will be taken up by the low paid or single parents or

---

Exercise 4.2   UK labour market statistics

The labour market described above is apt to change. To ensure that you and your organisation are prepared for these changes, it is important to monitor developments within the labour market. This exercise is designed to make you familiar with some of the key sources of labour market statistics. By answering some of the questions below you should become more acquainted with the variety of statistics available and some of the problems associated with them.

(a) Unemployment in Great Britain (seasonally adjusted)
(b) Unemployment in your region (seasonally adjusted)
(c) Male employees in employment in the UK (seasonally adjusted)
(d) Female employees in employment in the UK (seasonally adjusted)
(e) The number of working days lost per thousand employees
(f) Monthly growth of average earnings

fathers. According to the House of Commons Social Services Select Committee, without an element of payment there is low take-up. Comparisons made with continental countries have shown that while male (and female) take-up does rise if parental leave is paid, there remains a significant gap between the two sexes. For example, in Sweden, which has a relatively generous paid scheme, the take-up rate among women is almost 100 per cent; for men it is 50 per cent.

☐ Summary and conclusion

This chapter began with a review of recent trends within the UK labour market. Among the trends noted in this section were the changing patterns of ownership and sectoral shifts within the economy, the declining presence of trade unions and the continuing increase in the number of women at work, as well as the emergence of 'flexible' forms of employment.

These developments have important implications for organisations and their employees. The UK labour market has moved from one characterised by employers competing to attract male employees who will work full-time for one or two employers for most of their adult years. A more diverse pattern of employment has emerged, in which men and women compete for a variety of types of employment and one that is often more insecure. Some 'flexible' work patterns are no more than a palatable way of describing poorly paid and insecure jobs. As we have seen, the employment prospects for women at senior levels of organisations are often, in practice, very limited. The same can be said for ethnic minority and disabled workers.

In the wake of our 'long hours' culture, pressures for a greater 'work–life' balance have been growing. Similarly, the absence of adequate 'voice mechanisms' within the workplace is arguably assisting the growth of some of the emerging 'partnership' deals and the modest revival of trade unions.

☐ Useful websites

A leading family friendly pressure group
www.parentsatwork.org.uk

The EOC web site. Useful for factual information
www.eoc.org.uk

The government's Women's Unit website which produces (free) briefings on many issues.
www.womens-unit.gov.uk

The House of Commons library produces excellent briefing papers on many issues, including employment.
www.parliament.uk/commons/lib/research

The Industrial Society is a leading think tank on workplace issues.
www.indsoc.co.uk

The main employers' representative organisation
www.cbi.org.uk

The main trade union representative organisation
www.tuc.org.uk

05 Economics and the UK economy

Chapter

☐ Introduction

The citizens of all developed countries are faced with difficult choices about how to organise their activities. An important area within which these decisions are made concerns the planning of work and the creation of wealth. Over the past three hundred years, economics has developed as a field of study devoted to analysing these decisions and their consequences. Derived originally from the Greek word for 'housekeeping', the term 'economics' is generally used today to refer to the study of firms, industries, regions, nations and international trading relationships.

When applied to the UK in the post-war period, this form of analysis has typically sought to explain the reasons for the country's relative economic decline, and to outline ways in which policy could be improved to prevent a continuation of this decay. The main focus of this debate has been upon the steps which national governments can take to maintain and enhance the economic well-being of people and companies in this country. As this chapter aims to demonstrate, governments of different political persuasions have adopted different priorities and policy instruments in their pursuit of this objective of increased economic growth.

☐ Focus and scope

This chapter aims to explain some key economic concepts and to describe the current operation of the UK economy. Throughout this analysis the principal focus is the national economy although, as noted in earlier chapters, the increasing globalisation of business means that considerable attention is also devoted to key features of the emerging international economy.

Learning objectives

Once you have read through this chapter and completed the associated exercises, you should be able to:

☐ comment on the three principal questions in economics;

☐ outline the principal features of market and command economies;

- [ ] describe six key economic indicators currently used to measure the performance of the UK economy; and
- [ ] comment critically on the economic goals pursued by the UK government in recent years.

☐ First principles in economics

Despite tremendous growth in the economic wealth of developed countries over the past three hundred years, there is little evidence that the wants of individuals within these societies have been satisfied. In the last century, cars, telephones and colour televisions have been added to the list of goods and services that many people feel they need.

By contrast, more than half the world's population live in countries where people continue to die each year from starvation and a lack of basic health care. Despite calls from some socialist and environmental campaigners for individuals in rich countries to reduce their demands, it seems likely that the wants of people will continue to exceed the world's scarce resources for the foreseeable future. These contradictory pressures give rise to the fundamental problem at the heart of economics – how to reconcile unlimited demand by consumers with the world's limited supply of resources.

The limited supply of resources forces those who make decisions to answer the following three important economic questions:

- [ ] What goods and services should be produced?
- [ ] How will these goods or services be produced?
- [ ] How can these products be distributed?

In tackling these questions the people involved are deciding how resources will be used and how they will not be used. Allocating resources to meet one set of consumer wants will inevitably mean that another set of demands are not satisfied. For example, an individual deciding how to spend his or her wages may have to choose between having a holiday or buying a new car. Similarly, an employer may have to choose between giving employees a pay rise or investing in new equipment. Economists refer to this type of choice as the *opportunity cost* – the cost of the options given up in order to pursue the preferred course of action. For example, the opportunity cost of a government decision to cut taxation on petrol may be a cutback in, or delay in the improvement of, public transport.

When analysing how the basic problems of economics are tackled, it is possible to discern two basic approaches: market and command economies. In practice there are few countries in which either of these systems operate in its pure form; most developed economies have struck some balance between the two and operate what is called a mixed economy.

Market economies

The market system works on the basis of people deciding for themselves what, when, how and where they are going to produce and consume goods and services. Under such a system, what will be produced, how it will be produced and the method of distribution are determined by individuals and companies. These different groups within the economy choose what to do by comparing the price of different options and considering which course of action will lead to the biggest improvement in their level of satisfaction.

Many economists use demand and supply analyses to examine the operation of this market system. This approach begins by recognising that consumers will place different values on different goods and services. These differences will be reflected in the prices that they are prepared to pay.

Demand

Some people will value a particular good or service so much that they will be prepared to pay considerably more than others to ensure that they satisfy their demands. Similarly, with other categories of goods some people will be prepared to buy more of the goods as the price of this product falls. For example, if we look at the demand for apples in the UK over a one-week period, we might find that when the price is £1 per kilo the overall demand is 200 tonnes. When the price falls to 20p per kilo, the overall demand increases to 1000 tonnes. This relationship between the price and demand for apples is mapped out in the form of a demand function in Fig 5.1.

In addition to the price, the demand for apples, as set out in Fig 5.1, will also respond to movements in the price of other goods, changes in consumer preferences (fashion) and shifts in the size and distribution of household income. Change in any one of these variables can alter the shape of the demand function. Figure 5.2 illustrates how the demand function responds when the demand for apples reduces.

As Fig 5.2 demonstrates, at any given price the quantity demanded by consumers has decreased. This relationship is represented by the shift in the demand function from D1 to D2. Thus at a constant price of 0P1, the quantity of apples demanded by consumers has fallen back from 0Q1 to 0Q2.

Apart from uniform shifts in the demand curve, as denoted by the movement from D1 to D2 in Fig 5.2, the slope of the demand function may also change. The gradient of the demand function is referred to by economists as the *price elasticity of demand*. If the demand function becomes steeper, as illustrated by the movement from D1 to D3 in Fig 5.3, the demand for the goods being sold will become less price sensitive. In these situations people will continue to buy similar quantities of the good despite large increases or decreases in its price. This phenomenon is referred to by economists as *inelastic demand*.

Figure 5.1
The demand
function

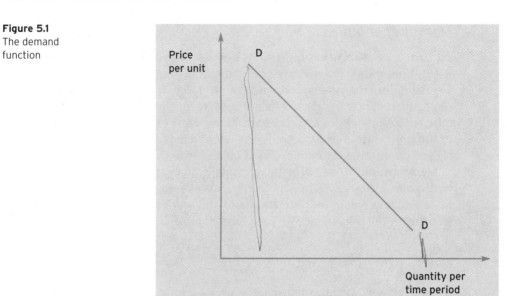

Figure 5.2
Shift in the
demand function
due to a change in
consumer
preferences

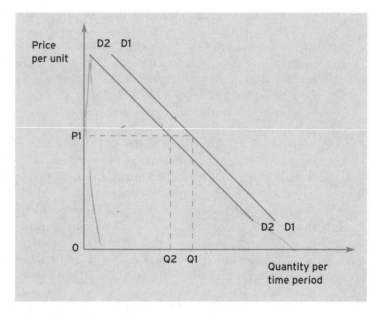

If we reverse these changes and the slope of the demand function becomes less severe, as illustrated by the movement from D1 to D4 in Fig 5.3, the quantity of goods demanded will become much more sensitive to price changes. Thus, if the price increases marginally, the quantity of goods demanded may decrease markedly. Economists refer to this form of relationship as *elastic demand*.

Figure 5.3
The elasticity of
demand

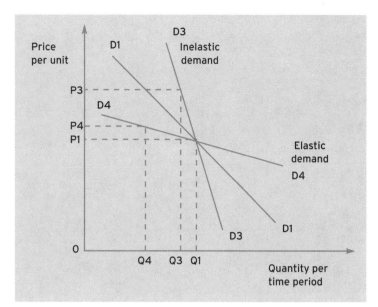

Supply

The supply of goods and services in any market also responds to fluctuations in the price. Other things being equal, when the price of a particular good or service increases in relation to the costs of production, more resources will be devoted to supplying this product. Among the other important variables affecting the supply of a particular product are the prices and profits available from producing other products, the cost of raw materials, the objectives pursued by company managers and, finally, the state of the technology available. If we return to the previous example, the general relationship between the price and supply of apples over one week in the UK is demonstrated by the supply function in Fig 5.4.

Like the demand function, the gradient of the supply function may change, giving rise to *elastic* or *inelastic supply*. For example, the supply of many precious metals and stones is relatively inelastic because there are limited amounts of these materials and it is not possible to increase the supply markedly, even if the price rises substantially. By contrast, the quantity of magazines and newspapers supplied may be more sensitive to changes in the price of these products. Thus, other things being equal, an increase in the price consumers are prepared to pay may lead to a substantial increase in the quantity supplied.

The interaction of demand and supply

If we now bring together the two sides of the equation and examine the interaction of supply and demand, we find that where the two lines intersect supply equals demand, which is backed by a willingness to purchase at that price. Economists refer to the intersection of the demand and supply functions as the

Figure 5.4
The supply
function

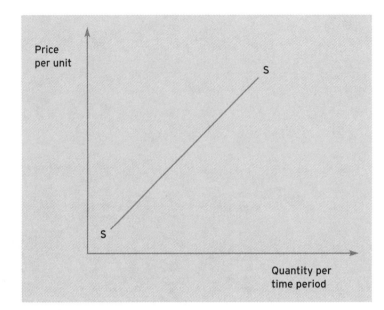

equilibrium position. At this point the market should clear. In other words everything that is supplied will be purchased. In Fig 5.5, at the equilibrium position the quantity of apples actually supplied is 0Q1 at the price 0P1. The total revenue available to suppliers from all these sales can be calculated using the following formula: 0P1 × 0Q1.

Thus according to free market economists, prices respond, more or less, to the forces of demand and supply. The end result tends to be the equilibrium of demand and supply and therefore the coordination of the economic activities of countless individual consumers and companies. In the words of Adam Smith, 'the invisible hand of the market' guides the best utilisation, production and distribution of goods and services.

However, the market system is not without its failings and critics. Among the most commonly cited problems are the following.

Market domination

The free interaction of demand and supply may be subject to distortions caused by the collusion of a few producers or consumers. In these situations prices may be kept artificially high, or the quantity of goods supplied may be restricted, in order to ensure that a few firms or individuals make very substantial profits or gains.

Inequality

This may arise because goods and services are distributed according to ability to pay, rather than the need of the consumer. This will mean that poorer members of a society may not receive the goods and services they need. In the short term, this may appear economic, but in the longer term the costs of dealing with the crime and disease which result from poor housing, education and health will be considerable.

Figure 5.5
The interaction of
demand and
supply

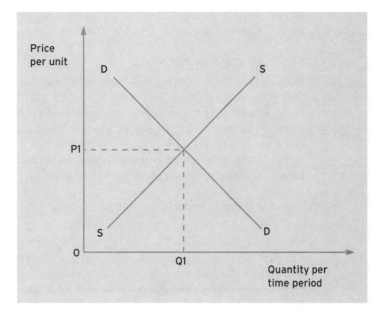

Economic dislocation

Rapid changes within a particular market may have very detrimental effects upon the employees or immediate neighbours of a particular business. For example, a fall in the international price of coal has led to the closure of a number of collieries. These closures have meant that not only have many miners lost their jobs, but also that other local shops and companies have experienced significant losses of business.

Externalities

The market system provides an ineffective means of controlling and reducing the environmental and social costs associated with modern business activity. For example, individuals and companies who pollute the atmosphere may be able to avoid the costs of this activity. In these situations the final costs of dealing with the consequences of this pollution may have to be met by people who live many miles away.

Public goods

There are many goods and services which are best provided collectively, either because the costs would be prohibitive if they had to be borne by small groups or individuals, or, alternatively, because it would not be possible to enjoy fully the benefits of these products unless everyone else had access. Examples of public goods include the fire, health and sanitation services. In a market system it may be tempting for an individual to avoid paying for these public goods because they rarely, if ever, need them, or alternatively, because they feel that the services provided by other people's contributions are sufficient to ensure that they are covered. However, this so-called *free-rider* approach only works if the number of people who avoid paying for the service is relatively small. When the number of free-riders increases there is a danger that the limited cover provided by a few people will be insufficient to cover the needs of those who have opted out.

The failure of the price mechanism

Market systems do not work perfectly because there are limits to the availability of information about the prices of particular goods and services. Furthermore, even when price information is available, people rarely, if ever, have the time, capacity or ability to react and alter their behaviour as a consequence (Omerod, 1994). For example, when people choose a job, they rarely conduct their own comprehensive survey of the relative wages on offer before deciding upon which employer to work for.

Price is not the only indicator of worth

Traditional economic analysis suggests that consumers and producers are motivated primarily by the cost or price of a product. Thus workers will seek the highest wage, consumers will hunt for the lowest prices, and producers will pursue the lowest costs. However, reducing all human behaviour to this form of economic calculus has its dangers. As a number of social commentators have pointed out, this form of analysis ignores wider social and ethical motivations in human behaviour (Etzioni, 1988). For example, wages are affected by feelings of fairness, established internal pay scales, the cost of living, general wage increases, and a number of other factors which are not related to the state of the employer's capital, labour or product markets. As a consequence, employers will rarely lower or increase the pay of their employees purely in response to changes in the general price of labour, costs of their raw materials, or the price of their finished goods and services.

The myth of the free market

The operation of market economies relies on a system of law and social customs which defines ownership rights, regulates the exchange of property, and controls the exchange of labour for wages. In the absence of these legal and social regulations there would be considerable incentives for people to steal, renege on commercial agreements, or engage in fraud. Thus the view that markets are part of the natural order and that they would emerge in their present form without any regulation is misplaced. Instead it is more appropriate to see markets as relying on centralised controls or cultural norms which ensure that everyone knows and abides by the rules of the game. The presence of these laws, regulations and customs in turn create its own anomalies which prevent markets from behaving in the manner suggested by traditional economic analyses.

Exercise 5.1   Market economies

Draw a diagram to map out the effects of the following changes to the demand for and supply of apples:

(a) A change in fashion which leads to an increased desire for apples.
(b) An improvement in technology which makes it cheaper to grow and supply apples.

Command economies

Command economies are managed by a central authority which determines what, when, how and where goods and services should be produced and consumed. This central authority decides what resources to use, what to produce and how to distribute on the basis of cost, anticipated demand and wider economic, social and political objectives. For much of the twentieth century, countries within the Communist Bloc operated as command economies.

The advent of *glasnost*, *perestroika* and the gradual break-up of the USSR and its satellite states in Eastern Europe have generally been viewed as signalling an end to the centrally planned system. The old warnings of Nikita Khrushchev, leader of the USSR in the early 1960s, that Communism would bury Capitalism, appear to have been turned on their head. Today, no country in the world operates a pure command economy. Indeed, in recent years all of the former communist states have adopted some form of market-based approach modelled on established practice in western economies. This movement away from command economy structures was based upon a recognition of the following problems associated with centrally planned systems.

□ *Difficulties in forecasting future demands*. The problems associated with producing accurate centralised forecasts of consumer demand led to the over-provision of some goods and chronic shortages of others. The gaps in supply were then frequently filled by the growth of black market activity.

□ *Lack of focus on the customer*. Increasing wealth leads to a wider variety of tastes and a more discerning approach by consumers. It is therefore difficult for central planners to anticipate and accommodate these changes in fashion.

□ *Lack of incentives for producers*. The central determination of the level of supply and the prices that will be charged means that local managers and employees have few economic incentives to operate more effectively and efficiently. As a consequence, the quantity and quality of products may be lower than expected.

□ *Low investment*. The desire to minimise costs leads to a lack of investment in improving technology.

□ *Bureaucracy*. The need to produce complex central plans may increase bureaucracy as a large number of staff are employed to draw up and issue these documents. Furthermore, if these planners are not democratically accountable the plans will not only ignore the demands of consumers, but may also fail to take account of the environmental and social concerns of the wider population.

Mixed economies

Mixed economies combine elements of the market-based and centrally planned systems outlined above. Thus some areas of economic activity are centrally planned, e.g. the armed services and police force, while others are left to centrally or locally regulated markets, e.g. groceries and telecommunication services.

The relative balance between these two forms of provision usually reflects political decisions about the best means to provide certain goods and services. As we have seen in earlier sections, markets tend to respond more quickly to changes in consumer demands because they provide strong incentives to producers to alter their output as tastes change. However, democratically accountable centrally planned systems tend to provide a more effective means of taking social and environmental costs into account when deciding what to produce, how it is to be made and what is the most effective means of distributing it.

In the UK, despite concerted efforts by recent Conservative administrations to introduce the discipline of the market into an increasingly wider sphere of economic activity, the State oversees the planned provision of goods and services in a number of areas. Thus the UK can still be characterised as a mixed economy. The areas of economic activity within the UK which are still planned or heavily regulated by the State include:

☐ *Provision of essential services.* The government provides health, education, sanitation, policing and national defence for everyone, regardless of their ability to pay. These services benefit all members of society and there is a general political consensus that a market system would not produce the same level of provision.

☐ *Transfer payments.* Various forms of taxation and government borrowing are used to redirect resources within the economy to more desired ends, e.g. pensions and social security payments.

☐ *Regulation of monopolies and cartels.* Whether privately or publicly owned, the government monitors, regulates and places limits on the activities of monopolies in the UK, e.g. the Office of Gas and Electricity Markets (Ofgem), the Office of Telecommunications (Oftel), Competition Commission and the Office of Fair Trading.

☐ *Social costs and benefits.* The government intervenes in the market to protect consumers from certain goods and services which are deemed to produce high social costs, e.g. drugs and alcohol. In addition, a growing awareness of the damage done to the environment by the activities of industry has led to government proposals to control pollution by taxing or prosecuting polluters.

☐ *Support for industry and commerce.* Regional, industry and organisation-level grants may be made by governments to support economic or social goals, e.g. assisted areas and small business grants.

☐ *Management of economic activity.* Governments intervene in the economy to encourage balanced economic growth, control the level of inflation and to promote acceptable uses of the nation's scarce resources. This area of government activity is commonly referred to as macroeconomic policy. The following section examines government activity in this area in more detail.

☐ The goals of macroeconomic policy

Governments normally pursue a number of economic objectives simultaneously, although the importance of each and the trade-offs between them vary, reflecting the political orientation of the people in power and the external pressures facing these policy makers. Furthermore, most countries are subject to international economic pressures as a consequence of trade with other nations and the movement of capital across borders. The list below sets out some of the more commonly sought objectives of macroeconomic policy.

- ☐ *Economic growth*. As measured by national income and other indices, consistent economic growth usually leads to increases in the living standards of the general population.
- ☐ *High employment*. Persistent unemployment represents wasted resources and may be politically damaging to the political party in power.
- ☐ *Low inflation*. High levels of inflation create uncertainty and may erode standards of living and the value of investments and savings.
- ☐ *A sound balance of payments coupled with a strong and stable currency value in foreign exchange markets*. The balance of payments refers to the flows of money in and out of a national economy. Governments normally strive to avoid a deficit balance.

In addition to the above list, at different times in post-war UK history, governments have pursued their own subsidiary goals. Among the more noteworthy have been attempts to influence the distribution of wealth and income and increase or decrease the level of state ownership of industry and commerce.

In order to measure progress towards their preferred economic goals, governments use a range of economic indicators. The definition and calculation of six of these measures – economic growth, inflation, money supply, balance of payments, exchange rates and employment – and the operation of associated policy instruments form the focus of the remainder of this section.

Economic growth

Economic growth is the term used to describe expansion of the productive capacity of an economy. In general it is assumed by most economic commentators that economic growth will lead to a general improvement in people's living standards, if the population of a country remains relatively stable. As a consequence, in the post-war period, governments of all political persuasions have sought to promote economic growth within the UK. In determining specific objectives for this economic growth these administrations have relied upon one or more of the following three measures of economic growth.

- ☐ *Gross domestic product (GDP)* measures what is produced in the domestic economy.
- ☐ *Gross national product (GNP)* adds to GDP property income from abroad.

☐ *National income* deducts capital consumption, including the sale of investments in housing and shares, from GNP.

Despite their apparent simplicity and common usage, there are three important problems associated with the use of these measures as an indication of the economic performance of a country.

1 *There are difficulties associated with the measurement of these indices.* Gross domestic product and the other two measures of economic growth can be measured in three ways: either by counting output, expenditure or income. In theory all three measures should produce the same result, but in practice they rarely do. For example, between 1980 and 1999 differences between the highest and lowest of the three measures of annual growth in GDP averaged 0.5 per cent. This may appear to be a small figure, but when we consider it in the context of the average annual rate of GDP growth in the UK over the last 50 years the effects are more marked. The addition or subtraction of 0.6 per cent to or from the 2.2 per cent average annual rate of GDP growth produces significantly different perceptions of the performance of the British economy in recent years.

2 *Some important areas of productive human activity are excluded.* For example, the official measures take no account of housework, do-it-yourself, voluntary work or any other form of work which is not sold for money. Similarly, in the UK, but interestingly not in Italy, these figures ignore the contribution of the 'black economy' and other unlawful or illegal activity. If measures of the contribution made by these forms of activity were included in the country's national accounts it is possible that different conclusions could be reached about the performance of UK PLC in recent years.

3 *The primacy attached to these measures by government ministers and other policy makers can have negative consequences.* According to a number of critics, this focus upon economic growth has detracted attention from other important gauges of the social well-being of the population. Although measures exist to monitor people's health, education, housing, general satisfaction and the state of the natural environment, these have not generally been given the same priority as economic growth. As a consequence, a number of economists have suggested alternative measures of economic and social progress. For example, the United Nation's Human Development Index, which ranks countries by a measure combining life expectancy, educational attainment and basic purchasing power, placed the UK in 14th position in a list of 162 countries compiled in 1995. The top three positions in this league table were held by Canada, the USA and Japan (United Nations, 2001).

Despite these problems with measures of the UK's economic performance, GDP, GNP and National Income remain the principal yardsticks for estimates of improvements in the UK economy. By these measures in the post-war period UK economic growth has been very variable. As Fig 5.6 indicates, the level of economic growth within the UK has been subject to periodic booms and cyclical recessions. During the nineteenth century this economic or business cycle

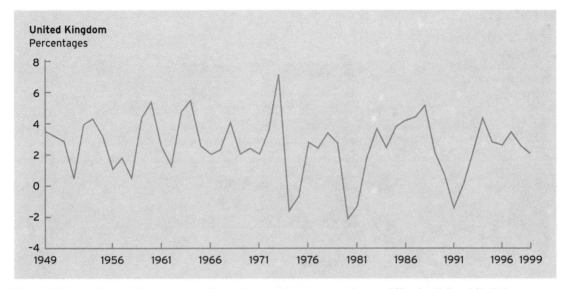

Figure 5.6 Annual growth in gross domestic product at constant prices. *Source:* Office for National Statistics

appeared to occur every seven to ten years. After the First World War this pattern ceased and for nearly twenty years the UK and much of the western world experienced a sustained depression in economic activity. This economic collapse was reversed in the USA and much of Europe during the 1930s by massive programmes of public spending and rearmament. The recovery resumed after the Second World War and continued until the early 1970s. Although the UK experienced declines in economic growth over this period they never lasted more than one year, and rarely involved more than a 1 per cent decline in GDP. In most of these downturns GDP merely grew at a slower rate, rather than declining in real terms. This pattern changed again in the early 1970s and for the last 20 or more years the UK has once again experienced alternating periods of economic growth and recession on a seven- to ten-year cycle.

Apart from wrestling with the problems of managing cyclical variations in the economic growth rate, post-war governments of the UK have also been concerned with the overall level of growth. Although the economy has grown, the rate of this growth has until very recently been lower than that of many competitor nations. As Fig 5.7 indicates, this relative decline continued during the 1980s and 1990s. According to recent figures compiled by the Organisation of Economic Cooperation and Development (OECD) – a grouping of 24 of the world's largest industrial nations – although the UK remains the world's sixth largest economy, it lies in 22nd position in terms of GDP per head of population.

In order to cope with the twin problems of variable and low rates of economic growth, government ministers and policy makers in the UK have looked to economists for proposals to improve the situation. Economists' views of how to increase a nation's economic growth may be divided roughly into two schools of thought: *Keynesian* and *Monetarist*. The ideas of the first group evolved from the work of John Maynard Keynes and had a profound effect upon the economic policies of governments of all political persuasions between 1945 and 1976. Put simply, Keynesian economists believe that the level of

Figure 5.7
Gross domestic product in OECD nations
Source: (OECD, 2001) http://www.oecd.org/std/nahome.htm

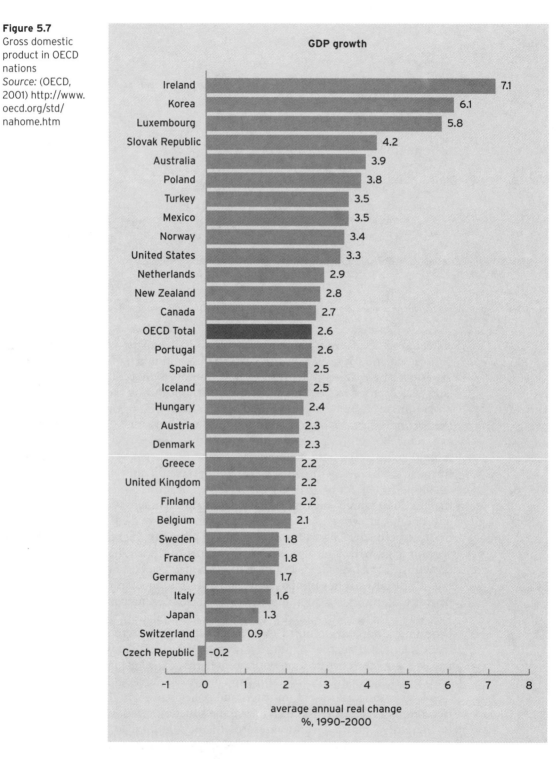

economic growth within an economy is determined by the overall level of consumer demand for goods and services. Today, Keynesian economists still believe that when an economy has spare productive capacity (people and capital), investment and output can be stimulated to create more jobs without increasing inflation by changing levels of government expenditure. They argue that this can be achieved by altering taxation or government borrowing in order to finance public projects which will inject money into the economy and therefore fuel demand.

The apparent failure of Keynesian policies in the mid-1970s, when both inflation and unemployment remained persistently high (circumstances referred to as *stagflation*), led policy makers to focus their attention on an alternative Monetarist approach. Monetarist policies owe much to the work of Milton Friedman in the USA. He conducted a number of studies examining the relationship between the supply of money in an economy and the overall level of inflation and economic growth. He argued that increasing government expenditure inevitably led to increases in the money supply and an increase in inflation in the longer term, with any stimulus to real growth being only short term. As a consequence of this line of thought, Monetarists have argued that you cannot buck the market. The proper job of government is twofold: first, to limit the growth in the money supply to changes in the level of productive capacity in the economy; and second, to ensure that there are few barriers to the effective operation of markets within the economy. The second of these objectives can be achieved by reducing taxation, benefits and regulations on the free movement of labour and the competitive behaviour of organisations. In addition, the operation of the market may be improved by regulating the behaviour of large companies, trade unions and professional associations to ensure that they do not engage in restrictive practices. By adopting this approach, inflation may be limited and appropriate conditions for the growth of private enterprise can be created.

Although the Monetarist approach was initially successful in reducing inflation in the late 1970s, in 1979 international and national economic pressures coupled with the tight monetary stance of the UK's new Conservative administration led directly to a deep recession between 1980 and 1982. Having recovered from this recession, the UK enjoyed a period of rapid growth during the mid-1980s.

In 1987, the UK economy began to experience new problems. The combination of an international stock market crisis, the relaxation of controls on individual credit, and inadequate or inaccurate measures of the economy's performance conspired to produce an unsustainable consumer spending boom. In the fallout from the so-called Lawson boom, the government once again pursued a policy of attempting to control inflation through the combination of interest rates and maintaining a specified exchange rate against the Deutschmark. By 1990, however, separate wrangles about the role of the UK within the European Community led directly to the resignation of Margaret Thatcher and a fundamental switch in government economic policy. When the UK joined the exchange rate mechanism (ERM) in October 1990, the primary policy goal became the maintenance of a stable exchange rate. Unfortunately, the decision to enter the ERM coincided with the onset of recession in the UK and elsewhere in the western world. This recession was prompted, at least in part, by austerity measures introduced in Germany to ease the process of reunification with the East, and concerns about government debt in the USA. The ensuing recession became the longest, although not the deepest, in UK post-war history and together with uncertainty about

Britain's commitment to the European Community led to speculation about the government's ability and commitment to sustain the chosen Sterling/ Deutschmark exchange rate. In early September 1992 increased speculation on the international money markets led to the UK's withdrawal from the ERM. With the abandonment of this policy the Conservative government at that time reaffirmed its commitment to moderate and sustainable economic growth within strict inflation targets.

Economics and the UK economy

After sterling's exit from the ERM, the then Conservative Government introduced for the first time an explicit target for inflation instead of targeting growth in the money supply or the exchange rate as a means of controlling inflation. Interest rates were set to ensure demand in the economy was kept at a level consistent with a certain level of inflation. The first inflation target was set by the Chancellor of the Exchequer to be an annual inflation rate of 1–4 per cent with an objective to be in the lower half of that range by the end of the 1992–97 parliament. The inflation target was subsequently revised to be 2.5 per cent or less.

In the period between 1992 and 1997, interest rate decisions were taken by the Chancellor of the Exchequer. However, the Bank of England was asked to publish its own economic appraisals in a quarterly Inflation Report, and was given the task of deciding the timing of interest rate changes. Each month the then Chancellor – Kenneth Clarke – met the Governor of the Bank of England to discuss the level of interest rates. Although the Governor could offer the Bank's advice about the level of interest rates necessary to meet the Government's inflation target, the decision remained the Chancellor's. These arrangements continued until May 1997 when an incoming Labour government announced that it was setting an inflation target of 2.5 per cent.

As well as modifying the inflation target, the new Government gave the Bank of England independence to set interest rates. This meant that interest rates would no longer be set by politicians. The Bank would act independently of Government, although the inflation target would be set by the Chancellor. The Bank would be accountable to parliament and the wider public. The objective given to the Bank of England was initially explained in a letter from the Chancellor. This objective was then formalised in 1998 with the passing of the Bank of England Act. This Act codified the requirement for the Bank 'to maintain price stability, and to support the economic policy of HM Government including its objectives for growth and employment'.

Inflation

In general there is agreement between economists about how inflation manifests itself. In essence, it is seen as an increase in the price of any factor of production or output, e.g. price or wage inflation. Thus an annual rate of inflation of 10 per cent will increase the price of a £300 fridge by £30 to £330 over a twelve-month period. However, this general agreement between economists masks some important areas of disagreement: how to measure inflation; what is an acceptable level of inflation; what causes increases in prices and wages; and how to control inflation.

Measures of inflation

In the UK economy a range of indices are used to measure inflation; these include the Retail Prices Index (RPI) the Tax and Prices Index (TPI), the Consumers' Expenditure Deflator and the Producer Output Prices Index.

The *RPI* is sometimes referred to as the headline rate of inflation as it is most commonly quoted in the media. As an index it measures the total cost of a notional basket of goods and services of the sort bought by the great majority of UK households (excluding pensioners dependent on state benefits and the wealthiest 4 per cent of the population). It is constructed by collecting the prices of around 600 items on a specified day every month (including mortgage interest payments and council tax). These are then weighted according to their importance within household budgets. To avoid seasonality in the figures (e.g. the effect of changes in the price of fruit and vegetables, etc.), the increase in retail prices is expressed as a percentage change since the same month a year earlier (*see* Fig 5.8).

Although the RPI is the measure of inflation most commonly referred to, there are a number of problems with this index which may be overcome by alternative measures.

First, the RPI takes no account of changes in direct taxation. This means that reductions in personal tax allowances and increases in income tax rates or the level of national insurance contributions are not reflected in changes in the RPI's measure of inflation. This failing is overcome by the *Tax and Prices Index* which takes account of these changes and is therefore often favoured by trade union negotiators who are anxious to protect their members' real standards of living in annual wage negotiations.

Second, the RPI is based upon the contents of a notional basket of goods and services which is updated infrequently and may therefore not be representative of an average family's purchases. More worryingly, this measure tends to exaggerate the effects of inflation during periods of rapid price increases, because it fails to take account of the fact that consumers alter their buying behaviour by purchasing fewer of the most inflationary goods and services.

These problems are overcome by the *Consumer Expenditure Deflator (CED)* which provides a measure of real purchasing activity within the economy. In addition, this measure has the added benefit of including an estimate of housing costs which is based on notional rental values of owner-occupied housing rather than mortgage interest payments. This is beneficial because a reliance on interest payments may mean that the inflation rate as measured by the RPI will increase at a time when governments are using interest-rate changes as a means of reducing inflation. In these circumstances the cure (higher interest rates) may appear to make the symptoms (the level of price inflation) worse.

Third, the RPI only deals with consumer prices and therefore does not deal with inflation as it affects the price of wholesale goods. As these price rises may feed through into the rest of the economy at a later date, the RPI is best treated as an historic measure rather than as an indication of what might happen in the future. For these reasons many management negotiators may prefer to focus their attention on the Producer Output Prices Index as this may give an indication of future trends in inflation.

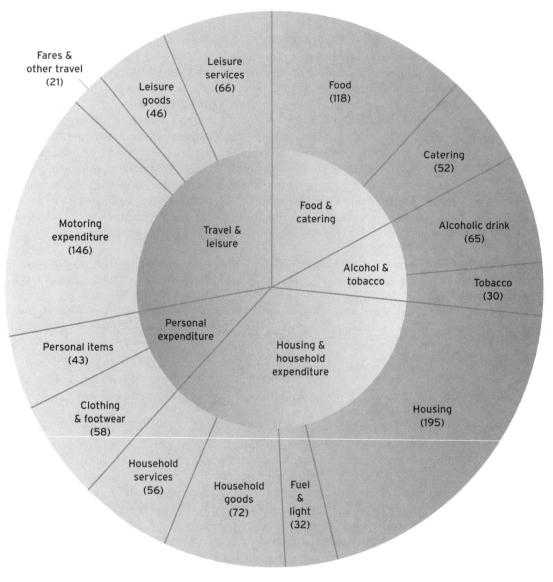

(The figures in brackets represent the 'weights' out of a total of 1000 and are revised annually by the Office for National Statistics)

Figure 5.8 The components of the Retail Prices Index (RPI). *Source*: http://www.statistics.gov.uk/themes/economy/articles/brief guides

As the preceding discussion has illustrated, there are a variety of ways in which inflation can be measured. It is not surprising, therefore, that these different measures produce different indications of the level of inflation in the economy. Obviously, the combination of estimates of future economic growth and inflation will have an immediate effect upon decisions within many organisations. In the short term we might expect these measures to affect decisions about the price of products and the level of salaries and wages. In the longer term, it is perhaps more important to consider what, in an economy like the UK's, an acceptable level of inflation is.

What is an acceptable level of inflation?

Inflation is not a new phenomenon in the UK. In 1990, the Retail Prices Index was 45 times higher than its level in 1900. However, this significant increase in the level of consumer prices conceals variations in the rates of increase at different points in time. During the first 90 years of the twentieth century the level of inflation fell in 13 years, most notably during periods of recession or depression – 1920–23 and 1925–33. Meanwhile, during the periods of moderate and sustained economic growth in the 1950s and 1960s inflation stood at averages of 3 and 4 per cent respectively. It was not until the mid-1970s that inflation became really serious, with a record rate of 25 per cent in 1975 and an average rate for the decade of 13 per cent. During the 1980s the inflation rate fell from 19 per cent to 3 per cent in 1986 before rising again to 9 per cent in 1990. Over the last ten years stability has returned, with average annual inflation rates rarely exceeding 3 per cent but still high by international comparisons.

These fluctuations in the rate of inflation have led a number of economists to suggest that the UK economy is inherently inflationary – a tendency which appears most marked when compared with the consistently lower levels of inflation experienced by some of our main economic competitors. According to this view, periods of economic boom have brought price rises in their aftermath which eventually wipe away the benefits of the earlier growth. By this standard, inflation should be avoided at all costs because it erodes the benefits of earlier improvements in the economy as well as making it difficult for employers and employees to predict how their production or living costs will alter in the near future. By contrast, a number of other economists suggest that moderate levels of inflation may be acceptable or even beneficial. They argue that if the level of inflation is predictable, producers and consumers can adjust their behaviour to take account of possible future price rises. Furthermore, the presence of low levels of inflation is preferable to periods of sustained price falls, because rising prices can increase consumer confidence. The recent decline of the UK housing market is used as one example of how falling prices can undermine this confidence and thereby restrict or delay a more general expansion of the economy.

This disagreement between economists about what is an acceptable level of inflation reflects deeper-seated differences in their analyses of the causes of inflation. Here, once again, there are a variety of different views; however, the most fundamental differences exist between Keynesian and Monetarist economists.

Causes of inflation

For many Keynesian economists the fundamental cause of inflation is excess demand (*demand pull*) or cost increases (*cost push*); therefore, the most efficient means of reducing inflation is through one or more of the following mechanisms: limiting demand via taxation, quotas and rationing, or constraints on cost increases through prices and incomes policies. In periods of relatively high economic growth and rising inflation, excessive consumer spending is reined in by increases in indirect purchase taxes and direct income taxes. Similarly, mortgages and other forms of credit which might create inflation are controlled through strict limits on the availability of this form of finance. Meanwhile, incomes policies are used to limit the level of pay rises in the economy by setting national guidelines or going rates. Finally, price controls discourage companies from passing on to the consumer the effects of increases in the price of their raw materials and labour.

By contrast, Monetarist economists argue that inflation arises from the presence of too much money in an economy. If the presence of paper money exceeds the real value of goods and services in any economy then the price of goods, in terms of paper money, will increase giving rise to inflation. Thus Monetarists argue that governments can reduce inflation by restricting the money supply through the use of interest rates (increasing the cost of money), prudent fiscal policies and tight controls on public spending.

Money supply

Any attempt to restrict the supply of money requires an accurate measure of the money supply so that the success of policy can be determined. In a modern economy like the UK, however, a universal definition of money is not available, as money exists in several different forms, e.g. cash (notes and coins), bank deposits and credit arrangements. In order to cope with this diversity of forms the government has developed a series of ways of measuring the money supply. These different measures are known as the *monetary aggregates* (*see* Table 5.1).

Table 5.1
Money aggregates and their components

M0	Cash in circulation, in banks' tills, money deposits and deposits with the Bank of England. (Non-interest bearing component of M1.)
M1	M0 plus private sector interest-bearing sterling bank deposits.
M2	M0 plus private sector interest-bearing retail sterling bank deposits plus private sector holdings of retail building society shares, deposits, national savings bank ordinary accounts.
£M3	M1 plus private sector sterling bank deposits and private sector holdings of sterling bank certificates of deposit.
M3c	£M3 plus private sector holdings of foreign currency bank deposits.
M4	£M3 plus building society shares, deposits, sterling certificates of deposit and holdings of foreign currency bank deposits. Less building society holdings of bank deposits, bank certificates of deposit, notes and coin.
M5	M4 plus holdings by the private sector (excluding building societies) of money-market instruments (bank bills, treasury bills, local authority deposits) certificates of tax deposit and national savings instruments (excluding certificates, SAYE and other long-term deposits).

Balance of payments

The UK economy relies heavily on trade and the international flow of capital to generate the nation's income and meet the demands of the country's consumers for goods and services. The balance of payments provides a summarised statement of a country's international trade transactions in goods and services and capital transactions with all other countries.

The UK's balance of payments account is divided into two parts.

☐ *The current account.* This records visible and invisible import and export activity. Visible imports and exports are those goods which can be physically seen and counted, e.g. aeroplanes, cars and hairdryers. The invisible balance consists of the sale and purchase of services between the UK and other countries, plus interest on investments, profits and dividends paid and transfer payments. The term 'transfer payments' refers to non-trading and non-commercial payments, e.g. private gifts, international aid and subscriptions to international organisations.

☐ *The capital account.* This is the balance of payments statement and covers changes in a nation's external assets, and liabilities, including foreign exchange reserves and borrowings.

By definition, the sum of these two parts of the balance of payments must be equal to zero (the overall balance of payments always balances). Thus media reports of a balance of payments deficit refer only to the current account which necessarily will be financed by a reduction in foreign currency reserves or an increase in borrowings from overseas so that the overall balance remains zero.

At the bottom of the statement of the UK's balance of payments account is the *balancing item*. This relates to discrepancies between the total value of recorded transactions and the actual flow of money, i.e. it is the total of errors and omissions arising within the balance of payments accounts. A positive value shows there have been unrecorded net inflows and a negative value that there have been unrecorded negative outflows. The size of the balancing item from any one period can be huge, highlighting the difficulties in interpreting the data, for any one single period.

An imbalance in the UK's current account balance of payments will have the following implications. In the case of a deficit, the country will face a drain on its foreign currency reserves and is likely to find itself getting into more and more debt with overseas monetary agencies and authorities. By contrast, a country experiencing a continuing balance of payments surplus will be accumulating reserves at the expense of the deficit countries. Eventually this inflow of currency may create inflationary pressures as the foreign currency is converted into own currency, increasing the overall money supply. Given these possible problems there are four policy measures available to control the overall balance of payments.

☐ *Demand management policies.* Expanding demand will generally lead to an increase in imports reducing a balance of payments surplus. Similarly, contracting demand should reduce the level of imports and consequently decrease a balance of payments deficit.

☐ *Supply side policies.* As previously mentioned, these policies focus on improving the efficiency and effectiveness of an economy. If successful, these policies will improve the international competitiveness of an economy and consequently gradually move the balance of trade into surplus.

☐ *International trade policy and protectionist measures.* Artificial barriers to trade with other countries will obviously reduce the level of imports. However, limits on imports are likely to lead to retaliatory action by the governments of the exporting countries. Furthermore, the growing globalisation of business activities has to lead to increased cooperation between the governments of different countries designed to reduce the barriers to international trade and thereby foster economic growth. There have been two important developments in this direction:

1 attempts by the World Trade Organisation (formerly known as the General Agreement on Tariffs and Trade) to promote free trade between all countries of the world;

2 the establishment of a number of international customs unions or trading blocks, including the European Union (EU), North American Free Trade Area (Nafta) and the Asia-Pacific Economic Cooperation Forum (APEC).

☐ *Exchange rate management policies.* The final option available to governments is the management of their exchange rate. The following section deals with the mechanisms by which countries attempt to manage their exchange rate in more detail.

Exchange rate

Exchange rates exist because one country's currency is not acceptable in another country and this leads to the need to exchange or convert money from one currency to another. Most developed western countries permit this form of exchange, but not all currencies may be freely traded. Some countries have non-convertible currencies, and others, like the UK before 1979, operate exchange controls which limit the amount of currency that may be traded or taken out of a country.

Exchange rates may be fixed, managed or free-floating. Over the past one hundred years, the UK has experimented with all of these approaches.

Under a managed or fixed exchange rate system, government ministers make a commitment to maintaining the value of their currency against another specified currency or international standard. This value is then defended by the country's central bank which buys or sells the domestic currency on international money markets. In the short term, the value of the currency may be reduced by sales on the international money markets; similarly, the value of the currency may be increased by buying the domestic currency with foreign currency reserves. It is in the longer term, however, that fixed exchange rates are supposed to help a country's economic planning. The main virtue of fixed/managed exchange rates is that they impose a discipline upon a country's economic policy makers, ensuring that governments do not use short-term currency devaluation to fuel short-term economic growth. In the long term, within a fixed or managed exchange rate system, currency stability may only be achieved by improvements in a country's international competitiveness, whether this is achieved through deflationary policies or economic restructuring.

There have been three periods over the past one hundred years during which the UK has been a member of a fixed or managed exchange rate system: the

Gold Standard (linking the value of sterling to the value of gold) from the late nineteenth century until the 1930s, The Bretton Woods Exchange Rate System (linking sterling to the value of the dollar) from 1944 to 1971, and the Exchange Rate Mechanism (ERM) (linking the value of sterling to the ECU and Deutschmark) from October 1990 to September 1992.

Fixed or managed exchange rate systems work most effectively when the economies of member states are performing in similar ways. When one or more

---

5.1 | **EXHIBIT**

European Monetary Union and the European Single Currency **FT**

The European Single Currency was launched on 1 January 1999 as the third stage in a process of Economic and Monetary Union originally initiated in 1992 by the Treaty of European Union (also known as the Maastricht Treaty). The single currency has been officially named as the Euro (€) and replaced the separate currencies of the European Union member states participating in European Monetary Union (EMU). At the beginning of 1999 in the run-up to the eventual launch of the new Euro notes and coins in 2002, twelve of the fifteen member states had their exchange rates 'irrevocably' fixed. Of the remaining three countries not currently committed to the Euro project, Britain and Denmark negotiated 'opt out' clauses from the Maastricht Treaty that meant that these countries reserved the right to take the final decision to join the Euro at a later date. Denmark held a referendum on 28 September 2000 and voted against joining the Euro. The British Labour Government has promised that there will be a British referendum before the final decision is taken. Sweden has not yet made a final decision on whether it wishes to participate in the Euro.

The Euro zone
The countries in the first wave of EMU: Austria, Belgium, Finland, France, Germany, Greece, Ireland, Italy, Luxembourg, Netherlands, Portugal and Spain. The euro notes and coins went into circulation on 'E day', 1 January 2002.

The European Central Bank
Another key element of the Maastricht Treaty in 1992 was the establishment of a European Central Bank (ECB) to administer the Euro. The ECB resides in Frankfurt. The powers of the ECB include:

☐ exclusive rights to authorise the issuing of banknotes and to approve the issuing of coins;

☐ the holding and managing of the official foreign reserves of the Euro-zone countries;

☐ the setting of interest rates to apply to all Euro-zone countries;

☐ the setting of monetary policy for all Euro-zone countries.

The terms of the Treaty of European Union state that the priority of the Bank is to deliver 'price stability', i.e. low inflation, but price stability is not defined. The Executive Board of the European Central Bank consists of a President, Vice president, and four other members. Board members have one vote each and decisions are reached by a simple majority. ECB Board Members are appointed and hold office for between four and eight years.

countries are experiencing higher rates of growth, inflation or public debt than other members, problems are likely to arise. For example, as one member's currency appreciates, that country's economic policy makers will be forced to sell their currency on the foreign exchange markets. This approach will inevitably lead to an expansion of the money supply and may force up the inflation rate. These problems confronted the UK in the late 1980s when the then Chancellor of the Exchequer, Nigel Lawson, pursued a policy of maintaining the UK exchange rate at £1=DM3. By contrast, when one member's economy experiences problems leading to a fall in its exchange rate, policy makers will be forced to buy their own currency through the money markets. In the long term this policy will not be sustainable as foreign currency reserves may become exhausted. Unless other more fundamental steps are taken to address the decline in the exchange rate, this member's currency will be forced to devalue against other currencies in the system. This problem confronted the UK in September 1992 when Norman Lamont, the then Chancellor of the Exchequer, decided to remove sterling from the ERM and allow it to float freely.

The term 'floating exchange rate' refers to situations where the exchange rate is determined by the interaction of supply and demand for a particular currency in international foreign exchange markets. Under this system the exchange rate reflects the relative price competitiveness of an economy and speculation about its future performance. This system offers governments the benefit of rapid movement in the exchange rate to reflect changes in the balance of trade and investment. For example, if a country experiences balance of payments problems reducing the exchange rate may help to bring the balance back into equilibrium. Decline in the value of the currency will make exports more attractive to overseas buyers, while imports to the home country will increase in price and decline in number. However, whether the effects of this devaluation can be maintained in the longer term depends upon the ability of governments, employers and employees to prevent these gains being lost through inflationary increases in domestic wages and prices.

Floating exchange rates also have political as well as economic benefits for national governments. Under a fixed or managed exchange rate system governments are required to sanction any change in the international value of their currency. In the UK these changes have typically involved a politically embarrassing devaluation of sterling. For example, the official devaluation of sterling by Harold Wilson in the late 1960s and Britain's exit from the ERM in 1992 were widely treated with dismay by many journalists and economic commentators. Meanwhile, between 1972 and 1986, and then again between 1992 and 1996, when sterling was allowed to float relatively freely in foreign exchange markets, the gradual devaluation of sterling was arguably just as damaging, but less contentious because it happened slowly.

For business people and tourists, floating exchange rates produce considerable extra costs as they are forced to pay in order to transfer money from one currency to another. Furthermore, there are additional risks for companies involved in doing business between countries with variable exchange rates. For example, the British car manufacturer Jaguar made considerable profits in the USA during the mid-1980s when the value of sterling was relatively weak *vis-à-vis* the dollar. When sterling subsequently strengthened, American consumers were less willing to buy what had become relatively more expensive British cars and Jaguar's profits declined markedly. The risks associated with these types of currency movement can be offset in the short term by speculation in foreign exchange and futures markets, but this activity merely adds to business costs. In the longer term, companies can avoid these costs of foreign exchange dealings by building production facilities in overseas markets. However, this type of activity may be seen by national governments as damaging to the level of employment in the company's home country.

Exercise 5.2   A single European currency?

Outline the principal arguments for and against the adoption of a single European currency. Useful information to help you answer this question is available from the websites listed at the end of this chapter.

Employment

It is common sense to suggest that stable and high economic growth depends on the fullest use of a nation's human resources. Therefore any level of unemployment reflects an inefficiency. However, economists disagree about what is a sustainable level of employment and what is an unacceptable level of unemployment.

Between 1945 and 1976, a broad consensus existed between all political parties about the importance of maintaining very low levels of unemployment. This political position drew on Keynesian analysis in which full employment was deemed an achievable goal, as unemployment was seen to represent a shortfall in the demand for goods and services.

From 1976 to the late 1980s the adoption of Monetarist economic policies led successive British governments to attach a lower priority to the maintenance of high levels of employment. According to many Monetarists, there is a link between the level of inflation and the level of unemployment. Adapting earlier arguments by non-Monetarist economists, Monetarists argue that, other things being equal, when the rate of inflation increases the level of unemployment will tend to rise. Similarly, when the rate of inflation decreases the level of unemployment will generally fall. By this reasoning there is, at least in the short to medium term, a natural rate of unemployment. This so-called *natural rate* is often referred to by economists as the non-accelerating-inflation rate of unemployment (NAIRU).

For Monetarist economists, the natural rate of unemployment in the UK during the 1980s and early 1990s was judged to be between 6 and 8 per cent – higher than the 1 to 3 per cent experienced between 1950 and the early 1970s. It was therefore not surprising that the official rate of unemployment consistently exceeded 1.5 million from the late 1970s onwards and reached a peak of 3.12 million in July 1986. This figure may have been even higher if account is taken of changes in the way unemployment statistics were collected over this period.

The theory of the NAIRU is a re-interpretation of the more famous, but now discredited, Phillips Curve which proposed that there was a straight trade-off between inflation and unemployment. Economies throughout the western world did appear to work like this in the 1950s and 1960s, but the relationship then broke down with the emergence of *stagflation* in the 1970s. In order to account for these new circumstances economists developed the theory of the NAIRU. This new approach suggested that there was a relationship between unemployment and the rate of change in inflation; and only one rate of unemployment is consistent with inflation that is neither rising nor falling. If unemployment is below this critical rate, workers will push for bigger pay increases, inflation will rise and keep rising. If it is above it, inflation will fall.

Believers in this natural rate of unemployment concede that it is not set in stone. It will vary with supply side policies. For example, minimum wages or more generous job benefits will tend to raise the rate. Indeed some have suggested that the high level of unemployment in Europe over the last two decades reflects the influence of these policies.

Critics of the theory of a natural rate of unemployment suggest that two recent changes in western economies have undermined the validity of this model. First, they suggest that the rapid globalisation of business has reduced inflationary pressures within domestic economies, by removing the bottlenecks in production which used to arise because of scarce labour during periods of low unemployment. They maintain that firms are now less reliant on local labour markets to supply their needs. If they cannot employ local staff to make a product, they can always buy the item from another firm in another country. Second, they argue that the rate of technological change has accelerated in recent years with the more widespread adoption of information technology. This computerisation has led to rapid increases in productivity which mean that firms can increase their output without increasing their staffing levels.

On the basis of these arguments a number of economists have suggested that full employment is once again a feasible economic objective. With appropriate international cooperation, governments can develop the skills of their domestic workforces and stimulate consumer demand, in order to promote non-inflationary growth with low levels of unemployment. Looking at the levels of unemployment in major western economies at the beginning of the 21st century, the link between these policies and employment is not wholly evident. While unemployment in the UK reached a 25-year low in 2000 of 5 per cent, it has recently begun to rise again and in many parts of Europe it remains above 10 per cent.

☐ Summary and conclusion

This chapter began with an outline of three important questions for economists, politicians and the wider population of any country. What should be produced? How should it be produced? And how should the results of productive activities be distributed? As we noted in the first half of this chapter, the answers to these questions vary.

For some, free markets provide the most effective means of deciding what to produce, ensuring that the productive activities of millions of people are coordinated and maintaining an efficient distribution system. The market may create temporary hardship for some, but it also provides incentives for entrepreneurs, encourages innovation by employees and offers choice for customers.

For others, markets provide an ineffective method for deciding what to produce and how to produce it. In the market place, things only have a value if they have a price and therefore there is a tendency to overlook important social and environmental objectives. Furthermore, markets do not distribute the results of economic activity fairly. To overcome these problems governments and other bodies are needed to regulate economic activity to ensure that everyone benefits.

In practice, despite continued disagreement between economists, most, if not all, economies are organised on the basis of some mix between market and planned provision of goods and services. The balance may vary between countries, and the emphasis may change over time, but today there are few politicians or business people who would seriously advocate a purely market-based or planned system.

In the second half of this chapter we moved on to consider the economic goals of politicians overseeing macroeconomic policy in mixed economies like the UK. Here we argued that the primary goal of UK economic policy in the post-war period has been sustained economic growth. Politicians of all political persuasions have explicitly or implicitly suggested that if everyone becomes wealthier they will be better placed to choose what they want to produce and how they wish to produce it. Despite this consensus, there has been disagreement about the balance to be struck between this objective and the other goals of containing inflation, maintaining high levels of employment and safeguarding a stable balance of trade and exchange rate. Here once again policy prescriptions have varied. While Keynesian economists and politicians have emphasised the importance of reducing unemployment, Monetarist economists have been more concerned with controlling and reducing inflation.

In recent years British governments have experimented with Keynesian and Monetarist approaches and as a consequence have used different economic policy instruments and indicators to map and chart their progress. Thus the emphasis on demand management in the 1950s, 1960s and 1970s gave way to monetary controls and supply side reforms in the 1980s, which in turn were replaced by a brief experiment with fixed exchange rates in the early 1990s before returning to a focus on low inflation and stable growth supported by supply side reforms in the late 1990s and first few years of the twenty-first century. These policies enabled, or, alternatively, did not prevent, the UK economy from growing in absolute terms. However, its relative position in international economic league tables deteriorated for much of this period. Whether this decline can be reversed in the future remains to be seen.

Exercise 5.3 **Economic indicators**

Choose one of the seven economic indicators listed in Table 5.2 and plot the movement of this variable over the last five years on a graph. You should be able to collect the raw data for this exercise from one or more of the statistical series listed.

When the graph is complete, write a very short account of the trends it reveals and the implications for a specified organisation if the trends continue.

Table 5.2
Some economic indicators and their sources

Economic indicators	Statistical series
1 UK annual aggregate GDP	www.statistics.gov.uk
2 UK annual aggregate retail price index	www.statistics.gov.uk
3 Minimum Lending Rate (interest rate)	www.bankofengland.co.uk
4 Growth in the monetary aggregate M0	www.bankofengland.co.uk
5 Annual average UK unemployment	www.statistics.gov.uk
6 UK annual aggregate current account balance	www.statistics.gov.uk
7 UK effective exchange rate *or* annual average sterling exchange rate index	www.statistics.gov.uk

☐ Useful website addresses

Bank of England: source of official information on inflation and monetary policy
http://www.bankofengland.co.uk/

BisEd: briefing notes for students on business and economics-related issues
http://www.bized.ac.uk

Euro: official European Union website promoting the Euro
http://europa.eu.int/euro/

European Single Currency: Website outlining arguments against single currency
europeansinglecurrency.com/

Office of National Statistics: a UK Government Agency charged with collating statistics
http://www.statistics.gov.uk/

Organisation of Economic Cooperation and Development: international and comparative data on national economic performance
http://www.oecd.org/

☐ Single currency sites

EmuNet
www.internet-prospector.org/intr0199.htm

EU Business
www.eubusiness.com/

Europarl: The Single Currency and the European Parliament
www.europarl.eu.int/euro/default_en.htm

Europe United through a Single Currency
http://home-4.worldonline.be/~ir004300/euro/euroamue.htm

European Central Bank
www.ecb.int/

The official euro website. Organised by the European Commission, this provides an official account of the operation of the Euro
http://europa.eu.int/euro/html/home5.html?lang=5

This site provides an overview of the operation of the single currency and an outline of the pros and cons associated with adoption
http://www.thesinglecurrency.net/Singlecurrency.net

Treasury Euro pages. Information provided by the Treasury on the operation of the Euro
http://www.euro.gov.uk/home.asp?f=1

06 Technology

Chapter

☐ Introduction

Technological developments have literally and metaphorically provided the motor for much of human development. In the past two hundred years the pace of this technological change has accelerated continuously. With each successive wave of innovations the lives of people as employees and citizens have been altered. Cars have offered people greater mobility, medical advances have provided relief from illness and disease, while telephones and computers have enabled people to gain access to enormous quantities of information. For many people these inventions and discoveries represent progress. The human race now has a better understanding and mastery of the world within which it lives, and this knowledge has been used to improve the health, wealth and well-being of societies across the globe. For others, these same innovations present problems as well as solutions. Industrialisation threatens to exhaust the natural resources of the planet; information technology threatens to reduce employment opportunities and dehumanise work; and medical advances pose difficult questions about the value of different people's lives.

☐ Focus and scope

This chapter begins the task of assessing and evaluating the effects of new and established technologies upon the lives of individual employees, the organisations they work for, and the societies of which they are a part. To this end, the chapter is arranged into two main sections. In the first section we attempt to define what is meant by the term technology and to analyse the nature of technological change. The second section then moves on to consider the characteristics of three recent technological changes: industrialisation, information technology and bio-technology. Here, as well as spelling out some of the benefits of these developments, we attempt to outline some of the many dangers.

Learning objectives

Once you have read through this chapter and completed the associated exercises, you should be able to:

☐ explain what is meant by the term 'technology';

☐ describe the nature and causes of technological change;

□ outline some of the problems associated with industrialisation, information technology and bio-technology; and

□ critically evaluate the introduction of new technologies within an organisation known to you.

☐ The nature of technological change

What do we mean by the term technology?

If we are to examine the effects of technology on employees, organisations and society in general we need to be clear about what we mean by the term. The term technology is now used to convey such a wide range of meanings that it has become ambiguous. One way of differentiating between the different meanings of this term is to consider the following three different ways in which it is used.

□ *Apparatus*   The tools, instruments, machines and other appliances which may be applied to a specific task. Examples include combustion engines, computers and chemical testing techniques.

□ *Technique*   Technical activities such as skills, methods, procedures or routines which people perform to achieve particular purposes. The focus here is the human agent that adopts new ways of accomplishing tasks.

□ *Organisation*   The social arrangement of work and machines designed to produce specific products and services. Examples include offices, factories, laboratories and other ways of organising the work of a large number of people.

When has technological change occurred?

Researchers examining the historical development of technology usually take the Industrial Revolution as their starting point. The following four stages of technological change can be identified in the UK since the late eighteenth century:

□ *First stage*   The use of machinery driven by steam power to replace human labour in the transformation of raw materials into products.

□ *Second stage*   The use of machines powered by electricity to accomplish the transfer of materials between machines and to run continuous flow assembly lines.

□ *Third stage*   The use of electronics-based computing and information technologies to coordinate and control the transformation and transfer of tasks.

□ *Fourth stage*   The use of bio-chemical techniques to analyse and synthesise the genetic basis of plant and animal life.

The distinction between these four stages in the technological development of western societies is based upon the assumption that the invention of steam-powered machinery produced a radical transformation in the way people lived and worked. While there is a truth in this assertion, technological innovation did not begin with the Industrial Revolution in the late eighteenth century. The developments at this time were merely an acceleration of the pace of invention and discovery. For example, progress in the development of energy sources had already led people to use horses, water and wind power as alternatives to their own muscles and brawn. The subsequent development of steam and petro-chemical engines as well as gas, electrical and nuclear turbines were a natural extension of these earlier innovations. Similar comments could be raised about the development of electrical, electronic and bio-technology processes and products. There are occasional scientific and technological breakthroughs which produce step changes in the way in which industry, commerce and social life is organised, but each of these changes normally involves the bringing together of a number of different inventions and innovations over a period of time. As a consequence, the speed of change is normally much slower than the division of developments into four stages might lead us to presume. At this point, it is also perhaps worth mentioning that other changes which appear to offer much promise at their start seem less significant in retrospect. One example of this is the development of nuclear fission technologies and atomic power in the second half of the twentieth century.

What causes technological change?

An important question for policy makers in government and business is, what causes technological change? The answer to this question has important implications for the research and development strategies pursued by different countries and companies. New inventions and discoveries offer people the opportunity of better standards of health and education. They also provide the physical basis for an expansion of the wealth of nations and their citizens.

Conventionally, the opinions of scientific and economic historians about the causes of technological change could be divided into roughly two groups. One group of writers believed that the role of the scientists and engineers engaged in pure research was central. The breakthroughs made by these specialists, they argued, produced the technological push for the development of new products, processes, and organisational forms. By contrast, another group tended to high-light the role of customers and financial backers who, they suggested, provided the demand for new ways of doing things. This approach emphasised the power of the marketplace and the importance of the final consumer, who, they maintained, provided the demand pull which inspired new approaches.

In recent years, the polarisation of the debate between advocates of the technological-push theory and believers in market pull has been superseded by more complex explanations which combine elements of each approach. Freeman (1987) provides a good example of this approach with his distinction between four forms of innovation:

1. ☐ incremental innovations;
2. ☐ radical innovations;

☐ changes of technology system;

☐ technology revolutions.

Incremental innovations

Incremental innovations happen continuously in any industry or service activity. They arise as a consequence of engineers, managers and workers making suggestions to improve the goods or services being produced. A number of research studies have demonstrated how this form of continuous improvement by quality circles, team briefing groups and individual suggestion schemes can lead to improvements in the efficiency and effectiveness of organisations. Although the effects of these changes often go unrecorded, the cumulative effect of these innovations can often be very dramatic.

Radical innovations

Radical innovations occur irregularly and often as a result of deliberate research and development activity by companies, universities or government laboratories. The causes of these developments are difficult to ascertain. Radical innovations often provide the stimulus for the development of new markets and industries. Thus, while the immediate effects of these inventions or discoveries may appear at different times in different industries over a period of time, they can have a profound influence over the way we live and work. An example of this phenomenon is provided by the development of information technologies over the past 50 years. The first programmable electronic computer, with a memory of 20 words, was built in 1946, but the IT revolution did not really start until the invention of the silicon chip in the early 1960s and the spread of mainframe computers later that decade. The pace of technological advance since then has been popularly summed up by Moore's Law. Gordon Moore, the co-founder of Intel, forecast in 1965 that the processing power of a silicon chip would double every 18 months, and so it has over the past 30 years. Accompanying improvements in processing power have been reductions in the costs of this technology. Scientists reckon that Moore's Law still has at least another decade to run. By 2010 a typical computer is likely to have 10m times the processing power of a computer in 1975, at a lower real cost.

With radical innovations the evidence of market pull is much weaker than in the case of incremental innovation, since by definition no established market exists. However, those responsible for these developments clearly have some idea of the potential applications of their research and the possible markets for its exploitation.

Changes of technology system

In this case a number of related innovations appear simultaneously and they can provoke fundamental changes in the corporate structure and composition of specific industries. Comprising of a combination of incremental and radical innovation, these developments can give rise to the emergence of new industrial sectors as well as rapid and turbulent restructuring or decline within established industries.

A recent example of this type of technological change is provided by the development of the Internet and multimedia forms of entertainment, which combine the computer technologies discussed above with digital communication and established television networks. According to a number of futurologists, one effect of these changes within the next 20 years will be the gradual replacement of television by entertainment and communication boxes which can be used to perform the following functions:

- broadcast programmes from a variety of sources (cable, satellite and video);
- play interactive games;
- visually and verbally communicate with other people;
- retrieve text, audio and graphical information from a variety of sources, including national and local libraries;
- manipulate images and text;
- store material; and
- buy and sell goods and services.

In addition, it has been suggested that the growing connectivity of previously free-standing computer-based systems will finally allow the productivity growth promised by information technology to be realised. Over the past 50 years the costs of telephone-based communication have fallen dramatically and more and more computers have been linked together. The Internet got going properly only with the invention of the World Wide Web in 1990 and the browser in 1993, but the number of users worldwide has already climbed to more than 350m, and may reach 1 billion within four years. However, it is not just the increase in the numbers of these computers that is enabling companies to improve the productivity of their operations. The benefit of being online increases exponentially with the number of connections. According to Metcalfe's Law, attributed to Robert Metcalfe, a pioneer of computer networking, the value of a network grows roughly in line with the square of the number of users.

There has been considerable speculation about the effects of these technological changes on the ways in which companies will undertake their business in the future. For the optimists, the emerging new e-economy will be increasingly based on businesses that produce text, images and other media which can be produced anywhere in the world at anytime and traded across continents at the touch of the button. They suggest that these 'weightless' commodities will escape the traditional constraints on business growth. These limitations in the past have included restricted access to skilled labour and raw materials as well as the high costs associated with producing finished products and transporting them to customers. Internet-based businesses, it has been argued, can escape these constraints because the services they provide are ubiquitous (available all over the world), improve rapidly (product and service life cycles are typically between 6 and 18 months in duration) and offer very high margins. Once the costs of developing a new piece of software have been met, the very low costs of producing each additional copy are so low that much of the purchase price is pure profit for the provider.

The sceptics, on the other hand, argue that these changes are not as profound as those introduced by electric light which lengthened the working day, the railways which enabled firms to gather and distribute materials across a wider area, the telegraph and telephone which speeded up communication, and the production line which made it cheaper to manufacture goods and services. In addition, it has been argued that the benefits of the Internet are far from ubiquitous. Differences in access to the machines that have made these advances available mean that societies across the globe are increasingly characterised by the information haves and the information have-nots and that this creates yet another divide within society. Finally, it has been suggested that the low costs of producing computing technology and software products mean that these technologies will not provide many employment opportunities in the future. For example, despite its global dominance in the software industry, Microsoft employs 31 000 people worldwide while Walmart, the world's largest retailer, employs over 1 million. For these critics, these differences in the pattern of employment mean that it is the industries that cannot be replaced by these technologies that will be important in the future. Service-based industries in the hotel, catering, security and leisure industries will be more important than computer-based organisations.

| 6.1 | **Fundamental change is now a real proposition: e-markets** | **FT** |

EXHIBIT

Even the most slow-moving companies are now aware of the immense opportunities being opened up by the Internet to reshape their businesses.

But how do they go about translating their ambitions into reality? The technology is there to do almost anything they want, whether it be opening up new sales channels to customers, streamlining and extending supply chains, collaborating with partners or shedding non-core activities.

Executives can, therefore, look beyond the technology and concentrate on what it can achieve. Foremost now in their minds should be the strategy to be pursued in an e-business age which is fast-moving, if less frenetic than during the heyday of the Internet boom. IT can then be fitted to suit the real business purpose.

'Businesses now have no excuse,' says Michael De Kare-Silver, head of e-business at PA Consulting. 'Before, they could say it (e-business implementation) was too expensive or not proven, but now it can be done. It doesn't have to be perfect. Nor does investment have to be a three-year exercise.'

For all the hoopla and upsets of the Internet, the new e-commerce companies spawned by it did at least show what could be achieved online. They brought a creative spirit to the often staid business world and shook up established companies, many of which thought that their whole existence would soon be undermined.

In the reflective aftermath of the Internet boom, it is clear that the real benefits will come not from snazzy new front-end links to the consumer but from more fundamental changes both within and beyond the enterprise.

'E-business is no longer being seen in terms of dotcoms prevailing over "old" traditional businesses, but in terms of a transformation of business models throughout the supply chain in every business sector,' says Digby Jones, director general of the Confederation of British Industry.

His comments are in the foreword to a survey on e-business in the UK called The quiet revolution, produced with KPMG Consulting. It talks of 'an emerging but clear consensus that business should be e-enabled at every level'.

The sectors feeling the greatest impact of e-business are currently telecoms/utilities and financial services, with retailing, professional/consulting and travel not far behind. But all businesses are likely to be transformed in the next two or three years.

The survey's findings showed that 21 per cent of UK businesses could be called 'e-pioneers', while 43 per cent were 'e-followers' and 36 per cent were 'e-laggards'. It concluded: 'Implementing advanced e-business is a complex task that requires not only a change in business strategy, but collaboration with customers, suppliers and employees.'

'Corporations have got to accept that e-business transformation is going to be the single biggest opportunity for them over the next three to five years in terms of improving shareholder value,' says Mr De Kare-Silver.

But behind the vision, companies must focus hard on the process of implementation. They have to overcome initial hesitancy, as well as the temptation to go it alone and exclude outside expertise or to invest heavily in systems which are too complex and specialised for their needs.

'It's a journey,' says Mr De Kare-Silver. 'Companies can be shape changers or surface scratchers.'

Whichever category they fall into, careful planning and project monitoring are vital, as are robust IT systems on which to build new applications. 'There has to be a plan and risk assessment as with any major IT project,' says Irfon Watkins, vice-president of sales and operations for the UK at US-based CommerceQuest, which provides e-business integration software.

Companies have to ensure that their data flows smoothly throughout the business, can be easily retrieved and is totally secure. Systems must be tested to the limit. 'A lot of companies put in systems without testing,' says Harry Harris, senior solutions architect at CommerceQuest. 'Then these break down when they're really needed. End-to-end testing is critical.'

Crucial to companies' e-business performance is strong commitment by the board. Formulating a coherent strategy and then carrying it out across varied and scattered operations is as much a question of people as of policy and technology.

'It has to be championed by the board as there's so much politics involved,' says Geoffrey Codd, managing partner at InterChange Associates, a consultancy which works with the UK's Institute of Directors. 'Part of e-business success is to garner all the experience in the business which can be relevant.'

Without the involvement of the chief executive and other key directors, e-business initiatives can lose their impetus. 'It's all about joined-up thinking,' says Charlie Blackburn, vice-president of Scient Europe, part of the California-based Scient consultancy. 'Clients are getting much smarter.'

Mark Reece, a partner at the Capital Markets Company (Capco), an e-business solutions provider for the financial sector, believes companies generally now have a much more mature attitude to online activities.

'They understand the advantages and drawbacks better,' he says. 'The internet will not go away – it will revolutionise business and services,' he adds. 'But past the hype, companies have got to identify how it takes the business forward.'

Source: Andrew Fisher: *Financial Times*, 30 March 2001

Exercise 6.1   E-business

By reference to the information and analysis contained in Exhibit 6.1, produce a short description of the approach towards e-business adopted by an organisation known to you. Is it an e-pioneer, an e-follower or an e-laggard? A shape changer or a surface scratcher?

Technology revolutions

In these circumstances changes in technology are so substantial and far reaching that they have the capacity to change the way in which people think and behave within an entire economy. These revolutions happen relatively infrequently and take many years to affect everyone; however, when they occur, they necessitate changes in the knowledge, skills and systems of working for entire populations.

A number of writers have suggested that technological revolutions occur in cycles or waves. These waves, it is argued, provide the impetus for economic growth as people find ways of exploiting these technologies.

One of the earliest and best-known proponents of this approach is Krondratieff. A Soviet economist, he observed in the 1920s that it took the world economy approximately 50 years to move through a boom-to-slump-to-boom cycle. Subsequently, economists have traced the development of 'Krondratieff cycles' into the latter part of the twentieth century (*see* Fig 6.1).

According to this long-wave theory, the world economy in the early part of the twenty-first century is beginning to move out of the downturn from the fourth Krondratieff cycle. As a consequence, a number of economists have devoted their attention to spotting the technologies which will provide the stimulus for the upturn of the fifth Krondratieff cycle. One of the most promising contenders at this stage appears to be the emerging bio-technologies.

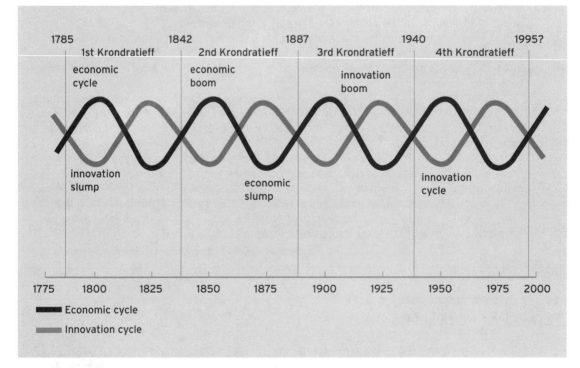

Fig 6.1 Krondratieff cycles and innovation waves (1775–2000), showing innovation peaks in troughs of long wave
Source: Open University, T362 Course Team (1986) Innovation Waves, T362, Block 5, Unit 13.

Research by the Science Policy Research Unit has demonstrated that the upturns in Krondratieff cycles are stimulated by the adoption of new technologies by pioneering new firms (Freeman *et al.*, 1982). These new technologies are then transferred to other parts of an economy, either by spin-off companies from the original pacesetter, or by the adaptation of existing mature firms. These established companies are apt to rely upon external consultants and training programmes to provide expertise in the new technologies.

6.2

EXHIBIT

Future perfect?
Genetic knowledge will change the world profoundly

Many discoveries and inventions shaped the 20th century, but there is a good case to argue that electricity was the most important of them. As the 19th was the steam century, the 20th was the electric one. There is at least a possibility that the 21st may be the DNA century.

Certainly, the technology is now at the new-born baby stage. But babies grow up. People now alive will witness the synthesis of completely artificial life forms (if only to show that it can be done) and the creation of new species, not merely new varieties, of living things. They will see the routine incorporation of biology into industrial processes. They will see a revolution in medicine for themselves, and the birth of people whose biology has been optimised from conception to be resistant to disease and old age. They may even see a world where children are tailored to the wishes of their parents.

They will also see a shift of mind-set. It will be brought home that living things, people included, are indeed no more than information-processing machines, while at the same time it will be shown just what it is that makes humans so special and different from their fellow creatures. The underlying unity of humanity will probably be emphasised in ways that might even help to dispel racial prejudice. In the longer term, the genetics of the neurobiology that underpins the predisposition to such prejudice, along with many other aspects of human behaviour, may yield itself up. Yet evil, or the capacity for it, will persist.

On the way, there will be accidents – especially accidents caused by the fact that biological inventions, unlike the physical inventions of the past, will frequently be able to reproduce themselves without human assistance. Dealing with these accidents, or adjusting perspectives to tolerate them, will require new ways of thinking. New ways of thinking of a different kind may be forced on people by the biological self-knowledge that the century will bring. It will be an interesting ride. And it may end up, literally, reshaping humanity.

Source: *The Economist*, 9 June 2000

☐ The human and environmental costs of industrialisation

The adoption and exploitation of mechanical, chemical, electrical and electronic technologies from the late eighteenth century onwards led to the gradual speed across the globe of new forms of work and patterns of leisure activity. As sophisticated technologies have been turned to the provision of goods and services, in the west at least, industry and commerce have replaced agriculture as the main source of income and wealth. Accompanying this industrialisation have been massive increases in population, urbanisation and the commitment of considerable resources to further innovations, inventions and discoveries.

Today one-fifth of the world's population are fortunate enough to live in highly developed western economies. Meanwhile, a further fifth of the world's population live in abject poverty as they toil on subsistence wages to produce many of the raw materials which feed western industry and commerce. Between these two extremes, the remaining three-fifths of the world's population live in developing countries with standards of living that provide far more than subsistence, but which would still be considered impoverished in the west.

In recent years, a number of writers have begun to question whether the relentless pursuit of technological progress and industrialisation should be tempered by a consideration of the physical and human effects of these changes. The following sections explore some of the more profound of these changes under the following headings: non-renewable resources; pollution; the greenhouse effect and ozone holes.

Non-renewable resources

The generation of power and the production of manufactured goods require large amounts of raw materials. Although many of these raw materials renew themselves, many more are scarce and cannot be replaced. In recent years, the realisation that the Earth's supply of fossil fuels, minerals, wood and many species of animals are limited has led to campaigns to increase awareness of the dangers associated with the uncontrolled use of these resources.

Fossil fuels

According to current projections, the earth's stocks of crude oil and natural gas will not last more than another century. Stocks of uranium and coal reserves are more plentiful, but the environmental costs associated with these forms of energy may make their use uneconomic in the foreseeable future.

Forests

Forests currently cover a little under one-fifth of the earth's land surface. This vegetation is crucial to the stability of soil systems and to the survival of innumerable animal and plant species as well as millions of people.

Fauna and flora

The number of animal species facing extinction increases every day. In 1998, the World Wildlife Fund for Nature (WWF) estimated that there were approximately 380 000 species of plant and between 5 and 10 million species of animal. In the same year, according to the WWF's World Conservation Monitoring Centre, 4589 species of animal were known to be in danger of extinction and close to 60 000 species of plant.

The destruction of these animal and plant species threatens to reduce the variety of life on earth (*bio-diversity*), with serious consequences for the stability of eco-systems around the world. This contraction threatens to rob us of a number of species which might have provided important new medical remedies and other innovations. Without a rich assortment of different plants and animals, the self-regulating stability of eco-systems may be in jeopardy. The extinction of natural predators may free some species to become dangerous new pests to people and their activities.

While the quality of life on earth is being denuded, the quantity of animals available for farming and fishing is threatened. Despite improvements in modern trawling techniques, the catch from modern fishing has levelled off. In response to these pressures, international agencies have attempted to regulate some forms of fishing, e.g. whaling, drift netting and herring fishing.

On the land, despite the conversion of increasing areas of land to arable and cattle farming, there are signs that advances in farming may not be able to keep pace with the exponential growth of the world's human population. Of particular importance is the declining availability of fresh drinking water in areas of the Middle East, Africa and Asia.

Conservation, managed farming, recycling and the exploitation of alternative resources have all been offered as possible solutions to the depletion of the world's natural resources. However, for a number of environmental campaigners these initiatives do not go far enough. They suggest that the fundamental problems are the exponential growth of the world's population and the rapid spread of industrialisation. Without more effective programmes of population control and limited or sustainable development, they argue that famine, pestilence, war and disease will increasingly blight the lives of people across the globe.

Pollution

While consuming the earth's limited natural resources in order to feed and equip a burgeoning population, the human race has been responsible for creating massive quantities of pollution. Chemical wastes and other byproducts of human activity belch onto the land and into the air and the seas. As these contaminants build up in the environment they threaten the continued lives of countless species of plants and animals. Two of the most damaging of these forms of pollution are high levels of acidity (acidification) and excess nitrogen and phosphates (eutrophication).

Acidification

Acidification is caused by sulphur and nitrogen oxide emissions from fossil-fuel-burning power stations, motor cars and heavy industry. Winds can disperse these pollutants over great distances until they eventually come down to earth as rain, snow, dry particles or gases.

Increases in the level of acid in the world's soils, rivers, lakes and seas have had dramatic effects on the types of plants and animals which are able to live and prosper in these environments. For example, the acidification of rivers and lakes in Northern Europe and Scandinavia has meant that many are unable to support fish life.

On land, low levels of acidification can produce beneficial effects for plants as it helps to free nutrients trapped in the soil. However, as the acidity level increases, vital chemicals are leached out of the earth while other more toxic chemicals are freed. The net effect of these changes is that increased acidification may kill or severely curtail plant growth and can have effects on the health of animals further up the food chain.

The worst effects of acidification can be temporarily neutralised by treatment with lime or other agents. However, this is an expensive and difficult process which is rarely applied to the areas of the natural wilderness most seriously affected by acidification.

Eutrophication

Modern fertilisers and other artificial soil and plant treatments have greatly improved crop and cattle yields, but the full costs of these innovations have only recently been realised.

One of the most damaging side effects is eutrophication. This is mainly caused by the over-use of chemical fertilisers. When rain falls after these nutrients have been applied, any surplus nitrogen or phosphates in the fertiliser are likely to be dissolved and will then leak into adjoining rivers or lakes. In eutrophied waters, algae and weeds feed on the nitrogen and phosphate and as they grow and multiply they use up oxygen, killing fish and other aquatic life.

The greenhouse effect

In the long term, the earth must shed energy into space at the same rate at which it absorbs energy from the sun if the temperature is to remain stable. Solar energy arrives on the earth in the form of short-wavelength radiation. Some of this radiation is reflected away by the earth's surface and atmosphere. Most of it, however, passes straight through the atmosphere to warm the earth's surface. The earth gets rid of this energy (sends it back out into space) in the form of long-wavelength, infra-red radiation.

Most of the infra-red radiation emitted upwards by the earth's surface is absorbed in the atmosphere by water vapour, carbon dioxide, methane and nitrous oxide. These so-called 'greenhouse' gases prevent energy from passing directly from the surface out into space. Instead, many interacting processes (including radiation, air currents, evaporation, cloud-formation, and rainfall) transport the energy high into the atmosphere. From there it can radiate into space. This slower, more indirect process is essential because if the surface of the earth could radiate energy into space unhindered, the earth would be a cold and lifeless place rather like Mars.

By increasing the atmosphere's ability to absorb infra-red energy, greenhouse gas emissions are disturbing the way the climate maintains a balance between incoming and outgoing energy. A doubling of the concentration of long-lived greenhouse gases would, if nothing else changed, reduce the rate at which the planet can shed energy into space by about 2 per cent. According to current estimates, if present trends continue, there will be a 'global warming' of between 1.5 and 4.5 degrees centigrade over the course of the next century. The effects of these temperature increases are difficult to predict but are likely to include the following:

☐ *Change in the regional pattern of rainfall.* At the global level the evapo-transpiration cycle is expected to speed up. In short, this means that it would rain more, but that the rain would evaporate faster, leaving soils drier during critical parts of the growing season. New or worsening droughts, especially in poorer countries where irrigation is less extensive and robust, could reduce supplies of clean fresh water to the point where there are major threats to public health.

☐ *Shifts in the world's agricultural zones.* In the mid-latitude regions there is expected to be a shift of between 200 and 300 kilometres towards the poles in the effective growing regions for each increase in average temperatures of one degree centigrade. In addition, increased summer dryness may reduce mid-latitude crop yields by as much as 10 to 30 per cent. These changes would be accompanied by increased desertification in equatorial regions, and more frequent droughts and heatwaves in the grain-producing areas of the Great Plains in the USA and arable areas of Europe.

☐ *Melting glaciers and thermal expansion of sea water.* The average global sea level has already risen by 15 centimetres over the past hundred years and is expected to rise by a further 18 centimetres by the year 2030 and 65 centimetres by the end of this century. As the sea level rises, an increasing amount of land will become vulnerable to flooding. Among the countries most at risk in the near future are poor and populous countries like Bangladesh and low-lying island states like the Maldives.

In order to tackle the effects of these potentially devastating changes a number of policy proposals have been brought forward by politicians and other pressure groups. These proposals include:

☐ a tax on those fuels and other substances most responsible for the release of greenhouse gases;
☐ restrictions on the use of fuels and other activities which release greenhouse gases and the promotion of energy conservation, e.g. speed limits for cars, insulation for houses, recycling initiatives and the expansion of public transport;
☐ the exploitation of new sources of energy which do not involve the release of greenhouse gases, i.e nuclear, wind, wave, solar and geo-thermal energy.

Despite much discussion of these different policy options over the past ten or fifteen years, efforts to effect these types of change have been relatively limited to date. The United Nations Framework Convention on Climate Change, which was originally agreed in Kyoto in 1992, commits its signatories to taking steps to stabilise greenhouse gas concentrations in the atmosphere at a level which prevents dangerous interference with the climate. In addition, the agreement promotes scientific research and education programmes as well as encouraging governments to take steps to reduce and limit activities which might lead to global warming. In particular, there is a requirement for the world's 24 leading industrial countries (members of the Organisation for Economic Cooperation and Development (OECD)) to reduce greenhouse gas emissions to 1990 levels by the year 2000.

Ozone holes

The ozone layer in the earth's upper atmosphere provides protection from harmful ultraviolet rays from the Sun, while letting enough light in to support the growth of plants and animals. However, this protective screen is beginning to break down. The major causes of ozone depletion are man-made chlorine and bromine compounds – notably cholorofluorocarbons (CFCs). These CFCs are found in aerosol cans, refrigeration coolants, fire extinguishers and the byproducts of plastic foam manufacture. When CFC molecules reach the upper atmosphere, ultraviolet light causes them to break down, releasing chlorine atoms. Each of these chlorine atoms can then destroy up to 100 000 ozone molecules.

The appearance of a hole in the ozone layer over the South Pole in 1985 and over the North Pole in 1994 drew the world's attention to the possible damaging effects of CFCs. Each year these holes have widened and every spring they now cover several million miles in the southern and northern hemispheres. Doctors and ecologists are worried that the depletion of the ozone layer will increase the level of ultraviolet light reaching the earth's surface, causing skin cancer and cataracts among humans, as well as destroying a number of species of plants and animals. In response to these worries the heads of several western governments signed the Montreal Protocol in 1989 which includes targets for the phased reduction of CFC production. In 1994, the UK and other members of the European Union took further steps by committing themselves to a complete ban on CFC production. Despite regular meetings of signatories to both of these agreements, a number of other ozone-depleting agents remain unregulated, e.g. m ethyl bromide and HCFCs.

6.3 **Green accounts and audits**

EXHIBIT

In the United States companies are required to inform the government authorities about their prospective environmental liabilities and their use of chemicals listed as toxic. As a result of these regulations, a growing number of American companies include some environmental information in their financial statements. Outside the USA there are few regulations governing the types of environmental information companies must release. Those companies that voluntarily choose to release information have adopted a variety of approaches, as the following examples demonstrate.

☐ Dow Europe - a division of an American multinational company - produces tabulations of the pollutants to air, water and soil from its individual plants and lists the extent to which they have been reduced or increased in recent years. They also list unwanted events, including accidents, spills, complaints and fines imposed.

☐ Union Carbide - the company responsible for the Bhopal disaster in India - tracks its performance against the 'Responsible Care' programme devised by the American chemical industry. Their reports give details of pollution prevention, safety and targets for future improvement.

☐ Kunert - a German textile manufacturer - has published an 'eco-balance sheet' for the past four years. This document weighs up the company's use of raw materials, including electricity, air and water, against its output of tights, socks and waste.

☐ B&Q - Britain's biggest chain of do-it-yourself retailers - has added to its own annual green audit by requiring its suppliers to complete a tough environmental questionnaire. Managers at this company believe that their customers are concerned about conserving the environment and are prepared to change their shopping habits in order to buy from companies that share these beliefs.

In the near future these voluntary arrangements are likely to be superseded by national regulations. As a consequence, several organisations, including the United Nations, the International Chambers of Commerce and the European Union as well as a variety of industry groups, are now trying to develop guidelines in an attempt to influence national regulations. The effects of these regulations will doubtless depend upon the force of the law attached to these rules.

The European Union's proposals will require companies to evaluate and improve their environmental performance. It is expected that these guidelines will be based on the 'Valdez Principles' drawn up by the Coalition for Environmentally Responsible Economics (CERES) in the USA.

CERES was formed in 1989 when a number of environmental groups, religious organisations and investors came together in response to the disastrous oil spill by the *Exxon Valdez* oil tanker in the Prince William Sound on the Alaskan coastline. One of the first actions of this group was to lay down a code of conduct which it has called the 'Valdez Principles'. This code encourages companies and other organisations to abide by the following ten proposals:

1 *Protection of the biosphere* - to strive to eliminate the release of harmful pollutants.

2 *Sustainable use of natural resources* - such as water, soils and forests.

3 *Reduction and disposal of waste* - to minimise the creation of waste and, wherever possible, recycle materials.

4 *Wide use of energy* - to make every effort to use environmentally safe and sustainable energy sources; invest in improved energy efficiency.

5 *Risk reduction* - to minimise risks to employees by employing safe technologies and operating procedures and by being constantly prepared for emergencies.

6 *Marketing of safe products and services* - to inform consumers of the environmental impact of products and services.

7 *Damage compensation* - every effort to be taken to restore the environment and to compensate those persons who were adversely affected.

8 *Environmental directors* - to have at least one member of the board of directors qualified in environmental issues.

9 *Disclosure* - to disclose to employees and to the public incidents relating to operations that cause environmental harm or pose health and safety hazards. To disclose potential environmental, health or safety hazards posed by operations and not to take any action against employees who report any condition that creates a danger to the environment or poses health and safety hazards.

10 *Assessment and annual audit* - to conduct and make public an annual self-evaluation of progress in implementing these principles and complying with all applicable laws and regulations.

Exercise 6.2   Eco-friendly organisations

How does an organisation known to you measure up to the Valdez Principles
listed above?

☐ Information and communications technology (ICT)

Having examined the effects of industrialisation and commercial activity on the
environment that surrounds us, we now move on to consider the effects and
communication of information technology – the most recent set of technological revolutions to affect people's work and social lives.

A post-industrial society, an information or a computer revolution, whatever
we call it, most people agree that the invention, exploitation and diffusion of
microchip and communications technologies have had a profound effect on
people's lives over the past 30 years. For some people, these new technologies
offer us all the prospect of more enjoyable jobs and more fulfilled lives. For
others, these advances are less worthwhile as they threaten to increase unemployment and create sharp distinctions between the information haves and the
information have-nots; the technologically literate and the technologically illit-
erate; the gods and the clods.

Whether these developments are seen as good or bad often depends upon
the perspective of the commentator. The following section aims to define what
it is we mean when we talk about new technologies and to examine their effects
upon employment and the skills of the workforce.

What is information technology?

According to Buchanan and Boddy (1983), computer-based information technologies have four unique characteristics which set them apart from older and
more established technologies.

☐ *Information capture*	Sensing, gathering, collecting, monitoring, detecting and measuring information
☐ *Information storage*	Converting text and numeric data into a digital form which can be stored and retrieved when required
☐ *Information by manipulation*	Organising large quantities of data and analysing this information, performing standard calcula-tions or operations
☐ *Information distribution*	Digitally stored information can be transmitted rapidly worldwide, e.g. through the transfer and storing of files; and through the display of infor-mation via websites on the Internet.

The introduction of such technologies can have a number of implications. For example, an increased trend towards e-commerce could result in a greater transfer of jobs from centralised high street retail locations to more dispersed wholesale locations along with resulting job losses.

Also, the knowledge, skills and attitudes of staff involved in the newer IT-based and e-business-based sectors differ markedly from those in the more traditional manufacturing and service industries.

Information and communications technology and employment

In the 1960s and 1970s, it was widely believed that the newly emerging computer-based technologies would herald an era of unmanned factories and people-less offices. It was argued that machines and robots would be able to take over the work of humans. Working around the clock in unlit buildings, these machines would be able to increase production levels and lower costs. These changes promised to solve the problems of production, leaving policy makers and business leaders free to worry about how the vast numbers of newly unemployed people would be able to afford to buy these manufactured goods. Thirty years later, despite the widespread adoption of computers, there is little evidence that this vision of the future is any nearer realization. According to Huczynski and Buchanan (1991), a number of compensatory mechanisms have prevented the introduction of new technology being accompanied by massive and sustained unemployment.

☐ *New products and services*. Technical innovation generates new products and services, like compact discs, multimedia PCs and mobile phones. These inventions change the pattern of consumer demand and this leads organisations to invest in factories and offices which in turn leads to new employment opportunities.

☐ *Productivity*. Higher productivity means producing more or the same level of output with the same or fewer resources. As productivity increases, the associated savings may be passed on to the consumer as lower prices; kept by the employer with increased wages and other expenses; or transferred to shareholders in the form of rising share prices and dividends. Whichever way these gains are distributed, there will be more money available to be spent on other goods and services within the economy.

☐ *Investment costs*. Many new technologies are still very expensive. Unless a company expects the demand for its products and services to expand, it may not be able to justify the expenses associated with the investment in new technology. Automating production and information flows does not guarantee profitability. Indeed, a number of studies have confirmed that the relationships between the adoption of information technologies, productivity and product quality are not straightforward. For example, some of the most effective and efficient automobile plants in the world have low levels of automation.

☐ *Technical limitations.* New technologies may not live up to the claims of their inventors, champions or salespeople. The new machines may not be able to do everything that the old technology was capable of doing. For example, no craftsperson would be without a screwdriver or hammer.

☐ *Time lags.* It takes time for existing organisations to adopt new technologies. They need to be made aware of the development, train their staff and carefully appraise the risks before investing in new equipment. Because of the time lags associated with these developments, technical changes take longer to permeate all areas of industrial and domestic life. The result of these delays is that employment losses caused by the introduction of new technologies take many years to have their full effect.

Information and communications technology and skill

According to McLoughlin and Clark (1994), there are three competing views of the effects of information technology upon job content, skill levels and status. They label these three different perspectives technological determinism, labour process and strategic choice.

Technological determinism

The work of Joan Woodward (1970) perhaps best exemplifies this approach. On the basis of a number of research studies in the early 1960s, she argued that technology determines the nature of the work people undertake and the systems of control they are subjected to by management. While she conceded that different technologies require different approaches, she maintained that competition determines which technology is the most economic. At the time of her investigations, Joan Woodward suggested that the emerging highly automated technologies of assembly line operations (characteristic of consumer goods factories) and continuous process production (common in refineries and large chemical works) would increasingly require impersonal management control systems. Under these new regimes, employees would be engaged in work which involved monitoring production processes, rather than directly intervening in them.

Labour process

Advocates of this approach argue that technology does not determine the form of managerial control systems or the nature of employees' work. Instead they argue that technology provides a means by which managers seek to impose control over the work of employees. Seen from this perspective, technology embodies management control systems which themselves arise from the class-based conflict between capital and labour. According to Braverman (1974), information technology is used to cheapen labour and deskill job content. Furthermore, this new technology is used to remove control over the execution of work from the worker, and place it in the hands of management. As a direct consequence of these processes, the work of employees is degraded.

Strategic choice

Writers adopting this perspective argue that the effects of introducing information and communications technology are not predetermined in any way. Instead they suggest that the outcomes of technological change are the products of choice. Different groups within the organisation – managers, unions and individual employees – will all have a preferred list of objectives for the new technology. The eventual outcomes will depend upon negotiations between these groups and will reflect the values, power and determination of these various parties (Child, 1972). Thus the introduction of electronic teller machines and price-scanning equipment in a supermarket may be undertaken in a human-centred or technology-centred way. Human-centred design begins with the needs of the employee rather than the needs of the equipment. Adopting this approach, technology will be designed to deal with the most laborious elements of the work, freeing the employee to engage in the more socially and intellectually rewarding aspects of the job. Furthermore, the layout and design of the new machinery will be determined by the physical and social needs of the operator, rather than the economic and technical demands of the equipment.

A more human-centred approach to technological innovation provides benefits for companies as well as employees. As Walton and Susman (1987) have argued, although the primary motive for the adoption of advanced manufacturing technology tends to be the search for cost reductions, many manufacturers still look for ways to enhance employees' capabilities and improve labour relations. They suggest that concern with these human aspects is based on the realisation that the adoption of new technology increases:

☐ the interdependence between different functions in the production process;

☐ the requirement for skill and commitment from employees;

☐ the need for capital investment;

☐ the speed, scope and cost of errors; and

☐ the sensitivity of overall organisational performance to changes in employees' skills and attitudes.

If the needs of human operators are overlooked, the introduction of new technology will merely increase the likelihood and cost of operator errors and poor performance.

Information and communications technology and health and safety

The effects of information technologies upon employees' health and safety have received considerable attention in recent years. Eye strain, migraine and repetitive strain injury (RSI) are just a few of the medical conditions which doctors have suggested are caused or aggravated by prolonged use of computer keyboards and mice, and video display screen equipment (*see* Table 6.1)

Table 6.1 Office automation hazards: a summary from the literature

Typical symptoms	Probable causes	Ergonomic solutions	Organisational solutions
Reproductive disorders			
Male infertility Abnormal pregnancy Miscarriage Still birth	Repetition Radiation Static electricity	Work design Screen filters Equipment earthed	Job enlargement/enrichment Job rotation Training
Eye sight			
Eye strain Blurred vision Flickering eyelids Migraine	Poor lighting Screen glare and flicker Intense concentration	Good lighting Good displays Work schedule	Office layout IT audits and assessments Working hours
Musculo-skeletal			
Stiff neck and shoulders Arm and wrist pains Backache and headache Repetitive strain injury	Repetition Inadequate desk and chair Work pace Poor posture Badly designed keyboard	Check posture Desk design Chair design Properly designed keyboard	Exercise routines Check rest periods More rest periods Increased job variety
Personal			
Heightened levels of stress Disturbed domestic life		Job design	Organisation and work design

Source: adapted from Huczynski, A and Buchanan, D (1991) *Organizational Behaviour: An Introductionary Text*.

In response to the perceived health hazards accompanying the use of some forms of information technology, the UK government, as a result of pressure from the European Union, introduced regulations governing the use of display screen equipment (DSE). These regulations contain detailed advice on appropriate computer design, operator seating and general workstation layout as well as advice on how to monitor the health and welfare of PC users.

Exercise 6.3 **Information technology health and safety**

What steps has your organisation taken to ensure compliance with the Display Screen Equipment Regulations and to reduce the health and safety risks associated with the use of personal computers?

ICT, control, surveillance and data protection

Information technology allows managers and employees greater access to information about their organisation, its employees, suppliers, customers and other stakeholders. When used appropriately, this information can be turned to competitive advantage over rival firms in the marketplace. This information can also be used, among other things, to match employees' skills and expectations to job opportunities, protect employees from health hazards, and tailor reward packages to individual demands.

Buchanan and McCalman (1989) suggest that computerised information systems offer the following benefits.

☐ They encourage managers and employees to share information previously protected in manual systems.

☐ This technology may enhance the motivation and confidence of managers as they now have access to accurate and shared information. The visibility of individual employees' work performance is increased as tasks may be monitored more effectively.　HR .

☐ The enhanced confidence of managers and visibility of work performance increase the pressure on managers to react quickly and appropriately to business opportunities and problems.

☐ Shared information, shared confidence, shared visibility and shared pressure encourage a cooperative approach to management decision making, reducing opportunities for power struggles and inter-departmental conflicts.

Other writers are more pessimistic about the effects of increased access to information (Zuboff, 1988; Sewell and Wilkinson, 1993). As they point out, there are dangers associated with unregulated access to information. The following five problems are among the most important mentioned by these authors.

☐ Information technology may enable managers to gain access to previously confidential records about their employees, customers and other parties. For example, computerised databases can provide people in positions of authority with easy access to personal information about credit ratings, school performance, housing and medical histories.

☐ Unrestrained access to information increases employees' fears and worries about what their employers know about them and their private lives.

☐ Surveillance techniques enable managers to keep their workforce under surveillance, monitoring work rates and comparing employees. The information produced by these techniques may not take sufficient account of differences between employees, and the contexts within which their work has been performed.

☐ Surveillance increases the pressure on employees to ensure that the performance indicators they are measured against show favourable results. It may also prevent employees from devoting attention to other issues, i.e. customer service and productivity improvement suggestions.

☐ Access to private information and secret surveillance may alienate employees, reduce their trust in managers and decrease commitment to the organisation. As employees become increasingly disgruntled and worried about their job security, there is a possibility that cooperation within teams will break down and power struggles will increase.

Data protection, surveillance and the law

The relevant legislation is:

☐ Data Protection Act 1998 (in force from March 2000)

☐ Human Rights Act 1998 (in force from October 2000)

☐ Regulation of Investigatory Powers Act 2000

☐ Telecommunications (Lawful Business Practice) (Interception of Communications) Regulations 2000 (in force from October 2000).

Data Protection Act 1998

What personal data is covered by the Act? This is any information relating to a living individual who can be identified from the information. It covers computer data about employees, documents such as appraisals, disciplinary records and medical information. It also includes CCTV images and voicemail messages.

What are the principles underlying the legislation? The Act contains eight data protection principles relating to the processing of personal data (*see* Figure 6.2).

How is sensitive personal data dealt with? This consists of information concerning: racial or ethnic origin; political opinions; religious or similar beliefs; union membership; physical or mental health; sexual life; and circumstances relating to actual or alleged criminal offences.

Are there specific provisions governing the employment relationship? Although the Act covers the processing of personal data in a wide range of busi-

Figure 6.2
Data protection
principles

Personal data must be processed fairly and lawfully. At least one of the following conditions must be met:

☐ The consent of the individual is obtained.

☐ There must be a contract with the individual.

☐ There must be a legal obligation.

☐ The processing must be to protect the vital interests of the individual.

☐ It must be necessary to carry out public functions, or necessary to pursue the legitimate interests of the business (unless prejudicial to the individual).

☐ Personal data must be obtained only for one or more specified and lawful purposes (and shall not be further processed in a manner incompatible with that purpose).

☐ Personal data must be adequate, relevant and not excessive for the purpose (or purposes) for which it is processed.

☐ Personal data must be accurate and, where necessary, kept up to date.

☐ Personal data must not be kept for longer than is necessary for that purpose.

☐ Personal data must be processed in accordance with the data subject's right under Data Protection Act 1998.

☐ Appropriate technical and organisational measures must be taken against unauthorised or unlawful processing and against accidental loss or destruction of, or damage to, personal data.

☐ Personal data must not be transferred to a country outside the European Economic Area unless that country ensures an adequate level of protection for data subjects in relation to the processing of personal data.

ness circumstances, human resources professionals will be particularly concerned with the Code of Practice, 'The use of personal data in employer–employee relationships', issued by the Office of the Information Commissionier in 2001.

The Code of Practice 2001: The use of personal data in employee–employer relationships

Monitoring of employees:

- ☐ A distinction is drawn between performance monitoring (i.e. the quantity and quality of and individual's work) and behavioural monitoring (i.e. compliance with workplace rules and standards).
- ☐ This must conform with data protection principles.
- ☐ Monitoring must not unnecessarily intrude on employee's privacy.
- ☐ Staff should be aware that monitoring is taking place (other than in exceptional circumstances).
- ☐ Employers are encouraged to establish a policy on the use of electronic communications.
- ☐ Clear corporate standards should be made explicit on: circumstances when an employer may access e-mails, the misuse of the Internet, the use of CCTV, vehicle monitoring, and screening for drug and alcohol consumption.

The Human Rights Act 1998

This Act incorporated into UK law the European Convention of Human Rights and Fundamental Freedoms 1950 (see Chapter 8). Only public authorities can face a direct claim under the Human Rights Act. However, because courts must, as far as possible, interpret all law in accordance with the Convention rights, these rights will apply indirectly to private organisations as well as public bodies.

The Convention Article most likely to have bearing on the processing of data is Article 8, which states that 'everyone shall have the right to respect for his private and family life, his home and his correspondence'. This is, however, a qualified right. It can be interfered with in certain circumstances under law where 'it is necessary in a democratic society in the interests of national security, public safety or the economic well being of the country, for the prevention of disorder or crime, for the protection of health or morals, or the protection of the rights and freedoms of others'.

Regulation of investigatory powers

This legislation implements part of the European Union's Telecommunications Data Protection Directive 1997. The directive requires member states to protect the confidentiality of communications and also to take account of the European Convention on Human Rights. The basic principle of this legislation is that interception of communications and covert surveillance require the consent of the sender and the recipient. Unlawful interception is a criminal offence. The Act covers circumstances where 'a person intentionally and without lawful authority' intercepts anywhere in the UK 'any communication in the course of its transmission by means of ... a public postal service or ... a public telecommunications system'. A public telecommunications system is defined as a system that, although not itself public, is attached, directly or indirectly, to a public system. This would include an e-mail system connected externally.

'Lawful authority' to incept has been outlined in the Telecommunications (Lawful Business Practice)(Interception of Communications) Regulations 2000. These regulations will be considered in relation to both the Data Protection Act and the Human Rights Act.

At the time of writing, it is fair to say that the interconnections between these three pieces of legislation is uncertain. Employers with problems and issues in respect of monitoring, surveillance and data protection will need to take up to date advice.

☐ Bio-technology

While managers and employees are still wrestling with the opportunities and problems presented by the new information technologies, another wave of technological change is beginning to take shape in laboratories and research establishments across the western world. These new bio-technologies offer the prospect of new products and services which will create new businesses and industries during the course of this century.

Since the discovery of DNA by Crick and Watson in the early 1950s, scientists have been engaged in the mammoth task of mapping and understanding the operation of the genes which form the building blocks of all life. The strands of DNA in each animal or plant cell contain unique codes which control the growth and reproduction of the organism. In recent years, biochemical research has established links between certain DNA sequences and specific physical characteristics, susceptibility to disease and, more contentiously, particular patterns of behaviour. As a consequence of these advances, scientists have been able to genetically engineer more productive farm animals and create disease-resistant crops as well as discover new pharmaceutical products, diagnostic tests and therapeutic procedures. Despite the obvious benefits associated with these new bio-technologies, a number of writers have expressed their concerns about the possible consequences of these developments.

Genetic profiling

There are currently a large number of research projects across the globe designed to identify and profile the genetic and bio-chemical make-up of animals and plants. By far the largest of these projects is the Human Genome Project. Begun in 1990, the Human Genome Project is a 13-year effort coordinated by the Department of Energy and the National Institutes of Health in the USA. The project originally was planned to last 15 years, but rapid technological advances have accelerated the expected completion date to 2003. The goals of this project include:

- identifying all the approximate 30 000 genes in human DNA;
- determining the sequences of the 3 billion chemical base pairs that make up human DNA;
- storing this information in databases;
- addressing the ethical, legal, and social issues that may arise from the project.

The development of genetic profiling techniques like those used in the Human Genome Project raise the possibility that within the not too distant future people will be able to assess their susceptibility to a range of common diseases and conditions, e.g cancer, heart disease and mental illness. If this information is used to provide affected individuals with better health care it is possible that the length and quality of their lives may be extended. However, if the information concerns diseases or conditions that are untreatable and unavoidable, being aware of the fact that you will develop a particular disease within the next ten years is unlikely to improve the quality of your life. Furthermore, unrestricted access to this information could present problems. For example, once employers have obtained this material, they may decide not to recruit certain individuals, while mortgage and insurance companies may decline to accept the risks associated with granting them a policy.

Genetically modified food

The development of genetic profiling and engineering techniques has enabled seed producers and chemicals companies to develop a range of new plant and animal varieties which grow more rapidly, produce larger yields and are less susceptible to disease. However, these benefits have not been without cost. The development of these new strains has required sizeable investment by these firms and associated research and development organisations, and according to some commentators has exposed other plants and animals to risks. Among the alleged problems caused by the development of genetically modified foods, the following are the most commonly mentioned.

- Crops that have been genetically modified to resist insects don't just kill the target pests (e.g. weevils), they also kill beneficial insects (e.g. Monarch butterfly). This has a knock-on effect of animals which rely on these insects for food.
- Where crops have been developed to be resistant to herbicides, this encourages greater use of these chemicals with consequent detrimental effects on other plants and animals.
- Genetically modified plants may crossbreed with wild species to produce 'superweeds' which cannot be eliminated using standard herbicides.
- Genetic material inserted into plants and animals can enter the human bloodstream through the intestines.
- The long-term effects of genetic modification are not well understood at present because these products have not been fully tested before being released. For example, in the USA until recently the Department of Agriculture approved the sale of a number of genetically modified crop seeds solely on the basis of test data provided by the manufacturers.

Bio-hazards

Advances in genetic engineering techniques have produced useful new types of bacteria, plants and animals. However, these developments have also raised people's fears about the prospect of generating dangerous organisms which could damage the environment or human health. Past experiences give little cause for comfort. Experiments with anthrax on islands off the Scottish coast during the Second World War have left at least one island uninhabitable to this day. Popular dramas, like *The Andromeda Strain*, have also outlined the possible risks associated with the release of new organisms which mutate or interact with other agents in the environment to produce dangerous side effects. The potentially damaging effects of these developments have recently been underlined by the spread of Bovine Spongiform Encephalopathy (BSE) and the associated Creutzfeldt-Jakob Disease (CJD). The protein particles (prions) which cause these diseases have only recently been identified by scientists. However, it is not just the disease agents that are a source of risk. Improved transportation and increases in the frequency with which people, animals, plants and other items are moved between different locations heighten the chances of any dangerous substances coming into contact with other people.

☐ Summary and conclusion

In this chapter we sought to demonstrate that technological change is an ambiguous term which can be used to describe new tools, ways of working and organisation. Over the past two centuries the pace of this change has accelerated as humans have adopted mechanical, electrical, electronic and biological technologies to improve the quality and productivity of their work. Each new wave of technological change has affected the numbers of people employed in different occupations and the skills they are required to use. These changes have also influenced the structure of employing organisations, the wider pattern of social relations and the physical environment within which firms operate.

However, these changes were not inevitable. As individuals, organisations and governments develop, assess and implement new technologies they are faced with important choices which will have important direct and indirect effects. For example, computers can be used either to intensify, deskill and degrade, or alternatively to improve, enhance and enrich the work of employees. Similarly, organisations can actively seek out new technologies or defensively protect established ways of operating. At a societal level, new technologies can be developed which either protect or undermine communities and the natural environment. In practice these choices are rarely presented in such stark terms. New technologies slowly permeate organisations and gradually alter the way in which people work and live their lives. It is therefore important that managers in general, and human resource managers in particular, are constantly involved in questioning the way in which new technologies are designed, implemented and evaluated within the workplace.

☐ Useful websites

Beginners Guide to the Internet: History of the development of the Internet and an outline of how various elements of this system work today.
http://www.northernwebs.com/bc/

Data protection and the Information Commissioner
http://www.dataprotection.gov.uk

Friends of the Earth: comprehensive set of materials dealing with, among other things, climate change and its effects.
http://www.foe.co.uk

Genetically modified food web site: Information about the alleged effects of genetically modified foods.
http://scope.educ.washington.edu/gmfood/

Greenpeace: conservationists' organisation.
http://www.greenpeace.org.

Human Genome Project: an overview of the project and progress to date.
http://www.ornl.gov/hgmis/

The industrial revolution: Introductory overview
http://www.fordham.edu/halsall/mod/modsbook14.html#

World Wildlife Fund: an organisation dedicated to animal and plant conservation.
http://www.panda.org/

Society and social trends

Chapter

☐ Introduction

What does the word 'society' mean? In practice, it tends to be a general term for the institutions and relationships within which a relatively large group of people live. The former prime minister, Margaret Thatcher, famously denied the very existence of society. To the seventeenth-century poet John Donne, 'No man is an island, entire of itself/ every man is a piece of the continent, a part of the main'. One of society's most obvious features is its complexity. It can embrace a vast array of issues, including ageing, ethnicity, migration, health and education. Some of the key issues lack consensus on fundamental terms; there are no universally accepted definitions of social inequality, poverty or social exclusion. However, poverty in Britain is commonly described in relation to average incomes or standards of living. Social exclusion is more than poverty; it often encompasses notions of participation in society.

What is clear is that such trends shape and influence organisations. Pay levels, recruitment and retention, employment practice are all powerfully affected by such developments. At the very minimum, strategic awareness within organisations requires a grasp of such matters.

☐ Focus and Scope

This chapter seeks to outline recent social trends and to comment upon their causes and implications for the management of people at work. To this end we focus on five key changes that have affected British society since the end of the Second World War.

Learning objectives

Once you have read through this chapter and completed the associated exercises, you should be able to:

☐ describe recent population trends;

☐ outline features of social class and social mobility;

☐ report on the changing composition of British households;

☐ comment upon the distribution of wealth and income within the UK.

☐ Demographic change

Changes in the demographic make-up of Britain shape changes in the labour market. In the last quarter of the twentieth century, the population of the United Kingdom grew from 56 million to 59.5 million in 1999. This is expected to increase to over 63 million by 2021.

Births

Britain's birth rate fluctuated rapidly in the twentieth century. Rapid growth characterised the start of the century, and again during the 1960s. Since 1990 there has been a steady decline in the number of births (a 10 per cent fall between 1990 and 1998). Many factors affect the age at which women have their first child. Education levels appear to be particularly important. Generally the pattern is the higher the qualification, the later the birth of the first child. The proportion of births occurring outside marriage has been rising rapidly. In 1968 one in twelve births were outside marriage; by 1998 one in three were.

An ageing population

The elderly population of Britain is expanding significantly; it is said to be 'greying'. We are leading longer lives. Improvements in mortality rates for older people and lower fertility rates have both contributed to an ageing population. One in seven of the population was aged 50 and over in 1901; by 1997 one in three were (*see* Table 7.1). It is projected that by 2021, 40 per cent of people will be aged 50 and over. Currently, about 18 per cent of people are over pensionable age (65 years for men, 60 for women; some 4 million men and 7 million women). Demographic projections suggest that by 2016 it is expected that the number of people aged 65 or more will exceed those aged under 16. Older people are more likely to be women than men; by the age of 89, there are around three women to every man.

Table 7.1
An ageing population

	All aged 50 and over (thousands)
1901	5,678
1951	13,845
1997	18,818
2021 (estimate)	25,107

Source: Social Focus on Older People (Office for National Statistics, 1999)

Households and families

One of the most striking of all post-war social trends in Britain has been the change in the make-up of a typical household. The so-called 'nuclear' family, a couple with dependent children (dependent children are those aged under 16 or between 16 and 18 and in full-time education) living in their own home has been in sharp decline since the 1960s. In 1961, two-fifths were 'nuclear' households. By 2000, this had fallen to less than a quarter of households (*see* Table 7.2). Over the same period, the proportion headed by a lone parent had more than quadrupled, from 2 per cent to 9 per cent; nine out of ten of these households are headed by women. Family sizes have fallen – the average size of households almost halved during the twentieth century – from 4.6 to 2.4 persons – and there is an increasing trend towards living alone, particularly among the elderly. The proportion of households made up of a single person more than doubled from 11 per cent in 1961 to 29 per cent in 2000. The extended family has also declined. Official projections suggest that all these trends will continue for the next twenty years.

Table 7.2
Households in Britain 1961-2000

	1961	1981	1998
Single pensioner	7	14	15
Single non-pensioner adult	4	8	14
Couple with no children	26	26	29
Couple with dependent children only	38	31	23
Couple with non-dependent children	10	8	6
Lone parent	2	5	9
Other households	12	10	6

Source: Social Trends 31 (Office for National Statistics 2001)

Declining marriage rates, increased divorce rates and changing fertility patterns

Since the mid-1970s the proportion of men and women who are marrying has been declining and the proportion cohabiting has been increasing. Thus in 1970 there were almost 390 000 marriages, by 1999 there were less than half this number (179 000). The government estimates that in 1996 there were just over a million cohabiting couples in England and Wales. This was expected to double by 2021. Divorce has also become much more common, in part due to changes in legislation in 1969 and 1984. Of those who married in the late 1980s, one in six women had separated within the first five years.

Fertility patterns have changed sharply since the 1960s and have been crucial in shaping changes in the labour market. The sale of the oral contraceptive pill, which began in 1961, was particularly important. Better contraception does not necessarily mean lower fertility, although it should mean less unwanted fertility. Birth rates have sharply fallen; by 1998 there were 59 live births per 1000 women of childbearing age, compared to 91 per thousand women in 1961. Birth is also now later in a woman's life. The mean age of childbirth rose from 26.2 years in 1971 to 29 in 1999. The number of women giving birth when aged between 30 and 34 has been rising, as is the number of childless women (nearly one in four of women born in 1974 are projected to be childless).

Ethnicity and race

Britain is a multicultural and multiracial society. Its diversity is present even within the so-called 'white' part of the population; it is estimated that 10 per cent of the population can trace their ancestry back to Ireland (Mason, 1995). There are some 300 000 Jews in Britain, many originating from Jewish refugees who came to the UK towards the end of the nineteenth century and in the 1930s. There are also large communities of Italians, Greeks and Turks in various parts of the country.

Members of non-white ethnic minority groups were present in the United Kingdom in small numbers throughout the period of the British Empire. However, their numbers increased dramatically after the Second World War before being curtailed by legislation passed in the 1960s and 1970s. Some 4 million people (one in every fifteen) are from a non-white minority ethnic group (*see* Table 7.3). In general, ethnic minority groups tend to have a younger age structure than the white population (this is particularly true of Bangladeshis and Pakistanis). Geographically there is a high concentration of ethnic minorities in certain areas: one in four people in London are from an ethnic minority, compared with one in 50 people in the South West, Wales and Scotland. Cities such as Leicester, Bradford and Coventry have large ethnic minority populations.

Table 7.3
Resident population by ethnic group in Great Britain 1999–2000

	No. of people (thousands)	%
White	53 082	93.2
All non-white ethnic minority groups	3 832	6.7
Black Caribbean	504	0.9
Black African	374	0.7
Black Other	124	0.2
Mixed	184	0.3
Indian	942	1.7
Pakistani	671	1.2
Bangladeshi	257	0.5
Chinese	133	0.2
Other	644	1.1
All	54 927	100

Source: Labour Force Survey (Office for National Statistics)

Unemployment rates are typically at least twice as high for ethnic minority groups as for white people (in 1999, the overall rate was 13 per cent for the former and 6 per cent for the latter). Among the young rates are particularly high; a government report in 1995 found that 62 per cent of black men, aged 16 to 24, in London, were out of work. There is also, for male workers from ethnic minorities, a particular concentration in the service sector; 60 per cent of men work in this sector, but for groups like Bangladeshi men, 91 per cent do so.

Geographical distribution

Britain has a high level of regional diversity. Income is significantly higher in the South East and lower in the north. In 1998–99 average gross weekly household income in London and the South East was almost one and a half times that of households income in the North East. While these overall regional comparisons give a broad picture, they also mask considerable variability within regions; some of the poorest areas in Britain are to be found in the heart of London. Of the 20 000 people in the United Kingdom who were known in 1999 to be infected with the HIV virus, more than half were residents of London (only 95 were in Northern Ireland).

Britain is a highly urbanised society. By 1991 almost 90 per cent of the population were living in urban areas, the largest of these being Greater London, with a resident population of 6.4 million (in the EU, London is second only to Brussels in terms of density of population).

Migration: an international labour market?

Migration flows influence the size, growth and profile of the population. Since 1983 there has been net migration into the United Kingdom; in 1998 there was a net inflow of 178 000 migrants.

Recently migration to the UK has increased. This rise appears to be largely driven by economic forces, reflecting economic globalisation, greater labour mobility within the EU and increased political instability around the world (Glover et al., 2001). There is considerable support for the view that migrants create new businesses and jobs, fill labour market shortages and reduce inflationary pressures. With no net migration, the population aged 16–65 is forecast to fall by two million in the next 25 years, while the population aged over 65 would rise by more than three million. The migration of skilled workers, for example doctors or nurses, might have a negative impact on the development of the poorer countries they come from.

Britain has a tradition of granting protection to those in need, and has certain obligations under the 1951 United Nations Convention, and the 1967 Protocol, relating to the status of refugees. These provide that refugees lawfully resident should enjoy treatment at least as favourable as that accorded to the indigenous population. The number of people seeking asylum varies considerably from year to year; 46 000 people claimed asylum in 1998. The greatest number of applicants in 1998 was from the Federal Republic of Yugoslavia.

Nationals of the European Economic Area (EU plus Norway, Iceland and Liechtenstein) have the right to reside in Britain provided they are working or able to support themselves financially. Some 117 000 UK nationals were living in Germany (1997) on this basis. In the post-war era there has always been substantial, two-way, Irish migration.

Exercise 7.1 **The consequences of demographic change**

List five possible consequences of the changes in the structure of the population and the composition of families for the personnel policies of an organisation known to you.

☐ Income, taxes and wealth

Income and wealth are central to any discussion of poverty or social inequality. For some inequality is a key issue. The philosopher John Rawls argued that 'All social primary goods – liberty and opportunity, income and wealth, and the bases of self-respect – are to be distributed equally unless an unequal distribution of any or all of these goods is to the advantage of the least favoured' (1971). To the political thinker R.H. Tawney, 'it is the mark of the civilised society to aim at eliminating such inequalities as have their source, not in individual differences, but in society's organisation'. One former prime minister, Margaret Thatcher, welcomed inequality: 'It's our job to glory in inequality, and see that talent and abilities are given vent and expression.' She believed that the rich were performing a public service by getting richer still as their prosperity would trickle down to the poor. In the words of the economist J.K. Galbraith, if one feeds a horse enough oats, some will pass through to feed the sparrows.

This section examines changes in the pattern and distribution of incomes. Income measures flows of money, which usually comes from wages or salaries or from state benefits like the state pension. Wealth is about the ownership of assets, including money saved, property and investments. Together, income and wealth determine how much money people have, which in turn is crucial to their standard and style of living.

Earnings

For most households the main source of income is income from employment (wages or salaries). In 2000 the average gross wage for full-time employees was £21 000 (for men the average was about £23 000; for women it was £16 000). The differential between the earnings of men and women has narrowed over the past 20 years, though women still earn significantly less than men. In 2000 women's weekly earnings were only 74 per cent of men's, but as even those women working full time tend not to work as many hours as men, the gap for hourly earnings is narrower than the gap measured by weekly or annual earnings, with women's earnings at 82 per cent of men's.

Earnings also vary across occupations, geographically and by age. Men and women in the managerial group earned the highest levels in 2000. In the hotel and restaurant sector, a low-paid sector, three-quarters of employees were on wage rates less than £6 an hour in Spring 2000, compared to a quarter in the economy as a whole (a third earned less than £4 an hour – compared to 6 per cent in the economy as a whole). Earnings in London, at £29 000, were 25 per cent higher than the national average; in the North East of England they were around 15 per cent lower than the national average.

Taxes

Taxation is as old as the organisation of society. In 1086 one of the main purposes of the Domesday Book was to register the country's landed wealth and thus determine the revenues due to the king. Taxes on income were first raised by the government of Pitt in the 1790s to finance the Napoleonic Wars.

The income tax regime for 2001–02 had three different rates. Taxable income of up to £1880 is charged at 10 per cent. Income above this level but below £29 400 is charged at 22 per cent, and income above this level is charged at 40 per cent. It is a mildly progressive system. The Inland Revenue estimates that in 2000–01 over half the adult population (28 million) paid income tax. Of these, roughly a tenth (2.7 million) paid tax only at the lower rate and the same number are higher rate tax payers.

Households also pay indirect taxes through their spending. Indirect taxes include value added tax (VAT) and customs and excise duties. These are included in the prices of consumer goods and services. These taxes are highly regressive as lower income households proportionally spend more on goods, while high income households devote a large proportion of their income to investments.

Income distribution

Until the 1980s the post-war years saw a gradual narrowing of income inequality. The 1980s and 1990s sharply reversed these trends. One authoritative study (Machin, 1996) found that wage inequality is greater now than it was a century ago. Among western countries, the UK stands out for the speed at which inequality grew. The Rowntree Inquiry into Income and Wealth found that 'the poorest 20–30% of the population failed to benefit from economic growth'. The nearer the top an income group lies, the faster its income has risen. Between 1981 and 1989, whereas average (median) income rose by 27 per cent, income for the top 10 per cent of earners rose by 38 per cent; for the bottom 10 per cent incomes rose by only 7 per cent. Lone parents, those of pensionable age and some ethnic minorities are particularly likely to have low incomes.

The Labour government, in its first three years of office, made little progress in reducing inequality. Poverty – defined as an income below 60 per cent of average earnings – affected ten million people in 2000. A third of single parents were in this category, as were 60 per cent of the Pakistani and Bangladeshi community (compared to 16 per cent of white families). A national minimum wage was introduced in 1999, which affected 1.3 million workers, but its relatively modest level meant that its impact on income inequality was limited. The adult rate (23 years old or more) rose to £4.10 in October 2001 and to £4.20 in October 2002. The development rate (for those aged 18 to 22) will rise to £3.60 in October 2002.

Will Hutton (1995: 193) has powerfully illustrated income inequality by using an analogy based on the height of people in an imaginary parade of Britain's working population (also known as the Gini coefficient). If, he suggests, the population were divided according to income, and if income were made equivalent to height and the population then marched past for an hour, it would take a full 37 minutes before the first adult of average height was seen. For the first fifteen minutes there would be a parade of dwarves. Fifty-seven minutes would have passed before we saw people of twice average height. Giants of 90 feet or more would appear in the last few seconds, with the last one or two literally miles high.

Wealth

Wealth refers to the stock of riches accrued by an individual, the ownership of assets. These riches may be held as cash or invested in a house, pension, life assurance, share holdings or other valuable items. Wealth is considerably less evenly distributed than income. It is estimated that the most wealthy 1 per cent of individuals own between a fifth and a quarter of all 'marketable wealth' (wealth that can be sold). In contrast, the bottom 50 per cent of the population have 6 per cent of total wealth. If the value of housing is omitted the distribution is even more skewed (*see* Table 7.4). In contrast, half of all households in 1998–99 reported having less than £1500 in savings, with 28 per cent reporting no savings at all. In contrast, many UK banks are now particularly keen to target what they call the 'mass affluent', that is those with investable wealth of £50 000 or more.

Table 7.4
Distribution of wealth

Marketable wealth less value of dwellings % of wealth owned by	1976	1991	1998
Most wealthy 1%	29	29	26
Most wealthy 5%	47	51	50
Most wealthy 10%	57	64	65
Most wealthy 25%	73	80	86
Most wealthy 50%	88	93	95

Source: *Social Trends 31* (Office for National Statistics 2001)

Health at work and well-being

It has been argued that reducing inequalities in health would significantly reduce the number of premature deaths (Mitchell *et al.*, 2000). Health in affluent societies seems to be less influenced by people's absolute standard of living than by their standard relative to others in society. Once the majority of the population is above some basic subsistence, then increasing standards of material comfort make less and less difference to health. What affects health most is the distribution of resources within each society (Wilkinson, 1994). Dr Wilkinson calculates that if income inequality in Britain were reduced to continental levels we could expect average life expectancy to rise by two years.

There are long-established links between health and the workplace. In 1898 Dr Thomas Legge was appointed the first Medical Inspector of Factories and Workshops. In that year 1287 cases of lead poisoning were notified. Since 1975 the Health and Safety Executive (HSE) has been responsible for health in the workplace. Injuries and work-related illnesses are debilitating and costly. The HSE estimate the total cost to society of work accidents and work-related illness at some £8 to 9 billion at 1990 prices. The WERS survey (Cully *et al.*, 1999) found that 61 per cent of workplaces had seen one or more employees suffer a serious injury or work-related illness in the past year. Most common of all was stress, reported in 30 per cent of workplaces. While some stress is a normal feature of everyone's working lives, high levels of prolonged stress can give rise to one of the following symptoms:

☐ tension and anxiety;

☐ excessive alcohol, tobacco and alcohol misuse;

☐ sleep problems;

☐ reduced job satisfaction;

☐ high blood pressure;

☐ eating disorders and digestive problems;

☐ forgetfulness;

☐ increased absenteeism.

While much of the media focus has been on stress as experienced by senior executives, stress levels tend to be highest among employees in the lowest echelons of an organisation. The causes of this stress may be many and varied, but typically include poor job design, difficult working relationships, lack of communication, work overload, time pressures and business reorganisation. These occupational pressures will heighten the stress that individuals experience as a consequence of their home or personal lives.

Exercise 7.2 A health awareness audit

Employers can do a lot to help improve the health and fitness of their staff. Whether their organisation is part of a large multinational or a recently established small business there are a number of steps that can be taken to increase health awareness. The following list sets out some of the measures available to employers. Read through the list and tick those steps which have been taken by an organisation known to you. What steps could be taken to improve the organisation's performance?

1 Use offices to put across health information and distribute information to staff about healthy living.
2 Publish articles in the company newsletter or magazine promoting health consciousness.
3 Provide smoke-free offices and other work areas.
4 Provide a healthy choice of food in staff canteens.
5 Introduce training and education programmes for employees in exercise, nutrition and stress management.
6 Provide more opportunities for staff to take exercise.
7 Arrange for staff to have a general medical and fitness testing including blood pressure monitoring and cholesterol testing.
8 Adopt practical, company-wide policies on smoking, nutrition, exercise, alcohol and stress management.
9 Take steps to encourage regular eye sight testing, dental check-ups, hearing examinations and screening for breast and cervical cancer.
10 Establish an Employee Assistance Programme (EAP) to provide confidential counselling, advice and welfare support for staff experiencing high levels of stress or other work and non-work related problems.

Productivity is rising and material wealth is growing. But often this is not always translating into more happiness or greater well-being. Some commentators write of a 'paradox of prosperity' in which the economic fortunes of the many are decoupled from consumer confidence and quality of life (Henley, 1999). High living standards do not always mean a high quality of life; the chief medical officer estimates that one in twenty-eight men and one in twelve women are on anti-depressants.

☐ Social class and mobility

The concept of social class has been central to social analysis in the UK for over 150 years. In 1848 one of the more radical thinkers, Karl Marx, argued that 'we find almost everywhere a complicated arrangement of society into various orders, a manifold gradation of social rank'. Despite the endurance of the concept, the meaning of the term and its implications for the structure of society are hotly contested.

Earlier attempts to define social class focused on the jobs and the labour market position of different groups in society. The social class of individuals reflected their position within the jobs hierarchy of companies or the pattern of market relationships between large and small organisations. For Marx, advanced capitalism had three key classes. The 'bourgeoisie' (the upper class) were able to use their position in order to exploit the poorer labouring 'proletariat' (the working class). Between these groups lay the petty bourgeoisie of shopkeepers and managers. Marx used this analysis of class differences to explain the historical and political changes which had given rise to a highly unequal distribution of wealth and income in Victorian Britain.

One of the most influential efforts to map and measure class differences has been the Registrar-General's classification of socio-economic groups. First used in 1911 and revised since then, this classification system places people into categories according to the occupation of the head of their household. The occupational structure of Britain changed considerably in the twentieth century. In 1900 the vast majority of Britons were elementary schooled proletarians; by 1970 the employed were equally divided between white and blue collar jobs. By 2000 the balance had been decisively tipped to form a white collar majority. In 2001 a new measure will be used, the National Statistics Socio-Economic Classification (NS-SEC). Table 7.5 outlines the new categories, some examples and the percentage of the working population said to be within them.

The new classification is not completely hierarchical, but has a significant element of this. It attempts to measure social mobility (movement between the different groups) in terms of class rather than income because income is only one dimension of social position. One could enjoy upward mobility without necessarily enjoying greater income. As well as income, the occupational categories are measured according to other 'labour market situation', economic security and prospects of economic advancement (status of job); and 'work situation', (level of control, authority and autonomy at work).

Table 7.5
The National Statistics Socio-Economic Classification

1 Higher managerial and professional occupations (**11%**)

   1.1 Large employers and higher managerial occupations, e.g. employers of more than 25 staff

   1.2 Higher professional occupations, e.g. doctors, lawyers

2 Lower managerial and professional occupations (**23.5%**), e.g. teachers, junior managers, social workers

3 Intermediate occupations (**14%**), e.g. Constables, firefighters

4 Small employers and own account workers (**9.9%**), e.g. non-professionals who employ fewer than 25 employees

5 Lower supervisory and technical occupations (**9.8%**), e.g. train drivers

6 Semi-routine occupations (**18.6%**), e.g. call centre workers, shop assistants

7 Routine occupations (**12.7%**), Drivers, cleaners

8 Never worked and long-term unemployed

Source: Office for National Statistics, 2001 (cited in Aldridge, 2001)

Some argue that these categories do not capture important social changes. For example, Adonis and Pollard (1998) have written of the emergence of a new, highly prosperous, largely private sector employed 'superclass' within the middle class who are not adequately represented in these categories. Furthermore, there are difficulties in classifying the social class of many people. Women who have never had a job (e.g. because they were child-rearing) or some economically inactive men are excluded from many analyses.

While there is significant social mobility in Britain, the association between class origins and class destinations is stronger; most working class sons have working class fathers. The same is true of the middle classes. Those who do move 'up' or 'down' tend to move one or two deciles up the income distribution but not, in general, much more. Since 1979–81 social mobility appears to have declined for men, but improved for women (Aldridge, 2001). Evidence suggests that higher rates of social mobility are associated with lower income inequalities; countries like Sweden have far higher rates of social mobility.

Exercise 7.3 Identify five measures that would increase social mobility in Britain. Give reasons as to why this would be a positive or a negative outcome.

☐ Summary and conclusion

In this chapter we have outlined a number of general trends in the structure of British society. Among the changes singled out for attention have been population growth and the shifting nature of demography, including increasing life expectancy in the UK, the demise of the traditional family unit, trends in migration and growing patterns of inequality in income and wealth.

These trends affect all of us in different ways as members of British society. They also have indirect implications for us as employees and managers. As people change the way in which they live their lives, policy makers within organisations are forced to respond. As in other areas of business practice, these policy makers have choices. They may decide to ignore the trends and continue to use policies that have worked well in the past. Alternatively, they may act on an ad hoc basis as general trends become evident when individual employees present the organisation with specific problems. However, it is our belief that more proactive managers and organisations will ensure that they are aware of these general and emerging trends so that they are in a position to think out the implications for their personnel policies before they emerge. By anticipating the possible future direction of these changes and being aware of different explanations of their causes, managers and employees should be better prepared to deal with their consequences.

☐ Useful Websites

Cabinet Office Women's Unit
 www.womens-unit.gov.uk

Institute of Fiscal Studies; the leading independent think-tank on tax and income issues
 www.ifs.org.uk

National Statistics
 www.statistics.gov.uk

Performance and Innovation Unit at the Cabinet Office
 www.cabinet-office.gov.uk/innovation

Social Exclusion Unit
 www.cabinet–office.gov.uk/seu/

08 The political context

Chapter

☐ Introduction

A country's political system is concerned with the exercise of power. Although some people find politics and politicking distasteful, most see institutionalised political processes as necessary and preferable to anarchy or war. By setting down ways in which decisions should be made in a framework of laws, rules and conventions, conflicts of opinion are consequently handled in more predictable and manageable ways.

☐ Focus and scope

This chapter explores a number of contemporary issues relating to the operation of Britain's political system. These issues are, to varying degrees, matters of concern for both employers and other interest groups within society (voters, employees, trade unions and pressure groups).
 The three contemporary issues selected are:

☐ the extent to which Britain can be said to be a representative democracy;

☐ the significance for Britain of membership of the European Union;

☐ the nature of the law-making processes within Britain.

These issues are interrelated. Decision making (including law making) in a representative democracy is expected, in theory, to reflect the interests of citizens in that society. As we shall see, however, the concept of 'representativeness' is not easy to define.
 Furthermore, the British political system is now locked into that of the European Union. Membership of the Union affects both political decision making and law making. Consequently, there can be tensions about the policies advocated and pursued. Questions can arise as to whether such laws and policies are in the interests of the British people as a whole or just particular segments of society. It is also frequently argued that the institutions of the European Union are not fully democratic and so cannot fully reflect the interests of European citizens.

Learning objectives

Once you have read through this chapter and completed the associated exercises, you should be able to:

☐ understand the concept of representative democracy;

☐ understand the significance of Britain's membership of the European Union;

☐ understand the processes used for law making by the European Union and the British Parliament and the extent to which these might be influenced by employers', consumers' and employees' organisations;

☐ understand the impact of political activity on private, public or voluntary sector organisations;

☐ advise on how employers might lobby within the political system.

☐ The context of the political system

Of course, a political system does not exist in a vacuum. It operates in an economy, which will influence it and which will have its own balance of power between employers, on the one hand, and employees and trade unions on the other. It operates in a society and so will be influenced by developing social attitudes. The political system is also affected by the legal system, which can determine the legality of certain political actions.

Of course, influence does not flow in one direction. Those operating in the political system, in their turn, invariably seek to influence the economy, society and the legal system. This reciprocal interplay of relationships can be seen in various ways.

In the economy, government policy may be affected by multinational companies. For example, Nissan, the car manufacturer, negotiated favourable investment incentives to locate its manufacturing base and entry into the European Union market in Britain. Government, on the other hand, can try to influence the behaviour of employers – either through law or taxation or through the advocacy of policies. In the mid-1980s, for example, the Conservative government, to promote a free labour market, successfully encouraged many employers to rescind industry-wide collective bargaining and to relate pay either to the business's economic performance or that of individual employees.

In terms of society, reciprocal influence is often quite complex. For example, as we shall see in Chapter 10, the enhancement of women's status in society derives from a number of factors. On the one hand, some women have challenged (through direct action and political campaigning) their subservient position – by demanding the right to vote, the right to equal pay and the right not to be discriminated against on grounds of sex, marital status and pregnancy. Legislation was eventually enacted to achieve certain standards of equal treatment. This legislation, in its turn, generated further demands for action to eradicate entrenched discriminatory practices by employers and within society at large.

Finally, in terms of the legal system, legislation is enacted by Parliament. This statute law frequently reflects the views and ideology of the predominant political party. In the 1980s, the Conservative governments introduced a rolling programme of legislation to curb trade union power and to limit the definition of lawful industrial action. In turn, the legal system, through the courts, can affect the actions of politicians by determining the legality of certain actions by government ministers or certain pieces of legislation. For example, in 1994, the House of Lords, under judicial review, ruled that the qualifying periods necessary for employees to invoke unfair dismissal complaints were contrary to European Union law.

The areas of contemporary debate

Three areas of contemporary debate concerning the British political system have been selected for examination. These are:

1 *The nature of representative democracy* – Britain's status as a liberal democracy; securing constitutional rights; the structure of government and the separation of powers; devolution; the values and policies of the main political parties; the role of pressure groups; and reforming the political system.

2 *Britain's membership of the European Union* – perceptions of the European Union; the philosophy underpinning social legislation; principal institutions of the EU; processes for implementing EU law.

3 *Making statute law in Parliament.*

☐ Britain's status as a liberal democracy

To consider this, it is necessary to explore the nature of 'liberal democracy', and examine it in comparison with other political systems. It is possible to categorise these systems in different ways. In this chapter, we use the model shown in Fig 8.1.

Figure 8.1
Political systems

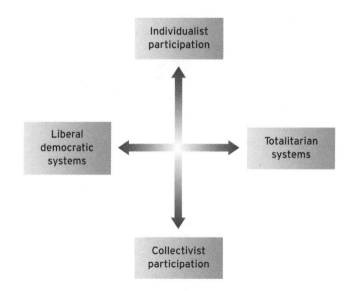

This links two broad characteristics:

☐ the fundamental ideological perspective embodied in the political system (on an axis ranging from 'liberal democratic' to 'totalitarian');
☐ the predominant form of participation by citizens (on the 'individualist'/ 'collectivist' axis).

The extremities of each axis refer to theoretical 'ideal types'. Political systems are unlikely to conform precisely to such 'pure forms'. Using this model, however, we should be able to plot the location of a country's political system by examining the extent to which it measures up to the characteristics set out below.

It should also be possible, broadly, to compare one country's political system with that of another and identify any shifts that may take place within any one country – that is, is a particular political culture becoming less 'collectivist'? Is it tending to adopt more 'totalitarian' measures?

Each of these axes will be considered in turn.

Liberal democratic societies

Liberal democratic societies are pluralist – in accepting the expression of various opinions – and they acknowledge a range of rights and duties for both the governors and the governed. The rights can be categorised as human rights, social rights, economic rights and political rights.

Human rights

These include the following basic rights (*see also* Fig 8.2):

☐ Freedom of thought, conscience and religion; and the right, individually and collectively, to practise such beliefs (provided this does not interfere with the freedom of others in a democratic society).
☐ Freedom of peaceful assembly and freedom of association with other people to join together in organisations (e.g. political pressure groups, political parties and trade unions).
☐ Freedom from arbitrary arrest; and access to effective judicial remedies to enforce all rights.

Political rights

Issues of economic, social and political policy are debated and opinions are sought from the electorate; and pressure groups are able to organise and influence the political process.

The electorate is widely drawn and the right to vote is not limited on grounds of, for example, property ownership, educational qualifications or sex. Political leaders are elected in individual secret ballots, free from intimidation. More than one political party competes for power and it is expected that opposing parties may replace governing parties from time to time.

Political power is spread across a number of different bodies. This may include the devolution of some power to local and/or regional government. There are safeguards to prevent the abuse of power (e.g. an independent judiciary, committees of inquiry, and the existence of investigatory agencies, like 'Ombudsmen').

Economic rights

These generally comprise a right to work and to job security; a right not to be conscripted into forced labour; a right to fair remuneration for work performed; a right to 'just conditions' at work; and also, adequate social security benefit protection (e.g. pensions, sickness, unemployment and disability). Furthermore, there should be effective judicial remedies to deal with complaints about infringement of these economic and employment-related rights.

Social rights

These include basic provisions for all citizens, equally, in respect of education, healthcare and accommodation. Furthermore, there is the right not to be discriminated against on such grounds as 'sex, race, colour, language, religion, political or other opinion, national or social origin, association with a national minority, property, birth or other status' (European Convention for the Protection of Human Rights 1950, Article 14).

Duties

It is generally acknowledged in liberal democratic societies that such rights should coexist with duties and obligations that, on the one hand, citizens owe to each other and to society in general and, on the other hand, the government owes to citizens. Some of the principal duties are:

☐ *Compliance with 'the rule of law'*. Members of society are expected to obey laws passed by democratically elected legislatures and adjudicated by an independent judiciary. They are likewise expected to cooperate with enforcing agencies, like the police service.

☐ *Restrictions on the exercise of rights*. Rights like freedom of thought, belief, speech, association and assembly may be qualified in various ways. The European Convention on Human Rights 1950, for example, refers to restrictions that 'are necessary in a democratic society in the interests of national security or public safety, for the prevention of disorder or crime, for the protection of health or morals or for the protection of the rights and freedoms of others' (Article 11).

☐ *Non-discriminatory speech and behaviour*. A further example of restricted rights can arise in respect of freedom of speech. This can be limited if it is to result in, for example, unfair discrimination and racist behaviour.

Totalitarian societies

At the other end of this axis (Figure 8.1) are totalitarian societies. Countries which have been described this way include the former Soviet Union, Nazi Germany, Fascist Italy and, currently, the People's Republic of China, Iran and Iraq. The characteristics of such political systems are:

☐ The society is committed to one overriding secular ideology or religious ideal – usually embodied in an all-powerful authoritarian leader (e.g. Stalin, Hitler, Mussolini, Mao Tse Tung, Ayatollah Khomeni and Saddam Hussein).

☐ A power élite exists that expects full compliance by the population to the ideology or religious belief. Dissent and critical questioning are not permitted. Citizens are required to follow the will of their political masters. Education, literature, the arts, the professions are likely to be subordinated to the ideology or religious dogma.

☐ Enforcement of the power élite's ideology is carried out by the police, armed forces and other agents of the government. The techniques used to ensure compliance can include a secret police force, surveillance of the population, the torture and murder of dissenters, and imprisonment in concentration camps.

☐ Commitment to the ideology or religious belief is reinforced by identifying an external enemy who must be mobilised against and destroyed (e.g. the United States of America has been demonised by Iran). Often, an enemy is also identified as disruptive or seditious within the particular society (e.g. the Jews in Nazi Germany).

☐ Any alternative focus of loyalty – e.g. non-approved religious organisations, trade unions, opposition political groups – is either suppressed or subverted. For example, in the former Soviet Union, trade unions became an administrative arm of the Communist power élite. They did not engage in free collective bargaining and the right to strike was deemed unnecessary.

☐ The right to vote freely in elections does not exist. If elections take place, they will be restricted in various ways. For example, voters may be physically intimidated; they may be required to ask for a separate ballot paper to oppose the governing party; or their choice may be restricted to rival candidates of the governing party.

The other axis in Fig 8.1 refers to participation within political systems – that is, the extent to which 'individual' as against 'collective' participation is actively encouraged or discouraged.

Individualist participation

Under a 'pure' individualist approach to participation, engagement in the political process will be as an individual citizen (e.g. by voting periodically in an election). Any collective involvement – through pressure groups – is likely to be minimal or non-existent.

The economic system in such a society will also perceive the individual as of paramount consideration as either consumer or worker. Individuals are expected to pursue their own economic well-being and ownership of private property is widely dispersed. Collective expressions of economic concern (e.g. in consumer groups and trade unions) will be of minimal significance.

As for the notion of 'society', its existence is denied. Margaret Thatcher exemplified this by stating that: 'There is no such thing as society. There are individual men and women and there are families' (quoted in Wedderburn, 1991: 209). This attitude reinforces the atomisation that is evident in the political and economic arenas.

Figure 8.2
The Human Rights
Act 1998

This legislation incorporates the European Convention on Human Rights and Fundamental Freedoms into the law of the United Kingdom. The Convention, drafted largely by British lawyers, was adopted by member countries of the Council of Europe in 1950. It was a response to the abuse of rights experienced in Europe under Nazism and Fascism. (The Council of Europe pre-dates the creation of what eventually became the European Union by some seven years. It remains a separate body).

From October 2000, all legislation and common law in Britain must be interpreted as far as possible to be compatible with the Convention. Also, certain bodies must behave, in all their decision making, in conformity with the Convention. These are *public authorities* (e.g. local authorities, hospital trusts, the civil service) and *courts and tribunals*. In addition, certain private organisations, which are carrying out public functions, must act in conformity with the Convention when carrying out public functions.

Some of the principal Convention rights (which have been incorporated) are:

Article 2:   The right to life

Article 3:   Prohibition of torture

Article 4:   Prohibition of slavery and forced labour

Article 5:   Right to liberty and security

Article 6:   Right to a fair trial

Article 7:   No punishment without law

Article 8:   Right to respect for private and family life

Article 9:   Freedom of thought, conscience and religion

Article 10: Freedom of expression

Article 11: Freedom of assembly and association

Article 12: Right to marry

Article 14: Prohibition of discrimination

The rights most likely to be involved in employment relations issues are Articles 8–11. These are also *qualified rights*. They are not absolute rights. So, a balance has often to be struck between one individual's right and the rights of other people. For example, the freedom of expression is limited lawfully if it is to prevent slander, libel; or racist abuse.

The prohibition of discrimination (Article 14) is very wide-ranging. It states that '*The enjoyment of the rights and freedoms set forth in this Convention shall be secured without discrimination on any ground such as sex, race, colour, language, religion, political or other opinion, national or social origin, association with a national minority, property, birth or other status.*' However, this is not a free-standing right. It can only be invoked where a person is alleging some infringement of another Convention right.

Convention rights are enforceable in the courts of the United Kingdom.

Collectivist participation

The 'pure' collectivist approach sees individual participation within the political system as minimal – possibly restricted to voting occasionally in elections. Most major political and economic decisions are likely to be taken by organisations, groups and committees established within the political process.

In liberal democracies, these may comprise the principal pressure groups (like employers' associations, consumer groups and trade unions). In totalitarian regimes, the collective groups will represent supporters of the power élite at particular levels. For example, in the former Soviet Union, such groups would involve Communist Party committees, Communist-run trade unions, and committees of local and regional Communist officials.

In the social arena, collective action is seen as the normal and legitimate form of participation. In liberal democracies, this may be reflected in the establishment of community groups, for example. In totalitarian societies, collective social activities may be designed to reinforce commitment to the political or religious 'ideal'.

(You may choose to undertake the following two exercises now or, alternatively, keep them in mind as you read the remainder of the chapter and complete them at the end.)

Exercise 8.1 **Liberal democratic rights**

Consider the extent to which you think Britain provides human, political, economic and social rights for particular social groups. Draw up a matrix similar to that shown in Table 8.1. Mark with a tick, a cross or, if you think the existence of the right is unclear, with a question mark.

Table 8.1

	Human rights	Political rights	Economic rights	Social rights
Men				
Women				
Pregnant workers				
Ethnic minorities				
The elderly				
The unemployed				
Full-timers				
Part-timers				
Trade unionists				
Homosexuals				
Religious groups				
Disabled persons				

Exercise 8.2   Political systems

Using your general knowledge, indicate on the model in Fig 8.1, by inserting the appropriate number, the location of the following political systems:

1 Britain in the 1980s and early 1990s.
2 Britain in 2001.
3 the United States of America.
4 the former Soviet Union (1917-91).
5 the People's Republic of China (1949 to date).
6 Nazi Germany (1933-45).
7 the Federal Republic of Germany (1949 to date).
8 Japan (since 1945).
9 Sweden.
10 Iran.
11 Iraq.

☐ Securing constitutional rights in a liberal democracy

As we have already seen, liberal democracies are characterised by the provision of various fundamental rights. Such societies can of course be differentiated both by the ways in which they secure these rights and by the nature of their democratic procedures. One important distinction is between those countries that have a written constitution (like the United States, France and Germany) and those that do not (like the United Kingdom).

This distinction can be important in respect of employment policies and law. For example, in France, Germany and Belgium, written constitutional provisions guarantee a core of fundamental rights and freedoms. These include the right to engage in collective bargaining and the right to form and join a trade union. Such rights come within the jurisdiction of a constitutional court. This can provide a protection against any government that seeks to infringe them.

In Britain, on the other hand, there is no written constitution. Each democratic right, enacted into statute law by one particular Parliament, can, technically, be repealed by a subsequent Parliament. For example, the wide protections for trade unions (when organising industrial action) that had developed over the past century were considerably eroded by successive Parliaments during the 1980s. With no constitutional 'right to strike' and no constitutional court, the actions of the government could be neither modified nor constrained.

Having said this, however, British governments do not have unfettered power. There are four possible constraints that can be brought to bear: the Human Rights Act 1998, the European Union, international conventions and the process of judicial review by British courts.

Britain, as a result of its membership of the European Union (since 1973) is obliged to conform to *European law*, whether it concerns competition, the free movement of labour, health and safety or employment protection for individual workers.

For example, as far as individual employees are concerned, the EU has set certain principles which should govern their treatment. Most significant in effect is the principle of equal treatment on grounds of sex. This principle has had a profound effect on British legislation and case law. It ensured that during the 1980s and 1990s these protections were guaranteed despite the Conservative governments' pursuit of free market deregulation. The principle of equal value was introduced into equal pay law; pregnant workers' rights were enacted; and access to unfair dismissal and redundancy rights could not be restricted to disadvantage part-timers, who were predominantly female, because this was held to constitute indirect sex discrimination.

International conventions, on the other hand, have provided a much weaker safeguard of rights. The most significant in respect of employment are those adopted by the International Labour Organisation (ILO). During the 1980s, Britain was found to have infringed certain of these conventions (Ewing, 1994) – for example, the removal of school teachers' collective bargaining rights. The weakness of these international standards lies not so much in the conventions themselves but in two related issues. First, governments can voluntarily subscribe to the conventions; and, second, the ILO has no enforcement mechanisms. It can investigate non-compliance and publish a report, but action beyond that is not possible.

In the European Union, by contrast, the Commission can initiate infringement proceedings against a government which fails to comply with EU law. In 1992 Britain was taken before the European Court of Justice for failing to implement fully the Directives on Collective Redundancies and on Transfers of Undertakings, and British law was changed as a consequence.

A final form of potential constraint on a British government is the *process of judicial review*, whereby the legality of certain policy decisions can be challenged – initially in the High Court.

A significant example of this process in the employment arena was the action of the House of Lords in declaring qualifying thresholds for unfair dismissal compensation and redundancy pay to be contrary to EU equal treatment law because of their differential impact upon women as against men. One writer has commented that this case has given Britain 'the taste of a constitutional court' (Szyszczak, 1995).

Direct and effective guarantees of civil rights, therefore, whether in employment or in society at large, are dependent on the attitudes and decisions of each successive British Parliament (apart from those specifically deriving from the European Union). They will be affected by the results of elections and political decision making.

The separation of powers

In liberal democracies there are four principal elements of government: the head of state; the executive; the legislature; and the judiciary.

The head of state oversees the political system and can be guardian of the constitution. The powers of the head of state can vary significantly from being largely ceremonial – either as a monarch or elected president – to being an important political actor, as in the elected presidencies of the United States and France.

The executive is charged with the formulation and implementation of policy. In Britain, Ireland and Germany, for example, the head of government is the Prime

Minister who appoints a Cabinet of ministers to carry out executive responsibilities. Normally, the Prime Minister is the leader of the largest party in the country's Parliament. In recent political analyses of Britain, it has been commented that the Prime Minister has at his or her disposal considerable patronage in terms of Cabinet and other political appointments. The Prime Minister is also central to the management of government business. Possible limitations on this power may arise when a political party is part of a coalition and, therefore, daily negotiations are required to determine policies and legislative priorities.

A further constraint can arise when the governing party has a slim parliamentary majority. Given that political parties are themselves 'coalitions of interests', well-organised minority groups of MPs can influence the direction of specific policies – for example, the 'Euro-sceptic' MPs in the Major government.

The legislature or parliament discusses, scrutinises and amends legislative proposals. Such measures are normally approved by a simple majority vote. In Britain, it has been usual in most of the post-war period for one political party, either the Conservatives or Labour, to form a majority government. Other western democracies have been characterised by coalition governments for most of their recent histories, e.g. Ireland and Germany.

The judiciary is responsible for interpreting law and adjudication on cases. Judges may have to decide whether particular laws are themselves lawful as well as whether they have been breached in specific circumstances.

The separation of powers in Britain

While the concept of 'separation of powers' is useful as a theoretical tool to analyse political systems, in practice the constitutions of most western democracies allow for overlap between these four functions. This can be considered by looking at the operation of certain parts of the British political system: the sovereign, the government, the official opposition, the House of Commons and the House of Lords.

The sovereign

Since the constitutional settlement of 1688, the powers of the monarch as head of state have been limited. Although the Queen keeps in touch with political developments, not least through weekly meetings with the Prime Minister, her only remaining substantial constitutional role is the formal granting of a dissolution of Parliament prior to a general election at the request of the Prime Minister. Technically, she gives the Royal Assent to any legislation passed by Parliament. However, the role of the monarch today is largely ceremonial and confined to providing a unifying figurehead for the different nations and cultures that comprise the United Kingdom.

The government

Most post-war British governments have been drawn from the party with a majority of seats in the House of Commons. If no party has a majority, then a coalition government can be formed. Alternatively, the largest party might govern as a minority government – making *ad hoc* deals with other parties to ensure that government business and legislation is approved – for example, the Wilson government in 1974 and the Callaghan government between 1977 and 1978.

A government comprises about 100 individuals. Most are drawn from the House of Commons. However, some are members of the House of Lords. These Secretaries of State, ministers and parliamentary secretaries are responsible for developing policy and tactics. The most senior members are the 20 or so members of the Cabinet, who include the Prime Minister, the Chancellor of the Exchequer, the Foreign Secretary and the Home Secretary. These senior ministers collectively discuss and agree policy – frequently in various Cabinet committees of a few members – before it is proposed to Parliament.

The Prime Minister appoints members of the Cabinet and presides over it. To this extent he or she exercises considerable control and patronage and can influence the political perspective of the government. He or she is the main public presenter of government policy and gives a government its identity. Prime Ministers usually take a special interest in economic, foreign and defence policy issues. Although the Cabinet is expected to operate on the basis of collective responsibility – by publicly accepting agreed courses of action – disagreements, sometimes quite strong ones, can exist between ministers from different wings of the governing political party.

In Britain, therefore, the separation of the executive and the legislature is blurred. Members of government are clearly part of the legislature and responsible for the organisation and control of its business. Individual MPs have little freedom of action. They are 'whipped' to support their political party. They are only likely to succeed in promoting a Private Member's Bill – e.g. in the early campaigns for disability discrimination legislation – if the government is supportive.

The official opposition

The official opposition comprises MPs from the second largest party in the House of Commons. The main roles of the opposition are to challenge the government, to make it explain its policies, to check that it undertakes the task of government properly and, of course, to defeat it in Parliament or at a general election. The Leader of the Opposition presides over a 'Shadow Cabinet' of MPs, each of whom is charged with following the work and department of a government Cabinet minister.

The House of Commons

There are 659 Members of Parliament representing different geographical constituencies. The House of Commons performs five major functions:

☐ *Law making*. Most of the proposed legislation is submitted by the government of the day (*see* below).

☐ *Controlling finance*. Before the government can raise or spend money, it must have the permission of the Commons. Each year, usually in March, the Chancellor of the Exchequer presents a Budget Statement and Public Expenditure Estimates which cover both taxes and spending together.

☐ *Scrutinising public administration.* This takes two forms. First, the government is required to explain its actions to the Public Accounts Committee and to Select Committees. Second, questions are asked of specific ministers and debates are organised, particularly by the opposition, on issues of concern.

☐ *Examining European Union proposals.* The Select Committee on European Legislation examines proposed European laws before they are passed into UK law.

☐ *Protecting the individual.* Petitions to the House of Commons from members of the public, together with the lobbying of pressure groups and opinions as monitored in the media, help ensure that Parliament is informed of the electorate's concerns. Furthermore, MPs may take up issues on behalf of individual constituents with the relevant minister.

The House of Lords

In 1999, the House of Lords was partially reformed. Hereditary peers (who numbered some 800) were disqualified from sitting. An exception was made, through a political compromise, for 90 to be elected by their fellows and also for the holders of the posts of Earl Marshall and Lord Great Chamberlain to remain. The composition of the House of Lords is 590 life peers, 92 hereditary peers and 26 archbishops and bishops – a total of 708 (March 2002). The political composition is recorded as 220 Conservative, 199 Labour, 65 Liberal Democrat, 180 cross-benchers (i.e. those who have no political allegiance). In April 2001, the first group of so-called 'people's peers' was announced. (These were people of some experience who had been nominated individually and had their nominations scrutinised by the House of Lords Appointments Commission.)

This chamber has limited legislative powers – and no power in relation to financial measures. It can vote against entire Bills and specific clauses. This is only a delaying power, however, because the House of Commons can subsequently return measures to the Lords and require them to be approved. Effectively then, the executive branch of government has considerable indirect control over this House.

The second important function of the Lords is to act in its judicial capacity as the supreme court – except in relation to European Union law where appeal is possible to the European Court of Justice. Law lords, who can sit as legislators in the House of Lords, can also adjudicate on appeals from lower courts.

Devolution

A significant constitutional development at the end of the twentieth century was the creation of various forms of devolved government in Scotland, Northern Ireland and Wales. The Labour Party committed itself explicitly in its 1997 general election manifesto to referenda on the creation of a Parliament in Scotland with law-making powers and an Assembly in Wales with more limited powers. As to Northern Ireland, the party supported the proposals of the then

Conservative government which included the creation of a new devolved legislative body. All these forms of devolved government required legislation in the Westminster Parliament to set them up. By the year 2000, progress had been achieved on all.

A further area of constitutional change related to regional government within England. In its 1997 election manifesto, the Labour Party acknowledged that 'demand for directly elected regional government so varies across England that it would be wrong to impose a uniform system'. It added that 'in time we will introduce legislation to allow the people, region by region, to decide in a referendum whether they want directly elected regional government'. Action to establish this level of local government has occurred, to date, only in the greater London area (see later). However, in certain regions (for example, the North-east of England), there is vocal support for some form of devolved regional government.

This interest in devolution within a nation state is evidence of a constitutional 'double shift' that is taking place within parts of western Europe. On the one hand, certain power is being centralised at European Union level, balanced by some efforts to maintain the principle of subsidiarity (see later section on the European Union). On the other hand, there is some popular demand for decentralisation to regional governments (and in some cases full independence). The latter movement is a reflection of the diversity of cultural traditions, languages and economic concerns that can exist in one nation state. Recognition of this devolutionary trend is evident in various policy action across Europe. In some instances, tensions (occasionally violent ones) erupt. Some examples are as follows:

☐ The constitution of Spain provides for formal regional assemblies. So, for example, partial autonomy was granted to Catalonia and Catalan was recognised as the primary language. Spain, for a number of years, has experienced a sustained terrorist campaign from those campaigning for independence for Basques.

☐ Germany is a federal republic with devolved political power to Lander (or states) like Baden-Wurtenburg, Bavaria, Saxony etc. West Germany was established in 1949 on this basis and, in 1990, the former East Germany was incorporated into this constitutional framework.

☐ Belgium became a federal state in the recent postwar period, granting a degree of autonomy (under the current 1994 constitution) to Flemish-speaking Flanders, French-speaking Wallonia and bilingual Brussels. In the 1960s there had been serious and violent social tensions between the two communities (exacerbated by the economic decline of Wallonia and the developing prosperity of Flanders).

Devolution in the United Kingdom

Scotland

The *Scottish Parliament*, which sits in Edinburgh, was first elected in May 1999 for a period of four years. It comprises 129 members. The composition is: Labour 56 Members of the Scottish Parliament (MSPs); Scottish National Party 35; Conservatives 18; Liberal Democrats 17; and 3 others. The election system differs from that for the Westminster Parliament. Whilst 73 MSPs were elected to represent local constituencies on a 'first past the post' basis, the remaining 56 were elected from regional lists. This was designed to link the number of votes each party received to their number of MSPs. So each voter had two votes.

There is only one chamber in the Scottish Parliament (unlike the Westminster Parliament). The *Scottish Executive* is drawn from the party, or coalition of parties, that has a majority of seats and can form a government. In 1999, the Executive comprises the Labour and Liberal Democrat parties. It is composed of the First Minister (nominated by the Parliament and appointed by the Queen), various other Ministers, Law Officers and various junior ministers.

The role of the Parliament is to legislate. Most proposals for legislation come from the Executive. Much of the scrutiny of proposed legislation takes place in specialist committees. These comprise between 5 and 15 MSPs (who are selected having regard to the political balance within the Parliament).

The key areas of devolved responsibility given to the Scottish Parliament are: economic development; transport; housing; education; health; agriculture; and environmental issues. The main areas still reserved to the Westminster Parliament are: constitutional matters; foreign and defence policy; European integration; most economic policy; and social security.

Northern Ireland

The *Northern Ireland Assembly* was provided for under the Good Friday Agreement 1998. This was achieved as a result of multi-party negotiations. A referendum (held in May 1998) resulted in a majority voting in favour of the Agreement and appropriate legislation was passed by the British Parliament. In June 1998, 108 members of the Assembly were elected under proportional representation (the single transferable vote system) within 18 constituencies. The composition of the Assembly is as follows: Ulster Unionist Party, 28 members; Social Democratic and Labour Party, 24; Democratic Unionist Party, 20; Sinn Fein, 18; Alliance Party, 6; and 12 other drawn from six smaller parties.

The Assembly has full legislative and executive authority in respect of the following matters: agriculture; economic development; education; the environment; finance; and health and social services. The Assembly elected David Trimble (UUP) as First Minister and Seamus Mallon (SDLP) as Deputy First Minister.

Wales

The *Welsh Assembly* was first elected in May 1999 for a four-year period. There are 60 Assembly Members: 40 were elected through the 'first past the post' system (one from each constituency); and 20 were elected on a regional basis under proportional representation (the additional member system).

The Assembly elects the First Minister. It has powers (more limited than those of the Scottish Parliament) across various areas: for example, agriculture, culture, economic development, the environment, education, housing, industry, tourism, transport.

Among the decisions that the Assembly can take are the following:

☐   to set the content of the National Curriculum in Wales;

☐   provide financial assistance to businesses;

☐   administer European structural funds;

☐   implement policies on care in the community.

London

The *Greater London Authority (GLA)* was established in 2000, after a referendum decision (in 1999) by the 8 million electorate in London. It covers the geographic area of the 32 London boroughs. The Authority comprises a directly elected full-time Mayor of London and an Assembly, elected separately under a system of proportional representation. The first Mayor to be elected was Ken Livingstone. The next elections are scheduled for May 2004.

The main responsibilities of the GLA are transport, policing, fire and emergency planning, economic development, planning, culture, environment and health.

There is a separation of powers between the Mayor (who has an executive role making decisions on behalf of the GLA) and the Assembly. The Mayor sets plans and policies for London covering transport, buildings and land use, economic development and regeneration, culture and environmental issues. He also sets the annual budget for the Greater London Authority, the Metropolitan Police, Transport for London, the London Development Agency and the London Fire Brigade. These budgets totalled £3.7 billion in the financial year 2001–2. The Mayor also has an Advisory Cabinet, comprising a wide range of interests and communities, which meets monthly in public to advise him on policies.

The Assembly scrutinises the activities of the Mayor and questions his decisions. It can also investigate other issues important to Londoners, publish its findings and recommendations and make proposals to the Mayor. The assembly is responsible for appointing GLA staff.

Political parties

Consensus on aspects of the political system?

Before we look at political parties in detail, it is important to note that there is broad acceptance, by the major parties in the political system, of certain basic tenets about that system:

☐   the sovereignty of Parliament;

☐   the preservation of parliamentary democracy;

☐   support for maintaining a constitutional monarchy;

☐   commitment to the rule of law;

☐   individual rights and responsibilities;

☐   the promotion of economic prosperity;

☐   the protection of British interests in the world.

What usually divides political parties are differences of opinion over the meaning of these basic tenets and whether particular policies conform to them. Even then, as we will see, within political parties there can also be differences of view. The successful implementation of specific policies can depend on the extent to which particular views are dominant within the governing party. Alternatively, they can be the result of strongly articulated public opinion which influences politicians.

So, for example, debates have been initiated and continue on the following:

☐ *Constitutional issues.* There are two aspects to this. The first involves the reconciliation of our Treaty obligations to the European Union (ceding some sovereignty) with the long-standing commitment to the sovereignty of Britain's national Parliament. The second concerns the nature and extent of devolution within the United Kingdom and the extent to which such developments erode the sovereignty of the Westminster Parliament and fragment the United Kingdom as a nation state. These constitutional shifts within the UK reflect trends that are taking place elsewhere in Europe towards two apparently opposed directions. towards greater policy coordination and concerted action at EU level, on the one hand; and towards great regionalism and, possibly, regional autonomy, on the other (*see* earlier section on devolution).

☐ *Constitutional monarchy.* The character and role of the monarchy does, periodically and in a fragmented way, surface as an issue in political discussion. Individual members of parliament may express republican sympathies. However, no political party is committed as a matter of policy to such radical constitutional change. The nature of political debate, generally, centres on such issues as the role and funding of the more peripheral members of the royal family; and occasionally, on the behaviour of certain family members. Public opinion is, generally, supportive of the monarchy. However, in a regular *Guardian*/ICM poll, the newspaper has reported that republicanism has attracted increased support from 13 per cent of those surveyed (1987) to 34 per cent (April 2001) Forty-eight per cent of people between the ages of 18 and 24 say that the country would be better off without the royal family (reported in the *Guardian*, 25 April 2001).

☐ *Parliamentary democracy.* Ways of preserving and reforming parliamentary democracy invariably divide politicians on party lines. The debates arise on broadly four levels. First, as indicated earlier, the issues of Britain's membership of the European Union and the question of parliamentary sovereignty infuse much of the discussions. Secondly, the balance of legislative power between the elected House of Commons and the appointed House of Lords invariably raises strong political passions. This arose particularly after the election, in 1997, of a Labour government with a substantial Commons majority. The Lords (under the former composition) still retained a marked political bias towards the Conservative Party. Thirdly, the nature and fairness of the electoral system are questioned. This, invariably, focuses on the issue of proportional representation for elections to the Westminster Parliament (given that such systems exist for elections to the Scottish Parliament, the Northern Ireland Assembly, the Welsh Assembly and for the European Parliament). Fourthly, on a more practical level, the 'nuts and bolts' of the Parliamentary machine are invariably raised in debate. These include such matters as freedom of information; the power of select committees to scrutinise the government of the day effectively; regulation of the outside interests of members of parliament; the hours the Commons sits; and the extent to which women are nominated as prospective parliamentary candidates of all major political parties.

Parties as coalitions

Different views about social policy, economic management and the nature of political and legal systems are, clearly, characteristic of liberal democracies. Political parties, both within Parliament and at constituency level, are organised expressions of political opinions and values. It is, however, a mistake to see such parties as homogeneous. They are not monolithic bodies with all activists, members and supporters having identical views. Each party is a coalition of different interests. It is better, therefore, to think of them as broad-based organisations encompassing a range of different values and attitudes rather than narrowly focused structures.

To illustrate this, we will look at the two political parties which have formed post-war governments in the UK: the Conservative Party and the Labour Party. Because they are coalitions, shifts take place over time and different groups – with different ideological values, views and interests – have predominated at different times in influencing the policy directions of the parties concerned (both in government and opposition).

Reciprocal influences

Also, it is important to remember that the experiences and policies of the two major political parties can affect each other. So, for example, many the fundamental radical reforms introduced by the Labour Government (1945–51) (e.g. the creation of the National Health Service, the development of the 'welfare state', a commitment to full employment and the nationalisation of certain basic industries) were broadly accepted by successive Conservative governments (1951–64). Likewise, certain policies of the Thatcher/Major Conservative governments (1979–97) were broadly adopted by the Labour government (elected in 1997). These included, for example, a commitment to the promotion of business interests within a free market, the adoption (in specific circumstances) of privatisation, the eradication of individual dependency on social security benefits, and the preservation of legislation constraining industrial action.

The reasons why political parties influence each other in this way is, in part, simple recognition that electoral success can only be achieved by responding to changing public opinion. All oppositions wish to become governments; and governments do not want to lose power. Importantly, parties – if they are to survive as credible political actors – need to respond to those fundamental shifts and developments that are taking place in, for example, the world and UK economy, in public opinion, in social trends, in technological change, in European and world politics, in defence strategies and in international environmental considerations.

The old divide: left vs. right?

For most of the twentieth century, politics has been characterised by a left–right divide. Put in broad terms, this reflected deep-rooted ideological disagreements about fundamental policy issues: economic ownership, the management of the economy, the distributive purposes of taxation policy, state responsibility for social welfare provision, even the structure and democratic character of the political system itself.

It also reflected different political values and aspirations. So, those on the left were concerned with reducing inequality and the pursuit of social justice. Those on the right accepted inequality as a part of the natural order. Collective action (through, for example, trade unions, pressure groups or other social groupings) was seen by those on the left as a way of challenging and redressing the imbalance of political and economic power within society (nationally and locally). Whilst this left–right division still has some residual importance, it is no longer adequate for considering contemporary politics, where there is some evidence of degrees of consensus on certain of these fundamental issues.

A new way?

A new model is proposed for considering the present-day Labour and Conservative parties (*see* Fig 8.3). In present-day politics, it is suggested that there are two fundamental divisions about broad policy which cut across both the Labour and Conservative parties: the *constitutional dimension*; and the *economic and social policy dimension*. These are represented on the two axes in the diagram.

It is important to remember that this diagram (Fig 8.3) does not represent the actual position of either party. It is a theoretical tool designed to help analyse the nature of support for certain general policy objectives by members of the particular party, its MPs, activists and voters. It is hoped that it will help achieve the following objectives:

☐ identify those areas where there appears to be *broad agreement* between the parties on direction and policy fundamentals
☐ highlight *the dominant group(s)* within each respective party;
☐ highlight the nature of *internal divisions* within each party;
☐ identify the *historical shifts* that have taken place.

Constitutional dimension: The vertical axis concerns the location of political and economic power. So, those people who tend towards the '*national power*' end of the spectrum will be opponents of Britain's membership of the Euro. They will support a limited role for the EU (as a free trade area only) and a curtailment of the jurisdiction of the European Court of Justice. Some advocate the country's withdrawal from the European Union. They are strong advocates of the sovereignty of the British Parliament and the maintenance of the UK as a nation state. If Britain is to remain as a member of the EU, it should be one of a number of sovereign nation states, benefiting from considerable subsidiarity.

Those who tend to the '*European/international power*' end of the axis are committed to supranational action through both the European Union and

Fig 8.3
Framework of
contemporary
political policies

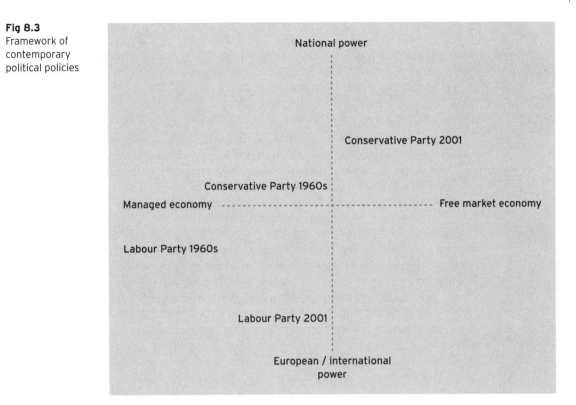

other international bodies (for example, the United Nations and the International Labour Organisation). This collaborative action is seen as necessary to promote, among other objectives, economic interests, social policy objectives, and ethical standards in the labour market. It is accepted that the 'pooling' of national sovereignty is essential in a global economy.

Economic and social policy dimension: Those who tend to the left-hand side of the horizontal axis, '*the managed economy*', have a commitment to several related policy strands:

☐ the management of the economy, through the imposition of taxation and the public expenditure, to promote full employment; to encourage new industries; to maintain competitiveness in global markets;

☐ a commitment to active, constructive membership of the European Union;

☐ the adoption, after debate within the EU, of its economic and social policy objectives;

☐ the creation of a regulatory framework to monitor the operation of certain sectors (particularly, those privatised, former public sector bodies, on the railways, in telecommunications and in the public utilities);

☐ a commitment to the preservation and public funding of certain 'public goods' (i.e. state health and social care systems, and a state school education);

- ❑ ensuring the provision of minimum social welfare entitlements which, wherever possible, encourage entry into the labour market by recipients and avoid dependency (for example, the Working Families' Tax Credit);

- ❑ an acceptance that this minimum state provision might be supplemented by individual private insurance and savings schemes;

- ❑ the regulation of the employment relationship through the enactment of specific (in many cases, minimum) employment standards and terms and conditions of employment (for example, the national minimum wage);

- ❑ the creation of a collaborative relationship of social partnership between government, employers and trade unions.

The right side of the horizontal axis, *'the free market market economy'*, attracts those who emphasise the following broad policy approaches.

- ❑ the creation of an economy where government plays a minimal role in economic management and promotes free trade through the EU (if the country is to remain a member state) as well as internationally;

- ❑ ensuring that businesses are not 'burdened' by regulation whether imposed for economic, social policy or environmental protection reasons;

- ❑ the creation of an unregulated labour market where employers are not constrained from offering employment and or deterred from job creation by 'excessive' employment protection legislation;

- ❑ emphasis on individuals providing for their own and their family's social welfare requirements (for example, private medical care, private pensions, private education, insurance against redundancies, schemes for private long-term residential care in old age).

We will now look at each party in turn and consider how it 'fits' into the model. It is our view that there are areas of overlap between the parties in terms of the policy objectives. Consequently, some individual politicians find cross-party political allies and may, in some instances, change political parties because they do not like the prevailing direction in their former party. (Examples of this can be found in a number of Conservative MPs or peers who have joined the Labour or Liberal parties in recent year.)

The Conservative Party

Moving from managed economy to regulated free market?

The Conservative Party has over the past thirty years, experienced marked shifts in its fundamental ideology as well as individual policies. On both economic management and social policy objectives, there have been some considerable, often vitriolic, intraparty tensions.

At government level (1951–64), particularly under the premiership of Harold Macmillan, the party was strongly located towards the left of the economic and social policy axis. There was a belief at the top of the party that some state intervention was desirable to reduce the social inequities resulting from the market system and a commitment to the achievement and maintenance of full employment. This intervention may be in the form of social security benefits; financial assistance to industry to ensure job creation and protection; and protective employment laws to promote minimum standards of fair treatment. Underlying this action was the view that if government fails to redress the imbalance against the economically disadvantaged, social conflicts and tensions may develop. So, many adherents to this view saw trade unions playing a legitimate and constructive role helping resolve workplace discontent. Indeed, collaboration between unions and employers in discussing economic objectives can be seen as a valuable tool for intervention in government economic policy.

Underpinning this general policy direction was the concept of 'one nation conservatism' (originally propounded by the nineteenth century Conservative prime minister, Benjamin Disraeli as a means of minimising class conflict and promoting social cohesion at a time when the urban working class was expanding and working men were organising into trade unions and given the vote).

Gradually, however, during the late 1960s and early 1970s, the Party began to shift, as more free market ideas took root. Margaret Thatcher as leader (1975–90) was the principal advocate of such policies. Supporters of these views see wide differences in wealth, income and social status in a market economy as natural and desirable. They believe that these differences should not be 'distorted' by government action. Such differences provide motivation for people to work hard and to better themselves. Government intervention is seen as rarely working in any effective way. For example, subsidies to declining industries merely delay the final day of reckoning; and social security benefits for the unemployed provide an incentive for people to stay at home and avoid work. Employment protection legislation is seen as a distortion of the free labour market. So, the tension between the Thatcher/Major governments and the European Union arose, in part, from a fundamental ideological conflict – particularly in respect of social policy objectives, where the EU promoted a wide range of social and employment protection legislation (*see* later section).

People tending to this end of the axis also saw individual interests as predominant and as the driving force for policy making. Collective social representation (for example, in trade unions) was seen as of marginal importance. In its extreme form, this tendency was expressed by Margaret Thatcher as prime minister (quoting the Austrian free market economist, Friedrich Hayek) when she said that 'there is no such thing as society, only individuals and families'.

The constitutional issue

The Conservative Party has, for well over a century, been the strong advocate of a unified United Kingdom. (Indeed, its official title is the Conservative and Unionist Party.) Furthermore, it is strongly monarchist. It has historically been resistant to devolution within the UK and fought in the 1997 election against the establishment of a Scottish Parliament and a Welsh Assembly. However, current party policy now accepts the devolved constitutional arrangements for Scotland, Wales and Northern Ireland.

The one constitutional issue which has caused deep rifts within the Party for the past thirty years has been Britain's membership of the European Union. It was a Conservative Prime Minister, Edward Heath, who negotiated and eventually agreed the terms for Britain's membership (effective on 1 January 1973 under the provisions of the European Communities Act 1972). In pursuing the UK's membership, Heath was following initiatives of previous prime ministers: Harold Macmillan (Conservative, 1957–63) and Harold Wilson (Labour, 1964–70).

Within the Conservative Party, there have continued to be significant groups who were strongly opposed to EU membership. In the early 1970s, one group was *the traditional right*. This is the pre-Thatcherite, aristocratic wing of the party which places defence of hierarchy, deference to social superiors and tradition at the core of its opinions. It is committed to national sovereignty, national defence and strong government. It shows strong reservations or hostility to the European Union. Now, this group is comparatively small. Of more significance, over subsequent years, has been the *Thatcherite right* – as proponents of a free market in goods and services, national sovereignty to make decisions in Britain's own economic and political interest, freedom from 'burdensome' regulation. Ironically, it was the government of Margaret Thatcher that in 1987 agreed to the Single European Act, which promoted the establishment of a single market and steps to further integration (including the adoption of the mechanism of qualified majority voting).

The tensions within the Conservative Party on the 'European issue' have not abated over the past thirty years. Many of the fundamental issues do not appear to have been resolved. Some (probably a minority of Conservatives) wish to leave the European Union – and find more in common with the UK Independence Party. At the other end of the spectrum, another minority find more in common with the Labour Party's policy of 'constructive engagement' and membership of the Euro (subject to the achievement of certain economic conditions and a positive vote in a referendum).

However, the active majority within the Conservative Party wish to retain as much freedom of manoeuvre as possible within the EU and to renegotiate Britain's relationship in respect of, for example, the Common Agricultural Policy and the jurisdiction of the European Court of Justice. As far as membership of the Euro is concerned, this has been ruled out for the duration of a Parliament, but not for ever.

Labour Party

The Labour Party has, likewise, experienced some considerable changes in policy objectives and also deep political rifts within its organisation over the past thirty years.

What kind of managed economy?

Historically, the Labour Party has been committed to the concept of nationalisation of key industries, redistributive taxation, and programmes of public expenditure to fund education, health and social welfare programmes. The Labour government under prime minister Clement Attlee (1945–51) was a high point of many of these political objectives. The National Health Service was created in 1948, and various major industries were nationalised – principally, coal, electricity, gas, water, the railways (primarily for economic reasons rather than merely on ideology).

Over many of the subsequent years, a number of factors required a reappraisal by the Labour Party of many of these fundamental objectives:

☐ deep-seated problems in the British economy: for example, low levels of private sector investment; the weakness of the pound on the foreign exchange markets; poor competitiveness; inadequate training provision; restrictive working practices;

☐ public concern about the perceived inefficiency and unresponsiveness of large public sector organisations to 'customer' expectations;

☐ a growing public unwillingness to accept what were seen as 'excessive' levels of direct taxation;

☐ a developing acceptance that some private funding of social welfare provision was desirable.

Political debate has increasingly, since the late 1970s, focused on fiscal policy, the balance of public and private expenditure, the measures necessary to manage (particularly, wage) inflation and unemployment, the 'privatisation' of services previously provided through the public sector, and the responsiveness of service providers to users.

The policies of the Thatcher and Major Governments (1979–97) provided the catalyst for much of the Labour Party's reappraisal. Labour lost four elections to the Conservatives in this period. The nature of the reappraisal was difficult and very bitter. It was compounded by internal policy and personality battles in the late 1970s and early 1980s with members of the extreme left-wing Militant Tendency who had infiltrated the local party organisation in parts of the country. Effectively, serious reappraisal began with the election (in 1983) of Neil Kinnock as party leader and continued under the leadership of John Smith (1992–94). It accelerated under the leadership of Tony Blair from 1994 onwards.

In brief, the position of the Labour Party in respect of economic management has shifted (in principle, if not in every detail) closer to that of the Conservative Party. Among the policy measures now accepted are:

☐ no commitment to nationalisation;

☐ commitments to privatisation and 'public–private partnership' in certain circumstances;

☐ the promotion of economic stability, low inflation and personal prosperity;

☐ a commitment not to raise income tax rates and towards reducing this direct taxation;

☐ the promotion of employment, flexibility and employability;

☐ regulation of the utilities (gas, electricity, water), of certain essential services (telecommunications and railways) and of certain public services (health, education and social care);

☐ the promotion of quality as a public service objective;

☐ performance standards and targets for public service providers;

☐ eradication of dependency on social welfare;

☐ targeting public expenditure on those in specific need.

In contrast, a significant difference of emphasis between the two parties exists about the statutory regulation of terms and conditions of employment. Conservatives emphasise that these constitute burdensome regulation on employers (particularly, small organisations). The Labour Party sees such protective legislation as necessary to promote fairness in a rapidly changing economy and labour market (although it has shown some sensitivity to the arguments of employers). However, even here, some concensus has arisen in respect of the National Minimum Wage. Having fought against the principle in the 1997 election, the Conservative Party now accepts this principle (if not the specific rate).

The constitutional issue

On the European Union, the Labour Party has moved a considerable way in the past thirty years – having, like the Conservatives, also experienced divisions within the Party. In 1962, when the Conservative Prime Minister, Harold Macmillan, was negotiating Britain's first attempt at entry into the (then) European Economic Community, the Labour leader, Hugh Gaitskell, strongly opposed it. However, by 1967, the party was shifting its stance when a Labour Prime Minister, Harold Wilson, attempted to reopen negotiations on British entry in the EEC. However, there was still substantial opposition within the party among MPs and members. By the early 1970s, the party reaffirmed its opposition to the EEC.

When the Heath government eventually succeeded in negotiating terms, the Conservatives were supported by a significant minority of Labour MPs (against party policy). The issue remained one of conflict until the Labour Government under Prime Minister Harold Wilson (1974–76) held, in June 1975, a referendum on continued membership of the EEC. The Labour Government supported continued membership and won the referendum.

It was not until the late 1980s that the Labour Party and its allies in the Trades Union Congress adopted a more positive approach. Nowadays, the political issues for debate within the Labour Party are no longer about continued membership or not. They are about the operation, effectiveness and specific policies of the European Union and their implications for Britain. The policy has been described, by the Labour Government (1997), as one of 'constructive engagement'.

The other constitutional issue that the Labour Party has addressed is the devolution of power within the United Kingdom. In the late 1970s unsuccessful attempts were made to establish Scottish and Welsh Parliaments. The commitment in principle to provide for devolution was implemented in new legislation in the late 1990s (see earlier).

The role of pressure groups

In Fig 8.1 the nature of participation within political systems was outlined: individual and collective. In Britain, there are two principal forms of individual participation – voting in general, local and European elections and activity as a member of a political party.

In the post-war period, these forms of participation have been gradually seen as less significant forms of influence on political decision making, both in central and local government. For example, the turnout in general elections has dropped since 1950 by about 10 per cent. There are estimated to be 1 million eligible voters who do not register. In terms of political party membership, these stand at approximately 300 000 (Conservative), 330 000 (Labour) and 100 000 (Liberal Democratic Party).

By contrast, activity in pressure groups and political campaigns is buoyant. There are numerous pressure, or interest, groups, many of which are widely acknowledged as a legitimate and valuable part of democratic society. These can be differentiated in the following ways: in terms of whether their organisational structure is 'formal' or 'informal'; and whether their primary activity is 'lobbying' or 'political campaigning' (*see* Fig 8.4).

Groups that are *formal* tend strongly towards the *lobbying* end of the spectrum. They include broad-based interest groups like employers' organisations, (such as the Confederation of British Industry and the Chartered Institute of Personnel and Development), trade union organisations (such as UNISON and the Trade Union Congress – an association of some 60 individual trade unions) and professional bodies (such as the British Medical Association).

It is, of course, possible that from time to time such groups might additionally engage in political campaigning. This might be through published survey reports, publicity and/or public demonstrations. In the early 1980s, for example, when the trade union movement was generally excluded from any discussions with the Thatcher government, it used marches and demonstrations against unemployment and privatisation as vehicles to influence public attitudes.

Formal organisations can develop a strong institutional link with government. Between elections, they manage the flow of influence between society and the government of the day. They articulate policy demands and opinions.

Fig 8.4
Pressure groups

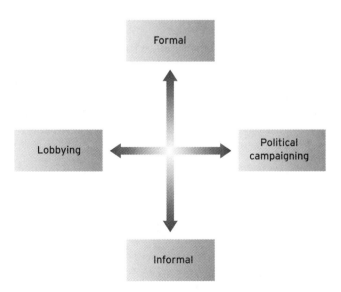

Some pressure groups (particularly those which are professional associations, like the British Medical Association) are reservoirs of considerable expertise that can make constructive contributions to the legislative and policy-making process. As a consequence, they receive much attention from senior civil servants and departmental ministers. Furthermore, there are quangos, such as the Equal Opportunities Commission and the Commission for Racial Equality, which have a statutory duty to put proposals for legislative reform to the appropriate Secretary of State.

There are also some formal organisations which are more specifically focused upon *political campaigning*. One such group is the *think tanks* which review economic, social and judicial policies and make recommendations. Normally, their aim is to influence the policies of either government or the opposition. During the 1980s, for example, the Adam Smith Institute and the Institute for Economic Affairs were particularly influential in promoting free market ideas and deregulation policies with the Thatcher governments. On the left of the political spectrum are organisations like the Fabian Society and Demos, which promote the welfare state and a social justice model of political policy.

There have been occasions, in recent years, when *ad hoc* organisations have been established to campaign against a specific issue. For example, protesters against various motorway extensions and bypasses (Twyford Down, the M11 extension, the Newbury bypass), using modern telecommunications, have developed sophisticated forms of physical obstruction to these works. Their objectives are twofold: to prevent the specific new roadworks and to raise public consciousness about the nature of transport policy. Such 'organisations' do not have the permanence of formal organisations, with premises and staff. However, in their activities, using the experience of previous campaigns, they are far from informal.

Furthermore, there are circumstances where existing formal groups create coalitions to push for particular policy changes – for example, in lobbying for disability discrimination legislation or improvements in overseas aid. Some groups involved see political lobbying as an ancilliary activity. For example, they may be a charity primarily, raising funds and promoting particular services and projects, e.g. Age Concern or Oxfam.

Finally, pressure can be exerted upon the political process in a generally informal, unorganised way – arising from various sources, i.e. letters to politicians and to the media, MPs' conversations with party activists and constituents, public opinion polls, newspaper editorials, etc. This amorphous concerted protest can arise from well-publicised and shocking criminal activities – for example where members of the public have been victims of knife attacks and the government is expected to implement new, tougher policy measures.

Pressure groups operate principally at the following access points in the political system:

☐ within the media to generate public support for a particular policy, as campaigning groups did to achieve disability discrimination legislation;

☐ within political parties to mould policy objectives;

☐ lobbying government departments in favour of particular economic or social policy or legislation – for example, employers' organisations trying to influence government tax and interest rate policies which affect economic activity and employment levels;

☐ responding to consultation opportunities provided by government through Green and White Papers (the case study towards the end of this chapter illustrates the opportunities available);

☐ pressing for specific legislative provisions and amendments as a Bill proceeds through Parliament;

☐ monitoring the implementation of legislation and administrative action and seeking consequential amendments as in the work of environmental groups such as Greenpeace and Friends of the Earth.

Exercise 8.3   Using pressure groups

Has your employer ever lobbied government - directly or through an employers' organisation - about any particular issue? If so, what was it? How did the organisation go about putting over its point of view?

If you were a member of a pressure group, e.g. a consumer group, a political campaigning group or a trade union, how would you go about representing specific interests?

☐ Britain's membership of the European Union

The European Union (known, variously, in its history, as the European Community, the European Economic Community and, colloquially, the Common Market) was given this title in 1993. It was originally created by France, Germany, Italy, Belgium, the Netherlands and Luxembourg on 1 January 1958 under the Treaty of Rome 1957. It now comprises 15 member states covering a population of almost 350 million people and a labour force of 140 million.

The European Economic Agreement, which came into force on 1 January 1994, now extends the *single market* to certain non-EU states – namely Norway, Iceland and Liechtenstein. They are covered by a majority of EU law, including social legislation. The EU is likely to be enlarged in the next ten years (*see* Fig 8.5).

Figure 8.5
EU: Candidate countries for membership

In advanced accession talks
Cyprus, Czech Republic, Estonia, Hungary, Poland and Slovenia

These countries could be in membership by 2003.

Other countries
Bulgaria, Latvia, Lithuania, Malta, Romania, Slovakia

The enlargement process will extend the European Union to 27 member states, as opposed to the present 15 members (2002). The total population will rise from 376 million to some 481 million.

This section will explore various perceptions about the nature of the European Union, the philosophy underpinning social legislation, the principal institutions of the European Union and the processes for implementing European Union law.

Perceptions of the European Union

The concept of European 'union', developed under the Treaty of Rome, is founded on the principles of liberal democracy – the provision of basic rights and plurality of opinion (*see* the discussion relating to Fig 8.1). New members are expected to conform to these principles. This determines the fundamental character of the present-day European Union. In terms of specific economic and social purposes, there are three broad 'schools of thought'. These perspectives are: the *single market* view, the *federalist* view, and the *integration* view.

The single market view

This view encompasses those who see the EU principally in economic terms – that is, as a single market of goods, services, labour and capital. The regulatory framework of law should be limited to that necessary to make this economic entity function effectively. Some members of the 'Euro-sceptic' right within the British Conservative Party generally accept this view.

The federalist view

The *federalist* view supports a European Union in which there are active and creative European political institutions and, counterbalancing these, independent nation states who constitute the membership of the Union. This perspective sees economic and social regulation throughout the Union as indissolubly linked. The issue which is often in contention, however, is the location of both decision-making and legislative authority.

In recent years, debate on this issue has revolved around the issue of *subsidiarity*. This concept relates to the question of which is the most appropriate level for legal regulation and decision making within the Union – that is, should these functions operate at the level of the member state or at the European Union-wide level.

For example, individual employment rights and laws on competition and the free movement of labour have tended to be adopted at Union level and, ultimately, enforced through the European Court of Justice. By contrast, economic decisions on taxation and public expenditure are generally the responsibility of individual governments in member states. Furthermore, collective rights – for example, relating to trade union status and membership, collective bargaining and the conduct of industrial action – have generally been determined at the level of each member state. This position is gradually changing, however, as the Union develops measures on the 'collective' issue of consultation.

Political debate in Britain in the 1980s and 1990s has been strongly affected by tensions between 'federal' decision making and subsidiarity.

The integration view

This sees a long-term shift in sovereignty from the governments and parliaments of member states to European institutions. The Maastricht Treaty 1992 was formulated to provide impetus in this direction. For example, it created forums for cooperation on police, crime, immigration and defence matters. It established European citizenship.

Of particular fundamental significance, the Treaty enacted the Economic and Monetary Union (EMU). It refers to 'the irrevocable fixing of exchange rates leading to the introduction of a single currency, the ECU [named the Euro in 1995], and ... a single monetary policy and exchange-rate policy' (Article 3a). A main consequence of this will be the alignment of the economies of member states and the transfer of economic decision-making power from the member states to central European institutions.

Member states proposing to join the EMU have to achieve four economic policy objectives. These 'convergence criteria' are designed to ensure that all EMU members are performing similarly. For each member, they are as follows:

☐ *Inflation.* Its rate should be within 1.5 per cent of the three best performing countries.

☐ *Budget deficit.* This should not exceed 3 per cent of Gross Domestic Product.

☐ *Debt.* This should not exceed 60 per cent of Gross Domestic Product.

☐ *Interest rates (long-term).* These should be within 2 per cent of the average of the three countries with the lowest inflation.

The achievement by a member state of these economic objectives will also have social and political consequences. In France, in 1995, attempts to reduce the budget deficit by cutting public expenditure resulted in large demonstrations and prolonged strikes in opposition to the government.

European treaties

The European Union has evolved over the past 50 years or so. The constitutional basis for the EU is found in a range of treaties agreed by member states and ratified by each country's Parliament (in some cases after a referendum). These treaties set out what is sometimes described as 'Community competence' (i.e. those areas of policy making where it is entitled to act). They consequently draw boundaries between between the policy making responsibilities of the EU and of individual member states.

In the immediate period after World War II, France, Germany, Italy and the Benelux countries agreed on the creation of the *European Coal and Steel Community*. The treaty establishing it came into force in 1952. This limited cooperation was supplemented by a more wide-ranging economic collaboration provided for under the *Treaty of Rome 1957*. As a result of this, the European Economic Community (or 'Common Market' was created on 1 January 1958. A treaty creating the *European Atomic Energy Community* (Euratom) was also implemented on that date.

These founding treaties have been amended on various occasions. Some changes have been a result of new member states joining the European Community (or European Union as it came to be called after 1993). The six founding member states were joined by new countries as follows:

1973: United Kingdom, Ireland, Denmark
1981: Greece
1986: Spain, Portugal
1995: Austria, Finland, Sweden

There have also been some far-reaching reforms to the treaties resulting in substantial institutional changes and introducing new responsibilities for European institutions. These changes have arisen as a result of.

☐ the *Single European Act* (which came into force in July 1987);

☐ the *Treaty on European Union 1991* (the Maastricht Treaty) which came into force on 1 November 1993);

☐ the *Treaty of Amsterdam 1997* (which came into force on 1 May 1999);

☐ the *Treaty of Nice 2000* (expected to come into force in 2002).

We will look at some of the specific provisions of these treaties:

☐ *Treaty of Rome 1957*. This gave limited attention to social policy measures (apart from free-movement of workers and equal pay). It defined the European Community's objectives strongly in economic terms: 'the Community shall have as its task, by establishing a common market and progressively approximating the economic policies of the member states, to promote throughout the Community a harmonious development of economic activities, a continuous and balanced expansion, an increase in stability, an accelerated raising of the standard of living and closer relations between the states belonging to it'.

☐ *Single European Act 1987*. This was the first substantial revision of the Treaties and laid the constitutional basis for the creation of the single market which came into force on 1 January 1993. Border controls on the movement of goods were removed.

It introduced the concept of qualified majority voting (in specific policy-making areas) as a means of speeding-up decision making in the Council of Ministers.

The Act also gave a new impetus to social policy. There was concern among member states that unless working conditions were harmonised across the Community, given free mobility of capital in a single market, there would be relocation from high standard/high cost countries to those with inferior standards. This is known as *social dumping*. Also, one particular area of workplace legislation enhanced by this Act was health and safety.

It also promoted social dialogue between the social partners (principally, employers' organisations and trade unions).

□ *Treaty on European Union 1991*. This provided for the establishment of the European Union. It set the framework for the achievement of Economic and Monetary Union by 1999 and the adoption of a common currency (eventually called the Euro). It set the convergence criteria to be achieved by member states joining EMU (*see* Chapter 5). It also enhanced the role of the European Parliament in decision making.

In respect of social policy, it was agreed that, at the instigation of the then Conservative government, the United Kingdom should be able to opt out of various measures which the remaining (then eleven) member states agreed upon. This 'opt out' covered the European Works Council Directive 1994, the Parental Leave Directive 1996, Posted Workers Directive 1996, and the Part-time Workers Directive 1997. After the election of the Labour government in 1997 these directives were eventually extended to the UK.

□ *Treaty of Amsterdam 1997*. In the area of social policy, this authorises the Council of the European Union, acting unanimously, to take appropriate action to combat any discrimination based on sex, race, ethnic origin, religion of belief, disability, age or sexual orientation. Furthermore, the Treaty enacts the promotion of employment as a Community objective – to be implemented through a coordinated strategy. The Treaty reaffirmed that pay, the right to association (in trade unions) and the right to strike would still be excluded from EU decision making.

□ *Treaty of Nice 2000*. This was agreed by the European Council and signed two months later by member states on 26 February 2001. It is awaiting ratification by each individual country. This is due to be complete by 2002. The principal amendments relate to changes to the institutions of the EU (*see* next section); and to procedures for enlargement of the EU by taking new countries into membership (*see* Fig 8.5). Qualified majority voting was extended. However, the UK obtained the right to veto on tax and social security questions and certain aspects concerning the regulation of asylum-seekers. A Charter of Fundamental Rights was also adopted (*see* Fig 8.6).

Figure 8.6
The European Union's Charter of Fundamental Rights: Treaty of Nice 2000

This is a *political declaration*, adopted by the Council of Ministers in December 2000. It is *not legally enforceable*. However, it is expected to mould behaviour within the member states of the EU and the European Court of Justice may refer to it when considering cases.

The Charter is said to reaffirm various rights found in a number of sources affecting the operation of the European Union. These include:

□ The Treaty of the European Union

□ The Council of Europe's Convention on Human Rights and Fundamental Freedoms 1950

□ The European Community Charter of the Fundamental Social Rights of Workers

□ The Council of Europe's Social Charter 1996

□ The case law of the European Court of Justice

□ The case law of the European Court of Human Rights

□ International obligations

Figure 8.6
continued

The provisions of the Charter of Fundamental Rights are aimed at:

☐ the institutions and bodies of the European Union; and

☐ member states only when they are implementing the law of the European Union.

Among the key rights affirmed are the following:

☐ Prohibition of discrimination on various wide-ranging grounds (Article 21).

☐ Equality between men and women in all areas including employment, work and pay (Article 23)

☐ A guarantee in certain circumstances for workers and their representatives of information and consultation in good time (Article 27)

☐ The right of workers to negotiate and conclude collective agreements in accordance with European and national law (Article 28)

☐ The right of workers to defend their interests, including through strike action (Article 28)

☐ The right of workers to be protected against unjustified dismissal (Article 30)

☐ The right of every worker to have working conditions which respect his or her health, safety and dignity (Article 31)

☐ The right of every worker to a limitation on maximum working hours, to rest periods and to paid annual leave (Article 31)

☐ Restrictions on the employment of children and young people (Article 32)

☐ Protection from dismissal related to pregnancy (Article 33)

☐ The right of workers to paid maternity leave and to parental leave (Article 33)

And

☐ Everyone shall have the possibility of being advised and represented in court proceedings. Legal aid shall be made available to those who lack sufficient resources to ensure effective access to justice (Article 47).

The philosophy underpinning social legislation

Social policy in the European Union has developed since 1957. The original Treaty of Rome contained few social policy measures. Substantial Social Action Programmes (1972–80; and 1987 to date) have developed a considerable framework. During that time the emphasis on particular social policy measures has changed. Initially, the focus was on employment protection measures. Then, in the late 1980s health and safety became a further important issue. Since the mid-1990s, the issues of labour market flexibility, investment in education and training, and the promotion of employment have featured more strongly.

The philosophy of European social policy now comprises a number of important strands:

☐ *Improvements in working conditions and standards of living.* The promotion of these by member states is a commitment in the Treaty of Rome 1957.

☐ *Harmonisation.* This is an established treaty goal associated with the aim of economic convergence.

☐ *Equal treatment for men and women.* This is a fundamental principle of the Treaty which has been elaborated in a 1975 Directive (on equal pay) and a 1976 Directive (on equal treatment). It has radically influenced equal opportunities for women – particularly as a result of interpretations and rulings by the European Court of Justice.

☐ *Non-discrimination.* The Treaty of Amsterdam 1997 includes a provision relating to action to combat wider grounds on which discrimination may be based – race, ethnic origin, religion or belief, disability, age or sexual orientation. Measures on these have been incorporated into new directives which come into force between 2003 and 2006.

☐ *Specific protections for individual workers.* Examples of these are maternity rights, display screen equipment regulations, working time restrictions and protections during collect redundancies and transfers of undertakings.

☐ *Social partnership.* Both the employers' organisations and trade unions are consulted widely in the formulation of, for example, new directives (*see* ECOSOC below).

☐ *Employee participation.* Social partnership is elaborated further in employee participation measures. These include directives on information and disclosure in multinational companies (the European Works Council Directive 1994); on consultation with employee representatives in respect of health and safety, collective redundancies and transfers of undertakings. A directive on company-level information and consultation (for organisations with 50 or more employees) was adopted in 2002.

☐ *The promotion of employment.* The objective of achieving a high level of employment without undermining competitiveness has been incorporated into EU objectives by the Treaty of Amsterdam. With member states, the EU responsible for developing a coordinated strategy for employment.

☐ *Labour market flexibility.* This is encouraged by the EU. At the same time, measures have been introduced to assist workers in this flexible labour market: the Part-time Workers Directive 1997; and the Fixed Term Contract Workers Directive 1999.

Influences on social policy

Social policy is affected by four, often interlocking, contextual factors: the views of member states about the balance between supranational and national interests; different social and political philosophies between governments of member states and within the EU; different traditions of legal regulation; and differences of interests between employers and trade unions.

☐ *Supranational and national interests.* A fundamental tension exists within this supranational organisation about the extent to which national interests are acknowledged and accommodated and the extent to which they are subsumed under a 'European' approach.

☐ *Social and political philosophies.* European social policy aims to achieve harmonised employment protection. The political philosophy underpinning this approach – deriving from Social Democrat, Socialist and Christian Democrat traditions – is markedly at variance with the free market ideology adopted by Conservative governments in Britain during the 1980s and 1990s. Consequently, in debates on social protection, at that time, several issues were dominant: the extent to which employment protection measures were costly and impeded competitiveness; and the appropriateness of European-wide regulation as against an approach based on the principle of subsidiarity. This tension can surface publicly, from time to time, depending on the political complexions of governments in any of the member states.

☐ *Traditions of legal regulation.* Employment protection measures within the European Union are implemented across 15 member states which, of course, have different traditions of legal regulation. This can be an additional source of tension. The original six member states were more accustomed to a prescriptive and interventionist legal approach to employment relations. Britain, on the other hand, has a more voluntarist tradition based on either the exercise of the management prerogative or, if an employer agrees, free collective bargaining.

☐ *The interests of employers and trade unions.* Throughout employment relations within the European Union, there is also evidence of the usual differences of interest between employers and trade unions. These differences usually focus around three sets of issues:

1 *Economic considerations* – for example, the extent to which EU policy facilitates or impedes job creation; the extent to which unit labour costs are perceived to rise as a result of employment protection laws and are seen to reduce business efficiency; the extent to which employment laws can provide protection for vulnerable employees in non-union organisations.

2 *Balance of power considerations* – for example, the extent to which EU employment protection affects the right to manage and so curtails managers' freedom to make decisions; the extent to which employee interests are accommodated through employee participation, in corporate decision making.

3 *Predominant values* – for example, the extent to which equal treatment, job security etc. are promoted within an organisation's employee relations.

Social Chapter of the Treaty

Prior to 1997, there was a complex legal arrangement for making social policy legislation because of the 'opt-out' secured in 1991 at Maastricht by the Conservative Government. The Labour Government, elected in 1997, agreed to end the 'opt-out' on social policy. As a consequence, the UK is now committed to the social policy arrangements agreed under the Treaty of Amsterdam 1997. The social policy objectives draw on earlier charters outlined by member states. In 2000, under the Treaty of Nice, the Charter of Fundamental Rights was adopted (*see* Fig 8.6). This consolidated social policy objectives, drawn from various European Union sources, into one document.

The principal institutions of the European Union

Six principal institutions within the European Union will be considered: the Commission, the Council of Ministers, the European Parliament, the European Court of Justice, the Economic and Social Committee and the Committee of the Regions.

The governments of member states operate directly and regularly through the Council of Ministers and can, consequently, have considerable influence over policy making. Additionally, they are responsible for nominating people to join such bodies as the Commission and the European Court of Justice. Their influence in the nomination process can shift the political emphasis either towards greater federalism or towards a greater recognition of subsidiarity. By contrast, the only direct influence exerted by citizens of the European Union is through elections to the European Parliament.

Governments of member states, of course, can have differing views about the relative powers of these institutions, e.g. should more power be granted to the European Parliament? Should the jurisdiction of the European Court of Justice be curtailed?

The Commission

This is the *executive* body of the Union. Its principal functions are to propose measures for discussion by the Council; to secure the implementation of decisions; and to monitor implementation of the Treaties by member states. It comprises 20 members, representing the 15 member states. Larger member states, like Britain, have two commissioners. Commissioners are obliged to be independent of national governments and to act only in the interests of the European Union. Each commissioner is responsible for one or more of the 23 Directorates General. (That which deals with employment policy matters is the Directorate of Employment and Social Affairs.) The President of the Commission is appointed by agreement between member state governments. The entire Commission has to be approved by a vote in the European Parliament. It can be required to resign on bloc by a parliamentary vote of censure. The Commission has some 16 000 staff.

The Treaty of Nice 2000 has initiated some changes:

☐ From 2005, the Commission will comprise one person per member state.

☐ At a future date (once EU membership reaches 27 countries) a ceiling will be placed on the size of the Commission.

☐ The President of the Commission is to be nominated by member states on the basis of qualified majority voting and then approved by the European Parliament.

☐ The President of the Commission is granted increased powers: to decide the internal organisation of the Commission; to allocate responsibilities to Commissioners; to appoint vice-presidents; and to require a commissioner's resignation, subject to the Commission's approval.

The rationale for these changes is essentially twofold: to make the machinery of the Commission more efficient; and to provide a speaker and more effective process for tackling corruption or inefficiency.

The Council of the European Union

This is the *decision-making body* of the Union. It adopts measures proposed by the Commission for enactment by member states. The Council legislates. It decides some matters by unanimity and some by qualified majority voting. The Council comprises several levels. Principal among them are:

☐ *The European Council* which comprises heads of government of member states. Summit meetings are held twice a year to discuss major issues and decide broad policy. It provides political direction through the creation of tactical alliances and the negotiation of deals. Changes in the governments of member states as a result of general elections can have a profound effect on the political direction of the EU.

☐ *The Presidency*, which is held by each member state in turn for a period of six months. As President, the member state sets Council agendas and can determine to some extent, therefore, which Commission proposals are progressed and prioritised.

☐ *Council of Ministers*. This comprises appropriate government ministers from each member state. The minister varies according to the subject matter under discussion. For example, an appropriate British employment minister attends meetings to discuss the free movement of labour, health and safety, or employment rights.

☐ COREPER is the Committee of Permanent Representatives of each member state in Brussels, comprising senior diplomats. It acts as a national embassy to the EU and negotiates on the details of Commission proposals in preparation for Council of Ministers' meetings and for the European Council.

The Treaty of Nice 2000 has initiated some changes:

☐ The definition and calculation of qualified majority voting will be changed from 2005 – reweighting the system in favour of the larger member states.
☐ A slight increase in the number of issues (27 in total) that might be determined by QMV.

The European Parliament

This comprises 626 members directly elected within member states every five years. Representation is according to population size. Germany has 99 Members of the European Parliament (MEPs); and France, Italy and the United Kingdom have 87 MEPs each. The next elections will be held in June 2004. The election procedures are determined in each member state. In 1999, Britain adopted a form of proportional representation for the first time.

The Parliament has three broad sets of powers:

☐ *Legislative power*. Originally, under the Treaty of Rome 1957, the Parliament only had a consultative role. Nowadays, it has acquired more decision-making responsibility (*see* next section).

☐ *Budgetary powers*. The Parliament approves the EU budget each year. It can make amendments to the Commission's proposals and to the position taken by member states. However, on most politically significant issues the European Council has the final word. The Parliament also monitors expenditure to ensure that it is properly spent.

☐ *Supervision of the Commission and the European Council*: The Commission and its President, as outlined earlier, hold office subject to parliamentary approval and the work of the Commission is scrutinised. The President of the Parliament regularly liaises with the European Council.

The Treaty of Nice 2000 has initiated some changes to redistribute seats and to prepare for the enlargement of the EU an additional 12 member states may join over the next few years.

The European Court of Justice

This rules on the interpretation and application of European law. It comprises 15 judges, nominated by member states for a six-year term. Cases appearing before the court can arise from any member state. The rulings of the ECJ are binding on all member states of the EU.

In some instances, the superior courts in a particular country can refer a matter to the ECJ for guidance on the applicability of European law. So, for example, the High Court referred the issue of whether the entitlement to parental leave (which is restricted to children born after 15 December 1999) was compatible with the Directive on Parental Leave 1996.

The court is assisted by nine Advocates-General. These provide reasoned submissions (an Opinion) in open court to help the ECJ to reach a decision by identifying points of law and by referring to relevant precedents. In most cases an Advocate-General's Opinion is followed by the court.

Following the ratification of the Treaty of Nice 2000, there will be some institutional changes to the ECJ to accommodate the entry of additional member states into the European Union.

The Economic and Social Committee

This is an advisory body to the Council of the European Union. It comprises 222 members – primarily employers, trade unionists and other interested parties, including consumers, agriculture and the professions. Members are nominated by national governments and appointed by the European Council for a renewable four-year term of office.

Its main task is to suggest amendments to proposed legislation. It has few formal powers. It delivers some 170 advisory opinions each year. Three representative industrial and public sector bodies contribute to this committee: UNICE (the Union of Industrial and Employers' Confederation of Europe); the CEEP (the European Centre of Enterprises with Public Participation); and the ETUC (the European Trade Union Confederation).

The Committee of the Regions

This was set up, in 1994, under the Treaty of European Union, to represent the interests of regional and local authorities. It has an advisory role in respect of the Council of the European Union and the European Commission. There are 222 members. They are nominated by member states for a four-year term of office and appointed by the Council of the European Union. The policy areas where the Committee must be consulted are: general and vocational training; culture; public health; trans-European networks and transport; and structural and regional policy.

Processes for making EU law

All EU policy proposals must be based on an Article in the Treaty of Rome 1957 (as amended). There are two principal procedures in the Treaty of Rome, for the making of European Union employment law (*see* Fig 8.7).

- ☐ *The Consultation Procedure* – for proposals on employment rights. Unanimity is required on the Council of the EU to approve such proposals.
- ☐ *The Cooperation Procedure* – introduced by the 1986 Single European Act, as an amendment to the Treaty of Rome, to strengthen the European Parliament in law making. It is used for proposals on health and safety of workers and free movement of workers. Such proposals can be adopted by *qualified majority voting* (QMV).

Within these procedures, there are considerable opportunities for the governments of member states to influence proposed legislation. The unanimity procedure provides an effective veto. One member state in the Council of the EU, therefore, may be in a strong position to achieve concessions from others to ensure that a consensus view is achieved. British Conservative governments in the 1980s and 1990s, concerned at the cost of employment protection legislation and the constraints imposed in a free labour market, frequently used this veto threat to achieve some concessions.

The wider public is represented by the European Parliament.

Sectional interests, like employers, trade unions and consumers, are formally represented on the Economic and Social Committee. This provides a direct opportunity to influence proposals. Indirectly, lobbying of the individual governments will also take place, by these groups, in favour of particular courses of action.

☐ Making statute law in Parliament

The preceding discussions have shown that law making is affected by political tensions both within and between political parties and also between member states of the European Union. There are, invariably, clashes of values and differences of interests to be taken into account.

This section and the related case study will consolidate the preceding discussion. We will first focus on the processes through which statute law is made in the British Parliament. By means of a case study, we will then show how different political interests and pressure groups can influence the character of specific legislation.

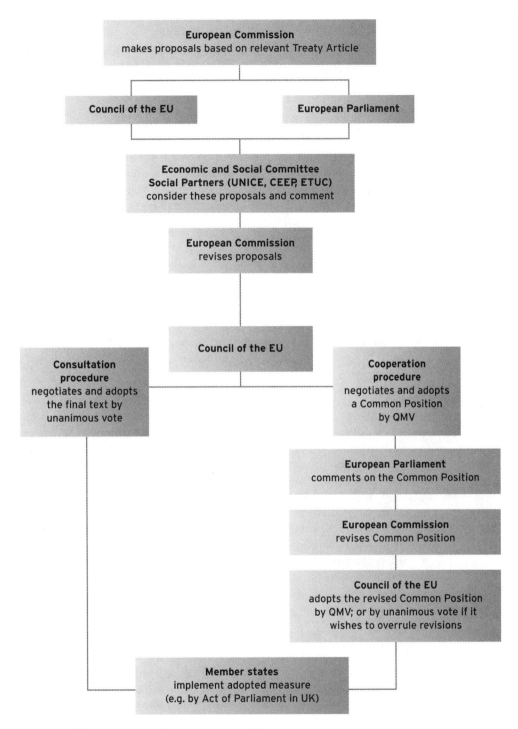

Figure 8.7 Consultation and cooperation procedures in EU law

Passing an Act of Parliament

Within Britain, most legislation originates in government departments and progresses through a number of stages, some of which are optional and some obligatory.

Publication of a Green Paper

This is an optional stage. A Green Paper is a consultative document for interested parties, such as employers' organisations, trade unions and pressure groups, to consider. It will set out the case for new legislation and the pros and cons of various courses of action. These Green Papers are prepared by government ministers and civil servants.

Publication of a White Paper

This is a firmer statement of government's legislative proposals. Again, it is an optional stage. Interested parties can still make representations. Sometimes, a government minister may change proposals as a result of reactions to the White Paper by either campaigning or other interest groups.

Publication of a Bill

This is a debating document, produced for Parliament to consider, amend and, if there is a sufficient majority of support, to enact. A Bill may reflect the results of consultation on Green and White Papers. Alternatively, it may be a direct reflection of government policy. Some Bills are introduced to give effect to EU directives. A Bill comprises various clauses and schedules and is drafted by specialist lawyers in the Parliamentary Counsel's Office. These parliamentary draughtsmen must ensure that the law is certain and unambiguous for judges and others who will interpret it and that no loopholes exist within the proposed legislation enabling certain groups to avoid the effect of the law.

A Bill must pass through the following formal stages of Parliamentary procedure.

☐ *The First Reading*. This is the formal presentation of the Bill to the House of Commons.

☐ *The Second Reading*. There is usually a full debate on both the principles and outlines of the Bill – rather than on its finer details. This is the most important stage through which a Bill has to pass. If a government has a working majority in the Commons, the result is usually predictable.

☐ *The Committee Stage*. Most Bills are dealt with by Standing Committees of between 15 and 20 MPs representing proportionately the various political parties in Parliament. At this stage detailed scrutiny of the Bill takes place and amendments may be proposed and voted upon. Some of these may represent the views of outside interests groups. If the government has a large majority in Parliament, it will control the committees and the Bill is likely to emerge with very few changes. Sometimes, government ministers, themselves, will initiate amendments at this stage.

Occasionally, with particularly important draft legislation – e.g. the Bill which subsequently became the European Communities Act 1972 – the Committee Stage can be taken on the floor of the whole House.

- ☐ *The Report Stage.* The amended Bill then returns to the House of Commons for scrutiny. Amendments can be made, or unmade, if the government has been defeated in Committee.

- ☐ *The Third Reading.* This is the final stage in the Commons. It usually follows the Report Stage immediately, and is often taken without debate.

- ☐ *The House of Lords.* The Bill is then passed to the Lords and progresses through substantially similar procedural stages. The Bill may be altered in the Lords. The Lords may, of course, reject a Bill. Under Parliamentary procedure, however, it may be presented again in the following session and must be passed by the Lords. Effectively, then, this chamber has a delaying power only.

- ☐ *Final reconsideration by the House of Commons.* This will involve consideration of whether to accept or reject amendments made in the House of Lords.

- ☐ *The Royal Assent.* This is the final stage of enactment. Normally, assent is signified on the sovereign's behalf by specially appointed commissioners. It is a formality – the last monarch to reject a Bill was Queen Anne. The Bill then becomes an Act of Parliament. Depending on the provisions in the legislation, it may be effective immediately or at a later date under a *Commencement Order*.

CASE STUDY

The politics of industrial action ballots

In 1984, the Conservative government, led by Margaret Thatcher, enacted a requirement that individual secret ballots of union members should be held before any industrial action to obtain their approval. The trade union(s) could be sued for damages and served with an injunction (a court order to stop the unlawful action) if they did not obtain this approval.

The political process that produced this legislation highlights some important issues in British Parliamentary democracy.

The standards in a liberal democracy
The International Labour Organisation affirmed the fundamental liberal democratic freedom of association in stating that governments should not interfere in any internal rule making (Convention 87, to which Britain is a signatory). This balloting requirement, therefore, raised the question, 'To what extent should the state in a liberal democracy interfere in the internal affairs of a voluntary organisation like a trade union?'

Responsibility of government for 'the public interest'

The ILO principle can pose certain dilemmas. Although trade unions are self-regulating voluntary organisations, their actions can have a 'public' effect – for example, disruption to services or the supply of goods to consumers and to other employers because of strike action.

Politicians then may ask, 'Have strikers willingly consented to and participated in the action? To what extent are the strike organisers' aims related to "industrial relations" or to "politics"?'

To answer these questions, others are raised:

(a) How far do union internal decision-making processes allow for full democratic participation?

(b) Are union members too heavily influenced by workplace and national leaders?

(c) Do individual union members fully understand the implications of industrial action?

The Thatcher government had these issues in mind. In a Green Paper, it stated that the external harms which unions could cause made it 'essential for their internal affairs to be conducted in a manner which commands public confidence' (para 3). Unions were being told that they must consider the 'public interest' as well as the 'sectional interests' of their members.

Conservative Party ideology

The Conservative Party has had a long-standing preoccupation with the economic consequences of industrial action. This became directly linked with concerns to *depoliticise* the trade union movement and reduce *militancy*.

Party policy on balloting developed during the 1980s. In 1980, James Prior, as Secretary of State for Employment, rejected compulsory strike ballots in favour of policy of cash reimbursement of expenses. He believed that, in practice, it was difficult to achieve a uniform arrangement for all unions. He also preferred unions to develop their own democratic arrangements voluntarily.

Indeed, in the 1970s and early 1980s there had been a general political debate about, on the one hand, the promotion of self-regulation and voluntary reform through the TUC and, on the other hand, the desirability of legislative action by government.

Public and pressure group attitudes

Generally, however, there was little public confidence in the effectiveness of TUC self- regulation and voluntary reform.

A Green Paper

In January 1983 a Green Paper, *Democracy in Trade Unions*, was published. It stressed the need for basic minimal protections for union members and for the government now to consider action in view of the lack of voluntary reforms.

It weighed up the pros and cons of employer-triggered and member-triggered ballots. The initial preference was for 'non-mandatory', 'member-triggered' ballots. There was 'considerable hesitancy' by the government for the idea of simply linking a ballot requirement to loss of union immunity, i.e. making unions liable to be sued.

Employer responses

Employer organisations like the Engineering Employers' Federation, the Confederation of British Industry, and the Institute of Personnel Management responded. Generally, these organisations did not see strike ballots as a central reform. If compulsory ballots were adopted, however, then these should be triggered by union members. Employers were lukewarm on the issue of improving union democracy. Their greater concern was strikes in essential services. Only the Institute of Directors advocated that loss of immunity should be a sanction for refusing to ballot.

1983 Conservative election manifesto

Despite the general reservations set out above, this manifesto stated that, 'We shall ... curb the legal immunity of unions to call strikes without the prior approval of those concerned through a fair and secret ballot'. This commitment was part of a wider undertaking to reform unions, ensuring that they acted democratically and responsibly. Simultaneously, it enabled the Conservatives to demonstrate publicly their intention to tackle the economic consequences of union militancy. The views of the IOD seemed to have prevailed.

The new legislation would mark 'a key shift in legislative technique from restriction to regulation' (Auerbach, 1990: 153). Whereas, in the previous four years, the government had restricted various industrial action - secondary action, political strikes, action to support workers overseas, inter-union strikes - it was now regulating the way unions behaved in calling and organising industrial action.

Proposed legislation on union democracy - July 1983

Following the manifesto commitment, ballots were to be a prerequisite for the preservation of immunity for all forms of industrial action.

The Bill

This included the ballot requirement. The government said it was a minimum level of intervention. Immunity was to be subject to certain minimum standards of conduct. The sanction would be action in the courts by employers, seeking an injunction and damages. Consumer actions were also contemplated. Member-triggered ballots were not to be introduced.

The continuing impact of the legislation

The Conservative Party continued to develop the regulation of balloting in subsequent legislation and also introduced a *Code of Practice on Balloting* which became ever more complex.

The Labour Party shifted its attitude in favour of accepting the principle of statutorily required ballots before industrial action. However, it has considered amending certain   provisions.

Public opinion, on the whole, was reconciled to statutory ballots as a fair means of determining the views of trade union members.

The International Labour Organisation criticised the complexity and some of the details of this British employment legislation. The principle of balloting was, however, consistent with freedom of association. The Labour Government, elected in 1997, did not repeal this legislation. However, it did make some modifications to the balloting process under Employment Relations Act 1999.

Exercise 8.4   ## Reforming the political system

Since the 1980s there has been increasing interest in reform proposals for the British political system. The most prominent issues have been:

- ☐ the nature of the voting system in Parliamentary elections;

- ☐ devolution of Scottish and Welsh government;

- ☐ the need to guarantee human rights within the British constitution;

- ☐ the degree of secrecy in government and the need for some freedom of information legislation;

- ☐ the character and role of the House of Lords in a two-chamber Parliament;

- ☐ the degree of effective scrutiny over proposed legislation from the European Union.

Many of these reform proposals have been considered earlier in the chapter. Select from the list above and find out what progress has been made on these issues.

Sources of information include the websites mentioned in this chapter.

☐ Summary and conclusion

This chapter has considered the British political system as a liberal democracy and a member state of the European Union. It has explored the complex network of different interests that exist in such a society and in political parties. It has considered the ways in which they may or may not be accommodated. It has also provided an outline of the context in which employment law is both formulated and enacted, which will be examined further in Chapters 9, 10 and 11. The case study is designed to illustrate some of these tensions and the processes within the political system.

Exercise 8.5   Review

Go back to Exercises 8.1 and 8.2 and consider any changes you would make in the light of what you have read in this chapter.

☐ Useful websites

Council of Ministers
    http://www.ue.eu.int/en/summ.htm
European Commission
    http://www.europa.eu.int/comm
European Court of Justice
    http://www.curia.eu.int
European Parliament
    http://www.europarl.eu.int/
European Union
    http://www.europa.eu.int
Greater London Authority
    http://www.london.gov.uk
Northern Ireland Assembly
    http://www.ni-assembly.gov.uk
Scottish Parliament
    http://www.scottish.parliament.uk/
UK Parliament
    http://www.parliament.uk/
Welsh Assembly
    http://www.wales.org.uk

09 Employment law in context

Chapter

☐ Introduction

This chapter opens up a consideration of the importance of employment law. It examines the context in which it is developed. In Chapters 10 and 11 the individual and collective frameworks of employment law will be discussed and their significance for employers explored.

It is important to remember that employment law does not emerge in a vacuum. It is moulded by various economic, political and social factors. These standards and requirements are subject to constant pressures. For example, governments may change and so may promote different values. Under one government, the economic interests of employers may predominate over the social and welfare interests of employees. Under another, more attention may be given to employee protection and fair treatment. Employment law is, therefore, enacted and implemented in a state of flux.

☐ Focus and scope

This chapter provides an understanding of the nature of the employment relationship, the 'politics' of employment law, the regulation of the employment relationship, the institutions for enforcing employment law and the impact of employment law on the managing of people.

Learning objectives

Once you have read through this chapter and completed the associated exercises, you should be able to:

☐ describe the main characteristics of the employment relationship;

☐ understand the political and economic context in which employment law develops;

☐ be aware of the balance between voluntary regulation and legal regulation of the employment relationship;

☐ understand the different forms of legal regulation;

☐ appreciate the impact of European Union law on legal regulation in Britain;

☐ understand the concept of minimum employment standards;

☐ be able to identify the processes that might be used for dealing with infringements of employment rights.

☐ The employment relationship

What is the nature of the employment relationship?

In historical terms, the concept of 'employment' is of relatively recent origin. From the beginning of the eighteenth century, in those societies that were transformed by the Industrial Revolution, it emerged as the dominant way of organising work. Before the development of a sizeable manufacturing sector, work was carried out by people having different statuses – as self-employed artisans and craftsmen, merchants, peasants subject to feudal relations, slaves, etc. Indeed, even today, the nature of work relations varies between societies. Compared with industrialised market economies, some developing societies are characterised less by employment and more by some of these other statuses.

As the nature of work relations has evolved, so the form of law governing workers has also changed over the past two hundred years. It has come to be based on *contract*. Previously, workers had their relationships

> ... shaped in part by criminal law, operating through a line of statutes which imposed compulsory labour and gave magistrates the power to fix wages and, in part, by civil law regulating the status of different categories of persons.

(Napier, 1986)

At the heart of this concept of status was the relationship of 'master and servant' – a relationship of submission. The jurist, Blackstone, writing in 1765, analysed this relationship as similar to the relationships of 'parent and child, guardian and ward, and husband and wife [sic!]'.

This submissive master and servant relationship contrasted with the *contractual relationship* which, in theory, was arrived at freely between two equal, independent parties. Progressively, *status* was superseded by *contract* as the basis for regulating the employment relationships. By 1875, the Master and Servant Acts had been repealed.

It is, of course, questionable whether the notion of equality underlying contract is realistic. This will be discussed later (*see* Chapter 10). It is necessary, first, to explore in more detail some views about the nature of the employment relationship.

By the late nineteenth and early twentieth centuries, various social scientists had begun analysing this relationship, identifying various aspects and proposing some theoretical perspectives to explain its character. These theories are concerned with the extent to which employees are motivated by purely economic concerns and the extent to which social values contribute to behaviour in the employment relationship. The analyses also considered such concepts as authority, control, power and conflict.

'Economic man'

In the nineteenth century, neo-classical economists in their model of the labour market put forward the concept of 'the economic man'. The implication of this notion was that:

... the employment relationship is a relationship between individual actors which can be understood largely without reference to the network of other social relations in which such actors might be involved; and that such actors will act in a self-interested way as utility maximisers.

(Brown, 1988: 34)

Under this model, individualism and self-interest were seen as the fundamental ingredients of the employment relationship and any notions that collective interests were of significance were disdained. Employees were seen as factors of production to be controlled. The *scientific management* of *Taylorism* provided the management techniques aimed to achieve this. This was based upon the detailed study of work processes to promote the more effective and efficient use of labour by breaking jobs up into narrow component tasks.

Social factors

Throughout the twentieth century, various social scientists evaluated this 'economic man' model critically. They drew attention to other key elements in the employment relationship. However, there is, as yet, no synthesis of these critiques into a single model.

In broad terms, the essential observations of these studies can be summarised as follows. Working people enter the employment relationship as social beings. They have been socialised through the family, the education system, possibly, religious organisations, community bodies, etc. They have learned social norms of behaviour; they have accepted certain values; and they bring to the employment relationship a range of expectations – some social, some economic.

Elton Mayo's research in the 1930s – *the Hawthorne experiments* – was the first to throw doubt on the economists' 'economic man' model. It was found that because of social norms, people might behave in economically non-rational ways.

Subsequent work by *systems theorist*, Talcott Parsons, argued that the employment relationship is clearly located in a social system. Brown (1988: 40) suggests that four features of his discussion of the employment relationship can be regarded as of particular value:

☐ the emphasis on the employment contract as involving more than just an exchange of wages for labour (i.e. it has a social as well as an economic dimension);

☐ the recognition that individual employees commonly enter employment as members of households towards which they have important responsibilities;

☐ the importance of the values which surround and support employment relations;

☐ the identification of significant differences in the employment relationship for workers making different types of contribution to the organisation and/or with different positions in the employment hierarchy.

Further work – deriving from social psychology – has also contributed to this analysis. This work has elaborated on the needs and motivations that employees bring to the employment relationship.

Pre-eminent in this area is the work of Maslow, who asserted that basic human needs were organised in a *hierarchy of needs*:

☐ physiological;

☐ security and safety;

☐ love, affection and belongingness;

☐ self-respect and self-esteem; and

☐ self-actualisation, developing one's full potential.

He accepted that such a hierarchy was not fixed in all circumstances. In this context, then, the social psychologist, Schein (1988), has proposed the existence of a *psychological contract* between the employee and his/her employer.

Overall, four general points can be made from sociological studies about working people's attitudes to the employment relationship:

☐ Individuals are already 'socialised' on entering the employment relationship as a result of their experiences in their family, schools, with friends and, possibly, religious and community organisations.

☐ Social influences on employees' expectations and priorities at work are important.

☐ Employees' attitudes and actions towards their employer are influenced by their orientation to work – that is, do they come to work for money alone and to what extent do they achieve other personal objectives at work?

☐ An employee's orientation to work derives from non-work life as well as from his/her experiences in the labour market and in employment itself.

If this social dimension is acknowledged, then a fuller understanding of the employment relationship can only be arrived at if certain other social phenomena are explored. These are authority, control and power relations; conflicts of interest; and individualism and collectivism.

Authority, control and power relations

There are differing views about the significance of power relations within employment. The question at the heart of this debate is whether the employment relationship should be seen as a continuing power relationship wherein the individual employee normally has little power relative to the employer. Some subsidiary questions might assist in coming to a view. For example:

☐ Who is responsible for formulating the terms and conditions of employment?

☐ Who is responsible for initiating changes to existing terms and conditions of employment?

☐ Who is responsible for organising the deployment of the workforce?

☐ Who is responsible for determining manpower requirements?

☐ Who is responsible for terminating the employment relationship?

☐ What degree of influence do employees, individually and collectively, have in the making of these decisions?

Exercise 9.1 **Power relations**

1 What answers would you give to these questions in relation to your own organisation?

2 What overall view do you come to about the balance of power between employees, both individually and collectively, and their employer?

The view adopted in this text is that the balance of economic and social power is clearly in favour of the employer. The employer also can – and does – exercise considerable authority in this relationship.

In his discussion about the formulation of contracts of employment, Wedderburn (1986) illustrates the fundamental imbalance. He comments that:

> The 'individual' employer is from the outset an aggregate of resources, already a 'collective power' in social terms ... In reality, save in exceptional circumstances, the individual worker brings no equality of bargaining power to the labour market and to this transaction central to his life whereby the employer buys his labour.

Such a power imbalance would probably be of minor importance if the employment relationship could be characterised as entirely consensual and harmonious. Even casual observation of the employment relationship reveals endemic conflicts of interest between the employer and the employee – for example, in pay claims, in redundancies, and in the implementation of health and safety standards.

Conflicts of interest

The issue of whether there is consensus or conflict at the heart of the employment relationship has been widely discussed by sociologists and industrial relations academics. Alan Fox (1974) contributed to the discussion by defining three perspectives:

☐ *The unitarists*. People adopting this view believe that the interests of employees and of employers are fundamentally the same. Conflict is not seen as inherent. It arises from various distortions such as poor communications or the existence of 'troublemakers'.

☐ *The pluralists*. People adopting this view believe that, within limits, the interests of employees and employers differ. However, there is likely to be agreement on such fundamental issues as the survival of the business. Conflicts, such as they are – about pay, hours and conditions of employment – can be 'institutionalised', i.e. processed through grievance procedures, through consultation mechanisms, or through negotiations, conciliation or arbitration.

☐ *The radicals*. People adopting this view believe that the balance of power is fundamentally unequal. Even negotiated settlements will reflect that imbalance of economic power, so they are more likely to be resolved in the employer's interests.

If the existence of conflicts of interest is accepted, it is possible, then, to distinguish between different sources of conflict which occur in the employment relationship. Allan Flanders (1968) suggested that they arise around three sets of issues:

☐ *Economic issues*. This source concerns the allocation of financial resources between pay and other labour costs, on the one hand, and investment, taxation, interest payments and dividends, etc. on the other hand.

☐ *Political issues*. This concerns the distribution of power and authority within an organisation. Such conflict usually concerns the question, 'Who has decision-making power to determine aspects of terms and conditions of employment?' It involves the extent to which management is prepared to share power or be influenced. For example, should there be negotiation and agreement with unions about pay, manning levels, working practices, etc., or should there be meaningful consultation with employee representatives about conditions of employment?

☐ *Values*. This relates to those standards that are used for judging management decision making. The most graphic conflict, in this respect, surfaces where a dispute involves, on the one hand, the employees' concern about security of employment and, on the other hand, the employer's pursuit of cost-effectiveness and efficiency.

Individualism and collectivism

The discussion so far has considered some of the context in which legal standards and rights are located. One further dimension and area of debate that needs to be identified concerns *individualism* and *collectivism*. A proper appreciation of the employment relationship, it is argued, recognises that it has both an individual and a collective dimension.

There has been a tendency in the past 20 years or so to downplay the importance of collective interests and to see individual interests as the primary focus of the employment relationship. This view was driven both politically and as a result of the employment policies of some employers. The anti-union philosophy of Thatcherism stressed individualism as central to its overall policy of *decollectivisation*. Simultaneously, at the workplace, the concept of *human resource management*, in its pure form, emphasised individualism and a unitarist approach to employment relations.

However, in their exploration of contemporary human resource management and industrial relations, Storey and Sisson (1993: 4) argue that 'the handling of both collective and individual issues (in unison) is likely to be the essential management requirement during the forthcoming period'. Certainly, any realistic assessment of HR the employment relationship must take into account both dimensions.

Asserting employees' interests

Having explored these characteristics of the employment relationship, we now consider the mechanisms available to employees to exert countervailing influence, power and control in this relationship.

There are two ways in which employees can attempt to rectify the power imbalance and deal with conflicts of interest – one depends on legal action and the other on voluntary action:

☐ by taking legal action through courts and tribunals against the employer, claiming the infringement of either an individual or collective right, e.g. unfair dismissal or consultation with employee representatives about redundancies;

☐ by organising collectively at the workplace, through a trade union or through a non-union committee of employee representatives.

The nature and effectiveness of these will be considered in more detail in Chapters 10 and 11.

The stakeholders in the employment relationship

From the discussion so far, it is possible to see that, arising out of the operation of the employment relationship, there are likely to be various issues of fundamental concern to the different stakeholders in employee relations. Principally, the stakeholders with a direct interest will be employers (and their associations), employees, and trade unions; and, those with an indirect interest will be customers (internal and external), government and the European Union.

The questions that are likely to arise, in varying ways, for these stakeholders are:

☐ What is the appropriate balance of power between an employer and his employees?

☐ What countervailing protections in law does an employee need in relation to his/her employer?

☐ Should there be a right to express collective interests at work?

☐ Should there be a complementary right to express collective interests in the political system?

☐ How might collective interests be expressed in the workplace and in the political arena?

☐ What values and standards should be promoted in the conduct of employee relations?

☐ What mechanisms need to be adopted to help in the management of employment conflict?

The answers to these questions will inevitably reflect a person's view in relation to a number of issues:

☐ the extent to which employers and employees, and trade unions, should voluntarily regulate themselves;

☐ the extent to which public policy should set standards to judge managerial behaviour;

☐ the extent to which employees should be entitled to job security and protection;

☐ the extent to which the collective interests of employees should be protected;

☐ the extent to which trade unions should play a role in employee relations;

☐ the extent to which employees are permitted to engage in industrial action.

In the next section, the political context of employment law will be discussed. The issues that have just been outlined will be considered against the backdrop of different ideological perspectives.

Exercise 9.2 Stakeholders

At this point think about the list of questions for stakeholders which appears above and make a brief note of how you would answer these questions.

☐ The 'politics' of employment law

The legislators

The legislators of UK employment law are Parliament, European institutions and the judiciary. In understanding employment law, it is essential to recognise that it originates in a political context. There are three aspects to this: statute law, Treaty articles and case law.

Statute law is clearly created in a political process. It can, and frequently does, reflect government policies, which themselves may be influenced by pressure group interests (*see* Chapter 8). These policies may not necessarily reflect a wide consensus of opinion in society and indeed may be partial to one interest group as against another.

In the past 25 years, fundamentally differing political views – for example, about the legitimacy of industrial action, the right to be a trade union member, minimum wages protection and, in some respects, equal opportunities – have resulted in certain pieces of employment law being highly contentious.

The judiciary provides another aspect of the political context of employment law. Judges are appointed after soundings made by the Lord Chancellor – a Cabinet member and a political appointee.

Anthony Scrivener QC, a former Chairman of the Bar, is reported as being critical of this secret appointments system:

Judges were chosen mainly from barristers who had concentrated on prosecuting cases for the government rather than defending civil liberties ... the secret appointments system was known only to involve taking soundings from the Bar Chairman and the heads of four High Court divisions ... You can only make representations.

(Reported in the **Guardian**, 21 September 1991.)

The appointments system, however, has begun to change. For example, it has become open to application, as a result of advertisements. Lord MacKay, as Lord Chancellor, said that the bench in 10 or 20 years' time should look very different in terms of racial and gender composition (reported in the *Financial Times*, 7 November 1990).

However, despite this optimistic prediction, progress to a more socially representative judiciary is still slow. The Lord Chancellor's Department reports the profile of the senior judicial appointments (March 2002) as shown in Fig 9.1.

Figure 9.1
Profile of senior
judiciary

□ *Lords of Appeal in Ordinary*
12 in post (all male)

□ *Heads of Divisions* (Lord Chancellor, Lord Chief Justice, Master of the Rolls, President of the Family Division and the Vice Chancellor)
5 in post (one female)

□ *Lord Justices of Appeal*
35 in post (two female)

□ *High Court Judges*
105 in post (6 female)

The only ethnic representation is below High Court level among circuit judges, recorders and district judges.

(This information is regularly updated on the website of the Lord Chancellor's Department: http://www.open.gov.uk/lcd/judicial/judapp.htm)

At the lower levels of the judiciary, it is rare for women to exceed 20 per cent in the particular grades of appointment (i.e. Recorders and District Judges). The highest percentages of ethnic representation are at 5 per cent among Recorders in Training and Deputy District Judges (Magistrates Courts).

By contrast, the 30 000 members of the non-professional (in terms of legal qualifications) lay magistracy (who deal with some 96 per cent of criminal matters) are, according to recent research, 'gender balanced' and ethnically representative of the national population. However, they are drawn overwhelmingly from professional and managerial people. Also, two-fifths are retired from full-time employment (Morgan and Russell, 2000).

The concerns about the professional judiciary are not usually related to direct political control. They are about two sets of related issues: attitudes and values; and the use of certain legal mechanisms which enable particular attitudes and values to become entrenched.

Attitudes and values

In a profile of the judiciary, John Griffith (1997: 21) drew attention to their educational background, class, gender and age:

> In summary, four out of five full-time professional judges are products of public schools and of Oxford or Cambridge, with an average age of about sixty.

Such a profile has provoked critical questions about the extent to which the judiciary is accommodating to changing social attitudes, to the changing role of women in society and to the evolution of a multiracial society. Furthermore, questions are asked about their understanding of intricate social sub-systems like employee relations.

There can be no simple appropriate response. Some judges, irrespective of this profile, show great facility in appreciating social changes. Others show a lack of understanding and, occasionally, marked prejudice.

To help promote an understanding of employee relations within the legal system, one innovation has injected some appropriate workplace experience decisions on certain employment issues. In 1975, the then newly created Employment Appeals Tribunal was established with panels of High Court judges and lay members representing experience of both sides of industry. Some commentators have advocated the extension of this model into a system of Labour Courts (McCarthy, 1989).

Precedent and tests

The second area which occasionally raises some concern, in respect of the judiciary, relates to the continuing influence of judicial decisions, unless they are overturned by Parliament. This arises in two principal areas: under the doctrine of *precedent* and, as a result, the creation of *tests*.

Precedent refers to the use by a court of a previous judgement or court decision, normally recorded in approved law reports, which can be used as an authority for reaching a decision in subsequent cases. For example, the decisions of the House of Lords are binding upon the Court of Appeal and all lower courts. Under appropriate employment law, the Employment Appeals Tribunal can bind employment tribunals, unless a superior court – for example, the House of Lords or the Court of Appeal – has previously ruled on the matter. In these circumstances, the EAT must follow the superior court.

In reaching decisions, judges may also formulate *tests* to help determine particular cases. These continue to influence employee relations under the doctrine of precedent. For example, a test has been developed, over a number of years, to determine whether or not a person is an employee and, consequently, is entitled to make certain claims before an employment tribunal (*see* the discussion in Chapter 10 on contracts of employment).

This judicial role in creating precedents and formulating tests can be helpful and influential in the longer-term implementation of employment law. Such tests may not necessarily ossify. The law-making process is dynamic after all.

Tests may be amended in the light of changing circumstances indicated in new cases; precedents may be overturned by an Act of Parliament or a ruling of the European Court of Justice.

The politics of employment law: three models

Parliament, the European institutions and judges, then, are the legislators. They operate in arenas where there are likely to be conflicts of values and ideological perspectives. Any brief consideration of the policies of the Conservative and Labour parties in recent years will show clear divergences concerning the aims and character of employment law. Likewise, there has also been a similar marked conflict of view between recent Conservative governments and the European Union about social policy and its economic effects.

The approaches, ideologies and attitudes of government, particularly, to the framework of employment law can be encapsulated in three different models:

☐ The *free collective bargaining* model

☐ The *free labour market* model

☐ The *employee protection* or *social justice* model.

Each model addresses, in differing ways and with significantly different emphases, a range of important economic, social, political and civil rights issues – for example, the management of the economy, the economic consequences of collective bargaining, the concept of social justice, the entitlement to job security, anti-discrimination policies, the civil rights of freedom of association and representation.

The free collective bargaining model

This might be characterised as the traditional British model. It became increasingly predominant following the First World War. Its central process for handling employee relations was collective bargaining. Consultation was seen as comparatively marginal, although occasionally it may have been supportive of collective bargaining. In part, this model also reflected the international standards on freedom of association set in the 1940s and 1950s by the International Labour Organisation (*see* Chapter 8).

Philosophically, this model emphasised *voluntarism*, which was characterised by the general, though not complete, 'abstention of the law' (Kahn-Freund, 1954) and limited state intervention, primarily in helping resolve industrial disputes.

The limited law that was enacted had two principal functions. First, it provided a permissive framework which enabled trade unions to exist lawfully, to operate, to engage in collective bargaining and, also, to call for and organise industrial action. For example, in the public sector and through the statutory duty of the Advisory Conciliation and Arbitration Service (ACAS), between 1974 and 1993, the State aimed to promote collective bargaining. The second function was to provide limited support for workers in vulnerable situations, e.g. through minimum pay set by Wages Councils (until 1993) and through health and safety legislation.

A consensus on voluntarism was broadly subscribed to by employers, unions and governments of both major political parties. The accepted view was that employers and trade unions should be free voluntarily to negotiate and agree both terms and conditions and also the procedures for handling their industrial relations.

Voluntarism was subject to numerous strains in the post-war years. Government increasingly tried to balance sectional interests and the public interest. For example, when the level of pay settlements through free collective bargaining was perceived to be inflationary and economically damaging, governments, both Conservative and Labour, enacted statutory incomes policies and introduced legislative attempts to limit trade union power. Since 1979, this free collective bargaining model has been subject to a major political onslaught.

The free labour market model

From 1979, this Thatcherite model was gradually implemented in Britain. It broke the prevailing consensus on a range of important industrial relations issues. The principles underlying this model emphasised the following:

- [ ] deregulation of the labour market, removing certain protective measures for employees, which were seen as 'burdens on business';
- [ ] the primary importance of individualism in the employment relationship (and the consequential marginalisation of collective interests);
- [ ] the curbing of trade union power;
- [ ] the advocacy of policies promoting cost-effectiveness, competitiveness, and flexibility in the use of labour;
- [ ] the limiting of external constraints (especially from the European Union) on the operation of this model – through both a commitment to the principle of *subsidiarity* and also through the *opt-out* mechanism that existed under the Maastricht Treaty until 1997.

In terms of employee relations, the following were the key consequences:

- [ ] Statutory recognition rights for trade unions were repealed.
- [ ] Non-unionism and derecognition of trade unions were encouraged.
- [ ] Lawful industrial action became increasingly difficult to undertake.
- [ ] Various statutory employment protections were rescinded.
- [ ] The individual employment relationship was emphasised in preference to collective representation.

In addition, large public sector organisations (which had provided the traditional base for trade union organisation) were fragmented by policies designed to promote competition and cost-effectiveness – for example, the introduction of profit centres, the contracting out of local authority services, the establishment of trusts in the National Health Service and agencies in the Civil Service.

These policies were principally driven by the economic interests of employers. Arguably, the countervailing interests of working people received little consideration – except, perhaps, in the areas of sex, race and disability anti-discrimination policies, and health and safety at work. To a considerable extent, however, in the areas of both sex discrimination and health and safety at work, the extended protections were a result of European Union policies and rulings by the European Court of Justice.

The employee protection or social justice model

This third model reflects the approach adopted, largely, by the European Union. As a consequence of Britain's membership, and obligations to implement EU Directives, it infuses certain pieces of legislation enacted in the UK.

In devising its legislative framework, the European Union places considerable emphasis on consensus – not only between member states, but also between employers' organisations and trade unions. Both are described as *social partners* and are explicitly involved in preliminary consultations about proposed new legislative initiatives. Under the Maastricht Treaty 1992, European Union-wide collective agreements were permitted and encouraged as a means of promoting EU social policy objectives. The negotiators and signatories of these deals would be UNICE, CEEP and the ETUC. An agreement on parental rights was signed in 1996 for example.

The principles underlying EU law are as follows:

☐ protection of employees throughout the employment relationship by creating a regulatory framework;

☐ a recognition that employees have both individual and collective interests and that these have to be accommodated in a framework of employment law;

☐ harmonisation of conditions of employment across member states – an aim which complements the objective of economic convergence;

☐ an acceptance of the principle of subsidiarity – that is, that some issues are more appropriately regulated at the level of the member state rather than at the level of the European Union;

☐ some regard paid to the economic issues of cost-effectiveness, competitiveness and labour flexibility.

As a consequence, various EU policies, outlined in Articles in the 1957 Treaty of Rome and in a range of Directives, have been enacted which provide for the equal treatment of women and men, for equal pay, for the protection of pregnant workers, for the establishment of health and safety standards, for restrictions on working time, for job security and for the protection of part-timers.

As far as the procedures of employee relations, such as trade union recognition, collective bargaining, dispute resolution, etc. are concerned, the European Union has been less interventionist, leaving the detailed arrangements to be devised in accordance with practice in each member state.

For example, it has established only the principle of consultation with employee representatives in respect of collective redundancies, business transfers and health and safety. The detailed mechanisms are a matter for determination in member states. Two exceptions to this more voluntarist approach are the prescriptive Directive on the establishment of European Works

Councils by multinational companies operating within at least two member states and with a given number of employees and the Information and Consultation Directive (2002) concerned with workplace level consultations.

The interlocking of the models

None of these models exists in its pure form. Contemporary employment relations in Britain are, in fact, governed by the inter-penetration of the three models.

There is evidence of the free collective bargaining model continuing to cover about half the workforce. However, the major tension over recent years has been between advocates of the free labour market and employee protection models. In terms of domestic politics, this ideological dissonance is broadly reflected in the policies and perspectives of the Conservative and Labour parties. On a European level, it has been a marked source of conflict between the European Union and the Thatcher/Major governments.

Since Britain's entry into the European Community in 1973, no government has been a free agent in respect of certain policies that it wishes to pursue. To that extent sovereignty has been limited. In terms of social policy, of which employee relations is a major part, signatories to the EC's founding Treaty of Rome (1957) must conform to Articles of that Treaty and to Regulations and Directives of the Union.

Inevitably, this obligation to conform can cause tensions and conflict between the government of a member state and the EU – particularly if there is a fundamental ideological gulf between them. The continuation and intensity of Britain's tensions are dependent, in large part, on which party will be in power in the coming years (*see* Chapter 8).

Which approach operates today?

The employment relations policies introduced by the Labour Government, elected in 1997, broadly conformed to the employment protection or social justice model. However, elements of the other models were evident. For example, reflecting the 'traditional model', there was an acceptance of the statutory right of recognition for collective bargaining (which came into force in July 2000). Secondly, there was a commitment to the continued operation of the flexible labour market, which, on the face of it, appeared to have associations with the free market model. In practice, though, there was no stark return either to traditionalism nor a continuation of an unbridled Thatcherite approach.

The Government's approach was set out in the White Paper, *Fairness at Work* (1998). This sought to bridge the economic interests of business and the aspirations of working people. It saw employment protection law as one element in a process of cultural change. It stated that

'Within Britain's flexible and efficient labour market, the Government is proposing in this White Paper a framework in which the development of strong partnerships at work can flourish as the best way of improving fairness at work. But the framework it proposes is not just about the application of employment law. It is designed to help develop a culture in all business and organisations in which fairness is second nature and underpins competitiveness. Such cultural change will lead in due course to more positive relationships between employers and employees than the letter of the law can even achieve.'

(para 1.8).

Three main elements in the framework were identified.

☐ *Basic fair treatment of employees*. 'Unless minimum rights are established, effective relationships in companies cannot prosper. The White Paper establishes new ground rules for fair treatment, allowing employees to form effective relationships with employers – including rights which recognise the changing nature of work. People must not be deterred from contributing to competitiveness through flexible working arrangements' (para 1.9).

☐ *New procedures for collective representation at work*. There is acknowledgement that a diverse range of representation can be available. The choice of arrangements will be dependent upon the circumstances within a specific organisation. In order to widen this range, the Government proposed 'a new settlement which will enable trade unions to be recognised for collective bargaining where the relevant workforce chooses such representation' (para 1.9). The general thrust in this policy area is the promotion of partnership.

☐ *Accommodation of non-work life*. This involved the promotion of 'policies that enhance family life while making it easier for people – both men and women – to go to work with less conflict between their responsibilities at home and at work' (para 1.9).

☐ Regulating the employment relationship

During the past century, as we have seen, when governments have attempted to regulate the employment relationship, different interests have prevailed at different times. Employer interests were dominant in some periods; at some times, trade union and employee interests were influential. On other occasions, a more consensual approach was attempted.

The interlocking of the three models outlined above has resulted, in practice, in a system of regulation of the employment relationship that combines both voluntary action and action deriving from law. Indeed, at any time, in any workplace, it is possible to see the coexistence and interplay of these two different methods.

Voluntary action

Traditionally, voluntary action to regulate the employment relationship was seen as the preferred approach by employer, trade unions and government. This was reflected in three principal ways:

☐ *Promotion of collective bargaining*. The process of collective bargaining was entered into voluntarily by employers. The range of issues to be bargained about – pay and various conditions – could be determined by the employer. Collective agreements were (and continue to be) voluntary, rather than legally enforceable, agreements.

☐ *Adoption of voluntary codes of practice*. Such codes have been adopted by bodies, such as the Chartered Institute of Personnel and Development, in order to set standards in the various stages of the employment relationship, e.g. in recruitment, occupational testing, equal opportunities, employee involvement.

☐ *Observance of international standards*. Principal among these standards have been those promulgated by the International Labour Organisation (*see* Chapter 8). These tend to reflect a free collective bargaining perspective.

So significant was this voluntary approach that, in the early 1950s, Kahn-Freund stated that collective bargaining was more important as a form of regulating the employment relationship than statute law (Kahn-Freund, 1954).

Legal regulation

Forty years on, the predominant form of regulation has changed substantially. It is now, clearly, the law. It infuses every term and condition of employment – for example, pay, health and safety standards, criteria for redundancy selection – and also, many of the processes used in the employment relationship – for example, disciplinary and dismissal procedures, consultation about redundancy and health and safety. In addition, it regulates trade union membership and various forms of industrial action.

Of course, to talk about 'the law' is an over-simplification. Lord Wedderburn (1986) has remarked that:

> It is never enough to call an act 'unlawful'. We must know what kind of illegality is in issue. Nor, for parallel reasons, should we speak of 'the law' without distinguishing what kind of obligation and sanction is involved.

The legal regulation of the employment relationship derives from a number of sources – some of which are long-standing and others of which are of more recent origin. These are common law, statute law, European Union treaties, the 'direct effect' of EU Directives, rulings of the European Court of Justice and ministerial rules and regulations.

☐ *Common law*. This embodies the principles and precedents derived from judicial decisions over many centuries and used in the interpretation of statute law.

☐ *Statute law*. This describes Acts of Parliament. These laws govern people's behaviour and are enforced by various agencies, e.g. government departments, local authorities, the police service, the Health and Safety Executive. Compliance with or infringement of these laws are generally determined by the courts. Case law is created as a consequence. Some statutes give effect to EU Directives.

On occasion, under employment law, Parliament may approve a statutory code of practice. Notable examples are the ACAS Code on disciplinary procedures, the Equal Opportunities Commission Code on Sex Discrimination, the Commission for Race Equality Code on Race Discrimination. Such codes are not enforceable as statute law. They are for practical guidance only. However, a tribunal or court may take into account any evidence of an employer's breach of the standards or guidance set out in a code.

☐ *European Union Treaties*. These have provided a new source of law since Britain became a member in 1973. Where a provision of the European Treaties is 'sufficiently clear, precise and unconditional as to require no further interpretation' it becomes a direct right enforceable by an individual in the national courts. One notable Treaty provision is Article 141 of the Treaty of Amsterdam (formerly Article 119 of the Treaty of Rome) which provides for equal pay. It can be relied on directly by a person claiming infringement of equal pay rights before a British court of tribunal. It has been used in several influential cases.

☐ *Direct effect of Directives*. Generally, these are not enforceable between individual persons but only against the State. They must be enacted, therefore, in national law and enforced in national courts. However, where an employee is employed by the State or 'an emanation of the state', then the individual can directly invoke the Directive in his or her national courts where that directive is 'sufficiently precise and unconditional'.

☐ *Rulings of the European Court of Justice*. These are binding on all member states, irrespective of where a case originates. They are concerned with the interpretation of and compliance with EU law. For example, the Article on equal pay has been interpreted in various cases to encompass a wide range of remuneration.

☐ *Ministerial rules and regulations*. Statute law may confer powers upon ministers to adopt rules and regulations to suit changing circumstances without using full Parliamentary procedures. The regulations removing the ceiling on compensation in sex discrimination claims were made under European Communities Act 1972. Other regulations (on display screen equipment) have been made under the Health and Safety at Work Act 1974.

Under the unwritten British constitution, through convention, Parliament has been seen as sovereign. This means that statute law stands above judge-made law or ministerial regulations, because statutes can overturn these other two sources of law.

However, Britain's membership of the European Union has modified this position. In those policy areas where the EU is empowered to act, then both Parliament and the British courts are bound by the EU Treaties and rulings of the European Court of Justice.

Common law and statute law

The differences and functions of these two sources of law can be seen by considering two broad types of law: criminal law and civil law.

Criminal law

Criminal law is mainly statutory. It deals with wrongs against society in general – for example, theft, burglary, actual bodily harm, public order offences – for which someone is prosecuted. In order to convict someone of a crime, the prosecution – usually, the Crown Prosecution Service (the Procurator Fiscal in Scotland) – has to prove the case *beyond all reasonable doubt* – a high standard of proof. Such offences are primarily dealt with in magistrates' courts or in the Crown Court. Punishment can be a fine, a community rehabilitation order, a community punishment order or imprisonment.

Criminal law has various implications for the employment relationship. For example, under an organisation's disciplinary procedure, certain acts of gross misconduct are likely to be specified under disciplinary rules, e.g. theft or acts of violence. These are also crimes. An employee who commits such an offence may, therefore, face two consequences:

☐ arrest by the police, prosecution, and a penalty imposed by the court; and

☐ disciplinary action by the employer – possibly dismissal without notice which, in turn, depending on all the circumstances and the conduct of the dismissal, could lead to an application by the ex-employee to an employment tribunal alleging unfair dismissal.

Employers, themselves, are also subject to criminal law in some employment relations matters. For example, an employer can be prosecuted by the Health and Safety Executive, under the Health and Safety at Work Act 1974 (s39), for using unsafe machinery.

Civil law

This is a mixture of statute law and common law. It concerns disputes between private individuals (including organisations). In these cases someone is sued. There are two branches of civil law: the law of contract and the law of tort.

The *law of contract* determines that a contract is an agreement between two or more parties. These parties voluntarily decide the content of the contract, i.e. create their own rights and duties. Courts may be involved in discovering the intention of the parties when they agreed particular provisions.

A civil wrong is committed when one party breaches the contract. In establishing whether or not a breach occurred, the standard of proof is *the balance of probabilities*, i.e. whether something is more likely to have happened than not.

The *law of tort* relates to civil wrongs other than breach of contract. This branch of law concerns the interests of one person that may be injured by another. Usually, it is related to obligations imposed by law. For example, a person may be injured by another's negligence, his/her property may be injured by nuisance or trespass or his/her reputation by defamation.

The bulk of employment law in Britain is civil and so is subsumed under either the law of contract or the law of tort. The most obvious example of contract law is the contract of employment or those contracts offered to self-employed workers. Courts and tribunals may be called on to consider allegations of breach of contract, and other complaints relating to variation and termination of contracts. (The contract of employment is discussed further in Chapter 10.)

The law of tort is especially important for trade unions in relation to industrial disputes, where Parliament has prohibited certain forms of industrial action (*see* Chapter 11). As far as employers are concerned, they may have allegations for negligence (a tort) made against them for failure to provide proper standards and procedures for health and safety at work.

The principal remedies for an aggrieved party under civil law are damages – compensation for the injury sustained – and an injunction – a court order to stop the unlawful act.

Who has employment protection?

The current framework of individual statutory employment rights developed from the 1960s onwards. Initially, full-time permanent employees were the principal beneficiaries of these rights. Part-time employees (unless they had completed a given period of continuous employment and worked a specified number of hours per week) had very limited rights. Other groups of so-called non-standard or 'atypical' workers (i.e. temporary workers, agency staff, casual workers and homeworkers) were generally outside employment protection. Indeed, employment rights were only accorded to 'employees' (i.e. those who had a contract of employment). So, those who worked on other contractual arrangements (and the self-employed) were excluded.

Since the 1990s, this discrimination in access to employment rights has begun to be tackled. The main instruments used have been the law on equal pay and indirect sex discrimination. This was potentially useful because the majority of workers with nonstandard employment status were female and the majority of standard workers were male. So, comparisons could be made. One example was the challenge concerning access to the statutory right to complain about unfair dismissal (R v Secretary of State for Employment ex parte Equal Opportunities Commission [1994] IRLR 176). Until 1994, part-time employees who worked less than 16 hours had to have five years' continuous service with an employer. Employees working in excess of 16 hours needed only two years' service. Part-time employees with less than eight hours' service had no statutory right of complaint. The House of Lords ruled that this differential access to making an unfair dismissal claim was discriminatory. The qualifying period was amended so as not to discriminate on grounds of hours worked.

In more recent years, employment rights for 'atypical' workers have been enacted in some pieces of legislation (*see* Chapter 10 for more detailed discussion on some of the following examples):

☐ Part-time Workers Regulations 2000, which prohibits discrimination and promotes pro-rata treatment under employment contracts;

☐ European Directive on Fixed-term Contracts 1999 (implemented through the Fixed-term Employees Regulations 2002);

☐ Working-time Regulations 1998, which extends protections to casual workers and homeworkers;

☐ National Minimum Wage Act 1998, which covers agency workers, homeworkers, part-time and temporary workers.

Additionally, the artificial division between those who are 'employees' and those who have some other form of 'employment relationship' has begun to be dealt with by legislators and the courts. The tendency, nowadays, is for statutory employment rights to be increasingly available to anyone who has an employment relationship (usually, described in legislation as a 'worker'). Even so, unfair dismissal and maternity rights are still restricted to 'employees'. Eventually, however, it is anticipated that the only category of working people excluded will be the 'genuinely self-employed'. The Employment Relations Act 1999 (s.23) gives the Secretary of State power to extend employment rights to such categories of working people. Although not implemented yet (April 2002), this provision reflects the policy in favour of a more inclusive framework of employment rights.

☐ The institutions for enforcing employment law

In the discussion so far, references have been made to particular courts and tribunals. The next section provides short descriptions of these bodies and their relationships. The administration of employment law is undertaken in two sets of bodies:

☐ courts and tribunals; and

☐ statutory agencies.

The court and tribunal system is set out in Fig 9.2. This shows the location of those dealing with employment rights.

Normally, complaints on individual employment rights are made to an employment tribunal and may proceed, through appeals on points of law, from the Employment Appeals Tribunal up to the House of Lords. A complaint may go to the European Court of Justice if the case involves specific European Union law – for example, on sex discrimination, redundancies or transfers of undertakings.

The statutory agencies have responsibilities for various pieces of employment law. Among such bodies the most notable are the Advisory Conciliation and Arbitration Service, the Equal Opportunities Commission, the Commission on Racial Equality and the Health and Safety Commission.

Courts and tribunals

Employment tribunals

Originally set up in 1964, (as industrial tribunals) these tribunals have been extended to cover a very wide range of employment rights. For example:

Figure 9.2
The court and
tribunal system

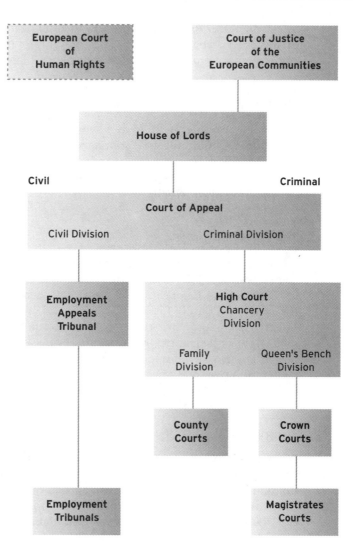

- ☐ unfair dismissal
- ☐ sex discrimination
- ☐ race discrimination
- ☐ equal pay
- ☐ discrimination on the grounds of disability
- ☐ maternity rights
- ☐ trade union membership rights
- ☐ unlawful pay deductions.

A tribunal comprises three people – the chair being legally qualified and the two lay members being drawn from either side of industry.

Over 100 000 applications are made each year, almost 50 per cent of which are unfair dismissal claims. Two-thirds of these are either withdrawn or settled by conciliation. Of those that proceed to a full hearing, about 20 per cent result in success for the applicant. (The role employment tribunals play in the enforcement of individual employment rights is discussed in Chapter 10.)

The Employment Appeals Tribunal

This was established in 1976 as a superior court of record to hear appeals on points of law from industrial tribunals. It comprises judges, nominated by the Lord Chancellor, from the High Court and Court of Appeal, together with other lay members who have experience of employee relations as either an employers' or employees' representative.

The House of Lords

A panel of Law Lords – either three or five – sit to hear appeals from 'inferior' courts. For most British cases, this is the final court of appeal. However, if the law derives from European Union law, then there is a further stage of appeal to the European Court of Justice.

There is no automatic right of appeal to the House of Lords. Leave, or permission, must be granted by the Court of Appeal or the House of Lords itself. It has, in recent years, produced a number of significant judgements on employment law in relation to business transfers, sex discrimination and equal pay and on the access of part-time employees to statutory rights.

European Court of Justice

Located in Luxembourg, it is officially known as the Court of Justice of the European Communities. It has jurisdiction in Britain under the European Communities Act 1972. It deals with appeals on matters within its competence. In terms of employment law, this includes, for example, collective redundancies, the rights of part-time workers, health and safety, working time, pregnant workers, sex discrimination, transfers of undertakings. In matters of European Union law it is superior to the House of Lords. Its rulings on points of law are binding (*see* Chapter 8).

European Court of Human Rights

Located in Strasbourg, this court exists under the Council of Europe, which is separate from the EU, although all EU member states do participate in this Council. Its responsibility is to adjudicate on alleged violations of the 1950 European Convention on Human Rights, of which Britain is a signatory. Its decisions do not automatically become part of British law. It has dealt with employment-related matters which have been said to be breaches of civil rights – for example, the British Rail closed shop and the withdrawal of union recognition rights from GCHQ.

Under the Human Rights Act 1998, the Convention has been incorporated into UK law (*see* Chapter 8). This will have significant implications for employment law.

Statutory agencies

Advisory Conciliation and Arbitration Service

Established in 1974, the Advisory Conciliation and Arbitration Service (ACAS) is an independent service, charged with a general duty to promote the improvement of industrial relations. It is governed by a Council, comprising a full-time Chair, three members appointed after consultation with the Confederation of British Industry, three after consultation with the Trade Union Congress, and three appointed by the Secretary of State for Trade and Industry. It publishes an Annual Report.

Among its functions are the following:

- to offer conciliation in disputes over individual statutory employment rights between individual employees and their employers (e.g. unfair dismissal, equal pay, discrimination);
- to provide collective conciliation for industrial disputes;
- to provide facilities for arbitration, mediation and committees of investigation;
- to issue codes of practice providing guidance, e.g. on disciplinary rules and procedures.

Equal Opportunities Commission

Established in 1976, under the Sex Discrimination Act 1975, the duties of the Equal Opportunities Commission involve:

- working towards the elimination of discrimination;
- promoting equality of opportunity between men and women;
- keeping relevant legislation under review and making proposals for change.

It is headed by a Chair and Deputy Chair and has 13 part-time commissioners. It operates through a series of committees and working parties.

It advises people of their rights in law and, in certain circumstances, can assist them to take cases to a tribunal or court; this is usually where there is a legal point to be tested. It can conduct formal investigations, issue non-discrimination notices enforceable in the courts, issue codes of practice and institute proceedings both in relation to advertising and in cases where there have been instructions or pressure to discriminate. It publishes an Annual Report.

Commission for Racial Equality

The Commission for Racial Equality was established in 1977 (replacing the previous Community Relations Commission and the Race Relations Board). Its objectives include working towards the elimination of discrimination and to promote equal opportunity and good relations between different racial groups. It has similar powers and duties to the Equal Opportunities Commission. It provides advice to employers, unions and other bodies. It supports and coordinates the work of about 100 local community relations councils operating in areas with significant ethnic groups. It publishes an Annual Report.

Health and Safety Commission

The Health and Safety Commission was established in 1974 under the Health and Safety at Work Act. It is responsible to the Secretary of State for the Environment for taking appropriate steps to secure the health, safety and welfare of people at work and to protect the public generally against dangers to health and safety arising from work activities.

It is headed by a Chair and up to nine commissioners. In formulating its policies, the Commission organises widespread consultation on all aspects of health and safety. It is advised by a number of Industry Advisory Committees as well as by experts within its own Executive. It publishes an Annual Report.

Disability Rights Commission

This was established in April 2000 and replaced the National Disability Council. The Commission comprises 15 members of whom 10 have a disability. They have been recruited for the particular expertise that they can bring to the work of the Commission.

It is under the following duties:

☐ to work towards the elimination of discrimination against disabled persons;
☐ to promote the equalisation of opportunities for disabled persons in all fields of activity;
☐ to encourage good practice in the treatment of disabled persons; and
☐ to review the working of the Disability Discrimination Act 1995.

As with the EOC and the CRE, it has the power to conduct formal investigations; issue non-discrimination notices; and can assist individual claims of unlawful discrimination.

Low Pay Commission

This was initially set up in July 1997 to report on the introduction of a national minimum wage. It is now established on a statutory basis. It comprises a chairman and eight other members, reflecting a wide range of knowledge and experience as employers, trade unions and working people.

One of the key tasks of the Commission is to review the impact of the statutory national minimum wage since its introduction in April 1999. In carrying out reviews, the Commission is required to pay particular reference to:

☐ the effect on pay, employment and competitiveness in low-paying sectors and small firms;
☐ the effect on particular groups of workers, such as young people, women, ethnic minorities, homeworkers and small firms;

- ☐ the effect on pay structure, including the effect on differentials and different pay systems, and the impact of the special rules for output work, unmeasured-hours work and salaried-hours work;
- ☐ the interaction between the NMW and the tax and benefit system; and
- ☐ the interaction between the NMW and the New Deal.

Overall, the Commission should have regard to the wider economic and social implications; the likely effect on employment and inflation; the impact on the costs and competitiveness of the small firms sector, and the potential costs to industry and the exchequer.

Central Arbitration Committee

This Committee has been in existence since the mid-1970s. It is an independent tribunal with statutory powers to adjudicate in various disputes relating to statutory employment rights.

In recent years, it has played a low-profile role in employment relations. Its principal responsibility has been dealing with complaints relating to the disclosure of information for collective bargaining. It could also provide voluntary arbitration in industrial disputes.

However, in 2000, it assumed significant additional responsibilities for two important areas of collective representation: statutory rights of recognition for collective bargaining; and information and consultation rights in respect of European-based multinational companies.

The current Chairman is a High Court judge (Sir Michael Burton). There are 9 Deputy Chairmen and 32 members of the Committee. They reflect a wide range of experience in human resource management, trade union representation, academic life and the legal profession.

☐ The impact of law on the employment relationship

In this chapter, we have discussed the nature of the employment relationship, the sources of employment law and the political, economic and social context in which it develops. This concluding section is in two parts. First, it draws out some general comments on the impact that the law has had on the employment relationship. Second, it will outline a case study that brings together a number of elements from the context within which employment relations operate – both British and European.

The development of employment law in Britain has been a gradual process. The present framework owes its origins to a number of key phases:

- ☐ the legalisation of trade unions and industrial action in the 1870s;
- ☐ defining the legal status of industrial action in 1906;
- ☐ the introduction of some piecemeal employment rights in the 1960s, e.g. on employment contracts and redundancies;
- ☐ a substantial growth of individual employment rights in the 1970s, e.g. sex and race discrimination, health and safety;

- ☐ legal constraints on trade union power in the 1980s;
- ☐ the significant expansion of European individual employment rights in the 1980s and 1990s, e.g. in transfers of undertakings, redundancies, working time, pregnant workers, health and safety, part-time workers.

The major expansion has been within the past 25 years – so much so that nowadays, employment law is a significant influence on the responsibilities of both personnel departments and line managers in their dealings with staff. The significance of this influence is seen in three ways:

- ☐ the standards used for determining managerial behaviour and action;
- ☐ proceduralisation;
- ☐ sources of advice.

Standards of practice

In the past, managers tended, usually, as part of day-to-day managerial decision making, to set voluntarily their own standards of practice, and their own rules and procedures for dealing with staff. Sometimes these reflected agreed standards of good practice; sometimes they were standards incorporated in collective agreements negotiated with trade unions; sometimes they were bad standards reflecting managerial prejudice and unfairness.

Increasingly, however, managers take account of those norms, standards and procedures set by Acts of Parliament and in case law. This tendency is called *juridification* – that is, the extent to which the behaviour of employers and unions is determined by reference to the law. It is a trend in all western industrialised countries and is strongly evident in Britain, where it can be seen in the following areas:

- ☐ *Individual rights*. There has been legislation in respect of dismissal, employment documentation, discrimination, the payment of wages and the legal regulation of health and safety.

- ☐ *Collective relations*. Collective relations between employees and their employer have been influenced by the law on such issues as discipline, redundancy, union membership and non-membership, equal pay and consultation rights.

- ☐ *Collective industrial disputes*. These have been made subject to a range of legal restrictions and requirements, including balloting provisions.

One other trend that is also clear is the evolution of the concept of *a minimum standards approach*. This is integral to what might be described as a *model employment contract* which has increasingly been defined in statute. Parliament has, over the past 30 years or more, developed a basic contract of employment, provisions of which can be enforced under statute. Key elements of this model contract are:

- ☐ the right to contractual information;
- ☐ the right not to have the contract unfairly terminated;
- ☐ the right that no term under the contract shall be discriminatory under sex discrimination law;
- ☐ the right not to have pay deducted unlawfully;
- ☐ the right to minimum periods of notice;
- ☐ the right to a minimum wage;
- ☐ the right to a maximum working week;
- ☐ the right to minimum paid annual leave;
- ☐ the right to minimum rest breaks;
- ☐ the right to minimum maternity leave;
- ☐ the right to minimum parental leave;
- ☐ the right to minimum time off for emergencies.

(Some of these rights are subject to specified qualifications under the appropriate legislation.)

Procedural standards

Legislation has also been influential on the nature and development of employment relations procedures. (Some of these issues will be discussed in more detail in Chapter 11.) It is arguable that, in certain respects but by no means all, there has been a move towards *minimum procedural standards*. These will be considered under the following headings: information disclosure; consultation duties; negotiation; grievance handling; and discipline handing. (In legislation enacted in 2002, statutory dismissal and disciplinary procedures and statutory grievance procedures are to be implied in all contracts of employment.)

Information disclosure

These rights include information on contracts of employment and any changes; about health and safety hazards, standards and procedures; on reasons for dismissal.

Duties to consult

These statutory duties to consult placed on employers concern particular issues – e.g. on collective redundancies and on transfers of undertakings with a view to agreement; and on health and safety.

Negotiation

Duties to negotiate with trade unions changed in 2000. For the previous twenty years, the decision of an employer whether to negotiate with a trade union on pay and conditions of employment has been voluntary. The Employment Relations Act 1999 implemented a new statutory right on recognition for collective bargaining purposes. It covers organisations with more than twenty workers.

The procedure aims to encourage voluntary agreements between the employer and the independent union(s) concerned. If, however, that fails then the union(s) can apply to the Central Arbitration Committee to decide the appropriate bargaining unit and also whether a majority or the workers in that unit support recognition. If a majority of those voting in a secret ballot (and 40 per cent of the workers in the bargaining unit support recognition), the CAC will declare the union recognised to conduct collective bargaining on behalf of the workers.

Grievance handing

This has become more important for employers. Effective procedures can help solve problems and prevent matters being raised at employment tribunal. So, for example, allegations of discrimination or harassment should be dealt with through in-company procedures. Indeed, it can be a defence against liability for an employer to show that he took such steps (e.g. using a fair and effective grievance procedure) to deal with the complaint.

Until 2000, there were voluntary standards of good practice concerning the structure and operation of the grievance process. Now, a statutory code of practice is in force (Code of Practice on Disciplinary and Grievance Procedures published by the Advisory Conciliation and Arbitration Service). This also includes guidance on the supportive *statutory right to be accompanied* (by either a trade union official or by a fellow worker).

Discipline handling

Disciplinary action has, since 1977, been subject to good practice guidance under the former ACAS Code of Practice. The revised Code (adopted in 2000) has replaced the earlier version. A key amendment in this area is that the new *statutory right to be accompanied* has been substituted for the previous recommendation about accompaniment.

Figure 9.3
Procedural
arrangements: the
overall picture

> By the end of the 1990s, research evidence (published in the Workplace Employee Relations Survey, 1998) reported the following:
>
> ☐ 91 per cent of workplaces had a formal procedure in place for dealing with individual grievances raised by non-managerial employees.
>
> ☐ 92 per cent of workplaces had a disciplinary procedure.
>
> ☐ Only 4 per cent of workplaces did not allow a worker to be accompanied in disciplinary action.
>
> ☐ Just over half of workplaces had a joint consultative committee which operated either at workplace level or elsewhere within the organisation.
>
> ☐ Only 2 per cent of workplaces have no consultation about health and safety. Where it existed it took the form of either direct consultation with employees, with safety representatives or through a joint health and safety committee.
>
> ☐ Union recognition for collective bargaining was evident in 45 per cent of workplaces and was more common in larger workplaces. So, some 62 per cent of workers were in workplaces with union recognition. However, it tended to be a public sector phenomenon.

Sources of advice

The context in which the HR function has evolved in the past 20 years has had a number of significant consequences for the work of practitioners. Many of these are discussed elsewhere in this textbook. Here, the impact of employment legislation can be summarised from data in the Workplace Employee Relations Surveys collated over the past twenty years. There are two aspects to this: the extent to which expertise exists within the HR function; and the extent to which external sources of advice are used.

Use of external advice

Over the past 20 years, the use of external advice to the HR function has grown significantly (Millward *et al.*, 2000: 73). In 1980, 69 per cent of organisations surveyed reported not using external advice. By 1998, this figure had dropped significantly to 44 per cent. The latest survey shows that the principal source of external advice (reported by 32 per cent of employee relations managers) was external lawyers. The use of lawyers has doubled since 1990. In 1980, only 1 per cent reported their use. The other key sources were ACAS and other government agencies (at 23 per cent) and other professional bodies (at 19 per cent).

Expertise within the HR function

Personnel management specialists, in defining their job responsibilities (Millward *et al.*, 2000: 63), pointed to the following in well over 80 per cent of cases: handling grievances; recruitment or selection; equal opportunities; pay or conditions of employment; performance appraisals; and staffing or manpower planning. All of these issues have, to a greater or lesser extent, employment law dimensions. This calls for expertise in-house from those able to apply legal standards and requirements to, often complex, HR situations. The 1984 Workplace Industrial Relations Survey observed that industrial relations and employment legislation was 'the single most common contextual factor cited as enhancing the role of personnel management' (Millward and Stevens, 1986: 41). The significance attached to employment law persists. Legal standards and processes, as we have seen are now finely woven into the fabric of much human resource decision making.

CASE STUDY

The Marshall cases

This case study draws on a pair of related influential cases – known as the Marshall cases. These involve a complaint about a discriminatory retirement age (as between men and women) and the available level of compensation for sex discrimination in British tribunals and courts.

The two Marshall cases deal with incompatibilities between British and European law. They also reveal the processes used to enforce the law. Furthermore, they provide examples of how British law had to be amended to comply. In the first case, British differential retirement ages for men and women were tested against European law. In the second case, the level of available compensation was determined.

EU equal treatment law

In 1976, the European Community implemented the Equal Treatment Directive. This concerned the eradication of discrimination on grounds of sex or marital or family status in access to employment, vocational training and working conditions.

Member states were required, by 1978, to enact legislation in their own Parliaments to ensure there was no provision contrary to the principle of equal treatment in:

☐ all legislative provisions;

☐ the terms of collective agreements;

☐ individual contracts of employment;

☐ the internal rules of undertakings.

If so, such a provision would be declared null and void or amended.

The Equal Treatment Directive, like all Directives, imposes obligations on the member state – not on private persons such as employers. Consequently, to regulate the behaviour of employers, trade unions and working people, the member state must enact the Directive into its own legislation. If a Directive is not fully implemented by a member state, then the EU Commission may start *infringement proceedings* against the member state before the European Court of Justice. In respect of equal treatment, Britain did have legislation (the Sex Discrimination Act 1975).

The first Marshall case

Up to the early 1980s, the policy of the South-West Hampshire Area Health Authority was that 'normal retirement age will be the age at which social security pensions become available' – that is, 60 years for women and 65 for men. Miss Marshall argued, before an industrial tribunal, that this policy constituted less favourable treatment under the Sex Discrimination Act. Her case was dismissed by the industrial tribunal and, on appeal, by the Employment Appeals Tribunal. British legislation, at that time, permitted these differential retirement ages.

However, Miss Marshall made an alternative claim that her compulsory retirement, at 62 years, was also contrary to the EU Equal Treatment Directive. She was able to invoke this, directly, because she worked for 'an emanation of the State' – that is, an organisation subject to state control and regulation. Had she worked for a private company, she would not have been able to.

The industrial tribunal agreed with this claim. The EAT rejected it, however, arguing that the Equal Treatment Directive did not have *direct effect* in Miss Marshall's case. The matter was referred to the European Court of Justice for a ruling. This ruled that direct effect was appropriate in this case.

The consequence of this first Marshall case was that those who worked for the State, or an emanation of the State, were entitled to harmonised retirement ages between men and women, under the direct effect of EU law. Those who worked for private organisations were exempt because British law – the Sex Discrimination Act 1975 – permitted differential retirement ages.

The European Union could have started infringement proceedings against Britain for non-compliance with the Equal Treatment Directive. However, the discrepancy was rectified when the Sex Discrimination Act 1986 was enacted. This required harmonised retirement ages throughout all sectors of employment.

The second Marshall case

When the issue of compensation for Miss Marshall's loss was considered, the compensation limit stood at £8500. However, this could not compensate her fully for a loss estimated to be

£19 405, including interest. Eventually, after various appeals, in 1991, the House of Lords referred the issue of compensation to the European Court of Justice for a ruling on compatibility with European Equal Treatment law.

In August 1993, the ECJ gave its historic ruling. It stated that a fixed upper limit on compensation, which was awarded for loss and damage suffered as a result of sex discrimination, was contrary to equal treatment law. Compensation must be 'adequate'. It must enable the loss, including interest for reduced value as time passes, and damage actually sustained as a result of the discriminatory dismissal 'to be made good in full'.

The consequence of this ruling was that all complaints would benefit from a change in the law in sex discrimination compensation. The compensation limit was repealed and industrial tribunals were also given the power to award interest with effect from 22 November 1993, under the Sex Discrimination and Equal Pay (Remedies) Regulations 1993. Comparable action was taken to remove limits in race discrimination complaints, under the Race Relations (Remedies) Act 1994. This came into effect from 3 July 1994.

Exercise 9.3 **The implementation of employment law**

In this section, we have considered a number of broad trends in personnel management and employment relations that have arisen from the implementation of employment law. The Marshall case study illustrates the importance for employers of a number of factors examined in this chapter

Read the case study again and note down how the following factors affect the Marshall cases:

(a) social policy standards about equal treatment;

(b) the regulation of the employment relationship;

(c) sources of employment law;

(d) the political and legislative significance of Britain's membership of the European union;

(e) the operation of the judicial process;

(f) the impact of judicial decisions and consequential legislative action for employers.

☐ Summary and conclusion

Employees are not one-dimensional individuals concerned solely with their own economic interests and rewards. They are social beings who import into the employment relationship values, expectations, experiences, external social and family obligations and differing standards of physical and mental health.

At work, employees will have many individual interests; but they will also have numerous interests in common with fellow-workers. These interests will not always coincide with those of their employer. In such conflicts of interest, employees are disadvantaged because of the scale of their employer's economic power.

The effective working of the employment relationship, therefore, requires reconciliation and accommodation:

☐ *Accommodation* by the employer to individual employees, with a proper recognition of their wider social concerns as parents, carers, breadwinners, etc. and their interests in both job and income security.

☐ *Reconciliation* between the values and expectations of employees with those of employers for productive, high quality, cost-effective, flexible working.

Given the underlying imbalance of power in the employment relationship, three questions inevitably arise:

☐ To what extent should employers and employees be free to work out the necessary accommodation and the reconciliation of interests?

☐ To what extent should government intervene, setting appropriate standards of public policy to deal with, for example, unfair discrimination and treatment, exploitation in terms of low pay and long hours, poor health and safety standards?

☐ To what extent should government intervene to promote, by encouragement or by statutory requirements, the representation of both individuals and groups of people at work through either trade unions or non-union employee representation systems?

These tensions between voluntarism and legal regulation have been explored in this chapter. In addition, three models reflecting different political perspectives on the balance between voluntary action and legal regulation were considered. It has been concluded that, at the present time, manifestations of all three models coexist in British employee relations. In addition, it has been noted that, over the past 20 years or so, there has been a marked shift from voluntarism towards considerable legal intervention and juridification.

☐ Useful websites

Advisory Conciliation and Arbitration Service
    http://www.acas.org.uk
Central Arbitration Committee
    http://www.cac.gov.uk
Commission for Racial Equality
    http://www.cre.gov.uk
Department of Trade and Industry (employment relations site)
    http://www.dti.gov.uk/er
Disability Rights Commission
    http://www.drc-gb.org/drc/default.asp
Equal Opportunities Commission
    http://www.eoc.gov.uk
Health and Safety Commission
    http://www.hse.gov.uk
Low Pay Commission
    http:www//lowpay.gov.uk

10

Chapter

Implementing individual employment rights

◆

☐ Introduction

This chapter will concentrate on the context in which four key sets of individual employment rights continue to be developed. The employment rights that will be used to illustrate the importance of these various contextual factors are:

☐ equal treatment and equal opportunities in employment;
☐ the creation and operation of the contract of employment;
☐ minimum standards for terms and conditions of employment;
☐ the termination of employment.

Together they provide a broad framework of law that reflects the flow of the employment relationship from start to finish. They will also highlight the interaction and importance of both statute law and the common law of contract.

Why have these been chosen?

☐ The principle of equal treatment is a theme which is fundamental to the entire employment relationship.
☐ The contract of employment is central to the regulation of the employment relationship.
☐ The development of statutory minimum standards has grown in significance.
☐ The termination of employment is likely to involve considerable loss of benefits to employees and result in a significant deterioration in living standards.

These areas of employment law give some protection for employees, who may otherwise be vulnerable to arbitrary treatment by their employer. This protection is provided, in theory:

☐ by outlawing unfair discrimination throughout the employment;
☐ by integrating *natural justice* into the employment relationship, e.g. in relation to dismissal;
☐ by recognising the value to employees of job security and the rights and benefits that accrue with length of service, e.g. in relation to redundancy;
☐ by requiring *reasonable treatment* by employers; and
☐ by requiring certain minimum standards in contractual terms.

All these issues have been at the forefront of public policy debates during the past 30 years.

☐ Focus and scope

This chapter is not designed to provide a detailed outline of employment law. The focus will be on the political, social and economic context that has affected employment rights in recent years. The principal issues are:

☐ social attitudes about good employment practice and fair treatment;

☐ social attitudes about work and its relationship to an employee's domestic responsibilities;

☐ social attitudes about women's role in society and the economy;

☐ employers' economic objectives and the pursuit of cost-effectiveness and flexibility in the use of labour;

☐ the standards of public policy set by various British governments and the European Union to promote fairness, reasonableness and non-discriminatory treatment;

☐ the extent to which labour market conditions encourage or discourage observance of these standards of good practice;

In the subsequent discussion, the following issues will be considered:

☐ the extent to which the law influences the policies and practices of employers in the management of their staff;

☐ the justifications for developing statutory individual employment rights;

☐ the costs and resource implications for employers of compliance with the law;

☐ the enforcement processes and their significance for good personnel management practice.

Learning objectives

Once you have read through this chapter and completed the associated exercises, you should be able to:

☐ understand the fundamental importance of equal opportunities as a theme in the employment relationship;

☐ understand the social and economic factors that influence the development of equal opportunities;

☐ analyse particular employment policies and practices in terms of equal opportunities and suggest action that might be taken;

☐ understand the central importance of the contract of employment in the regulation of the employment relationship;

☐ understand the legal principles underpinning this contract;

- [ ] advise an employer on issues to be considered when contractual terms have to be changed;
- [ ] understand the contribution of minimum employment standards;
- [ ] understand the concepts of *fairness* and *reasonableness* in termination of employment.

CASE STUDY

Seymour Aerial and Cable Installations

Seymour Aerial and Cable Installations employs about 30 staff at its office in Merton. There are three word processor operators, who carry out some ancillary tasks. Together with four other administrators, they work in the Central Administrative Services Department.

The company was founded in 1955, as Seymour Aerials, by Sid Seymour. It was initially a small business run from his home and then from a lock-up. In the early 1980s, his more entre-preneurial son, Warren, began to expand the business and Sid retired to the Costa del Sol.

The personnel management and employee relations approach of the company reflected Warren's buccaneering attitude. He had no time for formal procedures or policies. He was a great admirer of Margaret Thatcher. Like her, he regarded trade unions as 'the enemy within' and employment protection law as 'a burden on business'. Staff, consequently, were treated in an arbitrary manner. They were well paid when times were good and they were expected to work hard. When times were tough, exercising his right to manage, Warren would change con-ditions of employment unilaterally – cutting back what he saw as expensive, fringe benefits.

The company expanded considerably during the 1980s and was renamed Seymour Aerial and Cable Installations. In late 2001, however, it put a freeze on recruitment and the Engineering Manager had been overheard by one of the reception staff talking about poss-ible redundancies.

Personnel management, such as it was, was undertaken by Terry Daley, the Administration Manager. He was assisted by Sharon James, a secretary/PA who joined the company in 2000 to handle personnel administration. In her previous job, Sharon had successfully completed the Certificate in Personnel Practice course at the local further education college. She tried to make some simple changes at Seymour's such as providing every employee with a Section 1 *written statement* of their terms and conditions and introducing a disciplinary procedure. Terry said, 'We're not interested in all that stuff; we've got a business to run.'

Selena Charles, aged 23 years, had been employed by the company since 21 May 2001 as a full-time WP operator in the Merton office.

Selena was a moderately good employee. She had only been late twice. Her standard of performance at work was reasonable. She took some time to settle in. Her probationary period of three months was extended by a further three months because some of her work was sloppy and she was slow. By September 2001 she was doing a reasonably competent job.

She was known to the other staff as a friendly and helpful person, although Terry Daley found her surly. He had commented to Warren that 'she's one of those people who are always going on about their rights.' This arose for two reasons.

Selena had mentioned casually at coffee break to the other staff about the law on VDUs. Her father had read about it in an article in his union journal.

A few weeks later, when the company decided to impose a 1 per cent pay increase, Selena had been vociferous in an office discussion. She had said, 'If there was a union here, they wouldn't get away with this exploitation.' She told colleagues that her father was a shop steward at London Underground, where he had worked for 30 years since coming from Barbados. He had said that they should get organised into a union. Terry Daley was passing and said that they 'needn't try that here. Warren wouldn't stand for it.'

Returning from her holidays, on 13 May 2002, Selena was delighted to tell the other staff in the office that she was pregnant. The baby was due in November. The other staff asked if she was giving up work or taking maternity leave. She said that she wanted to carry on working because she and Winston, her boyfriend, were saving to buy a small flat. Her mother would look after the baby during the day.

Selena did not formally tell Terry about her pregnancy. He found out from Sharon, who, at Selena's request, was looking up the law on maternity leave. 'Bye bye, blackbird,' Terry commented. 'She's too much of a troublemaker, that one.' He told Sharon to tell Selena that she would have to finish work when the baby was due. Sharon tried to explain that Selena might have some rights. 'Look,' said Terry, 'they're all the same, these people. Their rights – that's all they go on about. It's probably her father putting her up to it. One of these militants, isn't he?' Later Sharon told Selena what he had said.

At the end of June, two weeks after this incident, Selena was late for work three days in succession because she was suffering from morning sickness. Terry seized his opportunity. 'We can't have this,' he told her. 'You'd better leave now. There's work to be done here and you're not up to it. Pick up your P45 and any money owing on Friday. You're finished.'

On the advice of her father, Selena decided to complain to an employment tribunal about unfair dismissal.

Exercise 10.1 **Individual employment rights**

The case study covers a number of individual employment rights discussed within this chapter. It can be used in various ways, depending on how much detailed exploration is required:

1 Note the individual rights issues that you think arise from the case study and then check them off as you read through the remainder of the chapter. Think about the importance of the underlying principles of fairness and non-discrimination in the case.

2 Check, in an employment law text or guide, the rights that Selena has and how they have been infringed.

3 Obtain an IT1 form and imagine that you are assisting Selena to complete it.

4 Obtain an IT3 form and imagine that you are assisting Terry Daley to complete it.

Both forms can be downloaded from the Employment Tribunals Service website: http://www.ets.gov.uk

☐ Equal treatment and equal opportunities

This section will examine the interplay of social, political and economic factors on the development of equal opportunities law. It will consider, first of all, the responsiveness of the political system to social pressures for change; and then it will explore the impact of various contextual pressures on employing organisations. Finally, it will examine those issues that are present within the workplace which facilitate or obstruct the implementation of equal opportunities objectives.

The political context

Equal treatment law concerns the eradication of both policies and practices based on stereotyping and also unfair discriminatory treatment of particular groups, e.g. women, pregnant women, people from various ethnic groups, and disabled people. The law, consequently, advocates effective equal opportunities policies. These are expected to reflect standards of social justice and good human resource management practice.

The concept of *equal opportunities* is set in the context of often negative, long-established, social attitudes, expectations and stereotyping. It is important to remember that, under this concept, it is not implied that, for example, all women must seek promotion and have full-time permanent jobs or even undertake paid employment at all. The concept is not prescriptive. It is founded on the notion of freedom of choice in decisions about employment. Such freedom can, of course, only be genuinely effective if stereotyping and entrenched discriminatory employment practices are eliminated.

Over the past 30 years, there has been a strong political impetus to outlaw discrimination – particularly sex discrimination. This has been derived primarily from the policies of various British governments, and supported by a framework of European Union law.

The initial areas of discrimination outlawed in Britain in the 1970s were those on grounds of sex, marital status, race, colour, nationality and ethnic origins. By the mid-1990s, the legal framework had expanded substantially to cover pregnancy, sexual harassment, disability and trade union membership and non-membership. The European Union had also reinforced this legal protection in respect of sex discrimination, pregnancy, maternity and parental rights.

By 2000–01, three further significant developments were evident. First, discrimination against part-time workers and fixed-term contract workers was outlawed. This followed the transposition into British law of two European Directives. Such legislation was designed, as part of European social policy, to provide some protection for workers in the growing flexible labour market.

Secondly, in October 2000, the Council of the European Union adopted a wide-ranging Directive on equal treatment, encompassing areas other than sex discrimination. Under this Directive, the UK government must introduce the following new laws:

☐ By October 2003: preventing employers discriminating against workers because of sexual orientation or religion.

☐ By October 2006: outlawing unequal treatment on the grounds of age or disability.

Thirdly, the Council of the European Union adopted a Race Discrimination Directive which came into force in July 2000 and has to be implemented into national law by 19 July 2003.

It might be argued that over the past 20 years or so a loose bipartisan political consensus has existed on some important areas of discrimination. Disagreement has arisen principally on details – the mechanisms used to ensure compliance by employers – and also on the degree of financial commitment necessary to implement them.

The organisational context

In the following section, several issues are explored about employers' attitudes to effective implementation. When implemented in organisations, equal opportunities policies are likely to confront numerous constraints and tensions – particularly financial costs, the degree of managerial commitment and social attitudes. In many organisations, equal opportunities continue to exist on paper only and not in reality.

For example, in 1990 the Equal Opportunities Commission reported that 93 per cent of Health Authorities stated they had an equal opportunities statement or policy. However, 75 per cent did not monitor the policy and 30 per cent did not communicate the policy to staff.

Employer attitudes to the economics of equal opportunities fall under two related headings:

☐ the degree to which the achievement of equal opportunities objectives is seen as a cost to the organisation;

☐ the degree to which it is seen as a contribution to the business objectives of the organisation.

Cost consciousness

A clear tension exists within organisations between the requirements to be cost-effective and competitive and the cost of compliance with social policy standards. The severity of economic pressures confronting employers is dependent on the state of their product markets and the labour markets in which they operate. A highly competitive product market will increase pressure on an organisation to trim unit labour costs. Adherence to social policy standards is likely, then, to be a lower priority, particularly for small organisations.

Employer resistance to these standards could, of course, be misplaced. Compliance might result in a better motivated, more creative and productive workforce. Nevertheless, this tension is a reality.

The possible costs facing an employer include both those which are directly quantifiable and those which are indirect and dispersed within the organisation.

Directly quantifiable costs can include, for example:

☐ the cost of compliance with improved terms and conditions of employment set out in law, e.g. equal pay, statutory redundancy pay, and working time requirements;

☐ resources and time involved in both providing advice and training on standards of good practice;

☐ establishing and operating monitoring procedures;

☐ the potential *opportunity cost* of non-compliance, e.g. representation at an employment tribunal, an award of compensation to a successful applicant, and the likelihood of anyone taking this course of action.

Indirect costs, by their very nature, are much less easy to discern and quantify. On the one hand, low compliance with standards of good practice might have a range of adverse employee relations consequences – low productivity, low quality standards, low morale, high labour turnover, poor attendance records, a sense of job insecurity, etc. On the other hand, compliance might result in higher unit labour costs than competitor companies and consequential difficulties in gaining orders.

Business strategy considerations

Some organisations are taking steps forward in the implementation and evolution of equal opportunities policies. One innovative concept centres around the *management of diversity*. This concept is located within the context of strategic business issues. It is concerned with the management of a workforce as a diverse group of people. It considers not just groups identified in those areas of outlawed discrimination but also includes people with differences on many other grounds – e.g. age, social background, personality, sexual orientation.

Its business focus means that consideration is to be given by all managers:

- to the promotion of greater creativity among staff;
- to problem solving;
- to the reduction of the costs of staff recruitment and retention by reducing labour turnover; and
- to assistance in marketing goods and services to a diverse range of customers.

As an approach towards operationalising equal opportunities, the management of diversity is commendably broad. It recognises the social heterogeneity of British society, is inclusive of wide ranges of groups and is not merely restricted to those defined by anti-discrimination law. However, although described as a step in the evolution of equal opportunities policies, it does not use one set of the equal opportunities measures – positive action and targets.

The justification for this has been put as follows:

> ... if managing diversity is truly about creating an environment where everyone feels valued and their talents are being fully utilised, then actions ought to be targeted on any individual who has a particular development need and not restricted to those who are members of a particular group.

(Rajvinder Kandola *et al.* 1995)

Although its significance must be recognised, the management of diversity is at present in its infancy in Britain. The focus in this chapter will be towards the implementation of equal opportunities policies as conventionally understood.

Implementing equal treatment in employment relations

As indicated earlier, equal treatment must be acknowledged as an ingredient in the entire employment relationship. It infuses the terms and conditions offered under the contract of employment; and it can be a factor in the termination of employment. It is, of course, central to the first stage in the employment relationship – recruitment and selection. It is this first stage, therefore, that will be used as an illustration, in the following section, of the interplay between recruitment policies and equal treatment.

A number of external and internal factors influence an organisation's recruitment policy and practice. Principally, these include:

☐ changes in social attitudes;

☐ the characteristics of the external labour market;

☐ the characteristics of the internal labour market;

☐ the extent to which positive action is promoted to deal with historic patterns of discriminatory treatment;

☐ the specific requirements that employers have for skill, experience, particular patterns of working-time and the deployment of labour.

The significance of and interplay between these factors is now considered under the following headings:

☐ Occupational segregation

☐ Positive action

☐ Social attitudes

☐ The external labour market

☐ Legal provisions

☐ Good human resource management practice

Occupational segregation

In considering their recruitment policy, employers should identify, first of all, the existing profile of their workforce. This will probably reveal both an inheritance of previous, often inadvertent, discriminatory practice and also prevailing social attitudes that have resulted in occupational segregation.

Within workforces, such segregation exists in respect of both women and ethnic groups. There are two kinds: vertical and horizontal (*see also* Chapter 4).

Vertical segregation describes the situation where, for example, men predominate in the higher graded posts in an organisation and women in the lower graded posts.

> For many women there is a glass ceiling blocking their aspirations, allowing them to see where they might go, but stopping them from arriving there. In any given occupation and in any given public office, the higher the rank, prestige or influence, the smaller the proportion of women.
>
> (Hansard Society, 1990).

This phenomenon is common to most large organisations.

Exercise 10.2 **Vertical segregation**

Look at your own organisation's workforce profile and see how extensive vertical occupational segregation is.

Horizontal segregation describes the situation where, for example, men and women in an organisation may work in different types of jobs – *men's work* and *women's work*. Workforce surveys, published by the Equal Opportunities Commission, indicate heavy concentrations of women workers in relatively few occupations – frequently those with a large demand for part-time labour.

The following occupations are identified as significantly female:

clerical and related; catering; cleaning; hairdressing; personal services; professional and related in education, welfare and health; selling; and, in manufacturing industry, painting, repetitive assembly and product packaging.

It is interesting to note that this occupational segregation also reflects in large part the stereotypical female domestic responsibilities – caring, cleaning, menial repetitive tasks and the provision of personal services.

Exercise 10.3 **Horizontal segregation**

Look at your own organisation's workforce profile and see how extensive horizontal occupational segregation is.

Positive action

If occupational segregation is a characteristic of an organisation's internal labour market, then, in preparing for future recruitment initiatives, an employer may consider whether positive action is appropriate. This involves the identification of targets for the recruitment of particular social groups and, consequently, the encouragement of those under-represented groups to apply for particular positions. It is permitted under both sex and race anti-discrimination law.

An organisation carrying out such a diagnosis of its workforce profile and proposing a proactive equal opportunities policy does not, of course, operate in a vacuum. The external context includes three related aspects, all of which are inevitably, by their nature, in a state of some flux: social attitudes; the external labour market; and legal provisions. These form the next part of the discussion.

Social attitudes

Social attitudes influence both the size and nature of the external labour market – that is, the characteristics of available recruits. In addition, attitudes and expectations are imported into the organisations and managers have to deal with them. The significance of this can be illustrated by exploring, as an example, the attitudes both of women and towards women.

Historically, certainly for the first half of the twentieth century, apart from during the two world wars, predominant social attitudes regarded women's contribution to society (outside the home) as largely peripheral. In society generally, the emphasis was on the importance of male roles. For example, government and political activity were male preserves. Full and equal civil rights to vote in elections were not granted to women until 1928. Education was seen as more important for boys. Both full-time work and the breadwinner role were usually ascribed to men.

In recent years, particularly with the emergence of greater feminist consciousness in the late 1960s, there have been some marked shifts in social attitudes among both women and men. In large part, this has arisen both from women's own preferences for changing their role in society and also the identification of particular barriers and discriminatory practices that have to be eradicated.

Labour market data provides some interesting evidence of certain social changes. For example, the economic activity rates of married women have grown significantly from 22 per cent in 1951 to 55 per cent in 1995. This has been a major contributor both to shifts in social attitudes as well as a consequence of such shifts.

Economic activity rates by women's age show that increasingly women in child-bearing and child-rearing years are taking much shorter breaks from employment (*see* Table 10.1).

Table 10.1 Women's economic activity by age groups (%)	**1971**	**1991**	**2006 (est.)**
25-34 years	45.5	69.7	80.6
35-44 years	59.6	76.7	85.2

Source: Ellison (1994)

For example, whereas in 1971 less than half of 25 to 34-year-old women saw themselves as participants in the labour market, by 1991, the proportion was over two-thirds. Two factors are suggested as contributing to this: a decline in childbearing, together with a stronger preference to continue in employment after a short maternity career break.

Both sets of statistics, then, provide some explanation of the increasing feminisation of the labour market. By December 1993 women accounted for 44 per cent of the working population (11.7 million). By 2006, it is estimated that the proportion will be 45.8 per cent (12.9 million).

By contrast, the number of males in the labour force is projected to stay relatively static or decline slightly as the chances increase of men being permanently out of work once they are over the age of 55 years. In 1993, there were 15.4 million men of working age. By 2006, it is estimated that there will be a marginal increase to 15.7 million.

However, although social attitudes are changing and so enhancing women's roles in both society and work, there are two factors that constrain the achievement of equal opportunities. The first is the existence of residual traditionalism among both men and also some women. The second is the generally inferior status of much female work.

An illustration of traditional stereotyping was reported in an Equal Opportunities Commission survey, where a British Rail manager was reported as saying:

> I have a number of ladies in my establishment and they are quite happy being routine booking clerks, travel centre clerks, and that's not to say they don't do a good job. But they're possibly there because it's basically pin money to them. So they do a good job by their pleasant personality and they get job satisfaction from it, but no way do they wish to go forward and take greater responsibility.
>
> (Robbins, 1986)

In a further survey in Barclays Bank, Tina Boyden and Lorraine Paddison (1986) commented:

> We recently asked a sample of male managers what they saw as the major factors inhibiting the progress of women in the bank and they replied that women lacked ambition and confidence, were reluctant to obtain professional qualifications, did not make long-term career plans and tended to put their husband and families first. More to the point, women staff, surveyed independently, also volunteered these reasons for lack of progress.

The comparative inferior standing of much female work is seen, frequently but not always, in terms of:

☐ employment status, much being part-time, temporary and homeworking;
☐ lower levels of earnings compared with men;
☐ low levels of skill; and
☐ limited or non-existent promotion and development opportunities.

The legacy of these attitudes and practices has to be recognised in society generally and also within the cultures of particular employing organisations. The law assists in setting standards of public policy which condemn such attitudes and

---

Exercise 10.4 **Social attitudes**

Ask female relatives from different generations about their experiences of work. For example, were they encouraged or expected to work? Were they expected to give up work on marriage or when they had children? If they wanted to work, what barriers and other difficulties were there to employment or to a career?

practices as unacceptable. However, the eradication of bad human resource management practice is, of course, both morally and in law, the responsibility of the employer concerned.

The external labour market

The interplay between social attitudes to women and the external labour market is particularly important. We will consider two further aspects:

☐ general levels of employment and the existence of skill and labour shortages;
☐ the type of employment status required by employers.

One significant facilitator for the overall promotion of equal opportunities is the general state of the labour market and, associated with this, the labour markets experienced by particular organisations. For example, the impetus for tackling sex discrimination and for advancing equal opportunities for women was considerably greater between the mid-1980s and the onset of the recession in 1990–91.

The two principal reasons for this were:

☐ employers needed to meet immediate skill and labour shortages; and
☐ their longer term need to anticipate the effect of the *demographic time bomb* which involves a decline in the number of young people (16 to 24-year-olds) in the labour market – from 21 per cent in 1990 to 17 per cent in 2001.

These supply side factors, in terms of the availability of labour, were matched by a range of practices by employers to encourage women to return to employment after maternity breaks or, alternatively, to remain in employment. These measures included either particular working-time arrangements – such as job sharing, term-time contracts, flexible working hours, career-break schemes – or specific fringe benefits – for example, workplace nurseries or other assistance with child-care provision.

Interestingly, there is in many of these arrangements an implicit, and sometimes explicit, assumption about women's continuing established roles as mother, wife and carer. Indeed, it can be argued that unless such arrangements are also genuinely available to men, they are not well-founded in a commitment to the principle of equal treatment. They merely reinforce traditional female roles.

The successful integration of female workers into an organisation's workforce, then, involves recognition of many considerations. The four most significant are listed below.

☐ Women are still the predominant family carers in our society.
☐ The working life of a woman is normally characterised by a career break, for childbirth and/or child-rearing.
☐ There is a marked overall preference among women (81 per cent of respondents) to work part-time (*Employment Gazette*, April 1994). After maternity leave, there is some evidence that women are now more likely to return to

full-time employment and to the same job, working for the same employer, than they were in 1981.

☐ Working-time flexibility is a key feature of employment conditions widely favoured by women workers.

Recognition of these issues and genuine attempts to incorporate them into equal opportunities policies will go a long way to comply with the requirements of sex discrimination law.

Legal provisions

For an employer, there are three factors that need to be considered in respect of anti-discrimination law:

☐ the extent to which it is a response to changing social attitudes;

☐ the extent to which it is moulding social behaviour;

☐ the extent to which it is fixed or is changing.

Responding to social change

Social changes continue to take place which give rise to developing expectations among women. Principal among these are preferences for flexibility in working time; the acknowledgement by employers of the need to reconcile work and domestic responsibilities; expectations of fair treatment and fair rewards; a growing preference for continuous career progression.

As a result of these evolutionary changes in social attitudes, the employment role of women is increasingly being redefined. Consequently, the law will inevitably be further developed and amended. For example, case law has affirmed the possibility of women, after maternity leave, to return to part-time employment if the employer cannot justify employment on a full-time basis. In this way, then, the legal framework is responsive.

However, it is important to remember that the law is a technique used to modify social behaviour. Two processes are at work.

☐ On the one hand, changes in social attitudes develop resulting in new laws and standards of public policy and acceptable practice.

☐ On the other hand, social behaviour then has to be modified to conform with these new standards of practice.

Moulding social behaviour

The manner in which social behaviour might be influenced by legal standards is seen in the recruitment and selection process. This is a process where choices are made. Discrimination – distinguishing or making choices between people – is a normal part of employee relations. If employers adopt standards of good practice, they will normally discriminate on the grounds of a person's work experience, skills and educational qualifications relevant to the job concerned.

However, any casual review of employee relations reveals that, when choices are made, discrimination is not always carried out using such objective criteria.

Employees or potential employees can often be judged according to qualities they are presumed to have because they belong to a particular social group, e.g. single women, Asians, older workers, people of Afro-Caribbean origin, disabled workers. This stereotyping prevents managers from considering objectively the qualities that a person might bring to a job. Such unfair discrimination is generally unlawful if it relates to sex, marital status, pregnancy and maternity, race, colour, ethnic origin, nationality, disability and, in Northern Ireland, religion.

In recruitment practice, this discriminatory treatment can be of two kinds. The first is intentional and direct. For example, an employer may, illegally, tell an employment agency that it does not wish to employ any black or Asian workers.

The second kind of discriminatory treatment may result, unintentionally and indirectly, from an existing employment practice. For example, an organisation may recruit staff by 'word of mouth'. In such circumstances, it is probable that those recruited will broadly reflect the gender, ethnic origin and social background of those employed in the organisation. The Sex Discrimination Act 1975 and the Race Relations Act 1976 outlaw both *direct discrimination* and *indirect discrimination*.

These provisions on direct and indirect discrimination are central to the effective enforcement of public policy in this area. The legislation, therefore, intervenes to set out principles of behaviour. It does not proscribe detailed practices. It is the responsibility of employers to scrutinise their own policies and practices and, if a complaint is made to an employment tribunal, to justify their actions and those of their managers and other staff.

Direct discrimination, by its very nature, is more obvious and may, therefore, be more easily tackled. By contrast, indirect discrimination may be more difficult to diagnose and root out. It is a more subtle form of bias and consists of treatment which may appear to be fair, but is discriminatory in operation and in its effect. It is largely the cause of the continuing absence of women and of ethnic minority groups from important areas of employment. Without this provision, the bulk of our anti-discrimination legislation would have been severely weakened and probably discredited.

Law in a state of flux

There is a danger in considering the law governing any aspect of the employment relationship as being fixed. Clearly, there are fixed principles and certain statutory provisions can have a long life-span. It is important to remember, however, that the law is constantly being interpreted in the light of particular circumstances. Case law and Acts of Parliament change year in and year out. As with other elements in an organisation's context, change and evolution are critical ingredients.

For example, within the past few years, British courts and the European Court of Justice have:

- refined the rights of pregnant workers;
- developed the framework of maternity rights;
- enhanced some of the rights of part-time workers;
- determined eligibility for pension rights.

In addition, there are current debates on possible anti-discrimination law in respect of age and sexuality.

Good human resource management practice

A number of critical problems can arise for employers at the recruitment and selection stage, in respect of discriminatory treatment. It is a stage which involves a number of steps:

- the drafting and distribution of a job description and a person specification;
- the publishing of advertisements;
- the drafting of application forms;
- the organisation of interviews;
- the establishment of a monitoring process.

Consequently, it requires clear standards of good practice at each step.

These standards are outlined in the statutory codes of practice from the Equal Opportunities Commission, the Commission for Racial Equality and the Disability Rights Commission.

The preceding discussion on equal treatment has focused, principally, on statute law – legislation passed by Parliament to achieve some particular economic and/or social purpose. It has shown that the character of this employment legislation is frequently determined by an interplay between changing social attitudes, public pressure, and a recognition that certain standards of good practice should be adopted and applied.

An additional form of employment regulation derives from common law. This is judge-made law, enunciated through specific cases. Under the common law of contract various principles have been developed. In two respects, these have had a clear impact on the development of the contract of employment: when it is formulated and when it is changed. The next section, will explore these issues.

☐ Contracts to regulate the employment relationship

Different forms of contract

In contemporary society, an employment relationship is invariably governed by some form of contract. Usually, this is a *contract of employment*. However, in the current flexible labour market another form of contractual relationship is developing in importance: *the contract for services*. A person working under such a contract is usually described as self-employed. The person who works under a contract of employment is an *employee*; while, the person who works under a contract for services may be called either an *independent contractor* or a *worker*.

An employer's reasons for choosing one contractual form over another are largely economic, deriving from concern about cost-effectiveness. Several factors influence employers. Self-employed workers can be responsible, for example, for their own training, tools, equipment and office overheads and for providing their own benefits, like pensions. They are less likely to be a direct cost for an employer. The employer can also have greater flexibility to terminate such contracts and so limit access to unfair dismissal rights.

Given different forms of employment status, as an employee or a self-employed person, and atypical forms of employment, e.g. part-time or temporary work or homeworking, it is understandable that some uncertainties will arise over a person's access to employment tribunals to claim infringement of a particular statutory right.

The groups covered by these rights vary. Unfair dismissal protection is limited to *employees*. Anti-discrimination law, however, extends to all *workers*. Over recent years, arising from various cases, judges have developed a test to determine whether or not an individual is an employee and is, therefore, eligible, for example, to submit a claim alleging unfair dismissal.

This test involves a number of factors:

- [ ] the degree of control exercised by the employer;
- [ ] the integration of the person into the business, including the extent to which the employer bears risk and provides tools;
- [ ] the extent to which a person is obliged to work;
- [ ] whether the work is on a continuing basis;
- [ ] whether the employer deducts income tax and social security.

According to this test, the finding of a contract of employment depends on considering all these factors. None is sufficient in itself and all do not have to be complied with.

An illustration of how the test may operate in practice is seen in the case *Airfix Footwear* v *Cope* (1978). Mrs Cope worked at home making shoe heels. The company provided her with tools and issued instructions. Over a seven-year period, she generally worked a five day-week. She was paid on a piecework basis, without deductions for tax and national insurance. She was held by the Employment Appeals Tribunal to be an employee and therefore eligible to claim unfair dismissal.

Exercise 10.5 Contracts

1 Carry out an audit of the workforce in an organisation known to you.

2 Find out whether your organisation uses both contracts of employment and contracts for services.

3 How many people are on the different forms of contract? What work do they do? What proportions of your workforce are on full-time, part-time and temporary contracts? Does your employer use homeworkers or teleworkers? What proportions of these groups are male and female?

4 What are your employer's reasons for these different employment arrangements?

Despite the gradual increase in self-employment in the past 15 years – now settling at about 12 per cent of the labour market – most working people are individual parties to contracts of employment. It is this form of contract, then, that will be considered further in this section. It will be explored under two headings:

❑ *What is the contract of employment?* This section will consider the sources of the contract of employment and those key legal principles that infuse it.

❑ *How can it be changed?* This section will discuss the interplay between contract law and employers' continuing needs to make employment changes.

What is a contract of employment?

The contract of employment is an agreement, legally enforceable in the courts, between an individual employee and his/her employer under which the employee promises to be ready, willing and able to undertake the agreed work and the employer promises to pay the agreed wage. The contract may be in writing, verbally agreed or part verbal and part in writing.

The terms of a contract of employment are usually of primary concern in any grievance, disciplinary case, dismissal, redundancy, sex or race discrimination allegation, etc. Attention will quickly turn to the provisions of the individual's contract of employment – whether those terms are in writing or not.

The contract of employment, on the one hand, enables the employer to assert power and control over the employee – for example, in explicitly requiring mobility and implicitly requiring adaptation to new methods of work. On the other hand, it also confers certain limited rights upon the employee – for example, payment for work performed and implicitly a duty of care by the employer.

It is arrived at freely. This is so to the extent that the employee has a choice whether to accept or reject the contract. As discussed in Chapter 9, however, it is formulated and agreed in the context of a power relationship. So significant can this imbalance of power be that the contract of employment has been described, for the employee, as 'a command under the guise of an agreement' (Kahn-Freund, 1983: 18). Other writers, however, would contend that it aims at a more accommodating and consensual form of employment relationship by providing an agreed framework of rights and obligations for each party. To help promote a more equitable balance of power, employees have a right to information about certain key contractual terms. This can be of assistance in any claim before a court or tribunal (*see* Fig 10.1).

The interplay between the law and employment practice can be seen, in the first instance, in the sources of the contract of employment. These are likely to include all or some of the following:

❑ managerial decisions on terms and conditions of employment;
❑ collective agreements negotiated between the employer and recognised trade unions;
❑ workplace rules;
❑ custom and practice;
❑ statute law;
❑ implied terms deriving from common law.

❑ *Managerial decisions on terms and conditions of employment.* Employers will want to set specific provisions in a contract of employment. They will want

Figure 10.1
Written statement
of particulars of
employment

1   Names of the employer and employee.

2   Date employment began.

3   Date when continuous employment began (this may include previous employment with that employer; or the consequences of transfers between companies within a group).

4   Scale or rate of remuneration, or the method of calculating remuneration.

5   Intervals at which remuneration is paid.

6   Hours of work and normal working hours.

7   Holiday entitlement, public holidays and holiday pay.

8   Job title or brief job description.

9   Place or places of work.

10 Terms relating to sickness, injury and sick pay.*

11 Pensions and pension schemes.

12 Notice periods to terminate the contract.

13 If employment is temporary, how long it is to last; or termination date of the fixed-term contract.

14 Collective agreements which directly affect terms and conditions.

15 Where employees are sent to work outside the UK for more than one month:

    – the period of work outside the UK;

    – the currency in which they will be paid;

    – special benefits available while they work abroad;

    – any terms relating to their return.

16 Disciplinary rules and procedures.*

17 Grievance procedure. *

In these cases it is possible to cross-refer to other documents, provided there is reasonable access and opportunity to read.

an individual employee to carry out specific tasks, work certain hours and meet other obligations. For example, an employer may require mobility from an employee, e.g. to work between a number of sites, or may require him/her to be available for night work. Within certain limitations, discussed below, an employer has considerable freedom to prescribe terms and conditions of employment.

☐ *Collective agreements negotiated between the employer and recognised trade unions.* These agreements on substantive terms – that is, pay, working time, holidays, etc. – are not usually legally enforceable. They are voluntary agreements. However, the provisions are *incorporated*, as appropriate, into each individual's contract of employment. For example, if a union recognised by the employer for negotiations agrees increases across a salary scale, the rate of pay of each individual employee will then change. The new rate becomes part of the contract.

☐ *Workplace rules.* An employer may set certain rules of conduct which an employee agrees to. Often these relate to such serious matters as harassment, theft, drunkenness and substance abuse at work.

☐ *Custom and practice.* Certain customary ways of working can become binding as contractual if they are well-known, reasonable and the employee is certain of the effect of the custom.

☐ *Statute law.* Statute law can influence contractual terms in a number of ways. It can set minimum conditions which must be complied with, e.g. notice to terminate employment, maternity leave provisions. It may also set general obligations on employers' behaviour in the employment relationship – e.g. equal treatment, provision of a healthy and safe working environment 'as far as is reasonably practicable'. Finally, statute law may directly intervene into the contract of employment. For example, the Equal Pay Act 1970 states:

> if the terms of a contract under which a woman is employed at an establishment in Great Britain do not include (directly or by reference to a collective agreement or otherwise) an equality clause, they shall be deemed to include one (s1).

☐ *Implied terms deriving from common law.* Common law provides terms implied into contracts of employment. These are in the form of general duties placed upon both employers and individual employees. For example, employers have duties to pay wages and salaries and not to make unauthorised deductions. Employees have duties to obey lawful and reasonable instructions and to be trustworthy.

As indicated above, then, employers have some considerable freedom to set and implement terms and conditions of employment. However, they are subject to certain specific constraints: statute law requirements, common law principles and duties, and, if appropriate, the provisions of collective agreements. In the circumstances of specific employee relations problems all three can interlock.

For example, this interlocking could be evident in an application to an employment tribunal where there is an allegation of unfair dismissal relating to redundancy. If unfair selection on grounds of race is alleged, then statute law is brought into play. The common law principle of *reasonableness* will be considered – particularly as to whether the employer behaves like a *reasonable employer*. In terms of dismissal, the tribunal would also need to be satisfied that the ex-employee had been treated in accordance with the principles of *natural justice*. Furthermore, issues relating to collective agreements on the handling of redundancies may also be invoked.

How can the contract of employment be changed?

Both the employer and the employee operate this contractual relationship against a backdrop of change: technology develops; product markets decline; working practices need to adapt; pay rates must be varied. The terms of any contract of employment are, therefore, from the start, subject to continual pressure for change – normally to take account of the economic and operational interests of the employer and in unionised organisations to respond to new pay and conditions settlements.

Tension invariably exists, therefore, between these employer interests and those of employees for job and income security. These conflicts of interest can be reconciled through negotiation with trade unions or by an employee's individual agreement to change. In some cases, however, the problems seem intractable. As a consequence, for employers concerned about cost-effectiveness and product and labour market conditions, a key question has to be: 'How can contracts of employment be varied within the law?'

Two courses of action are available:

☐ to change provisions in existing contracts of employment by agreement with the employee(s) in question;

☐ to terminate existing contracts with due notice and offer contracts embodying the changed conditions of employment.

Changing existing contracts

Case law, particularly in recent years, has elaborated a number of principles and practices that employers should adhere to. These relate to such issues as consent, unilateral variation, consultation and negotiation, and reasonableness. In brief, an employer must not change terms and conditions unilaterally. He must obtain consent from the employee(s) in question. He is expected to discuss proposals for change either through consultation or negotiating procedures. Three sets of examples are given below to illustrate how, in recent years, courts have approached the issue of contractual change.

First, in one set of circumstances, courts have tended to support applications by employees. This is where the employer has unilaterally varied a contract without agreement. For example, unilaterally imposed pay cuts have been ruled by the House of Lords as repudiatory, or fundamental, breaches of the contract of employment by the employer. In these cases, the court was not concerned with questions of the employer's economic necessity. Their concern was with the terms of the contract, with the failure to achieve consent to the variation and with the employer's repudiation of the original contract. Damages in the form of back-pay were awarded to the plaintiffs.

Second, in some other cases, the courts have favoured employers' concern about flexibility to introduce change. For example, in one important case the adaptation to new methods and techniques by employees has clearly been determined as an expectation in the contract of employment. In this case, arising from the computerisation of certain clerical and administrative tasks in the Inland Revenue, the High Court judge commented that employees could not conceivably have a right to preserve their working obligations completely unchanged during their employment. They could reasonably be expected, after proper training, to adapt to new techniques. All that would happen with computerisation was that jobs would remain 'recognisably the same but done in a different way'.

Finally, another set of cases concerns those circumstances where an employee might resign if an employer insists on a particular contractual change. The employee can allege constructive dismissal before an employment tribunal. Critical to the ex-employee's success will be whether or not the employer breached, fundamentally, the contract of employment. In the case of an unagreed imposed pay cut, the employee would probably be successful. However, if the employer is found not to be changing the terms of the contract but giving new 'lawful and reasonable instructions' then the employee is unlikely to succeed.

Offering new contracts

The alternative strategy that might be adopted by an employer is to terminate existing contracts of employment with due notice, i.e. what is appropriate for each individual employee. It is then open to the employer to offer a new contract incorporating the desired changes. The employee is free to accept or not.

If the employee does not accept the new contract then the dismissal can be tested in an industrial tribunal under the framework of unfair dismissal law. Tribunals have usually accepted 'business need' as 'some other substantial reason' for dismissal – provided that the employer adduces evidence to show why the changes were required. Reasonableness in handling the whole process is also expected – with the employer showing that the employee's interests had been considered and that reasonable procedures had been followed before the employer insisted on the adoption of the changes.

From the preceding discussion, it is evident that employers in handling change are confronted by a complex network of factors: their own economic and operational objectives; the interests of employees for job and income security; statutory employment protection requirements; and the principles relating to contractual variation which have been elaborated under common law. Each individual tribunal/court case will be considered on its own facts and will be tested against the precedents of previous case law and the interpretation of statute law in the present case.

Although there is no failsafe process in respect of contractual change, it is possible to summarise best practice guidelines:

- ☐ Plan the process of change.
- ☐ Decide on the nature and scale of contractual changes.
- ☐ Avoid unilateral variation.
- ☐ Decide whether existing contracts are to be varied or, if appropriate, terminated and new ones offered.
- ☐ Give information on the proposed changes to each affected individual employee.
- ☐ Be prepared to discuss, consult and/or negotiate.
- ☐ Try to obtain the employee's consent.
- ☐ Be prepared to justify contractual changes against the organisation's operational and economic requirements.
- ☐ Anticipate some of the arguments that might be put at a court or tribunal in terms of, for example, reasonableness or business need.

☐ Minimum standards for terms and conditions of employment

The contract of employment considered in the previous section has, in recent years, been affected considerably by the growth in statutory minimum standards and, in some cases, by the requirement to meet certain absolute standards.

The key statutory provisions considered below are: pay; working time; health, safety and welfare; harassment and bullying; and leave.

Pay

This is affected by various pieces of legislation. First is the requirement, under the Equal Pay Act 1970, that each contract of employment is deemed to include an equality clause. So, no term of a contract of employment can be discriminatory as between men and women. (It is important to remember that the European Court of Justice has defined 'pay' under this European law to cover a wide range of financial rewards – not just basic pay). Secondly, the National Minimum Wage Act 1998 enacts a range of provisions to ensure that no worker (depending upon his/her age) is paid less than the prevailing national minimum wage. Thirdly, the Employment Rights Act 1996 (Part 11) prohibits the unlawful deduction of wages. Complaints about these rights can be made to an employment tribunal.

Working time

Principally, this is governed by the Working Time Regulations 1998 (as amended). These cover maximum working week; periods of rest; paid annual leave; and health and safety considerations in respect of shift working and night work. There are some specific provisions for young workers (i.e. those above the school leaving age and under 18 years). Complaints can be made, as appropriate, to an employment tribunal or to the Health and Safety Executive.

Health, safety and welfare

The duty of care (by the employer to the employee) is an implied term of employment contracts. The Health and Safety at Work Act 1974 (and the various Regulations made under that legislation) together provide a structured and detailed set of standards against which it is possible to test an employer's compliance. Generally, complaints are made to the Health and Safety Executive. However, emphasis is placed in the legislation on the significance of workplace safety representation as a means of dealing with the enforcement of standards, problems and individual grievances at the workplace level.

Harassment and bullying

Such behaviour could be regarded as a breach of the implied term (in the contract of employment) of mutual trust and confidence. In more recent years, statutory discrimination law (the Sex Discrimination Act 1975 and the Race Relations Act 1976) has been used to tackle both sexual and racial harassment through employment tribunal complaints. Additionally, if an employer fails to deal seriously with harassment or bullying – by investigation and by taking appropriate action against the perpetrator, then, a victimised employee might resign and claim constructive dismissal. Taking no action to deal with harassment could amount to a fundamental breach of the contract of employment.

Leave

The Working Time Regulations 1998, as already mentioned, entitle workers to minimum paid annual leave. Additionally, the Maternity and Parental Leave etc Regulations 1999 provide for three sets of leave: ordinary and extended maternity leave (which is paid to some extent); unpaid parental leave; and unpaid dependency leave. Complaints can be made to an employment tribunal.

Why were statutory minimum standards created?

There are a number of reasons for the creation of statutory minimum standards. These reasons relate to some of the themes introduced in Chapter 9. First is the inability of the contract of employment in itself to ensure fairness and equal treatment. The contract of employment regulates what is essentially an imbalanced power relationship between an employer and an employee. The ability of an employee to influence the terms of the contract are very limited. Often a contract is offered and accepted on a 'take it or leave it' basis. Traditionally, contracts of employment, under the common law, have not had to be constructed in a non-discriminatory way; did not have to operate on the basis of fairness; did not have to avoid exploitation of workers through poor pay and long hours; did not provide detailed guidance on the ways in which an employer might comply with the duty of care; and could have been terminated in an arbitrary manner. Essentially, they were instruments which operated primarily in the interests of employers.

Against the background of this traditional context, then, statute law has been used (particularly over the past 30 years) to ensure that a number of social purposes are achieved:

- creating a fairer balance between the employer and the employee in deciding on the terms of the contract of employment;
- aiming to balance more fairly both the economic interests of the employer and those of the employee;
- attempting to limit potential exploitation of employees in respect of the terms and conditions of employment;
- taking account of any special considerations for young workers who could be regarded as particularly vulnerable in the employment relationship;
- providing for a more detailed elaboration on the standards expected of employers in the treatment of their employees (e.g. under health and safety legislation; or in respect of harassment);

☐ providing more detailed elaboration of implied contractual terms (e.g. the duty of care; and the duty of mutual trust and confidence);

☐ facilitating the achievement of a better balance between work and non-work life.

☐ Termination of employment

When an employment relationship ends a number of factors that have been explored earlier in this chapter can been seen as interacting. These derive from the interests of the employer, from the interests of the employee, from the nature of the contractual relationship and from standards of public policy. Illustrations of these can be summarised as follows:

The interests of the employer

☐ The need for a cost-effective organisation.

☐ Employees who perform effectively.

☐ Acceptable standards of conduct by employees.

☐ Operational flexibility and responsiveness.

☐ The ability to manage change.

The interests of the employee

☐ Protection of job security.

☐ Non-discriminatory treatment.

☐ Fair treatment and fair decisions.

☐ Income security.

☐ Workplace safety.

The nature of the employment relationship

☐ The exercise of control by the employer.

☐ The balance of power.

☐ Differences of interest.

☐ Accommodation and agreement between the employer and the employee.

☐ Public policy.

☐ Equal treatment.

☐ Natural justice.

☐ Fair disciplinary procedures.

☐ Reasonableness of decisions.

☐ Consent to change.

Nowadays, in any unfair dismissal application before an employment tribunal many of these issues will, implicitly or explicitly, be reflected in both the presentation of cases and also the cross-examination. The tribunal will then make its decision on the facts of the case, particularly having regard to the standards of public policy. It is only in the past 25 years, however, that this has been possible. It was only in 1971 that the concept of *unfair dismissal* was enacted. Prior to that date, most employees were vulnerable to unfair termination of employment.

Setting standards of public policy

During the 1960s, various proposals for improvements in the legal protections for employees were being put forward. One influential voice was the Royal Commission on Trade Unions and Employers' Associations – the Donovan Commission. In its 1968 Report, it stated:

> there is ... a very general feeling, shared by employers as well as trade unions, that the present situation is unsatisfactory and it was reflected in the submissions of many who gave evidence to us.

The Donovan Commission's review coincided with the publication by the (then) Ministry of Labour of an advisory council's report on dismissal procedures. This drew unfavourable comparisons between Britain and other industrialised countries in terms of procedural arrangements for contesting arbitrary dismissal. It stated that 'in other countries more elaborate concepts of the rights of employer and employee have been developed'.

Indeed, in the early 1960s, the International Labour Organisation had found that in most of the 68 countries they investigated there were provisions by statute or otherwise for protection from unjust or arbitrary dismissal. Subsequently, in 1963, the ILO published a Recommendation on Termination of Employment to which the British government subscribed.

In Britain, then, until 1971, employees were vulnerable to arbitrary and unjustified treatment by their employer – with only limited redress. The available legal redress was at common law and was generally inadequate.

The general legal position of employees was that, as long as the employer gave proper notice, under the contract, to terminate the employment, then he was able to sack the employee for whatever reason he wished. No obligations were imposed upon the employer either to provide reasons for the dismissal or to justify the dismissal. The only remedy available to an employee was to claim wrongful dismissal in the ordinary courts.

Wrongful dismissal is a relatively weak form of redress. Normally, it is alleged in circumstances where the employer gives inadequate or no notice to terminate the contract of employment. The employee may receive damages from the employer – generally limited to pay for the appropriate period of notice. The Donovan Report commented:

> '... beyond this, the employee has no legal claim at common law, whatever hardship he suffers as a result of his dismissal. Even if the way in which he is dismissed constituted an imputation on his

honesty and his ability to get another job is correspondingly reduced, he cannot - except through an action for defamation - obtain any redress'

(para 522).

As a result of these criticisms and the subsequent debate, a bipartisan political consensus emerged in favour of the principle of limited protection against unfair dismissal. The legislation was introduced by a Conservative government. It has been accepted by subsequent Labour and Conservative governments – although with some modifications, particularly in relation to access. These modifications have reflected commitment to either the *employee protection* or the *free market* model of employment law.

Unfair dismissal protection is available to all employees who have the necessary service qualifications, currently one years' length of service. There are no such qualifications if the dismissal relates to an automatically unfair reason. The only remedy, for short service employees, may still be a wrongful dismissal claim – if applicable. (*see* Fig 10.2 on p. 277.)

Although the majority of employers may aim to behave fairly towards employees, the potential for using arbitrary treatment, victimisation and for ignoring the principles of natural justice is still largely present in the legal regime governing the employment relationship.

Arguably, in certain sectors of employment today, the situation does not appear to have moved on much since the beginning of the nineteenth century where 'the legal regime in a factory could fairly be described as that of a private legislative kingdom in which the employer was sovereign, judge, jury and executioner' (Clark, 1970). The employee is vulnerable not just to loss of job but also to loss of income, loss of status and, possibly, loss of reputation.

☐ The enforcement of public policy standards

The individual employment rights cited in the preceding sections of this chapter, were enacted to establish standards of good practice and, accordingly, modify the behaviour of employers, particularly in the employment relationship. Clearly, behaviour will not change if enforcement of these rights is seen to be weak.

There are two ways in which enforcement of these public policy standards will be reviewed:

☐ the political perspectives of the legislators; and
☐ the effectiveness of those existing procedures which provide remedies.

Political perspectives of legislators

There are probably three significant elements in this area: the universal application of the standards; the question of whose interests influence public policy enforcement; and political commitment to effective remedies.

Figure 10.2
Testing the
fairness of
dismissals

Employment tribunals, which hear unfair dismissal claims, consider the following issues in assessing fairness.

Reason

☐ Is the dismissal for a 'fair' reason, i.e. capability, misconduct, redundancy, a statutory bar on employment, or some other substantial reason?

☐ Is the dismissal for an 'automatically unfair' reason, e.g. sex, race and disability discrimination, or is the dismissal on the grounds of trade union membership or the voicing of certain health and safety matters?

Reasonableness

Whether in the circumstances, including the size and administrative resources of the undertaking, the employer acted reasonably or unreasonably in treating it as a sufficient reason for dismissing the employee; and that question shall be determined in accordance with equity and the substantial merits of the case (Employment Rights Act 1996).

Procedural fairness

☐ Compliance with the guidance in the ACAS Code of Practice: Disciplinary and Grievance Procedures (2000)

☐ Compliance with the organisation's disciplinary procedure, if one exists.

☐ Compliance with the statutory dismissal and disciplinary procedure under employment legislation (2002).

Much individual employment law is designed to protect employees against discrimination, infringements of natural justice, arbitrary treatment and victimisation. It might be presumed, therefore, that such standards would be available universally. This has not always been so. Remedies available under sex and race discrimination law, certainly, have been available to any employee, self-employed person or contractor irrespective of the number of hours worked each week or the length of service. However, access to unfair dismissal proceedings has been limited by both the number of hours worked (until 1995) and by length of service.

The reason for this is associated with the second factor – whose interests influence public policy enforcement? The Major government resisted the extension of unfair dismissal and redundancy rights to part-time employees who worked less than sixteen hours, in three court hearings, in the High Court, the Court of Appeal and the House of Lords. Eventually, the House of Lords ruled that such qualifying provisions were discriminatory against women, who were preponderant in this group. The government's arguments had revolved around two sets of economic issues: the discouragement of job creation and the burdens imposed on business by further regulation. The social justice issues of employment protection and fair treatment were seen as lower order matters.

It can never be presumed that employee interests are of paramount concern for legislators. There will always be a tension between, on the one hand, these standards of social justice and good employment practice and, on the other hand, the economic consequences for employers of employment protection.

Political commitment to effective remedies is inevitably conditioned by a government's attitude to the relative importance of employer and employee interests. Government can, in fact, use two complementary measures. First, it can provide both enforcement procedures and specific remedies for individual applicants. Second, it can use its economic power to ensure compliance with public policy standards.

The procedures available for aggrieved individual employees will be considered more fully below. As far as remedies are concerned, these tend to be financial – in the form of compensation. Until 1993, there was a ceiling on compensation levels. However, this was ruled by the European Court of Justice to be unlawful in sex discrimination cases (*see* the case study in Chapter 9). As a result, the ceilings were removed in both sex and race discrimination cases. Although a ceiling remains for unfair dismissal compensation, this was raised significantly in October 1999 to £50 000 (and it is subject to period review through a link with the retail price index). There are occasional well-publicised cases of high levels of compensation, particularly in respect of sex and race discrimination. However, the most recent surveys suggest that these do not represent the overall situation (*see* Fig 10.3).

Figure 10.3
Compensation awarded at employment tribunal (1999)

Unfair dismissal
- Median: £2422 (1997/8)
- Median: £2388 (1998/9)

These figures were published in Labour Market Trends (September 1999)

Sex discrimination
- Average: £7 208
- Median: £3 713

Race discrimination
- Average: £9 948
- Median: £6 000

Disability discrimination
- Average: £9 981
- Median: £5 500

These figures are from a survey published by Equal Opportunities Review (September 2000)

It has been argued that compensation is an insufficient remedy given the loss of job, income, benefits and status experienced by the former employee. Technically, of course, an employment tribunal can order the reinstatement of an unfairly dismissed ex-employee. However, if the employer objects, then the only available sanction is to increase compensation.

The use of government economic power can be seen in respect of the adoption of *contract compliance*. In using its purchasing power, government and local authorities could require the providers of goods and services to give assurances that they are complying with, for example, equal opportunities policy in respect of sex and race discrimination.

Such steps were taken, for example, by the United States Federal Government, initially in the 1940s, to contribute to the slow process of eradicating race discrimination. Similar measures were introduced in Britain on a voluntary basis by some local authorities in the 1980s – covering sex and race discrimination.

The general approach of the Thatcher/Major Conservative governments was hostile to these measures. For example, when initiating its compulsory competitive tendering (CCT) policies it was indicated that non-commercial considerations should not be used to determine the award of contracts. Recent evidence from the Equal Opportunities Commission (1995) has pointed to a weakening of equal opportunities as a result of CCT. The Labour Government in 1997, has not promoted contract compliance.

Effective procedures?

Standards set in employment law can be enforced at two levels: within the workplace and through the legal processes of the court and tribunal system.

At workplace level, the principal arrangements for implementing, processing and monitoring employment standards are, as appropriate, collective agreements, disciplinary and grievance procedures, equal opportunities policies.

Collective agreements have diminished in their incidence over the past 20 years, although it is still calculated that just under half of the workforce is covered by such agreements (*see* Chapter 11).

Disciplinary procedures can be useful instruments in dealing with the enforcement of standards of good conduct in the workplace as well as performance standards. Grievance procedures are designed to enable the ventilation and resolution of workplace concerns (which may concern an individual or a work-group). The Workplace Employee Relations Survey (Cully *et al.*, 1998) reports that over 90 per cent of workplaces have procedures for both discipline and dismissal and for the handling of grievances.

Both procedures, since September 2000, have been covered by a statutory code of practice (Code of Practice on Disciplinary and Grievance Procedures, 2000), published by ACAS (the Advisory Conciliation and Arbitration Service). It covers the operation of grievance and disciplinary procedures and also the statutory right to be accompanied. It gives detailed guidance on how such procedures should operate. The right of a worker to be accompanied in this context can be valuable in achieving the more orderly resolution of a grievance. The worker may be accompanied by either a trade union official or by a fellow worker. The code states that 'the statutory right to accompaniment applies only to grievance hearings which concern the performance of a duty in relation to a worker. This means a legal duty arising from statute or common law (e.g. contractual commitments)' (para 55).

The development of statutory guidance on internal grievance procedures and the enactment of a right to be accompanied together acknowledge the role that such procedures can play in minimising and resolving conflict; filtering issues that might otherwise become tribunal claims; ensuring more orderly employment relations; and reinforcing management responsibilities for dealing with employment matters.

The incidence of equal opportunities has also been reported on in the Workplace Employee Relations Survey (Cully *et al.*, 1998). Some 64 per cent of workplaces have formal written equal opportunities policies. Workplaces without a policy were predominantly small. Workplaces with a formal policy were more likely to engage in monitoring gender and ethnicity, collect statistics, review selection procedures, and make adjustments to accommodate disabled people.

It is important to remember, furthermore, that this workplace stage can be supplemented by independent assistance, possibly in the form of investigations, from outside organisations like the Equal Opportunities Commission, the Commission for Racial Equality, and the Advisory Conciliation and Arbitration Service.

The legal processes are, of course, available to individual employees. Normally, this will involve an application to an employment tribunal about a discrimination allegation, dismissal or certain breach of contract issues. The effectiveness of this form of complaint can be considered under a number of headings. The principal concerns that have been raised by various commentators are as follows:

☐ *Restrictions on access to the statutory right in question.* There are certain statutory rights which are available widely to workers, irrespective of their length of service or hours of work. Key examples are the right to be paid not less than the national minimum wage (apart from a limited age restriction); the entitlements in respect of the maximum working week and periods of rest; the provisions of the equality clause under the Equal Pay Act; and the right not to suffer unlawful pay deduction.

However, under some legislation certain restrictions do apply. For example, there is a qualifying period of continuous service required in respect of entitlement to statutory redundancy pay (two years). In addition, some legislation on leave entitlements permits considerable discretion for an employer as to whether the leave should be paid (e.g. parental and dependency leave). It might, then, be argued that certain minimum standards are incomplete.

However, in recent years there has been a considerable extension of employment rights to certain groups of workers as a result of the removal in 1995 of hours limitations. Clearly, these requirements discriminated significantly against many part-time workers. (Because part-time workers are overwhelmingly female, it was possible successfully to challenge the restrictions in the courts as indirect sex discrimination).

☐ *The characteristics of the tribunal process.* When they first became responsible for employment rights in 1972, industrial tribunals (as they were then called) were seen as offering 'cheapness, accessibility, freedom from technicality, expedition and expert knowledge of a particular subject'. These characteristics, originally expounded by the Franks Committee in 1957 in respect of tribunals generally, have been used frequently as a yardstick to evaluate the current effectiveness of industrial tribunal operation.

Various researchers have commented on the extent to which industrial tribunals have now diverged from these original characteristics (Dickens *et al.*, 1985; Leonard, 1987; Lewis and Clarke, 1993). In an extensive survey of unfair dismissal applications it was reported that:

> Although the tribunals were found to display the Franks characteristics, the extent to which they were displayed was found to be constrained by the quasi-court nature of the ITs and their location within a legal framework involving the ordinary courts.
>
> (Dickens *et al.*, 1985)

Clearly, then, there are serious questions about the extent to which the tribunal process can discourage applicants who are seeking quick and simple justice – particularly in the less legally complex unfair dismissal claims.

Exploration of this issue led Lewis and Clarke (1993) to propose the option of arbitration for those applicants who preferred it.

In 2001, an arbitration alternative to employment tribunals began, operating under the auspices of the Advisory, Conciliation and Arbitration Service. It is a statutory scheme and, initially, is restricted to unfair dismissal cases that are not associated with discrimination law.

☐ *The insistence on individual application.* The insistence on individual application can cause some concern and difficulties for individual applicants in discrimination cases. Invariably, discriminatory practices affect more than one person and so patterns need to be established.

☐ *The balance of resources.* The balance of resources between individual employees or ex-employees and the employer is uneven. Although an employer may be concerned about the costs involved in an employment tribunal hearing, he can bear the cost of legal representation more easily than an employee, who is not a trade union member. Legal aid is not available to tribunal applicants.

☐ *The standards used by employment tribunals.* Various comments have been made about the standards used by employment tribunals. For example, in deciding reasonableness, tribunals are not using their own test. They determine it by reference to 'the range of reasonable employers'. As Anderman (1986) has commented:

> the net effect of this approach is to require employment tribunals to adopt a standard of fairness which reflects the lower reaches of acceptable managerial practice, rather than to allow tribunals to establish standards which reflect their view of a more objective standard of fair industrial practice.

☐ Justifying individual employment rights

The framework of employment law considered in this chapter reflects the *employment protection/social justice* model described in Chapter 9. The appropriateness of this model has been at the centre of political debate for the past 20 years or so.

This debate is complex. It does not conform to a conventional left–right divide. A few on the free-market right wing of the Conservative Party argue in favour of the removal of much statutory employment protection legislation. It is said to be a constraint to economic success. They would leave the contract of employment as the only regulatory mechanism containing mutual obligations. However, a broad political consensus of opinion favours some framework of protective employment law. The debate among those subscribing to this view is about degree. In part, it concerns the extent to which such legislation is, and should be, a constraint and a cost upon employers.

Various factors have been highlighted regarding the merits or otherwise of employment protection legislation. These can be summarised as follows:

Social factors

☐ A democratic society should have standards of fair and equal treatment for its citizens both out of work and in work.

☐ Social attitudes and expectations change. To help meet these changing expectations legislative action is necessary to tackle traditional attitudes, prejudice and stereotyping.

☐ Regulation and standards are necessary to ensure that all participants in the employment relationship understand what is expected of them.

Economic factors

☐ The implementation of fair and equal treatment can improve the quality of working relationships and so make the organisation productive.

☐ Employment protection legislation ensures that employers generally provide terms and conditions comparable with other employers. This ensures that in competitive markets some employers do not achieve their market share by exploitation of their workforce.

☐ Each employment right has a price tag deriving from the cost of raising standards, the administrative costs of implementation and monitoring and the possible costs of dealing with complaints.

☐ The cost of employment protection legislation is a deterrent to employment creation.

☐ Employment protection legislation limits an employer's flexibility in responding to new initiatives, in introducing technological change, and in changing terms and conditions of employment and, therefore, increases an employer's unit labour costs.

Exercise 10.6 Employment protection

If it is accepted that some framework of employment protection law is required in a democratic society, then each individual citizen should think about the following questions. Consider your own answers.

1 What social and economic purposes should such employment protection achieve?
2 What obligations should be placed upon employees and employers?
3 How much weight should be given to employers' concerns about cost-effectiveness and flexible working practices and conditions of employment?
4 What procedures should be adopted for effectively enforcing these individual rights?

☐ Summary and conclusion

Various aspects of public policy have been examined. Two broad themes have been considered. First, the standards enacted in law are designed in many respects to balance the interests of employees and employers. While this law is designed to protect employees and promote some concept of social justice in the workplace, it also attempts to take account of employers' interests.

This balancing of interests is often most noticeable when employers seek to make changes in contractual terms. Provided they adhere to the principles set out in case law which protect employees' interests, the courts will generally confirm an employer's ability to make such changes.

Even in areas of employment protection where employee interests seem to be paramount, there are opportunities for employer interests to be considered. For example, in respect of equal treatment under sex discrimination law, an employer is able to put forward 'justifications' for indirect discrimination. In respect of dismissals and redundancies, the concept of 'fair treatment' still enables an employer to take action in his interest.

The second broad theme is that individual employment law exists in a state of continual flux. This arises from a number of causes. Social attitudes change. The economic demands of employers vary. Different political ideologies are predominant at different times. Case law sets new interpretations and standards. Judges may try to accommodate the law to changing social circumstances. The economic balance of power between employers and employees can change as a result of both economic and political factors.

Despite this state of flux, certain principles and standards of public policy are preserved, e.g. fairness, equal treatment, reasonableness. These will be interpreted in the circumstances of each case and in the changing social, economic and political context.

☐ Useful websites

Advisory Conciliation and Arbitration Service
http://www.acas.org.uk

Central Arbitration Committee
http://www.cac.gov.uk

Chartered Institute of Personnel and Development
http://www.cipd.co.uk

Commission for Racial Equality
http://www.cre.gov.uk

Confederation of British Industry
http://www.cbi.org.uk

Department of Trade and Industry (employment relations site)
http://ww.dti.gov.uk/er

Disability Rights Commission
http://www.drc-gb.org/drc/default.asp

Equal Opportunities Commission
http://www.eoc.gov.uk

Health and Safety Commission
http://www.hse.gov.uk

Low Pay Commission
http:www//lowpay.gov.uk

Trade Union Congress
http://www.tuc.org.uk

11 Collective interests and the law

Chapter

☐ Introduction

Historically, working people have organised themselves, either informally or formally, for various purposes. For example, early nineteenth-century trade unionism is littered with *ad hoc* groups of workers who petitioned their employers about low pay, hazardous working conditions or long hours. These groups often disbanded quickly. Occasionally, such a group might form the embryo of a more formal, continuing organisation – a trade union. Two principal constraints prevented both informal groups and the formal union organisations from becoming effective: employer resistance and legal prohibitions.

These early examples of collective work group pressure and representation find clear echoes in contemporary employment relations. Employers might still restrict collective representation. Legal rights and obligations in respect of collective representation are still subject to political debate.

☐ Focus and scope

This chapter will explore:

☐ the continuing significance of collective interests in employment relations;
☐ the influence of law on the ways employers manage their staff;
☐ the principles underpinning the law on collective representation at work;
☐ the importance of enforcement processes.

Learning objectives

Once you have read through this chapter and completed the associated exercises you should be able to:

☐ understand the arguments for and against setting up systems of collective representation, unionised or not;

☐ advise your employer on possible forms of collective representation and the implications for your organisation;

☐ understand the factors involved in regulating industrial action and providing a right to strike.

☐ Are collective interests still important?

One theme of this book is that the character of the employment relationship can only be properly understood if both individual and collective dimensions are recognised. To deny the existence of collectivism is a mistake. It takes many forms – both formal and informal.

Work itself is after all a social, collaborative activity which produces some common interests among groups of working people. Furthermore, on entering the employment relationship, people import into it a considerable range of social ties and the legacy of their social experiences. The social – the group or the collective – dimension is, therefore, inherently important in various ways to the overwhelming majority of employees.

By its very nature, the employment relationship is concerned with issues that affect both individuals and groups of people. Any single issue is likely to reflect both dimensions. This can be seen as we look at the practical steps necessary for managing redundancies.

☐ *Notice.* Has due notice of the proposed redundancies been given to the trade union or to employee representatives?

☐ *Alternative policies.* Have alternative policies been considered in relation to each affected individual member of staff? Has there been consultation about these proposals with either union or employee representatives?

☐ *The selection criteria.* What are they? Are they fair in terms of employment law? Have they been discussed and agreed with union or employee representatives? How does each individual measure up in relation to them?

☐ *Handling the redundancies.* Has there been consultation with union or employee representatives about the overall handling of the redundancies and also about individual cases? Has the consultation been 'with a view to agreement'?

☐ *Redundancy pay.* Is it proposed to pay merely the statutory minimum? Has there been consultation about any enhancements? What are the implications for individual employees?

It is simplistic, then, to talk of *individualism* replacing *collectivism*. What can change over any period of time is the balance between the two dimensions. This balance may be influenced by a number of factors – e.g. prevailing economic conditions, the impact of technological change on job design, employer preferences and government policy.

For example, during Conservative governments in the 1980s and 1990s, there was a political drive to emphasise individualism. The expression of collective interests was marginalised as far as possible. Individual performance-related pay heightened the individual dimension. Withdrawal of trade union recognition made collective representation more difficult to express. Employers were encouraged to withdraw from collective bargaining and to introduce personal contracts.

By contrast, during the term of office of the Labour government elected in 1997, there was greater support for the expression of collective interests. In particular, this is seen in the introduction of a statutory right of recognition for collective bargaining; the strengthening of collective consultation on redundancies and transfers of undertakings; the development of workforce agreements in non-union organisations under the Working Time Regulations; and the promotion of social partnership arrangements between employers and trade unions.

Employer preferences are varied and complex. Small and medium-sized non-union firms will tend to be individualistic in their employment relations. It is rare, however, to find large companies that have constructed coherent employee relations systems that deny any collectivism and promote entirely individually based arrangements. However, there are exceptions.

The most notable is IBM, which has operated a highly individualist employment relations model. Its approach comprises two elements: a strategic perspective and a view that employees should be 'looked after' by management.

> Implicitly, IBM sees in the concept of unionisation the assumption that the interests of the employed would inevitably be neglected by the employer in the absence of trade union representation. IBM does not accept this, arguing instead that its record shows that it is possible for a company to be successful, to be managed successfully, and for its employees' best interests to be a central part of that.
>
> (Bassett, 1986)

Among the elements of the IBM approach, described in the mid-1980s are:

1 *Contextual factors*: detailed and long-range manpower planning; guaranteed job security; reliance on full-time permanent employment.

2 *Conditions of employment*: single-status conditions of employment for all employees; within centrally determined salary ranges, individual pay recommended by an employee's manager taking into account merit and performance indicators.

3 *The processes of employment relations:*
   - ☐ Communications with employees are the responsibility of line managers.
   - ☐ Managers receive 40 days per year training on human resource management – covering, for example, performance appraisal, career prospects, etc.
   - ☐ Each manager is responsible for small groups of staff, between 9 and 17.
   - ☐ A biennial internal opinion survey is undertaken throughout the organisation, covering the employees' evaluation of the company, their satisfaction with their jobs, their rating of their manager, their views on their duties and responsibilities.
   - ☐ Two complaint systems exist, on business issues and on management decisions, with the emphasis on managers resolving any problems.
   - ☐ Trade unions are not recognised for either individual representation or collective bargaining.

Such an employee relations system will probably be tested at times of organisational crisis – that is, when product market problems arise, when technological change is accelerated, when redundancies are necessary. These changes can expose the contradictions inherent in individualised and paternal employee relations systems. For example, how is job security best protected? How are corporate interests and those of individual employees reconciled at times of crisis?

Arguably, then, no employing organisation can ignore the interplay between these two dimensions. If it is an organisation that approaches its employment relations strategically and systematically, then it is more likely to consider such issues as:

☐ the balance of individualism and collectivism required within the organisation's human resource management and employee relations policies;

☐ the extent to which individual interests, commitment and performance can contribute to organisational effectiveness;

☐ the extent to which collective interests can be harnessed towards organisational goals;

☐ the procedures that could be used to express collective interests – whether the organisation is unionised or not.

Exercise 11.1   Employee representation

1   Look at the work group of which you are a member. Consider the ways, if any, in which this group makes representations to your employer about terms and conditions of employment, and/or about the ways in which your work is carried out.

2   What views does both your work group and your employer have about the value of such representative arrangements?

☐ How are collective interests expressed?

The collective interests of working people may be expressed either on an *ad hoc* basis or through some form of continuing organisation. It is the organised expression of such interests that will be considered in this chapter.

Employees' interests may be expressed on three levels within employee relations using different processes.

☐ *An individual grievance to the employer.* This may concern an aspect of an employee's conditions of employment, e.g. grading, or the failure of the employer to meet some statutory obligation, e.g. maternity rights. Although the complaint may be specific to an individual, it could well concern a policy that also affects other staff. Consequently, there can be repercussions on the wider group of employees.

☐ *Consultation with employee or trade union representatives.* This may concern certain conditions of employment, e.g. health and safety, redundancy, technical change.

☐ *Negotiation with a trade union.* This may concern certain terms and conditions of employment, e.g. pay, hours of work, holidays.

The legal framework in which these three processes – grievance handling, consultation and negotiation – exist will be considered later in this chapter. Here, we will explore two background factors: employer attitudes to these processes, focusing around the concept of *the right to manage*; and the extent to which the various forms of employee involvement and participation reflect different power balances between employers and employees.

The right to manage and employee participation

Before deciding on whether or not to set up arrangements to deal with employees collectively, employers will have in mind a number of critical issues – principally, the balance of power and control in employee relations, and the freedom for an employer to pursue his economic objectives. These issues are often encapsulated into the short hand phrase, *the right to manage*.

While the phrase can be dismissed as part of the rhetoric of management – for example, when faced with a challenge to its power by either trade unions or legislation – it does draw attention to a number of important questions that need to be addressed:

☐ Should employers have unfettered power to make decisions because of their economic ownership of the organisation?

☐ To what extent should an employer's decisions be influenced by the views of employees?

☐ Are there specific issues over which employees should have some influence? Are these issues those which are directly related to employment, e.g. pay, hours and working conditions; or those which indirectly affect an individual employment, e.g. introduction of technological change, changes in products or services provided, closures of parts of the organisation?

☐ If employees are to be involved in influencing management decisions, should this be by negotiation – where agreement is reached with union representatives – or by consultation – where, after discussion, management still retains the right to decide?

Exercise 11.2   Consider the questions below on the right to manage and decide what your views are.
The forms of employee participation are usually considered in terms of the degree to which they might modify management's exercise of power. Some forms enable management to retain a considerable degree of power and so exercise 'the right to manage' in a relatively unconstrained manner. Others are based on the notion of power sharing.
A spectrum of employee participation is described in Fig 11.1. In outlining these forms, it starts with those where the right to manage is largely retained; and concludes with those that emphasise power sharing.

1   Look at employee relations in an organisation known to you and find out which of the forms of participation (see Fig 11.1) exist.
2   How effective are they seen to be by employees and by the employer?

Figure 11.1
Forms of
employee
participation

☐ *Financial participation*. Such systems are likely to provide individual employees with limited influence over corporate policy. They are more likely to be seen as providing additional remuneration through employee share ownership or profit sharing.

☐ *Communication systems*. These are likely to be one-way channels of communication like videos, e-mail, notice boards, conference presentations and team briefing. Their purpose is to disclose management information. (Employers are required in law to disclose certain information to employees.)

☐ *Operational participation*. This deals with ways to improve service delivery and production processes, through working parties, quality circles or team briefing that are two-way. Management responsiveness to any proposals will vary.

☐ *Consultation*. This process can be found in various forms. It can be pseudo-consultation, often about trivial issues. Here management is unlikely to be influenced. Alternatively, there may be genuine consultation resulting in changes to policies and achieving some consensus. (Employers are required in law to consult employees about certain matters.)

☐ *Negotiations*. Usually, negotiations about terms and conditions of employment take place where an employer agrees to recognise trade unions. The outcome is a joint agreement between the two parties. (There are some legal obligations on employers to recognise unions.)

☐ *Co-determination*. This kind of statutory framework exists in the works council system in Germany, where there is joint decision making between employers and employee representatives on specified employee relations issues.

Legal entitlements are discussed later in this chapter.

Despite the rhetoric of managerial prerogatives, some employers report that positive economic benefits can accrue from employee participation.

For example, in an analysis of the 1990 Workplace Industrial Relations Survey data, William Brown (1994) found that non-union companies have generally not adopted the best practice standards of human resource management. They are characterised by 'a tired old world of unrepresented labour'. Only unionised companies adopt best practice. He concludes that promoting collective organisation and bargaining is the best way to secure increased productivity and to control the growth in pay. Certainly, this analysis reflects other findings of employers' attitudes towards trade unions (Batstone and Gourlay, 1986; Daniel, 1987; Willey, 1986).

The significance of employee participation in its wider sense was also outlined in a report in the United States. In surveying the small number of high performance workplaces, the Commission on the Future of Worker–Management Relations (May 1994) pointed to a number of issues of relevance to Britain:

☐ Interest in participation can be expected to grow in future years as the education of the workforce rises, technology creates more opportunities to share information and delegate decision-making authority and the pressures of competition require continuous improvement in productivity and quality.

☐ Where employee participation is sustained over time and integrated with other policies and practices, the evidence suggests that it generally improves economic performance.

☐ Many managers, workers and union representatives believe employee participation and labour-management cooperation are essential to being competitive in their industries and to meeting employees' interests and expectations.

☐ Collective interests: the contemporary debate

During the early years of the 1990s, a number of factors began to coalesce to create the first significant debate for over 15 years on how the collective interests of employees might be represented and accommodated in employment relations. The principal contributions to this debate derive from the trade union movement, employer approaches to employee relations, employee attitudes and concerns, existing statutory rights and the impact of European Union law. Each one of these will be discussed and the consequences of the debates for contemporary employee relations will be outlined.

Trade unionism

In the two decades from 1980, there was a considerable change in the fortunes of trade unionism. This can be seen through three indicators: union membership levels; union density; and the incidence of union recognition.

In 1980, the Certification Officer reported that *union membership* stood at 12.6 million. By 2000 (the latest available figures), there were 7.9 million members. Workplace Employee Relations Surveys (WERS) over the period showed a drop in the average *union density of membership* in workplaces. In 1980, this was 65 per cent. By 1998, it had dropped to 36 per cent. Most significantly, there is a marked difference between the private sector and the public sector. Density of union membership in the private sector dropped from 56 per cent to 26 per cent; whilst in the public sector the fall was from 84 per cent to 57 per cent – still leaving trade unions a significant presence in the public sector (Millward *et al.*, 2000: 87–91). (These density figures exclude organisations with fewer than 25 employees.)

Finally, there has been a downward shift in the incidence of *trade union recognition*. In 1980, unions were recognised at 64 per cent of establishments (again excluding organisations employing fewer than 25 employees). By 1998, this had fallen to 42 per cent. The sharpest decline was in the private sector. So, in private manufacturing and extraction the incidence of union recognition fell from 65 per cent to 25 per cent; and in private services from 41 per cent to 23 per cent. The public sector, on the other hand, showed a small decrease in the incidence of union recognition from 94 per cent to 87 per cent (Millward *et al.*, 2000: 96). Indeed, 'it is fair to state that union recognition is predominantly a public sector phenomenon' (Cully *et al.*, 1999: 93).

During this 20-year period, a number of significant economic and political factors have influenced the state of collective representation through trade unions:

☐ The decline of manufacturing industry – a traditional heartland of trade unionism.

☐ Major structural changes in the public sector as a result of the Conservative government's policies of compulsory competitive tendering and market testing. One result of such policies has been the transfer of some former public sector employees to employment by private contractors.

☐ The creation in the National Health Service of Trusts and, in the Civil Service, the establishment of agencies.

☐ The marginalisation of trade unions from discussions with Conservative governments about macro-economic and social policy measures.

☐ Political encouragement, by Conservative governments, for employers to question the continuance of union recognition and to consider the reconstitution of employee relations on non-union lines.

☐ The enactment of legal measures to constrain union activity and the repeal of statutory trade union recognition. (Some of these, as we see later, have been rescinded)

One consequence of this 20-year decline of trade unionism and the expansion of non-union workplaces was the effort by the Trades Union Congress to develop a credible representation strategy that might influence action to be taken by a Labour Government. In 1995, a report was adopted by the TUC that explored various levels of representation (both collective and individual) and also considered the possibilities of statutory support for consultation and collective bargaining. Much of this report did influence the measures eventually adopted by the Labour government following its election in 1997.

Employers' approaches

It is difficult to determine a predominant view held by employers. Those which are most concerned about representational issues are larger companies. Their preferred form of representation tends not to be union-based collective bargaining.

Survey evidence has shown the slow but continuing implementation of employee involvement and participation initiatives at the instigation of employers. The focus of these has tended to be towards operational matters rather than consultation about terms and conditions of employment. For example, quality circles and team briefings have tended to attract some employers because they can be associated with cost-effectiveness. Such approaches to employee involvement have been commended and encouraged in, for example, the Code of Practice on Employee Involvement and Participation drafted by the Institute of Personnel and Development (1994).

Some multinational employers did establish arrangements for information disclosure and consultation under the European Works Council Directive, despite, at that time, the British opt-out from the Social Chapter. Among the motives for setting up such arrangements are consistency of practice across the organisation and the preference to achieve a wider understanding by employees of business developments.

The change in political climate, following the 1997 election and the enactment of statutory recognition legislation, may have begun to affect employer opinion. By 2001, there were signs of a growth in the incidence of *voluntary* recognition deals by employers. For example, the Advisory Conciliation and Arbitration Service (ACAS) has, since 1997, been involved in an increasing number of disputes about recognition. In the year to August 2000, the figure was 263. Around half of these disputes were resolved – resulting in an agreement for full trade union recognition. Prior to 1998, such a deal was the outcome in only around one-third of cases (and the number of disputes was around 150).

Employee attitudes and concerns

Employee attitudes to collective representation are complex. However, two sets of evidence suggest certain trends. The first relates to employees' experiences at work; and the second is their attitude to unions.

By the mid-1990s, many employees' experiences of employment were encapsulated in such terms as job insecurity, stress, overwork, exploitation, vulnerability. Of course, not all employees experienced these phenomena. Nevertheless, evidence suggests that such experiences were sufficiently widespread to provoke debates about the quality of employment relations.

These characteristics might be thought to create conditions under which collective action, and particularly trade union membership, might grow. However, other factors might constrain this: the lack of any legal rights to representation; employer hostility; employees' sense of their vulnerability to dismissal and victimisation, despite certain statutory protections; and, in the absence of unions' recognition, doubts by employees about the ability of unions to articulate their interests and achieve improvements.

Although trade unions, therefore, found difficulties in gaining recognition rights and so demonstrating their utility to members or potential members, they were increasingly seen in a more favourable light. There was some concern that decollectivisation had gone too far. For example, opinion poll evidence (MORI and Gallup, 1993) suggested a more positive public view of trade unions. Three out of four people thought trade unions were essential to protect workers' interests; 55 per cent believed the balance of power in industry had tilted much too far in the direction of management (Taylor, 1994).

Against this background, there is evidence that the 20-year decline in trade union membership has reached a plateau and is slowly being reversed. The 1998 membership figures published by the Certification Officer (the latest available) show that there was an increase of 0.6 per cent over the previous year. This was the first increase in these figures since 1979. A further similar increase was recorded in 1999–2000.

It is certainly arguable that there are now more opportunities available to unions to demonstrate their utility to working people. These include not just negotiated agreements on terms and conditions of employment but also participation in consultation, social partnership deals and also the opportunity to accompany workers under the statutory right to be accompanied.

European social policy

European social policy has had an impact on British employee relations and conditioned the debate on collective representation in several respects.

1 The general philosophical approach of the European Union reflects commitment to the participation of the *social partners* – that is, representative employer and trade union organisations – in its supra-national policy-making processes. For example, the UNICE, CEEP and ETUC are consulted in the drafting of Directives, e.g. on Working Time or on European Works Councils.

2 Certain Directives require employee participation at organisation level in specific circumstances. The principal examples are the Directives on Collective

Redundancies and on Transfers of Undertakings. These require the giving of information by employers and consultation with employee representatives 'with a view to agreement'. In addition the Directive on European Works Councils (1994) covering specific multinational companies provides for the development of information disclosure and consultation arrangements. In 2002, a directive on workplace information and consultation was adopted.

3 The Working Time Directive (1993) provides for the use of collective agreements for implementing some provisions. This creates some flexibility for employers (for example, in determining the time period over which the calculation of working time is averaged). Under the Work Time Regulation 1998, it is possible for non-union organisations to use workforce agreements as an alternative.

Can there be a consensus on employee participation?

The discussion in this section has illustrated the wide range of opinions held by employers, employees, trade unions and government about employee participation. This is likely to be a continuing growing area of political debate. Consequently, the key question is whether a consensus can be fully achieved on the steps to be taken.

To answer this, the different interests and objectives of the key actors in employee relations have to be addressed. These have been explored earlier and are summarised below.

Employers' responses to employee representation tend to stress three factors: the overriding importance of economic considerations, limited constraint on the right to manage and the need for flexibility. For example, the Institute of Personnel and Development Code, in outlining the aims of employee participation and involvement, highlights the success of the organisation; the improvement of performance and productivity; and the organisation's ability better to meet the needs of its customers and adapt to changing market requirements and hence maximise its future prospects and the prospects of those who work in it.

The right to manage and employee participation are theoretically incompatible. However, some employers are prepared to concede some limitation in their managerial freedom to achieve other objectives. It could be merely to promote greater understanding of business conditions through communication channels. In other circumstances, it could be to achieve compliance with managerial policies as a result of consultation. If collective bargaining is used, it could be designed to obtain formal consent to jointly determined policies.

Flexibility relates to the nature and form of employee representation. In its White Paper, *Fairness at Work* (1998), the government outlined policies 'designed to help develop a culture in all businesses and organisations in which fairness is second nature and underpins competitiveness'. It was stated that 'such cultural change will lead in due course to more positive relationships between employers and employees than the letter of the law can ever achieve' (para 1.8). One of the significant principles underlying these policies on representation was some degree of flexibility: 'the Government believes that each business should choose the form of relationship that suits it best'. However, it adds that 'freedom to choose must apply to employees as well as employers, otherwise any commitment will be hollow and will neither create trust nor underpin competitiveness. This means that employers should not deny trade union recognition where it has clear and demonstrated support of employees' (para 2.6).

From the perspective of employees and trade unions, economic success, power sharing and flexibility are likely to be regarded as important ingredients in processes of employee representation. However, other objectives will also be important: employee protection and the achievement of both job and income security.

Underlying these objectives are a range of specific values – fairness, the avoidance of unfair discrimination, victimisation and arbitrary treatment. The divergence between employee and employer attitudes may not be wide – particularly in those large organisations that try to adhere to the standards set out in statutory and voluntary codes of good practice.

As far as the form of employee representation is concerned, employees and, particularly, trade unions are likely to be concerned about the following issues: continuity of the representation arrangements, the independence of the representatives and the degree of power sharing or genuine consultation.

For example, in 1995 in discussing the impact of the European Court of Justice ruling on consultation in collective redundancies and the transfers of undertakings, the Trade Union Congress emphasised that representatives must be independent of employers and that representation must be part of some continuous system of employee participation and not specific to, for example, particular redundancies.

Trade unions would also be concerned to ensure that the character of employee participation was effective. This means that there would be shared decision making with the employer or genuine influence on managerial decision making.

☐ Collective representation: some legal issues

This section will review the factors that underpin the legal framework governing collective representation. This framework is significantly affected by government policy. In Chapter 8, three models were outlined: the *free collective bargaining* model; the *free labour market* model; and the *employee protection* or *social justice* model. The adoption of a particular model indicates a government's approach to collectivism in various policy measures: employers' duties to inform and consult; collective bargaining rights; trade union power; the balance between a statutory and voluntary approach for the promotion of employee representation and participation.

Clearly, collective employment law is highly political in all societies. It concerns not only the exercise of economic power by employers, but also the power of unions, not just in relation to employers, but in relation to the government of the country. In liberal democracies, this law will probably address itself, at a minimum, to four sets of often interlocking issues.

1 specified representation rights for employees (both individually and collectively);
2 rights for individuals to join a trade union, to have collective bargaining rights and to take industrial action against their employer;
3 rights for disclosure of information from employers for both employees and for trade unions;
4 rights to be consulted about specific workplace issues.

The detailed content of any country's law on these issues depends on a range of factors. Principally these are political and economic interests and concerns about civil liberties.

Democratic governments are expected to balance interests within their society. On the one hand, there will be employers' concerns about their ability to compete efficiently, to achieve cost-effectiveness and high levels of labour productivity and to retain considerable managerial decision-making freedom. On the other hand, there will be the interests of employees, most of whom will also be voters. These interests, as indicated above, concern job and income security, safety standards and the means by which employees can make effective representations about any of these issues to their employers and to the government.

In addition, the government may be obliged to take account of international standards from the International Labour Organisation, to which it is a signatory, and any relevant European Union Directive.

Governments may, of course, choose neither to balance interests nor aim at consensus. They may act in a less even-handed way and impose significant legislative constraints upon one party. Recent Conservative governments in Britain, for example, enacted policies to curb trade union power. Some of these policy measures have been criticised by the International Labour Organisation – for example, the removal of collective bargaining rights from school teachers, the failure to provide an individual right to strike, and the complexity of the law relating to industrial action (Ewing, 1994).

In formulating policies on representation and union membership rights, the kind of questions any democratic government is likely to be considering are the following:

☐ What is the proper role for trade unions in a democratic society?

☐ What representational rights should working people have in the determination of terms and conditions of employment; and in dealing with individual grievances?

☐ Should trade union activities be restricted to the workplace or do they have a legitimate representational role to play within the political system?

☐ How can democracy within trade unions be ensured?

☐ How can the accountability of trade union leaders to their members be guaranteed?

☐ Should there be complete freedom of choice in respect of trade union membership and non-membership; or, alternatively, should the closed shop be permitted?

☐ What is the legitimate role for industrial action in a democratic society?

The answers to these questions – as reflected in party political policy – will obviously vary according to ideological perspectives and the economic interests that the respective parties favour (see Chapter 8). So, for example, the Thatcher/ Major governments enacted policies designed to 'decollectivise' employment relations and to 'depoliticise' trade union activities. The Labour government has sought to balance employer and employee interests under the concept of 'partnership'. Nevertheless, it has accorded various individual rights to working people (often enacting European law) and provided for a statutory right for trade union recognition.

The legal framework in Britain

This section will consider four themes that have emerged in the development of the legal framework: the concept of social partnership; the single channel of representation; positive rights and immunities; and the independence of representatives.

Social partnership

The concept of social partnership is central to social policy in the European Union (*see also* Chapter 8). This view has infused collective representation law in Britain in a piecemeal way. Nowadays a range of specific statutory duties have been placed on employers to provide information to and consult with their employees. Some commentators argue that, in aggregate, these piecemeal duties could form the basis of a works council system (on lines already long-established in Germany and France). Existing duties are set out in Fig 11.2. Some of these reflect European law and some are more long-standing obligations required under British law.

Figure 11.2
Information and consultation duties

☐ *Information to individual employees*: on contracts of employment and any changes to the terms of the contract; about health and safety hazards, standards and procedures; on reasons for dismissal; on redundancies; on the right to opt out of Sunday working in shops.

☐ *Information to union or employee representatives*: on collective redundancies; on transfers of undertakings; and in European Works Councils.

☐ *Information to trade unions*: on collective bargaining matters.

☐ *Consultation with individual employees*: on changes to contracts of employment; on redundancy affecting the individual employee.

☐ *Consultation with union or employee representatives*: on collective redundancies with a view to agreement; on transfers of undertakings with a view to agreement; on health and safety; in European Works Councils. (Although not duties to consult, it is recommended in various statutory codes of practice that employers consult about equal opportunities policies and about disciplinary rules and procedures.)

(Note: some of these rights might be qualified by certain conditions)

The single channel of representation

Traditionally, the law on collective representation has focused on the rights and obligations of trade unions. They have been seen, both in law and in practice, as the single channel of representation for working people. In 1995, as a result of a challenge in the European Court of Justice to British consultation rights on redundancies and transfers of undertakings, there was a change in the law. Non-union employers were obliged (in specified circumstances) to consult with appropriate employee representatives. In 1996, a similar requirement was enacted for health and safety representation. In 1999, the arrangements for electing non-union employee representatives were amended to ensure greater independence and to prevent the undermining of any trade union recognition (where that might also exist in an organisation).

A further development has consolidated non-union employee representation. Under the Working Time Regulations 1998, it is possible for non-union employers to negotiate workforce agreements. Such agreements are negotiated either through employee representatives or directly with a specific workforce.

They must be in writing and are for a specified period (not exceeding five years). They can cover such matters as the length of night work, night work involving special hazards, and maximum working time.

Given all these developments, it is now no longer possible to characterise British employment relations of having a single channel of representation.

Positve rights and immunities

The legal framework for collective representation comprises the provision of both *positive rights*, normally for individual union members and officials, and immunities, for a trade union as an organisation.

The *positive rights* are set out explicitly in legislation and cover a wide range of employment situations and practices (*see* Fig 11.3).

Figure 11.3
Some key
collective rights

- ☐ To be a member of a trade union.
- ☐ Not to be a member of a trade union.
- ☐ Not to be excluded or expelled unreasonably from a union.
- ☐ To participate in trade union activities at an appropriate time.
- ☐ To be protected from dismissal and victimisation because of trade union membership and non-membership.
- ☐ To vote in elections for the union's principal executive committee.
- ☐ To scrutinise a union's accounts and financial affairs.
- ☐ To be consulted, through a representative, about collective redundancies, business transfers and health and safety.
- ☐ Time off for union activities, public duties, prior to redundancies and for antenatal care.
- ☐ Right to be accompanied in disciplinary and grievance hearings.

Note: These rights do not extend to the police, armed forces and intelligence services.

These rights are enforceable in law by lodging a complaint – usually at an employment tribunal. The remedies variously available to successful complainants include compensation, re-employment if dismissal has taken place, and a declaration of their rights.

Immunities are a legal device used to protect specified persons from legal proceedings. This device affects trade unions in the following way. Under common law, trade unions are 'in restraint of trade'. This is because they aim to regulate jointly the pay and conditions of employment offered by employers. By this action they are interfering with employers' economic freedom. In the 1870s, the legal protection of immunity was introduced in statute law to override the common law situation. This meant that the legal status of unions was clarified; they were permitted to exist and function lawfully. Furthermore, they could lawfully negotiate terms and conditions of employment with employers. In addition, the principle of immunities was adopted to enable unions to call for and organise industrial action. Immunities continue to provide the legal base for union activity and are enacted in the Trade Union and Labour Relations Consolidation Act 1992.

Independence

The law in relation to trade unions addresses this critical issue. This concerns the extent to which a union is solely responsible to its members and not under the domination and control of an employer. The Certification Officer will scrutinise the rule book and practice of unions to determine whether they can receive a certificate of independence. All TUC unions have this certificate – as do most outside the TUC. However, the circumstances of a few company-based staff associations has been problematical. In these cases, the employer has provided financial assistance and material support which tends towards control of the organisation.

☐ Industrial action: the legal framework

So far, the discussion in this chapter has focused on the primary issue of representation. However, any review of collective employment law would be incomplete without some consideration of the law and industrial action. This area of law changed considerably during the 1980s. This section will review the context within which it developed and also provides a case study to enable you to consider the impact of prevailing legislation.

Political concern about industrial action in Britain has been a continuing theme in both industrial relations and the political system for the past 40 years or so. Advocates of reform have tended to be identified with one of two broad views:

☐ *Those proposing a reformed voluntary system of free collective bargaining.* Under these proposals more effective grievance and dispute procedures would be established and independent conciliation and arbitration arrangements would be set up by Parliament. Employers and trade unions would be encouraged to review the quality of their industrial relations and introduce the necessary reforms voluntarily. Through these reforms, it was expected that the sources of discontent would be minimised.

☐ *Those proposing a more detailed and prescriptive legal framework for the conduct of industrial relations.* This would set out rights and duties for employers, trade unions and employees. Industrial relations would be conducted in the context of these public policy requirements. Certain requirements could be enacted to deal with industrial action and its economic effects.

Since 1979, those advocating a legalistic approach have been dominant in political policy making. Concern had been developing throughout the 1970s about the economic consequences of industrial action. Several issues had to be addressed and reformed.

☐ The voting systems to decide on industrial action were frequently seen as defective. Mass meetings were often used and secret ballots were the exception. There was concern that individuals might be coerced into supporting such action.

☐ There was some use of industrial action before negotiations had been completed and/or the disputes procedure had been exhausted.

☐ There was concern about the extent to which it was right for workers to take supportive, sympathetic, secondary action.

☐ The extent to which trade union leaders controlled their members who were taking industrial action was also a matter of public debate.

☐ The use of industrial action in essential services, such as hospitals, the fire service, etc., was being challenged.

As a result of the 1979 general election, it became the responsibility of a Conservative government to address these issues. Unlike previous post-war Conservative governments, the Thatcher government was characterised by a radical shift in political ideology and objectives. Its attitude to unions and industrial action was clearly hostile. The policy pursued in relation to industrial conflict reflects this.

It was described as a *dual-track* policy (Auerbach, 1990), comprising a policy of restriction and a policy of regulation. These policies were framed in the context of the government's economic objectives of deregulated labour markets, the promotion of an *enterprise culture*, greater cost-effectiveness and the assertion of the managerial right to manage.

The *policy of restriction* focused on trade union immunities. These were narrowed, so creating a wide set of circumstances whereby certain forms of industrial action could be declared unlawful. This policy of restriction had two associated underlying components: the promotion of enterprise confinement and the depoliticisation of trade union activity.

The notion of 'enterprise confinement' (Wedderburn, 1989) reflected the view that industrial action should only be lawful in respect of employees and their own employer. Sympathetic secondary industrial action was made generally unlawful. This reflected a widely held view in the Conservative Party that trade unions' only legitimate sphere of interest was workplace industrial relations. A corollary of this view was that unions should not pursue political objectives. Industrial action was therefore deemed unlawful if it was undertaken for political purposes, e.g. to resist privatisation.

The policy of regulation involved the use of extensive statutory regulations on trade unions in industrial action. They can be categorised under two headings: those relating to industrial action balloting; and those which concern a union's liability for the actions of its members and its officials.

This policy of regulation used a different technique. Detailed prescriptions on the conduct of ballots for approving industrial action were set out in legislation and a statutory code of practice. While these regulations may appear consistent with improving trade union democracy, they have in fact created a myriad of legal trip-wires. These mean that unions must approach balloting and industrial action cautiously.

As far as liability is concerned, this policy of regulation provided remedies, principally for employers, when unlawful industrial action takes place. An aggrieved employer may apply to the High Court for an injunction (a court order to stop the unlawful industrial action) and for limited damages from the union. Unions can escape liability if they repudiate the members concerned and tell them to return to work.

The Conservative government's framework of law governing trade union organisation of industrial action was continued by the Labour government after the 1997 general election. Addressing the Trade Union Congress in 1997, Tony Blair, as prime minister, stated that 'we will not go back to the days of industrial warfare, strikes without ballots, mass and flying pickets, secondary action and the rest of it'. The modifications enacted by the Labour government have been limited in effect: amendments and some simplification to the statutory Code of Practice on Balloting (implemented in 2000); and a further extension of the limited protection against dismissal when individual workers take part in industrial action (see below). Generally, therefore, the fundamental objectives and provisions of the Thatcher government's framework of law remained intact (*see* Fig 11.4).

The statutory changes outlined above were enacted to deal with trade unions as the organisers of industrial action. In tandem with these developments, the law relating to individual employees continued to be developed. This highlighted, particularly, their vulnerability in the absence of any legal right to strike. Three aspects of the law coalesced to illustrate this: breach of contract; dismissals for industrial action; and pay deduction.

Figure 11.4
What is lawful industrial action?

1   *Trade dispute.* There must be a lawful trade dispute – between workers and their employer – and it must be 'wholly or mainly' about employment-related matters: for example, pay and conditions, jobs, allocation of work, discipline, negotiating machinery. Industrial action must be called 'in contemplation or furtherance of this dispute'.

2   *Secondary action.* Sympathetic action is not lawful.

3   *Secret ballot.*

☐   There must be an individual secret ballot.

☐   Immunity for a union is conditional on approval in such a ballot.

☐   Code of practice sets specific requirements on organisation and timings of balloting process.

4   *Picketing.*

☐   Attendance at or near own place of work.

☐   Peacefully to persuade a person to work or not to work.

☐   Peacefully to communicate or obtain information.

☐   Police to enforce criminal law.

A code of practice sets out specific guidance on picketing.

Breach of contract

When an employee takes strike action – or participates in most other forms of industrial action – then he or she breaches the contract of employment. It can be regarded by the employer as a 'repudiatory' breach, so fundamental that it effectively destroys the contract. This will be particularly so if no work is carried out – as in a strike. As a consequence, an employer can dismiss the employee. This has always been the situation under common law.

Britain has been criticised by the International Labour Organisation for failing to enact an individual right to strike. One way of modifying the common law would be to introduce a rule that industrial action suspends rather than breaches the contract of employment. Many European countries have accepted the principle of suspension of contracts in industrial disputes as part of a positive right to strike. In these cases the strike usually has to be lawful. It has to meet some specific statutory requirements, e.g. approval in a secret ballot.

Dismissals for industrial action

Parliament has intervened to modify the situation whereby individuals may be dismissed for taking part in industrial action. However, it did not create an individual right to take industrial action. In the 1970s, it was determined that selective dismissal of those taking industrial action was unfair. An employer must sack all. A complaint may be made to an employment tribunal only about selective dismissal.

Three amendments have been made to this situation. The first amendment, in 1982, enables an employer to re-engage, three months after their termination, some but not necessarily all employees who have been dismissed. In 1990, selective dismissal was permitted of those who participated in industrial action not supported by their union.

In 2000, protection against dismissal was extended. The new statutory protection makes it automatically unfair for an employer to dismiss an employee (or to select that employee for redundancy) if the reason or the principal reason for the dismissal is that the employee took part in *protected industrial action* (*see* Fig 11.5). An employee who is sacked has the right to complain to an employment tribunal regardless of age or length of service with the employer. The complaint must be lodged within six months of the date of dismissal.

Pay deductions

The third area where the law has had an impact on individual employees has been in relation to pay deductions. Case law during the 1980s clarified various issues. Where there is strike action and the employer is not dismissing the strikers then it is accepted that they will not be paid for the duration of this action. The situation in relation to other forms of industrial action has been more problematical. The courts have differentiated between 'accepted partial performance' of the contract and 'rejected partial performance'. The decision to accept or reject is with the employer.

Figure 11.5
Industrial action
and dismissal

Protection against dismissal is provided for where an employee is taking part in official industrial action (i.e. supported by the union) in the following circumstances:

☐ Where the dismissal was during an eight-week period beginning with the day on which the employee started to take protected industrial action (whether this industrial action is continuous or intermittent).

☐ Where the dismissal was after the eight-week period and the employee had stopped participating in the protected industrial action before the end of that eight-week period.

☐ Where the dismissal was after the eight-week period and the employee continued to take part in the industrial action **and** the employer had not taken steps to try and resolve the dispute. These would include: an offer to start or restart negotiations; the use of conciliation services or mediation services.

If the official industrial action continues beyond the eight weeks and ceases to be protected, the existing provisions against selective dismissal will operate.

With *accepted partial performance,* the employer accepts that some, but not all, of the contracted work is carried out. The difficult issue has been to calculate appropriate remuneration for part-performance of the contract. Limited case law suggests a degree of rough justice.

With *rejected partial performance,* specific guidance has been given in a Court of Appeal case. The key points are:

☐ Employees are not entitled to pick and choose what work they do under their contracts of employment.

☐ An employee could not refuse to comply with his contract and demand pay under the contract.

☐ An employer could not give an employee instructions and refuse to pay him if he had told the employee that he was not required to attend for work, as a result of partial performance, and that if he did, it would be voluntary.

☐ The character and volume of work was also a consideration. Even if it is small when assessed in terms of time, it might be of some considerable importance.

Employers, clearly, have legal remedies available to them to respond to industrial action. Both statute and case law have tilted the balance of power in favour of the employer since the 1980s. It is on rare occasions – for example, at News International in 1986, in cross-Channel ferry companies in 1988 and at Timex in 1993 – that the full force of the law is used against both individuals and union organisations. Employers have to balance short-term victories in industrial disputes with the maintenance of working relationships and the improvement of industrial relations.

Exercise 11.3 The law and industrial action

The following exercise is a sequence of related scenarios. Answer each question in turn. To help you will find it usefull to refer to the *Code of Practice on Industrial Action Ballots and Notice to Employers* and also to the Department of Trade and Industry's guide on industrial action (*see* DTI website http:/www. dti.gov.uk).

1   *Is it a 'trade dispute'?*

Computer operators employed by the London Borough of Putney and Roehampton decided at a UNISON meeting on 10 November to ballot on industrial action about their hours of work.

2   *Have the regulations on balloting been adhered to?*

An individual secret ballot, supervised by the staff representatives, was held in the canteen on 11 November. The result was declared by the senior union representative, who announced that industrial action would take place the following Monday, 15 November. It would be a one-day strike.

3   *Is it an official or unofficial strike?*

Hearing of this, the full-time District Official of UNISON told his members, by phone and subsequently by letter, that the Union Executive would not support them and that they must go back to work.

4   *Why?*

The staff representatives demanded an explanation for the Union's policy. What would this be?

5   *Is it a fair dismissal?*

On 15 November, despite the Union executive's decision, the one-day strike takes place. The local authority sacks the senior union representative for taking part in the action.

6   *Is this lawful?*

The following day, the whole workforce in the Policy and Resources Directorate of the local authority decide spontaneously to walk out on strike in support of the sacked union representative.

☐ Summary and conclusion

The context of employment relations is being significantly affected by a number of legislative initiatives. These are prompted by political policies originating in either Britain or the European Union. At the centre of these policies is the exercise of power both by employers and by unions.

Trade unions, as the traditional vehicle for expressing the collective interests, have been subjected to various curbs on their power: in claiming bargaining rights; in representing employees; and in calling for and organising industrial action. New forms of collective representation are developing alongside trade unionism. Some have been introduced voluntarily, at the instigation of employers and some are set up under new statutory consultation rights. The effectiveness of such emerging organisations is as yet untested. Given the recognition of collective interests in employment that occurs in EU social policy, employers will increasingly be called upon to accommodate such collectivism in their employee-relations policies.

12 | Conclusion

□ Introduction

By its very nature, the subject matter of this textbook is very wide-ranging. Nevertheless, as an examination of the context in which organisations operate, it has identified a number of themes and trends which may be common to various contextual influences. One purpose of this concluding chapter, then, is to bring together certain of these key themes. An attempt will also be made to identify some likely future developments that will have an impact on organisations.

Before considering these themes, it is important to reaffirm the characteristics of the organisational environment that have featured throughout the text.

□ *Choice and determinism* – the extent to which employers, employees and governments have choice or are subject to constraints.

□ *Change and stability* – the extent to which this environment is in flux or is characterised by inertia.

□ *Objectivity and subjectivity* – the extent to which decisions and choices are made by objective criteria or may reflect personal opinions and prejudice.

□ *Power relationships* – the nature of power relationships between employers, employees and governments.

□ *Ethical considerations* – the extent to which moral values and concerns influence the behaviour and attitudes of managers and employees.

□ *Reciprocal relationships* – the extent to which action in one area, e.g. social attitudes, has an impact on another, e.g. legislation, which in turn has a reciprocal effect. For example, equal opportunities law modifies social attitudes and then creates demands for further legislative change.

□ *Integration* – the degree to which economic, technological, social, political, and legislative factors are interrelated.

□ Broad themes

It is always invidious to rank contemporary themes in order of importance. Each person's preferences will inevitably reflect his or her own values and ideological views. Consequently, those set out here reflect the authors' own experiences and ideological perspectives. The reader is, of course, free to disagree and determine his or her own preferences!

The broad sets of themes considered here are those deriving from the economy and those within society. There are two principal reasons for this selection. The economy provides the motor behind many other contextual developments in the organisational environment, i.e. social, political, legal and technological factors. Within society, values, attitudes, expectations and practices change – so affecting economic activity, attitudes to technological change and the environment, the political system and the legislative framework.

☐ Economic themes

The principal economic themes are considered under the following headings: objectives; management of the economy; and the global context.

Objectives

At the level of the macro-economy, one central unresolved issue is the extent to which the pursuit of economic objectives should be modified by concerns for certain social values. These social values might relate, for example, to the effects of technological change, threats to the environment and the conduct of employee relations. Such tension has been evident in, for instance, the concern over the character and extent of economic, political and social policy integration within the European Union.

This clash of objectives is also replicated at the level of any company or employing organisation. The question to be answered is 'How far should cost-effectiveness, productivity, efficiency and flexibilities be limited by, for example, policies designed to provide "decent" pay levels and job security?' Employees bring expectations of fair treatment and social justice into the employment relationship, and so employers are forced to respond to this question. They may do this explicitly, by adopting standards of good human resource practice or negotiating collective agreements with trade unions. Alternatively, management's response may be implicit in the practices (good or bad) that they adopt.

Associated with the issue of economic objectives is a further debate about the distribution of wealth. This debate occurs both at the level of the employing organisation and in the macro-economy. The central purpose of industrialised economies is wealth creation. Inevitably, however, questions arise about the distribution of this wealth and about the extent to which employees, as well as the owners of capital equipment, are considered as contributors to wealth creation. Furthermore, a supplementary question arises about the extent to which government should use some of this privately generated wealth for social purposes, such as schools, hospitals, houses, roads, defence, etc.

The issue of distribution of wealth is, consequently, highly political. It is concerned with the articulation and implementation of conflicting economic and social goals. The protagonists reflect often markedly different perspectives and values. One aspect of this debate centres on the notions of equality and inequality of treatment and also the concept of fairness. For example, at one level the public are critical about the disparate treatment of, on the one hand, chief executives and, on the other hand, the large number of employees whose security of income is jeopardised by cost-cutting measures.

At the level of the national economy, the debate on distribution understandably concerns not just pay but much wider issues like the scale of social security benefits, the levels of taxation and the availability of 'goods', such as education, health care and living accommodation. Associated with this is the issue concerning the extent to which government can promote further wealth creation through economic and social policy measures.

Government, then, has to generate its income through taxation and borrowing. It has to determine the amounts to be raised. It has to allocate resources to these social provisions. It has to decide the criteria for allocation. In formulating policy in these interlocking areas, government has to manage the achievement of social policy standards, economic objectives and the consequences of its taxation policy. Various fundamental questions, which balance economic and social considerations, have become the focus of political debate in recent years.

☐ To what extent should there be inequalities in the provision of basic goods, such as education, health care and living accommodation?

☐ To what extent should private as opposed to public provision of these basic goods be encouraged?

☐ To what extent should there be universal as opposed to selective provision of social security benefits?

☐ To what extent should individuals supplement or replace state provision of benefits with private provision, e.g. pensions, medical insurance?

☐ In raising revenue, what are appropriate levels of government borrowing, and what levels of personal and corporate taxation create disincentives for taxpayers?

Such questions are endemic in economic management in liberal democracies. There are no definitive answers. However, there are alternative answers. Those suggested will, of course, vary according to the governing party's political purposes and the interests it represents.

The management of the economy

In order to achieve its economic objectives, government may choose from a selection of instruments for economic management. In the *mixed* economies of liberal democracies – that is, those that have both a private and a public sector – there is a choice available to government. It can determine whether the balance of economic management tends towards a pure free market economy or towards one based on a degree of planning. The tendency to be located at one or other end of this spectrum depends upon the ideological perspective of the government.

A government's decision on specific economic policy objectives and particular instruments can have a substantial impact within that society. For example, new laws may be enacted to facilitate economic changes, e.g. compulsory equal pay audits. Changes in social behaviour may be promoted, e.g. the degree to which part-time work and flexible working practices are encouraged.

In addition to its promotion of a particular model of the economy, a government is likely to determine other related ancillary characteristics. The first is its choice of approach – whether this is to be characterised either by control mechanisms or by the encouragement of participation of the different interests in society. The second factor, which is closely associated with this first point, is the approach to any regulation – whether voluntary self-regulation is encouraged or whether an infrastructure for legal regulation will be enacted.

The global context

Just as companies are not free agents, able to manipulate policies across a range of areas, neither are governments of individual nation states. They are subject to wider contextual influences, which can constrain their economic freedom of action. At present, there are two significant discernible themes.

The international economy

The international economy has a number of facets. The economies of individual nation states are increasingly locked into a world economy and simultaneously these countries may be a member of a trading bloc – e.g. the North American Free Trade Area or, in a more developed form, the European Union.

Within this international economy, the exercise of power relations is important across a number of fronts: between member states within the trading blocs; between countries and trading blocs, on the one hand, and multi-national companies on the other; and between trading blocs themselves.

Such globalisation can have a number of possible consequences:

- a more vigorous pursuit of cost-effective international competition;
- footloose multinational companies jeopardising national or local economies by relocation;
- the development of laws, in the European Union, and codes of practice, under both the International Labour Organisation and the World Trade Organisation, to limit and regulate workforce exploitation and to establish protective rights;
- concern within individual countries about their sovereignty and freedom to act in their own perceived interests.

Environmentalism and sustainability

The crisis of global warming, the social and economic dislocation through deforestation, and the impact of microelectronic technology have, for example, heightened the recognition of global interdependence. Public concern and campaigning have resulted in some attempts to control and regulate the adverse effects of these developments. Such attempts are, of course, clearly affected by the power relations and vested interests that exist within and between individual countries and multinational companies.

□ Social themes

This second broad set of themes derives from the interaction of people in society at large – for example, as citizens, employees, parents, women, men, and members of specific organisations.

Five such themes have infused discussion in the text:

1 Equal treatment and fairness

This establishes, albeit unsatisfactorily, certain principles to guide social behaviour both in employment and in social relations generally. Both fairness and equal treatment have been inextricably associated with anti-discrimination policies. The principle that certain categories of people should not suffer detriments and stereotyping and should not be excluded from various forms of social participation has been established. Protective legislation has been enacted in certain key areas, e.g. sex and race discrimination, but significant exceptions in respect of age and sexual orientation will be rectified by forthcoming European anti-discrimination law.

2 Feminisation

The shift in public consciousness about women's role in society combined with legislative action has provided the impetus for growing and widespread feminisation. This is one of the most significant characteristics of contemporary society.

3 The management of diversity

As a result of combined demographic and social developments many, but certainly not all, European Union countries are both multiracial and also give recognition to the changing role of women. In the employment sphere, this has led to the concept of the management of diversity. Indeed, as a concept, it is arguably much wider and deserves to infuse broader social policies.

It can be conceived as an issue of citizenship. For example, do different ethnic groups have full citizenship rights or are these denied? It can be conceived as an issue of employment status. For example, how far are the skills, abilities and experiences of different groups – for example, the elderly and the disabled – used in employment? Finally, it can be conceived as a commercial issue. To what extent can businesses in marketing and selling target these differentiated groups of consumers?

4 Participation and enfranchisement

This concerns the basis of people's involvement in both civil society and employment.

Much of the language and rhetoric of liberal democracy is about citizenship and rights to participate in democratic decision making. Two important trends concern the quality of participation in democratic societies and the disenfranchisement of certain social groups.

The quality of participation by individual citizens can be poor. It is contended that the political processes that exist between elections to influence both legislators and the executive are, effectively, weak. Furthermore, cynicism about the political process and a lack of confidence in politicians as a group is frequently reported in some European countries (including Britain and France). There is, then, the danger of the atomisation of political participation – individuals voting once every four or five years in general elections and engaging in no other active involvement. Indeed the low turnouts in both the UK General Election (2001) and the election for the European Parliament (1999) have prompted wide concern about the degree of engagement between the electorate and their representatives.

The question of disenfranchisement of certain social groups has been remarked upon in several European countries. Sometimes, exclusion is a deliberate choice; sometimes it arises through force of economic circumstances; and sometimes it is a result of civic status. In Britain and France, there are sizable groups of homeless people who because they have no residence find participation in employment and political society difficult. This may be a differentiated group, but this aggregate phenomenon of *the underclass* or, in France, *les exclus* is an important political and social issue.

Some argue further that the political and industrial arenas should not be differentiated – that democratic participation should be extended to include the workplace. In Britain, particularly, this view is still contentious. It is less so in other European countries. In Britain, there is no consensus on the principle of participation at the workplace. If it is exists, it is subject to employer agreement and the enforcement of limited statutory rights.

5 The individual and collective dimensions of social activity

An associated theme is the basis upon which participation takes place: individual activity or collective action. Collectivism is seen as more acceptable in the wider political process; after all political parties and pressure groups are collective entities. In employment relations, however, these two bases of participation are frequently juxtaposed; and collectivism is seen by some as unacceptable. However, the reality of the employment relationship is that both individual and collective participation and representation are appropriate, depending upon the issue in question. Too great a shift to individualism would markedly increase the vulnerability of individual working people.

☐ Future trends

It is difficult and perhaps foolhardy to predict the future. Nevertheless, those interested in economic, social and political affairs need to be sensitive to probable future trends. However, sometimes the probable does not occur and the surprising happens. All of the major political developments listed here have in varying ways had profound effects upon businesses, particularly with the collapse of product markets and the growth of new ones. This, in turn, can affect employment opportunities and even the economic stability of specific countries.

In 1989, who would have thought that within ten years ...

☐ the Soviet Union would have ceased to exist and the Cold War would end?

☐ East and West Germany would have united?

☐ Communist China would be developing into a major world economy exporting a wide range of goods?

☐ Apartheid would have been abolished and Nelson Mandela would have been elected President of South Africa?

☐ Yugoslavia would have fragmented, leading to the first war on European soil since 1945.

With warnings in mind, then, there are some future trends that seem likely within the medium term (the next five years or so):

Political and economic

☐ There will be widening of the European Union to include more eastern European states.

☐ There will be continuing and probably unresolved debate about 'deepening' the European Union through greater integration.

☐ A growing backlash will develop against globalisation.

☐ Nation states – particularly in Europe – will be subject to twin pressures: the possible loss of further sovereignty to supranational bodies like the European Union; and internal pressures for decentralisation within the member state to regional governments.

☐ The balance of provision between private and public transport will be re-appraised.

Social

☐ There will be continued but slower improvement in equal opportunities for women as the more intractable obstacles are dealt with – for example, child care provision, training and development and equal pay.

☐ The ageing populations in European countries will provoke debates about social welfare costs.

☐ There will be increased potential for individualisation and atomisation both socially and as work is relocated to home as a result of technical change.

☐ There will be countervailing tendencies for collective action politically, through pressure groups and campaigns and at work through employee participation.

☐ There will be action to enfranchise further those groups disadvantaged on grounds of age and sexuality.

☐ There will be further action to promote 'work–life' balance.

☐ The level of crime and fear of crime will continue to grow and further security and surveillance techniques will be developed.

☐ The concept of *community* will be redefined with the growth of, for example, *network communities*.

☐ The concept of *life-long learning* will be developed.

Technology

☐ There will be wider diffusion of ICT competence throughout the population.

☐ Technologies will continue to converge, e.g. one instrument to provide TV, PC, audio system and telecommunications link.

☐ The sphere of bio-technology will grow in importance.

Exercise 12.1 1 From the perspective of your own organisation, what do you see as the principal trends and changes that will have an impact upon it during the next ten years?

2 What impact do you think that these changes will have on the conduct of human resource management?

Answers to exercises

The exercises in the text have various purposes. Some are to encourage you to investigate and review practice within your own organisation. Some ask you to think about your opinions on particular matters. A third group of exercises is designed to test knowledge. Suggested answers to many of the exercises are provided in this Appendix. Answers to the remaining exercises will vary according to the views of the reader and the nature of the organisation chosen by the reader.

☐ Chapter 1

Exercise 1.1 The external pressures facing Hodsons

Listed below are a few of the many external pressures currently confronting Hodsons. This is not intended to be an exhaustive list and you may have suggested a number of other specific or general issues which could also be included.

1   Worries about economic recession at the beginning of 2001 threatened to affect the housing and commercial property markets with knock-on effects on the level of construction activity and the size of the building industry.

2   Changing consumer tastes and growing interest in 'Do-It-Yourself' (DIY) home improvements have altered the types of goods and services that customers demand from builders and domestic suppliers.

3   Increased competition from large DIY centres based in out-of-town sites has drawn customers away from high street based building suppliers. These new centres are often owned by large retailers who have substantial marketing and advertising budgets – e.g. Homebase, and B&Q (Kingfisher). The size of these centres means that products can be ordered direct from source with a consequent reduction in the need for wholesalers and large warehousing facilities.

4   DIY centres tend to stock a more extensive range of basic building supplies and also sell highly profitable home furnishings, garden equipment and other recreational goods.

5   The growing use of Electronic Point of Sale (EPOS) equipment by retail companies allows customers to pay for their purchases using Credit and Debit cards as well as cheques and cash. It also enables staff to monitor sales and stock to ensure that the right goods are available at the right time at the right location. By forecasting sales on the basis of this information these companies can order in bulk from suppliers and thereby gain significant discounts.

6 Concern about green issues in general and fears about the effects of defor-estation on global warming specifically have influenced the demand for timber and wood products.

7 The relaxation of the controls on retail trading hours, including the legalisation of Sunday trading, and increased consumer demand for late-night 24-hour shopping has led to longer shop opening hours.

8 Changes in the staffing of retail organisations – such as the increased use of staff on part-time, temporary and other non-standard forms of employment and the increased participation of women in the workforce – have altered the mix of staff in most retail stores.

Exercise 1.2 Representing the external environment

Examples of the results of different forms of environmental scanning activity undertaken on the Hodsons case study material are shown below. In the interests of space these examples are limited to a PEST analysis and to Metaphors/images. The answer to Exercise 1.1 provides an example of the list-based approach.

Metaphors and images

Hodsons could be seen metaphorically as an iceberg. On the surface it appears that the company is melting away as sales decline, and it is dragged into less hospitable waters by a combination of recessionary currents, increased competition and John Hodson's view of the future of the company. However, these surface difficulties conceal a number of deeper problems which lie hidden below the surface, but which will ultimately determine the future direction of the company. These problems include the high level of skill and expertise among the workforce and their reluctance to downgrade the level of service and advice they provide to customers.

Categories

Political

Improved access to UK markets
  for competitors from overseas activity,
  especially the companies from
  EU countries
Relaxation of regulations
  on opening hours
Concerns that out-of-town shopping
  centres promote car use and lead
  to a decline in high-street shopping

Economic

Recession
Decline in building
Competition from
  Do-It-Yourself centres

Social

Growing interest in Do-It-Yourself
Concern about damage to the
  environment
Greater interest in out-of-town
  shopping centres

Technological

Electronic stock
  monitoring and sales technology
Just-in-time systems
Increased use of debit
  and credit card sales

Exercise 1.3 Choosing an appropriate response to declining sales at Hodsons

Some of the possible responses Hodsons could consider adopting in response to the current recession include: doing nothing, selling up, consolidating, changing the markets that it serves, altering its product range, agreeing a joint venture/merger, or lobbying central government in order to get changes in the laws governing the industry.

Decisions reflecting the appropriateness, feasibility and suitability of these different solutions will reflect differences of individual opinion.

☐ Chapter 2

Exercise 2.1 Reading the financial pages

(a) The most expensive shares: Sainsbury at 428¾p.

(b) The widest fluctuations in share price in the preceding year: Iceland.

(c) The greatest number of issued shares: Sainsbury.

(d) The appearance of high shareholder confidence in its future performance: Sainsbury with a P/E ratio of 23.8.

Exercise 2.2 Public or private?

Although it is tempting to think that all organisations are either publicly or privately owned, in practice the distinctions are not always easy to make. A number of organisations combine a mixture of publicly and privately owned assets. For example, the government has retained some shares in several recently privatised organisations. Similarly, a number of private organisations receive substantial grants, funding and support from either central or local government.

Table A.1 Flexington University: public or private?

	Ownership	Control	Objectives
Stanmead Technical College	Voluntary organisation	Mechanical Institute	Meet local demand for education and training
	Local authority	Local politicians	Meet local demand for education and training
Stanmead Institute of Technology	Local authority	Local politicians	Meet need for undergraduate technical education and training
Flexington Polytechnic	Local authority	Local politicians and CNAA	Meet need for undergraduate education and training
Flexington University	Public corporation	University governors	Meet need for undergraduate education and training
Flexington University Enterprises Ltd	Private limited company	Board of directors	Commercially exploit enterprises, patents, limited copyrights and other materials

Exercise 2.3 Changes in the public sector

The following list summarises how some of the changes in the public sector over the last 15 years have affected the staff and students at Flexington University. There is also a speculative list of possible future changes.

Examples of changes which might be introduced include the following:

- ☐ *Privatisation* of universities through sale of their assets to the private sector.
- ☐ *Liberalisation* of sector through sale of degree-awarding franchises.
- ☐ *Marketisation* through introduction of student voucher system so that fees are paid by the student.
- ☐ *Managerialism* through appointment of business managers to oversee university operations.

Privatisation	None to date
Deregulation	Relaxation of the rules governing the award of degrees. Controls devolved to institutions with the scrapping of the CNAA
Liberalisation	Establishment of Buckingham University
Marketisation	Universities and polytechnics encouraged to compete for students
Financial	Strict limits on the level of prudence student funding
Managerialism	Students' Charter, appraisals and performance-related pay
Commercialism	University encouraged to attract overseas students and to sell research and consultancy services as well as university merchandise

☐ Chapter 5

Exercise 5.1 Market economies

Figures A.1(a) and (b) show the demand and supply function diagrams.

Exercise 5.2 A single European currency?

Advocates of a single European currency suggest the following benefits. For business, European Monetary Union (EMU) would eliminate the cost of foreign exchange transactions and hedging on currency movements. At current exchange rates and prices this is estimated to exceed $30 billion per year. It would also make trade and investment between member states more attractive as the returns from these activities would be less susceptible to currency movements. For individual European citizens, it would remove the cost of similar transactions when travelling on business or holiday trips. Meanwhile, it would protect the governments of individual member states from the effects of

Figure A.1 (a)
Demand function

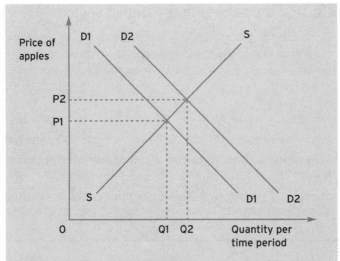

An increase in demand as denoted by the movement from D1 to D2 leads to an increase in both the price (P1 to P2) and the quantity demanded (Q1 to Q2).

Figure A.1 (b)
Supply function

An increase in supply as denoted by the movement from S1 to S2 leads to an decrease in both the price (P1 to P2) and an increase in the quantity demanded (Q1 to Q2).

speculation by money market traders. And in the longer term, it might also promote more stable economic growth as governments are prevented from devaluing and have to submit themselves to the tough monetary policies characteristic of Germany – the largest and most economically powerful member state of the European Union.

Opponents of EMU suggest that the movement of decision making on monetary policy from national governments and central banks to a new European

Central Bank represents an unacceptable reduction in national sovereignty. In short, they are concerned that this change will prevent their national politicians from taking short-term steps to correct local economic difficulties. There is also a fear that in the longer term European Union institutions will further reduce national sovereignty by taking a bigger role in determining fiscal policy. It is argued that without this central control or coordination of taxation and public spending, there is danger that economic problems in one country could have spill-over effects on others. To prevent this from happening, European Union institutions will therefore be forced to tax richer countries in order to promote investment and benefit spending in poorer regions. Over time there is a fear that this will lead to political union – the creation of a 'European Super State' – and an increase in the distance between individual citizens and the politicians who make decisions on their behalf.

☐ Chapter 8

Exercise 8.2 Political systems

See the scatter diagram in Fig A.2.

Figure A.2
Location on Fig 8.1 of the numbers representing the list of political systems

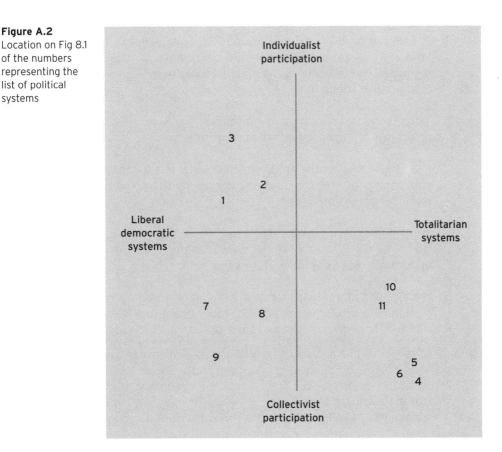

☐ Chapter 10

Exercise 10.1 Individual employment rights

The individual rights issues that arise in the Seymour Aerial and Cable Installations case study are:

General issues

☐ No 'Section 1 statements' setting out information on contractual terms.

☐ No formal procedures, e.g. discipline and equal opportunities.

☐ Unilateral changes in employment conditions by the employer are unacceptable.

☐ Health and safety standards in respect of VDUs are not being complied with, e.g. who are 'users', proper workstation, time spent at VDU, eye tests.

Issues specific to Selena

☐ As a pregnant worker with less than one years' service she is entitled to maternity leave.

☐ She cannot be dismissed on the grounds of pregnancy or for a reason associated with pregnancy. These would be an *automatically unfair* reason for dismissal. There is no service qualification to make an application to an employment tribunal.

☐ What is the real reason for her dismissal? It is said to be 'misconduct'. This might be a fair reason if it is the real reason.

☐ Is it reasonable for the employer to dismiss her for this reason in the circumstances of the case, having regard to the size and administrative resources of the employer?

☐ Was the dismissal handled fairly and in accordance with the guidance in the ACAS Code of Practice? She was not given a proper hearing and an opportunity to put her side of the case.

☐ She received no notice to terminate her employment. She might be entitled to claim *wrongful dismissal*. Suggestions that other discrimination law is infringed in respect of race and trade union membership.

☐ Chapter 11

Exercise 11.3 The law and industrial action

1 Is it a 'trade dispute'?

Yes. It is a dispute with their employer and is wholly or mainly about their hours of work.

2 Have the regulations on balloting been adhered to?

It is unlikely to be so. The scrutineers were not appropriate. The union Executive knew nothing about the ballot. It is doubtful that the ballot paper was properly drafted. The employer is unlikely to have received the appropriate notice.

3 Is it an official or unofficial strike?

The Union Executive has formerly repudiated the strike. So, it is unofficial.

4 Why?

The union is liable for industrial action that is not lawfully organised in compliance with the Code of Practice on Balloting. It can be sued by the employer. The employer can obtain an injunction to prevent the action. Repudiation is the way the union can avoid liability.

5 Is it a fair dismissal?

The industrial action is not 'protected industrial action' because it is unlawful and unofficial. So, it is possible for the employer to dismiss employees selectively

6 Is it lawful?

No. The industrial action is unlawful (no approval balloting having been held).

Backward integration when an organisation buys a stake in, or control over, one or more of its suppliers.

Balance of Payments a measure of the shortfall or surplus between exports and imports of visible and invisible goods and services as well as capital funds.

Business or economic cycle a measure of the period of time between successive phases of economic growth and recession.

Civilian labour force a statistical measure of the number of people either in employment or actively seeking paid work.

Closed shop an arrangement between employers and specific trade unions whereby trade union membership is a condition of employment for particular jobs. Given the freedom in law (since 1990) for employees to choose whether or not to be union members, such arrangements are now rare and difficult to enforce legally. Closed shops have been categorised as *pre-entry* (where only trade union members were considered for employment) or *post-entry* (where after an offer of employment, an employee was required to join a recognised union).

Codes of practice may be statutory or voluntary. The former (like the ACAS Code on Discipline and Grievances) are presented to Parliament and then approved. Breach of the provisions of such a code by an employer can be used in evidence before an employment tribunal. A voluntary code of practice is one formulated by an organisation like the Chartered Institute of Personnel Development. It has no legal force. But it can provide helpful guidance to employers in the conduct of employment relations.

Common law a term used to describe judge-made law, that is, laws which arise from precedents established in judicial decisions at the end of court hearings.

Contingency theory an approach to the analysis of organisations and their environments which attempts to specify influences (contingencies) which affect or constrain human decision making and action.

Corporatism a term used to describe political systems in which the state encourages participation by trade unions and employers' associations in national government. These bodies are consulted directly or indirectly by government ministers and in turn provide advice on general economic, employment and social policy issues.

Cyclical unemployment a term used to refer to fluctuations in the number of unemployed which arise as a consequence of the business cycle.

Demand function a measure of the relationship between the price of a good and the quantity demanded by consumers.

Deregulation a relaxation of statutory and other legal controls on the operation of organisations.

Determinism a belief that human choice and action is constrained or determined by external influences.

Devolution refers to the transfer of certain powers within nation states to subsidiary governing bodies. The powers may be to make law, to impose certain taxes or to administer certain social or economic activities. The governing bodies can include parliaments (like that in Scotland), assemblies (like those in Wales and Northern Ireland), or local government bodies (like the Greater London Authority). The powers transferred are determined by the national parliament and may by rescinded by that national parliament.

Economic growth increases in the productive capacity and wealth of a country or similar unit of economic activity. This is usually measured by changes in the Gross Domestic Product (GDP), Gross National Product (GNP) or National Income.

Economic and Monetary Union (EMU) the goal of the European Union, designed to create a single currency and European Central Bank.

Elasticity of demand or supply the degree to which the quantity of goods demanded or supplied is sensitive to changes in their price.

Employees in employment a measure of the number of the people who are actually in paid employment.

Exchange rate a comparative measure of the relative value of two currencies. For example, the dollar/sterling exchange rate specifies the rate at which dollars may be converted to sterling and vice versa.

Exchange rate mechanism (ERM) the official title of the European Union's managed exchange rate system. This system seeks to promote stability in the value of member state currencies in international money markets.

Externalities a term used by economists to refer to the social, environmental and other costs associated with production, which are not directly covered in the price of any resultant good or service.

Fatalism a belief that what will happen is bound to happen and that there is nothing humans can do to prevent it.

Feminisation used to refer to an increase in the representation of women or women's issues. This term is commonly used to describe increases in the number of women in the labour force over the last 50 or more years.

Financial short-termism a description of business policies which place an emphasis on the achievement of high profit and share performance objectives over a one- to three-year period.

Flexibility a term used to refer to a variety of forms of employment practice including numerical flexibility (varying the number of people employed); functional flexibility (expanding the range of tasks performed by individual employees); financial flexibility (adjusting pay and conditions to reflect local conditions, business or employee performance); temporal flexibility (allowing variety in the period of time employees spend at work); and geographical flexibility (moving staff within an organisation).

Footsie a colloquial phrase used to refer to the *Financial Times* Stock Exchange 100 Index. This index provides a measure of changes in the price of shares traded on the London Stock Exchange.

Fordism a system of production and distribution characterised by the manufacture of standardised goods by semiskilled and some skilled workers for a mass market of similar customers who have been persuaded to buy by big advertising campaigns.

Forward integration when an organisation buys a stake in, or control over, the buyers of its goods or services.

Free rider an individual who seeks the benefits of a public good while avoiding the costs associated with its provision.

Green Paper is a discussion paper published by government in which it outlines policy proposals (sometimes alternative proposals) for discussion by interest groups and members of the public. It is an early preliminary stage in the process to formulating legislation. It often proceeds the publication of a White Paper (q.v.). It is not necessary for government to publish a Green Paper.

Horizontal integration when an organisation buys a stake in, or control over, rivals in the same industry.

Ideology is a set of related beliefs, attitudes and opinions about economic, social and political activity.

Inflation an increase in the price of any raw materials, labour, land or finished goods and services.

International division of labour the splitting of work between employees in different countries. This term is used most frequently to describe the concentration of well-paid and high-skilled jobs in developed western countries and low-paid and low-skilled jobs in developing countries.

Japanisation the influence of the management practices used by Japanese multi-national enterprises on the policies and practices of their subsidiary operations in overseas countries.

Keynesianism an economic philosophy based on the belief that government intervention is needed to avoid the failings of free market systems and to ensure the most productive deployment of a nation's scarce resources.

Labour market a term used by economists to describe the interaction between employers and those employees who are either in work or are actively looking for work. A further distinction separates the behaviour of these individuals within firms (the internal labour market) and between firms (the external labour market).

Liberalisation a relaxation of laws and regulations which previously prevented private sector organisations from providing certain public services.

MAUT Multiple Attribute Utility Testing, a procedure for systematically evaluating the options available to an organisation when responding to a particular pressure or problem.

MNE a multinational enterprise referring to organisations which directly employ staff in two or more countries.

Monetarism an economic philosophy based on the belief that the appropriate role for governments in modern economies is the maintenance of sound money and the removal of barriers to the operation of free markets.

Nationalisation is also described as public ownership. It is form of economic ownership whereby the assets of a particular body are invested in a public (as opposed to a private) corporation. There are no shareholders. Revenue generated by the organisation is held by it, used for further investment and some may be paid to government in taxation. Some notable examples of nationalised organisations were British Rail and British Gas which were privatised (q.v.) in the 1980s and 1990s.

Opportunity cost refers to the cost of things that can not be done if a particular course of action is chosen.

Participation rate a measure of the percentage of the population in a particular category, i.e. women, ethnic minorities or all potential employees, who are actually in paid employment.

PEST an acronym used to describe analyses which consider the political, economic, social and technological pressures confronting an organisation.

Pluralism a belief that societies in general, and organisations in particular, consist of individuals and groups who have different and often conflicting objectives and interests.

Positive action a term used to describe steps taken to encourage the recruitment and progression of various disadvantaged groups including women and ethnic minorities. This approach may involve targeted job advertisements and training programmes, but it should not be confused with positive discrimination or quota schemes in which a particular number of jobs or opportunities are reserved for applicants from disadvantaged backgrounds.

Post-Fordism a system of production and distribution which relies upon the manufacture of specialised products by skilled workers for small markets of customers with particular demands who are persuaded to buy by targeted marketing.

Private Finance Initiative (PFI) is an arrangement whereby a consortium of private sector firms come together to provide an asset-based public service under contract to a public body. PFI falls within the definition of Public-Private Partnerships (PPPs) (q.v.). The principle sector contractor (often created for the purpose) funds any asset required and is then paid for the service provided. The public sector client pays a fee over the life of the contract to the private provider which is contingent upon services meeting specified standards. By June 2001, it was reported that almost 400 PFI deals had been signed with a capital value of £17 billion.

Privatisation transferring the ownership of an organisation from the public to the private sector.

Product life cycle a model of product sales which suggests that, like animals, the sales are born, grow, mature, decline and die.

Public good a good which is most effectively and efficiently provided if everyone is compelled to share in the costs of its provision.

Public–Private Partnership is a risk-sharing relationship between the public and the private sectors based on a shared aspiration to bring about a desired policy outcome. Contracting-out services, such as catering, is viewed as a form of PPP by some government departments, as are forms of joint venture, Private Finance Initiative schemes (q.v.) and strategic partnerships.

Recession a period of declining economic fortune characterised by a contraction of productive capacity and wealth which lasts for more than six months.

Seasonal adjustment a term used to refer to the smoothing out of seasonal variations from annual collections of statistics.

Seasonal unemployment a term used to describe annual fluctuations in the level of unemployment which arise as a consequence of seasonal variations in the number of available jobs and employees.

Segmentation a term used to describe divisions within the workforce which arise because of status differences and discrimination between groups of workers, e.g. differences of gender, ethnic origin and disability. Sociologists typically refer to three types of segmentation: horizontal segmentation between different occupational and industrial categories, e.g. teachers, secretaries and lorry drivers; vertical segmentation between different hierarchical levels in an organisation, e.g. sales assistants, departmental managers and directors in retail stores; and international segmentation between countries.

Segregation another term used to refer to vertical, horizontal and international segmentation.

Social partners refers to employers and trade unions and is used to characterise a more harmonious relationship between these two bodies in the contact of employment relations. A partnership approach is advocated by the social policy of the European Union. Employers and unions are encouraged to discuss the formulation of legislation, agree the content of employment directives and at the workplace to negotiate ways of implementing particular directives.

Stagflation a combination of high levels of inflation and unemployment.

Stakeholders groups inside and outside an organisation with an interest in its objectives and an influence over its operations.

Statute law a term used to describe laws made by the Houses of Parliament.

Structural unemployment a measure of the number of long term unemployed who are unable to find work because they lack relevant skills or alternatively because an insufficient number of appropriate jobs are available.

Supply function a measure of the relationship between the price of a good and the quantity supplied by producers.

Sustainable development is development that meets the needs of the present without compromising the ability of future generations to meet their needs. It generally concerns the introduction of environmentally friendly practices, processes and products.

SWOT an acronym used to describe analyses of the Strengths, Weaknesses, Opportunities and Threats confronting an organisation.

Systems theory an approach which uses techniques developed in biological and engineering sciences. This approach attempts to specify the nature and form of interactions between internal interrelated elements of an organisation and aspects of its external environment.

Trade union recognition refers to the decision by employers to agree to negotiate with one or more trade unions about specific terms and conditions of employment. Decisions to recognise unions have generally been voluntary. However, since 2000, a statutory recognition scheme has been in force. This provides for the imposition of recognition in certain specified circumstances.

Unitarism a belief that societies in general, and organisations in particular, consist of individuals and groups who share or should share the same objectives and interests.

Voluntarism a term used to describe societies in which the State leaves employers and employees free to determine the nature of the employment relationship either directly through management–employee contact or indirectly through the medium of trade unions and employers' associations.

White Paper is a firmer statement of government legislative proposals than a Green Paper (q.v.). Interest groups can make representations about these proposals and government may, as a consequence, amend proposed legislation as a result of critical detailed comments or as a result of campaigning. It is optional for the government to issue a White Paper.

References

Adonis, A and Pollard, S (1998) *A Class Act*, London: Penguin.

Advisory Conciliation and Arbitration Service (2000) *Code of Practice on Disciplinary and Grievance Procedures*, London: ACAS.

Aldridge, S (2001) *Social mobility: a discussion paper*, London: Performance and Innovation Unit.

Anderman, S (1986) 'Unfair Dismissals and Redundancy' in Lewis, R (ed) *Labour Law in Britain*, Oxford: Blackwell.

Ansoff, I (1987) *Corporate Strategy*, Maidenhead: McGraw Hill.

Auerbach, S (1990) *Legislating for Conflict*, Oxford: Clarendon Press.

Bassett, P (1986) *Strike Free*, London: Macmillan.

Batstone, E and Gourlay, S (1986) *Unions, Unemployment and Innovation*, Oxford: Blackwell.

Berle, A and Means, G (1932) *The Modern Corporation and Private Property*, New York: Macmillan.

Bohm, D (1980) *Wholeness and the Implicate Order*, London: Ark Books.

Boyden, T and Paddison, L (1986) 'Banking on Equal Opportunities', *Personnel Management Journal*, September.

Braverman, H (1974) *Labor and Monopoly Capitalism: The Degradation of Work in the Twentieth Century*, New York: Monthly Review Press.

Brown, R (1988) 'The Employment Relationship in Sociological Theory' in Gallie, D (ed) *Employment in Britain*, Oxford: Blackwell.

Brown, W (1994) *Bargaining for Full Employment*, Employment Policy Institute Economic Report, Employment Policy Institute.

Buchanan, D A and Boddy, D A (1983) *Organizations in the Computer Age: Technological Imperatives and Strategic Choice*, Aldershot: Gower Publishing.

Buchanan, D and McCalman, J (1989) 'Confidence, visibility and pressure: the effects of computer-aided hotel management' *New Technology, Work and Employment*, 3(1), pp 38–46.

Burawoy, M (1985) *The Politics of Production*, London: Verso.

Burns, T and Stalker, G (1961) *The Management of Innovation*, London: Tavistock Publications.

Campbell, A and Alexander M (1997) 'What's Wrong with Strategy?', *Harvard Business Review,* November–December, pages 42–51.

Capelli, P *et al.* (1997) *Change at Work*, New York: Oxford University Press.

Child, J (1972) 'Organization structure, environment and performance: the role of strategic choice', *Sociology*, 6(1), pp 1–22.

Clark, G de N (1970) *Remedies for Unfair Dismissal: proposals for legislation* (PEP Broadsheet 518) Policy Studies Institutes.

Collins, A (1994) 'Human Resource Management in Context' in Beardwell, I and Holden, L (eds) *Human Resource Management: A Contemporary Perspective*, London: Pitman Publishing.

Commission on Public Private Partnerships (2001) *Building Better Partnerships*, London: Institute of Public Policy Research.

Crompton, R (1993) *Class and Stratification: An Introduction to Current Debates*, Cambridge: Polity Press.

Cully, M *et al.* (1998) *The Workplace Employee Relations Survey (the first findings)*, London: Department of Trade and Industry.

Cully, M *et al.* (1999) *Britain at Work: the Workplace Employee Relations Survey*, London: Routledge.

Cully, M, Woodland, O'Reilly, A and Dix, G (1999) *Britain at Work: As depicted by the 1998 Workplace Employee Relations Survey*, London: Routledge

Cyert, R M and March, J G (1963) *A Behaviourial Theory of the Firm*, New York: Wiley.

Daniel, W W (1987) *Workplace Industrial Relations and Technical Change*, Policy Studies Institute.

Delacroix, J and Saudagaran, S (1991) 'Munificent Compensations as Disincentives: The Case of American CEOs', *Human Relations*, 44(7), pp 665–78.

Department of Trade and Industry (1998) *Fairness at Work*, Cmnd 3968, Stationery Office, London.

Dex, S and McCulloch, A (1997) *Flexible Employment*, Basington: Macmillan

Dickens, L, Jones, M, Weekes, B and Hart M (1985) *Dismissed*, Oxford: Blackwell.

Digman L (1990) *Strategic Management – Concepts, Decisions, Cases*, Maidenhead: Richard D Irwin inc.

Edwards, R (1978) *Contested Terrain: The Transformation of the Workplace in the Twentieth Century*, Oxford: Heinemann.

Ellison, R (1994) 'British Labour Force Projections 1994–2006', *Employment Gazette*, April.

Equal Opportunities Commission (1991) *Equality Management: women's employment in the National Health Service*, Equal Opportunities Commission.

Etzioni, A (1988) *The Moral Dimension: Toward a New Economics*, London: Collier Macmillan.

Ewing, K D (1994) *Britain and the ILO* (2nd edn) Institute of Employment Rights.

Flanders, A (1968) 'Collective Bargaining in Theoretical Analysis', *British Journal of Industrial Relations*, Vol. 6, No 1.

Fox, A (1974) *Beyond Contract: Work, Power and Trust Relations*, London: Faber & Faber.

Freeman, C, Clark, J and Soete, L (1982) *Unemployment and Technical Innovation*, London: Francis Pinter.

Freeman, C (1987) 'The Case for Technological Determinism' in Finnegan, R, Salaman, G and Thompson, K (eds) *Information Technology: Social Issues. A Reader*, Sevenoaks: Hodder and Stoughton/the Open University.

French, J and Raven, B (1959) 'The Social Bases of Power' in Cartwright, D (ed) *Studies in Social Power*, Ann Arbor: University of Michigan Press.

Friedman, M (1970) 'The Social Responsibility of Business is to Increase its Profits', *New York Times Magazine*, 13 September.

Gaffney, D *et al.* (1999) 'PFI in the NHS – is there an economic case?' *British Medical Journal*, 319.

Galbraith, J K (1967) *The New Industrial State*, London: Hamish Hamilton.

Gallie, D (1998) *Restructuring the Employment Relationship*, Oxford: Oxford University Press.

Giddens, A (1984) *The Constitution of Society: Outline of the Theory of Structuration*, Cambridge: Polity Press.

Giddens, A (1998) *The Third Way – The Renewal of Social Democracy*, Cambridge: Polity Press.

Gill, C (1985) *Work, Unemployment and New Technology*, Cambridge: Polity Press.

Gleick, J (1987) *Chaos*, New York: Viking Press.

Glover, S *et al.* (1999) 'PFI in the NHS – there an economic case?', *British Medical Journal*, 319.

Glover, S *et al.* (2001) Migration: an economic and social analysis, Research, Development ad Statistics Directorate Occasional paper No. 67, Home Office.

Greenlagh, L (1991) 'Organizational Coping Strategies' in Hartley, J, Jacobson, D, Klandermans, B and van Vuuren, T (eds) *Job Insecurity: Coping with Jobs at Risk*, London: Sage.

Gregg, P, Machins, S and Szymanski, S (1993) 'The Disappearing Relationship Between Directors' Pay and Corporate Performance', *British Journal of Industrial Relations*, 31(1), pp 1–9.

Greiner, L (1972) 'Evolution and Revolution as Organizations Grow', *Harvard Business Review*, July–August.

Griffith, J (1997) *The Politics of the Judiciary* (5th edn) London: Fontana.

Halsey, A H (1995) *Change in British Society*, London: Opus.

Hamel, G (1997) 'Strategy as Revolution', *Harvard Business Review*, July–August, p 69–82.

Hamel, G and Prahalad, C (1994) *Competing for the Future: Breakthrough Strategies for Seizing Control of Your Industry and Creating the Markets of Tomorrow*, Boston, MA: Harvard Business School Press.

Hampden-Turner, C and Fons Trompenaars, C (1993) *The Seven Cultures of Capitalism*, London: Piaktus.

Handy, C (1989) *The Age of Unreason* (1st edn) London: Century Business Books.

Handy, C (1991) *The Age of Unreason* (2nd edn) London: Century Business Books.

Handy, C (1994) *The Empty Raincoat: Making Sense of the Future*, London: Hutchinson.

Hannan, M T and Freeman, J (1988) *Organizational Ecology*, Boston, MA: Harvard University Press.

Hansard Society, The (1990) *Women on Top*, London: HMSO.

Hassard, J and Parker, M (eds) (1994) *Postmodernism and Organizations*, London: Sage.

Hay (1992) *Hay Compensation Report*, July, London: Hay Management Consultants.

Heery, E and Salmon, J (eds) (2000) *The Insecure Workforce*, London: Routledge.

Hendry, C (1994) *Human Resource Strategies for International Growth*, London: Routledge.

Henley Centre (1999) *The Paradox of Prosperity*, London: Henley/Salvation Army.

Hobsbawn, E (1998) *Uncommon People*, London: Abacus.

Hofstede, G (1980) *Culture's Consequences*, London: Sage.

Hofstede, G (1994) *Culture and Organizations: Software for the Mind, Intercultural Coop and its Importance for Survival*, London: Harper Collins.

Huczynski, A and Buchanan, D (1991) *Organizational Behaviour: An Introductory Text*, Hemel Hempstead: Prentice-Hall.

Hunt, J W and Downing, S (1991) 'Mergers acquisitions and Human Resource Management', *International Journal of Human Resource Management*, Vol 1, No 2, Spring.

Hutton, W (1995) *The State We're In*, London: Jonathan Cape.

Hyman, R (1987) 'Strategy or Structure: Capital, Labour and Control', *Work, Employment and Society*, Vol. 1, No. 1, p 25–28.

Johnson, G and Scholes, K (1993/2001) *Exploring Corporate Strategy* (5th edn) Harlow: FT Publishing, Pearson.

Kahn-Freund, O (1954) in Flanders, A and Clegg, H (eds) *The System of Industrial Relations in Great Britain*, Oxford: Blackwell.

Kahn-Freund, O (1983) in Davis and Freedland (eds) *Labour and the Law* (3rd edn) London: Stevens.

Kandola, R, Fullerton, J and Ahmed, Y (1995) 'Managing Diversity: succeeding where equal opportunities has failed', *Equal Opportunities Review*, 59.

Kanter, R M (1985) *The Change Masters: Corporate Entrepreneurs at Work*, New York: Counterpoint.

Kanter, R M (1989) *When Giants Learn to Dance: Mastering the Challenges of Strategy, Management and Careers in 1990s*, London: Unwin Paperbacks.

Katz, D and Kahn, R (1966) *The Social Psychology of Organizations*, New York: Wiley.

Kay, J (1993) *The Foundations of Corporate Success*, Oxford: Oxford University Press.

Kay, J (1996) *The Business of Economics*, Oxford: Oxford University Press.

Kelly, G (2000) *The New Partnership Agenda*, Commission on Public Private Partnerships, London: Institute for Public Policy Research.

Kelly, J (1998) *Rethinking Industrial Relations*, London: Routledge.

Klein, N (2000) *No Logo*, London: Flamingo.

Korten, D C (1995) *When Corporations Rule the World*, Connecticut: Kumarian Press.

Kuttner, R (1997) *Everything for Sale: The Virtues and Limits of Markets*, New York: Alfred A Knopf.

Labour Party (1997) *New Labour – Because Britain Deserves Better*, London: the Labour Party.

Labour Party (2001) *Ambitions for Britain*, London: The Labour Party.

Lash, S and Urry, J (1987) *The End of Organised Capitalism*, Cambridge: Polity Press.

Lawrence, P R and Lorsch, J W (1967) *Organization and Environment*, Boston, MA: Harvard University Press.

Leadbeater C (1999) *Living on Thin Air*, London: Viking.

Leavitt, H J (1975) 'Marketing Myopia', *Harvard Business Review*, September–October.

Leonard, A (1987) *Judging Inequality*, London: The Cobden Trust.

Lewis, R and Clark, J (1993) *Employment Rights, Industrial Tribunals and Arbitration: the case for alternative dispute resolution*, Institute of Employment Rights.

Lindbloom, C (1959) 'The Science of Muddling Through', *Public Administration Review*, 19, pp 79–88.

Lloyd, J (2000) 'Cultivating the World', *Financial Times*, 20 September.

Lovelock, J (1979) *Gaia: A New Look at Life on Earth*, Oxford: Oxford University Press.

Lukes, S (1974) *Power: A Radical Review*, London: Macmillan.

Machin, S (1996) 'Wage Inequality in the UK', *Oxford Review of Economic Policy*.

Marchington, M (1978) 'Shop Floor Control and Industrial relations' in Purcell, M and Smith, R (eds) *The Control of Work*, London: Macmillan.

Mason, D (1995) *Race and Ethnicity in Modern Britain*, Oxford: Oxford University Press.

McCarthy, Lord (1989) 'The Case for Labour Courts', *Industrial Relations Journal*, 20.

McLoughlin, I and Clark, J (1994) *Technological Change at Work*, Milton Keynes: Open University Press.

Miles, R and Snow, C (1978) *Organisation and Strategy, Structure and Process*, Maidenhead: McGraw Hill.

Millward, N and Stevens, M (1986) *British Workplace Industrial Relations 1980–1984*, Aldershot: Gower.

Millward, N, Bryson, A and Forth, J (2000) *All Change at Work? British employment relations 1980–1998, as portrayed by the Workplace Industrial Relations Survey series*, London: Routledge.

Mintzberg, H (1987) 'Five Ps for Strategy', *Californic Management Review*, June 30, (11), pp. 11–32.

Mintzberg, H, Quinn, J and Ghosal, S (1995) *The Strategy Process*, London: Prentice Hall.

Mitchell R *et al.* (2000) *Inequalities in Life and Death*, Bristol: Polity Press and Joseph Rowntree Foundations.

Monbiot, G (2000) *Captive State: The Corporate Takeover of Britain*, London: Macmillan.

Moore, J (1992) *Writers on Strategy and Strategic Management*, Harmondsworth: Penguin.

Morgan, G (1986) *Images of Organization*, London: Sage.

Morgan, G (1993) *Imaginisation: The Art of Creative Management*, London: Sage.

Morgan, R and Russell, L (2000) *The Judiciary on Magistrates' Courts*, London: Lord Chancellor's Department.

Murray, C (1990) *The Emerging British Underclass*, London: Institute of Economic Affairs.

Napier, B (1986) 'The Contract of Employment' in *Labour Law in Britain*, Oxford: Blackwell.

OECD (Organisation for Economic Co-operation and Development) (1994) *Main Economic Indicators*, Paris: OECD.

Office for National Statistics (1999) *Share Ownership*, London: The Stationery Office.

Office for National Statistics (1999) *Social Focus on Older People*, London: The Stationery Office.

Office for National Statistics (2000) *Social Inequalities*, London: The Stationery Office.

Office for National Statistics (2000) *Social Trends 2001*, No. 31, London: The Stationery Office.

Office for National Statistics (2001) *Regional Trends*, No. 36, London: The Stationery Office.

Office for National Statistics (2001) *Social Trends*, No. 3, London: The Stationery Office.

Omerod, P (1994) *The Death of Economics*, London: Faber and Faber.

O'Reilly, C, Main, B and Crystal, B (1988) 'CEO compensation as tournament and social comparison: a tale of two theories', *Administrative Science Quarterly*, 33, pp 257–74.

Packard, V (1957) *The Hidden Persuaders*, Harlow: Longman.

Pascale, R T and Athos, A G (1986) *The Art of Japanese Management*, Harmondsworth: Penguin.

Pensions Investment Research Consultants (2001) *Reporting on Employment Issues of the FTSE 100*, London: PIRC.

Peters, T (1989) *Thriving on Chaos: Handbook for a Management Revolution*, London: Guild Publishing.

Peters, T and Waterman, T (1982) *In Search of Excellence*, New York: Harper Row.

Pettrick, J A and Quinn, J F (1997) *Management Ethics: Integrity at Work*, London: Sage.

Pfeffer, J (1981) *Power in Organisations*, London: Pitman.

Pfeffer, J (1992) *Managing With Power: Politics and Influence in Organizations*, Boston, MA: Harvard Business School Press.

Piore, M and Sabel, C (1982) *The Second Industrial Divide – Possibilities for Prosperity*, London: Basic Books.

Pollack, A *et al.* (2001) *A response to the IPPR Commission on Public Private Partnerships*, 26 June, London: The Catalyst Trust.

Pond, C (1989) 'The Wealth of Two Nations', in McDowell, L, Sarre, P and Hamnett, C (eds) *Divided Nation: Social and Cultural Change in Britain*, London: Hodder and Stoughton/Open University.

Porter, M E (1980) *Competitive Strategy: Techniques for Analysing Industries and Competitors*, New York: Free Press.

Porter, M E (1985) *Competitive Advantage: Creating and Sustaining Superior Performance*, New York: Free Press.

Purcell, J and Ahlstrand, B (1994) *Human Resource Management in the Multi-Divisional Company*, Oxford: Oxford University Press.

Rawls, J (1971) *A Theory of Justice*, Oxford: Oxford University Press.

Reeves, R (2000) *Mothers Versus Men: why women lose at work*, London: The Industrial Society.

Reich, R (1991) *The Work of Nations: Preparing Ourselves for 21st Century Capitalism*, Hemel Hempstead: Simon & Schuster.

Robbins, D (1986) *Wanted Railman*, London: HMSO.

SEN (1995) *Labour Market and Skill Trends 1994/95*, Nottingham: Skills and Enterprise Network.

Saunders, P (1990) *Social Class and Stratification*, London: Routledge.

Schein, E H (1984) 'Coming to a new awareness of organizational culture', *Sloan Management Review*, winter, pp 3–16.

Schein, E (1988) *Organisational Psychology*, London: Prentice Hall.

Schuler R S and Jackson, S E (1987) 'Linking competitive strategies with Human Resource Management practices', *Academy of Management Executive*, Vol 1, No. 3, pp 209–13.

Schumacher, E (1977) *Small is Beautiful, Economics as if people mattered*, New York: Hartley and Marks.

Schumpeter, J A (1987) *Capitalism, Socialism and Democracy*, London: Unwin Paperbacks.

Scott, J (1985) *Corporations, Classes and Capitalism*, London: Hutchinson.

Sewell, G and Wilkinson, B (1993) 'Human Resource Management in "Surveillance" Companies' in Clark, J (ed) *Human Resource Management and Technical Change*, London: Sage.

Silverman, D (1970) *The Theory of Organizations*, Aldershot: Gower.

Simon, H (1976) *Administrative Behaviour: A Study of Decision-Making in Administrative Organization* (3rd edn) New York: Free Press.

Storey, J and Sisson, K (1993) *Managing Human Resources and Industrial Relations*, Milton Keynes: Open University Press.

Szyszczak, E (1995) 'Future Directions in European Union Social Policy Law', *Industrial Law Journal*, 24(1).

Tawney, R H (1961) *The Aquisitive Society*, London: Collins.

Taylor, R (1994) *The Future of the Trade Unions*, London: Andre Deutsch.

Thomas, K (1999) *The Oxford Book of Work*, Oxford: Oxford University Press.

Thompson, E P (1993 [1967]) 'Time, work discipline and industrial capitalism', in *Customs in Common*, London: Penguin Books.

Towers, B. (1997) *The Representation Gap*, Oxford: Oxford University.

Tregoe, B and Zimmerman, J (1980) *Top Management Strategy*, London: John Martin Publishing.

Tully, S (1992) 'What CEOs Really Make', *Fortune*, 125(12), pp 94–9.

United Nations (1995) *Human Development Report*, Oxford: Oxford University Press.

United Nations (2001) *Human Development Report*, Geneva: United Nations.

Vidal, J (1997) *McLibel: Burger Culture on Trial*, London Pan.

Vitols, S *et al.* (1997) *Corporate Governance in large British and German companies*, London: Anglo-German Foundation.

Von Bertalanffy, L (1967) 'General Systems Theory' in Demerath, N and Peterson, R (eds) *System, Change and Conflict*, New York: Free Press.

WEF (1995) *The World Competitiveness Report*, Geneva: World Economic Forum.

Walby, S (1990) *Theorising Patriarchy*, Oxford: Oxford University Press.

Walton, R and Susman, G (1987) 'People policies for the new machines', *Harvard Business Review*, 2, March–April, pp 98–106.

Wedderburn, Lord (1986) *The Worker and the Law* (3rd edn) London: Penguin.

Wedderburn, Lord (1989) 'Freedom of association and Philosophies of Labour Law', *Industrial Law Journal*.

Wedderburn, Lord (1991) *Employment Rights in Britain and Europe*, London: Lawrence and Wishart.

Whittington, R (1993) *What is Strategy: does it matter?* London: Routledge.

Wilkinson, R (1994) 'Health distribution and growth' in *Paying for Inequality*, Glyn, A and Miliband, A, (eds) London: Institute for Public Policy Research/Rivers Oram Press.

Willey, B (1986) *Union Recognition and Representation in Engineering*, London: Engineering Employers' Federation.

Women's Unit, The, Cabinet Office, London (2000) Women and Men in the UK – Facts and Figures, London: TSO.

Woodward, J (ed) (1970) *Industrial Organisation, Behaviour and Control*, Oxford: Oxford University Press.

Wright, E O (1985) *Classes*, Cambridge: Cambridge University Press.

Zuboff, S (1988) *In the Age of the Smart Machine: The Future of Work and Power*, Oxford: Heinemann Professional Publishing.

Website Index by Address

Website Index by Subject

Subject Index

Learning Resources
Centre